Senior Citizens
Behind Bars

Senior Citizens

Behind Bars

Challenges for the Criminal Justice System

edited by
John J. Kerbs
Jennifer M. Jolley

LYNNE
RIENNER
PUBLISHERS

BOULDER
LONDON

Published in the United States of America in 2014 by
Lynne Rienner Publishers, Inc.
1800 30th Street, Boulder, Colorado 80301
www.rienner.com

and in the United Kingdom by
Lynne Rienner Publishers, Inc.
3 Henrietta Street, Covent Garden, London WC2E 8LU

Library of Congress Cataloging-in-Publication Data
    Senior citizens behind bars : challenges for the criminal justice system /
[edited by] John J. Kerbs and Jennifer M. Jolley.
      p. cm.
    Includes bibliographical references and index.
    ISBN 978-1-62637-042-5 (hc : alk. paper)
    1. Older prisoners—United States. 2. Older prisoners—Services for—United
States. 3. Older prisoners—Government policy—United States. 4. Corrections—
Government policy—United States. 5. Criminal justice, Administration of United
States. I. Kerbs, John J. II. Jolley, Jennifer M.
    HV9469.S46 2014
    365'.608460973—dc23

                                                            2013031580

British Cataloguing in Publication Data
A Cataloguing in Publication record for this book
is available from the British Library.

Printed and bound in the United States of America

    The paper used in this publication meets the requirements
♾ of the American National Standard for Permanence of
    Paper for Printed Library Materials Z39.48-1992.

    5 4 3 2 1

To correctional staff members (correctional officers, counselors, administrators, and wardens) who aim to advance the quality of services for older prisoners in federal and state facilities across the United States.

To the community correctional officers (parole and postrelease supervision officers) who continue to provide services to aging prisoners after their release. Collectively, these individuals work—often without much public support or appreciation—to ensure that older offenders are not forgotten, that their needs are met, and that public safety is always maintained.

And, to our parents, who instilled in us a deep appreciation for education and the importance of asking those questions that will most likely benefit vulnerable individuals in need and society at large.

Contents

Tables and Figures

Figures

Acknowledgments

This book was funded in part by awards and grants from East Carolina University's Faculty Senate, the US Department of Health and Human Services, the Centers for Disease Control and Prevention, and the National Institute of Mental Health. We would like to express our sincere appreciation for this support. We would also like to thank the contributing authors for their hard work and diligence in the development of quality chapters for the book. Moreover, we would like to thank a number of people who assisted us on various levels. William Doerner, a friend and mentor, provided needed feedback and suggestions at numerous points throughout the development of this volume; we will forever be grateful for his academic insights, his knowledge of victimology, and his encouragement. J. H. Dautremont also deserves recognition for the invaluable feedback that he provided for many of the chapters. Christina Scarbel assisted us with the book's reference list and index. Howard Sapers, correctional investigator at the national headquarters of the Correctional Service of Canada, assisted us with the data on Canada's federal prisoners.

Despite the aforementioned assistance (financial and otherwise), the views and opinions in this book are solely those of the contributing authors and do not necessarily reflect the official positions or policies of the National Institute of Mental Health, the US Department of Health and Human Services, the Centers for Disease Control and Prevention, the Correctional Service of Canada, or any of the universities that serve as academic homes to the authors.

—*John J. Kerbs*
—*Jennifer M. Jolley*

1

A Path to Evidence-Based Policies and Practices

John J. Kerbs and Jennifer M. Jolley

This book is about older prisoners in federal and state correctional facilities in the United States. What makes this book unusual is that it takes an evidence-based approach to the synthesis and review of the extant scholarly research on older and aging prisoners' needs, policies, and procedures that govern their care and custody, and interventions and programs for older offenders inside prison and outside after their release. Such an approach also necessitates a longitudinal look at older inmates, from sentencing through imprisonment and potential release.

Building from the work of Golder et al. (2005) and Drake et al. (2001), this book generally defines evidence-based corrections as the use of scientifically rigorous *quantitative* evidence that is standardized and replicable in order to

- Improve our knowledge regarding older prisoners' specific criminogenic and bio-psycho-social needs, the prevalence of these needs, and the interventions that best address these needs.
- Inform specific policies and practices with particular populations of older prisoners who have specific problems.
- Develop effective evidence-based programs that improve specific outcomes (e.g., the reduction of recidivism rates) for older inmates with varying bio-psycho-social and criminogenic needs.
- Identify the limitations of prior research in a way that can inform future research to improve services and outcomes for aging inmates in the United States.

That said, evidence-based corrections in general and evidence-based programs in particular are often improved through accumulated knowledge from studies that span decades of research that ultimately defines the boundaries of what is and what is not known about older prisoners. Such studies should provide consistent scientific evidence demonstrating improved outcomes, including statistically significant reductions in recidivism (Drake et al., 2001).

Although quantitative evidence is essential to the advancement of evidence-based corrections and evidence-based programs (ideally rooted, when applicable, in randomized experiments with treatment and control groups), Sampson (2010) noted that there is a need to conjoin both observational (qualitative) methods and experimental (quantitative) methods to inform evidence-based corrections policy, in large part because we need to avoid equating evidence-based policy with experimental-based policy. Thus, there is room for mixed-method research (Sampson, 2010), but all studies should be rigorous as defined by their research designs, sampling methods, sample size, and analytic approaches (MacKenzie, 2000).

Such evidence-based discussions regarding older prisoners have materialized only recently, over the past four decades. Indeed, there has been an evolution in both the quantity and the quality of scholarship since the 1970s that cuts across four distinct periods in time. These historical periods, or stages of scientific progress, generally explore the relationship between older citizens and the criminal justice system, including in regard to correctional systems in the United States (Adams, 1995; Alston, 1986). To place the contribution of this book in historical context, and to give the reader a quick primer on the evolution of research concerning older prisoners, these four stages will be reviewed here. Thereafter, this introduction will focus on the structure of the book, providing a brief review of each chapter and the utility of each to inform policies and procedures related to the correctional treatment of older prisoners in the United States. Ultimately, this book aims to provide academics, correctional officials, policymakers, prison staff, and students from various disciplines and fields with the most current evidence-based discussion as developed from a multidisciplinary review of the scholarly literature in criminal justice, criminology, gerontology, law, medicine, penology, psychology, social work, and sociology.

While such a wide cross-section of disciplines may seem excessive and potentially unnecessary, such a review is actually essential if concerned academics, correctional practitioners, and policymakers are to understand and plan for the complex and multifaceted nature of the problems facing older offenders in each stage of the criminal justice system—that is, from sentencing and initial placement in prison to supervision behind bars and potential release thereafter. To gain an understanding of the complex vagaries of life facing older prisoners, one need look no further than the thousands of prison counselors and case managers who are charged with the daily care and custody of aging prisoners in the United States. As one prison counselor noted, older inmates "are a corrections problem, they're a parole problem, they're a welfare problem, they're a mental health problem, and no one takes care of them" (Alston, 1986, p. 219). This book, if successful, will empower readers and policymakers to better identify the problems facing older prisoners, develop more effective policies and procedures to address identified bio-psycho-social and criminogenic problems, develop evidence-based interventions and programs for treatment and rehabilitation, implement effective and efficient interventions, and evaluate policies, procedures, interventions, and programs. The culmination of these goals should also promote the humane treatment of older prisoners while maintaining and advancing public safety.

The Evolution of Scholarship on Older Prisoners

Although the academic and policy-focused literature on older inmates evolved slowly in the early 1970s, it has since grown to include a mix of national and international publications on a multiplicity of issues facing older prisoners in the United States (see, e.g., Aday, 2003; Aday and Krabill, 2011) and abroad (see, e.g., Dawes, 2009; Her Majesty's Inspectorate of Prisons, 2004; Turner and Trotter, 2010). That said, the literature still has a long way to go before it evolves to the level of sophistication that commonly typifies the literature on younger inmates in general. Nonetheless, each of the four stages in this evolution has been essential in advancing our understanding of critical issues facing older prisoners, their care and custody, and the professionals charged with their supervision, both in prison and after release. Each new stage integrates the scientific achievements of the earlier stages while advancing the level of scientific sophistication that is brought to the old and the new questions of each era of study. Thus, many of the issues that older prisoners faced in the early 1970s are still present today, but the most recent publications are much more advanced in relation to promoting best practices and evidence-based discussions.

Stage 1: Emergent Awareness of
Older Offenders and Aging Prisoners

The first stage—the awareness stage—began during the early 1970s and was characterized by a criminal justice system that appeared to be more concerned with older people as victims rather than as perpetrators of crime

(Adams, 1995; Alston, 1986). Thus, there was limited recognition in the scholarly literature of the plight of older prisoners in federal and state correctional facilities. Unlike poverty and other persistent and widely publicized social problems across the decades, the problems associated with older prisoners did not have a defined history in the scholarly literature until the early 1970s, when the Federal Bureau of Prisons recognized the "need for special programming" for older prisoners (Kratcoski and Pownall, 1989, p. 35). Still, older inmates were relatively invisible during this period, which was characterized by a concern more for elderly victims than for older prisoners. Their invisibility was so prominent in the 1970s that Ham (1976) called aging inmates the "forgotten minority."

Stage 2: Conceptualization of Older Offenders and Aging Prisoners

The second stage began in the early 1980s, when the elderly who were caught up in state and federal courts and prisons were viewed both as criminals and as inmates (Adams, 1995). Academics and the media followed this newfound geriatric deviance, and material published during the early 1980s (mostly in the popular press) incorrectly predicted a geriatric "crime wave" (Alston, 1986); not surprisingly, a revisionist movement in the academic and professional literature debunked this crime-wave myth during the middle to late 1980s (Cullen, Wozniak, and Frank, 1985; Forsyth and Shover, 1986; Long, 1992; Steffensmeier, 1987; Steffensmeier and Harer, 1987). During this stage, numerous academics rushed to publish the first books (edited and otherwise) to address the intersection of criminology and gerontology (Alston, 1986; Chambers et al., 1987; Chaneles and Burnett, 1989; Fattah and Sacco, 1989; Malinchak, 1980; Newman and Newman, 1984; Shover, 1985; Wilbanks and Kim, 1984). The books and journal articles of the 1980s characteristically included studies seeking to develop profiles of elderly crime, elderly offenders, elderly inmates, and treatment strategies for elderly offenders inside and outside of prison (Fry, 1987; Gallagher, 1990; Kratcoski and Pownall, 1989; Rosner et al., 1991; Rosner, Wiederlight, and Schneider, 1985; Rubenstein, 1982; Wilson and Vito, 1986).

During Stage 2, there was an emergent discussion regarding which prisoners and offenders qualified as "older" or "elderly." Outside the criminal justice system, governmental programs often recognize age 65 as the cutoff between younger and older citizens, because retirement and social security benefits are tied to age 65, but criminologists and criminal justice researchers (beginning in the 1980s) often considered younger ages as appropriate cutoffs for research concerning older offenders. Some studies used age 55 as the cutoff (Brahce and Bachand, 1989; Newman, 1984; Shichor,

1984) while others used age 60 (Champion, 1987; Feinberg, 1983; Wilbanks, 1984a, 1984b), but only rarely did researchers use age 65 as the cutoff (see, e.g., Chressanthis, 1988). Still, some used multiple categories (e.g., ages 55–59, 60–64, and 65 and older) for those aged 55 and older (Meyers, 1984; Sapp, 1989; Wilbanks and Murphy, 1984). Nonetheless, a general consensus started to form in the 1980s that age 55 was the most appropriate cutoff for designating an offender as elderly.

Beyond discussions concerning age-related cutoffs for criminal justice research, Stage 2 also included a number of published typologies (briefly discussed herein) for older prisoners' sentencing histories (see, e.g., Fry; 1987; Goetting, 1983, 1984; Metzler, 1981; Tobin and Metzler, 1983; Teller and Howell, 1981). One of the original typologies for older inmates found two distinct categories: those incarcerated for the first time, and those incarcerated more than once (Teller and Howell, 1981). Metzler (1981) found three types: those incarcerated for the first time at a young age who then grew old in prison, those incarcerated for the first time as older adults who then remained in prison, and those incarcerated multiple times. Finally, Goetting (1984) developed a four-category approach, one of the more advanced typologies published to date, based on a nationwide study of 11,397 inmates selected from two independent sample frames of males and females in state penal institutions in 1979. Goetting (1984, pp. 18–19) used a sample of 248 prisoners who were 55 years of age and older to construct her four-category typology as follows:

- Type 1: Old offenders. This category consisted of those inmates who were 55 years of age or older at their first incarceration. They constituted 41.38 percent of the sample.
- Type 2: Old-timers. This category consisted of those inmates who had grown old in prison. They had been incarcerated for their current offense before the age of 55, and had served at least twenty years on that sentence. They constituted 2.32 percent of the sample.
- Type 3: Career criminals. This category consisted of recidivists whose first incarceration had been before the age of 55, and excluded old-timers. They constituted 45.60 percent of the sample.
- Type 4: Young, short-term, first-time offenders. This category consisted of first-time offenders who were incarcerated before the age of 55, and excluded old-timers. They constituted 10.68 percent of the sample.

The importance of these age-based debates and related sentencing typologies should not be underestimated. In short, it is clear that older prisoners are not all the same. Some have long histories of experience with prison life, while others have little to no exposure to the vagaries of life in federal and state facilities. Such differences have profound implications for academics, policymakers, and correctional practitioners who hope to understand their needs and create effective and efficient programs for this diverse population of aging prisoners.

Stage 3: Advancement of Effective Correctional Treatment for Aging Prisoners

The third stage began in the late 1980s and ran through the late 1990s. During this period, debates regarding age-related cutoffs to define the line between younger and older offenders and prisoners had developed a consensus: most correctional researchers and practitioners used or advocated for age 50 as the operational cutoff to define the line between the young and old, especially in prison. For example, in a 1992 publication by Joan Morton, she argued "that correctional agencies nationwide adopt age 50 as the chronological starting point to define older offenders" (1992, p. 3). Proof of this emergent standard in correctional systems was found shortly thereafter by Aday (1999), who completed a national survey of state correctional departments and found that age 50 was the most common criterion that correctional officials utilized to define old age.

This standard was also readily adopted by researchers, who considered these age-based cutoffs to be appropriate because older prisoners (aged 50 and older) appeared to have different bio-psycho-social needs as compared to inmates who were younger than 50 years of age. For example, many older prisoners appeared to experience "accelerated" aging. Biologically speaking, the literature demonstrated that "their physical . . . condition has been found to deteriorate rapidly during their prison terms" (Rubenstein, 1984, p. 157). Older prisoners' rapid decline or accelerated aging was apparently due to two factors: they may not have had healthy lifestyles prior to incarceration, and life in prison was so harsh and stressful that it was seen as exacerbating the aging process (Fattah and Sacco, 1989). Consequently, older inmates were considered to have aged roughly ten years beyond that of the average citizen (Rosefield, 1993). Thus, a 50-year-old inmate is physiologically similar to a 60-year-old person outside of prison.

Stage 3 also included the publication of various studies regarding effective correctional strategies aimed at advancing the treatment of older offenders inside and outside of prison. The search for effective correctional strategies generally conformed to two schools of thought with respect to aging inmates. The first school of thought was primarily concerned with adapting existing prison programs to meet the special needs of geriatric inmates (Aday, 1994b; Anderson and McGehee, 1991, 1994; Dugger, 1988;

Florida Department of Corrections, 1993; Morton, 1993, 1994; Vito and Wilson, 1985). While adaptation advocates gave minor attention to discussions of decarceration (e.g., release via parole or commutation of sentences), they primarily promoted the adaptation of prisons to accommodate older inmates' needs. The second school was oriented primarily toward the diversion and decarceration of older offenders (Adams, 1995; James, 1992; Kerbs, 2000b; Lundstrom, 1994). Those in this school fundamentally questioned the initial placement and maintenance of aging inmates in secure forms of confinement, in large part because age-related illnesses and disabilities often reduced or nullified their threat to society.

While the adaptation versus decarceration debate continued in the 1990s, there was a well-documented and widespread recognition of the growing number of older prisoners in the United States, often referred to as the "graying of America's prisons" (Rosefield, 1993, p. 51). This recognition was the result of a myriad of factors, including (according to the scholarly literature) an increasing reliance upon sentencing strategies that were creating an unavoidable ballooning of the aging inmate population. Generally speaking, most states and the federal government had passed a number of sentencing statutes in the 1980s and 1990s that emphasized long-term mandatory-minimum sentences and "three-strikes" strategies mandating life sentences (often without potential for parole) for recidivists (Benekos and Merlo, 1995; Turner et al., 1995).

While such statutes targeting habitual offenders have been around since the colonial days, there was a renewed interest in the passage of such laws in large number beginning in the 1980s (Turner et al., 1995). Consequently, in 1993, Rosefield noted that "geriatric" inmates had arrived in US prisons, and that many more were "just over the horizon" (p. 57). The best available data from the 1990s supported this contention, and experts were already saying that various states would rename prisons as "centers for the treatment of old folks" (Rosefield, 1993, p. 57), and "old age homes for felons" (Zimbardo, 1994, p. 1). As shown in Table 1.1, the number of older prisoners in federal and state prisons grew by about 10,000 prisoners a year in the 1990s, from 34,845 prisoners aged 50 and older in 1991 to 113,358 older inmates in 2001 (C. G. Camp and G. M. Camp, 1994–2001; G. M. Camp and C. G. Camp 1991–1993). The proportion of older inmates also grew, from 5.3 percent of the total federal and state prison population in 1991 to 7.9 percent in 2001. These figures collectively demonstrated the start (beginning in the early 1990s) of a "stacking effect" whereby older inmates (aged 50 and older) multiplied in number and proportion in the 1990s due to sentencing statutes that required younger and older inmates (especially recidivists) to be incarcerated longer, often into their senior years, with or without hope of parole (Zimbardo, 1994). While the "stacking

Table 1.1 Number of Prisoners Aged 50 and Older in Federal and State Prisons, 1991–2001

Agency	1991	1992	1993	1994	1995	1996	1997	1998	1999	2000	2001
State[a]	28,948	35,032	37,058	41,309	45,226	50,896	62,272	69,994	77,146	87,358	97,292
Federal[b]	5,897	6,554	7,244	9,169	10,055	12,108	11,271	13,673	15,216	15,774	16,066
Total[c]	34,845	41,586	44,302	50,478	55,281	63,004	73,543	83,667	92,362	103,132	113,358
Percentage of total[d]	5.3	5.7	6.0	5.9	6.1	6.6	6.8	7.2	7.0	8.6	7.9

Sources: C. G. Camp and G. M. Camp, 1994–2001; G. M. Camp and C. G. Camp, 1991–1993.

Notes: a. Figures represent the aggregate of all inmates aged 50 and older in adult correctional agencies on January 1 of each year.

b. Figures represent the aggregate of all inmates aged 50 and older in the Federal Bureau of Prisons on January 1 of each year.

c. Figures reflect the aggregate of federal and state prison populations for each year.

d. Percentage of the total prison population in federal and state prisons on January 1 of each year.

effect" of the 1990s was well documented, the implications of this phenomenon had yet to be fully appreciated until the turn of the century. Thus, Stage 3 closed with a clear recognition that the United States would be housing an increasingly large population of older prisoners. It was not until Stage 4 that some of the commonly overlooked questions from the 1990s would begin to be answered.

Stage 4: Advancement of Specialized Research on Older Prisoners

Pragmatically speaking, the fourth stage began in 2000 and continues through the present day with an increased focus on the advancement of scientific research regarding the needs and service requirements for various subtypes of older prisoners, including older men, older women, older inmates with chronic illnesses and disabilities, older prisoners with terminal diseases, and older inmates in need of palliative and hospice care. Not surprisingly, this era of specialized research formed amid a continuation of the stacking effect across time, with the literature becoming more demographically sophisticated in relation to who was being stacked (largely sex offenders and violent offenders), what they needed, and the programs and services that would meet their specific needs (Aday, 2003; Aday and Krabill, 2011; Kerbs, 2000a, 2000b). That said, just measuring the counts for who was 50 years of age and older was not made simple until Stage 4. Unfortunately, the Bureau of Justice Statistics was very slow to alter its reporting patterns for age-based counts of federal and state prisoners, as evidenced by its reliance upon mid-decade cutoffs (e.g., 40–44, 45–54, and 55 and older) for age-based prison data (see, e.g., Sabol, Couture, and Harrison, 2007), which was counter to the suggested use of age 50 as the cutoff. Nonetheless, in 2008, the Bureau of Justice Statistics moved more appropriately to age-based cutoffs that started at age 50 (e.g., 50–54, 55–59, 60–64, and 65 and older) (West and Sabol, 2008). Hence, the tracking of stacking by demographic categories (i.e., tracking to include the intersection of gender, race, and age beginning at age 50) was not implemented in Bureau of Justice Statistics reports until after December 2008 (West and Sabol, 2008).

The tracking of stacking by demographic categories. According to the most recent release of Bureau of Justice Statistics data, federal and state correctional facilities housed about a quarter of a million inmates ($n = 246,600$) aged 50 and older on December 31, 2010; this figure translates into 15.9 percent of the combined federal and state prison populations, up from 8.6 percent in 2000 (a decade earlier), when state and federal prison collectively housed 103,132 prisoners in this age group (Camp and Camp, 2000; Guerino, Harrison, and Sabol, 2012). In relation to intersection of age and gender, the vast majority of older prisoners in 2010 were male (n = 233,000), but there was still a sizable population of women (n = 13,600) in federal and state facilities; proportionally, males constituted about 94.5 percent of all prisoners aged 50 and older in 2010, while females comprised about 5.5 percent of this prisoner population (Guerino, Harrison, and Sabol, 2012). Interestingly, the proportional representation of older males and females did not change across the two decades from 1990 to 2010 (see Kerbs, 2000b).

In relation to the intersection of age, gender, and race, Bureau of Justice Statistics data documented a significant amount of racial and ethnic diversity among older men and women (aged 50 and older) in prison (Guerino, Harrison, and Sabol, 2012). In 2010, whites constituted the highest proportion (41.2 percent) of all older men in federal and state prisons, but substantial proportions of older African American men (33.2 percent), older Hispanic men (15.2 percent), and older inmates who identified as multiracial (10.3 percent) were also present in US prisons. Similar to the proportional representation for older men in federal and state prisons in 2010, whites constituted the highest proportion (47.8 percent) of all older women in prisons, but substantial proportions of older African American women (25.7 percent), older Hispanic women (14.0 percent), and older women in prison who identified as multiracial (12.5 percent) were also present in US correctional facilities.

The exact numbers associated with these percentages are presented in Table 1.2. The largest group of older men behind bars on December 31, 2010, was white men (n = 96,100), followed by African American men (n = 77,400) and Hispanic men (n = 35,500). For older women in prison, the same pattern held, with white women representing the largest group (n = 6,500), followed by African American women (n = 3,500) and Hispanic women (n = 1,900). Interestingly, as one moved up the age brackets—from 50–54, to 55–59, to 60–64, to 65 and older—the number of older men and women decreased with each incremental step in age; starting at age 60, the number of older women in prison actually fell into the hundreds, regardless of their racial or ethnic identification.

Whereas older whites (regardless of gender) outnumbered older African Americans and Hispanics in federal and state prisons, the demographic trends were more complex in relation to the rates of incarceration per 100,000 US residents. Research by Guerino, Harrison, and Sabol (2012) found that older men (as compared to older women) were incarcerated at much higher rates across all age brackets and all racial/ethnic groups in 2010. Among males, Older African American men had the highest rates of

Table 1.2 Estimated Number of Sentenced Prisoners Aged 50 and Older Under State and Federal Jurisdiction, by Sex, Race, and Hispanic Origin, December 31, 2010 (incarceration rates per 100,000 population in parentheses)

Age	Male				Female			
	Total[a]	White[b]	Black[b]	Hispanic	Total[a]	White[b]	Black[b]	Hispanic
50–54	114,000 (1,015)	43,200 (552)	41,100 (3,441)	18,000 (1,495)	7,700 (68)	3,600 (45)	2,100 (150)	1,100 (88)
55–59	61,700 (650)	24,700 (347)	21,400 (2,239)	9,300 (1,031)	3,500 (34)	1,600 (22)	900 (76)	500 (55)
60–64	32,000 (391)	14,700 (233)	9,300 (1,262)	4,600 (679)	1,500 (17)	800 (12)	300 (33)	200 (29)
65 and older	25,300 (143)	13,500 (95)	5,600 (418)	3,600 (294)	900 (4)	500 (3)	200 (7)	100 (8)
Total	233,000	96,100	77,400	35,500	13,600	6,500	3,500	1,900

Source: Guerino, Harrison, and Sabol, 2012.
Notes: Data source used to estimate race and Hispanic origin was changed in 2010, and data source for age distributions was enhanced between 2009 and 2010. Use caution when comparing prior years. Counts based on prisoners with a sentence of more than one year.
a. Includes American Indians, Alaska Natives, Asians, Native Hawaiians, other Pacific Islanders, and persons self-identifying as two or more races.
b. Excludes persons of Hispanic or Latino origin.

incarceration per 100,000 residents within each age bracket in 2010, older Hispanic males had the second highest rates, and older white males had the lowest rates.

With one minor exception, Table 1.2 also documents the same pattern of rates for older women in prison, with older African American women having the highest rates of incarceration across almost all age brackets; the single exception was for the category of 65 and older, which was dominated by older Hispanic women. Older Hispanic women had the second highest rates of incarceration for the remaining categories, and older white women had the lowest rates of incarceration across all age brackets. In terms of ratios, generally, older African American and Hispanic women tended to be incarcerated at rates that were two to three or more times higher than the rates for older white women. For example, the rate of incarceration for older African American women who were 55 to 59 years of age on December 31, 2010, was 76 per 100,000 US residents, which was 3.45 times higher than the corresponding rate for older white women behind bars, at 22 per 100,000 residents. Within the same age bracket, the incarceration rate for older Hispanic women was 55 per 100,000 residents, which was 2.50 times higher than the corresponding rate for older white women, at 22 per 100,000 residents.

The national figures for incarcerated women as shown in Table 1.2 are clearly complex, and interpretations of these data can change radically when one moves from reviewing the number of women who are incarcerated to the rate of incarceration for women. Differences within and between groups that are delineated along sociodemographic lines (age, gender, race, and/or ethnicity) are indicative of disproportionate rates of incarceration for older nonwhite women, including older African American and older Hispanic women. Unfortunately, the data as released by the Bureau of Justice Statistics do not provide additional clarifications for the rates of incarceration as specifically applied to American Indians or Alaskan Natives, Asian Americans, and Hawaiian or Pacific Islanders (to name but a few groups). Nonetheless, such clarifications are needed as federal and state prisons continue their efforts to provide specialized programming for the diverse array of aging inmates in the United States.

Research regarding specific needs and specialized programming. During Stage 4, scientific and specialty literature started to mature on a variety of pressing topics. Although many of these topics were examined in publications from Stage 3, the fourth stage generally included more sophisticated examinations of sentencing practices resulting in the graying of America's prisons (see, e.g., Auerhahn, 2003), the bio-psycho-social needs of older prisoners (see, e.g., Marquart, Merianos, and Doucet, 2000; Maruschak, 2008; Leigey and Hodge, 2012), gender-specific issues (see, e.g.,

Aday and Krabill, 2011; Aday and Nation, 2001; Caldwell, Jarvis, and Rosefield, 2001; Leigey and Hodge, 2012), older prisoners' safety (see, e.g., Kerbs and Jolley, 2007), palliative and hospice care for aging inmates (Linder and Meyers, 2007, 2009), and so on.

In an effort to build upon this maturing base of literature, this book will provide the most up-to-date and scientifically informed discussions of policy-relevant topics facing older prisoners in the United States. This critical engagement of the scholarly literature aims to analyze correctional efforts to meet the needs of older inmates in prison systems that were inherently designed for relatively younger, less medically intensive, and more aggressive inmates. Therefore, this book examines the fit (or lack thereof at times) between the needs of older inmates and the correctional policies and practices that govern efforts to meet those needs. This examination will cover a wide range of practice and policy-relevant themes, including older prisoners' medical care, their psychological adjustment and mental health care in prison, their vulnerability to multiple forms of victimization, their access to theoretically informed programming that supports rehabilitation and reentry into society, and the overall poor standard of care for older inmates that has emerged within state and federal prisons. Solutions to the lack of fit between older inmates' needs and correctional policies and practices are discussed by proposing ways to advance evidence-based corrections and evidence-based programs for this complex and vulnerable population.

Overview of Chapters

The structure of this book and the organization of the chapters follow a logical order related to the correctional continuum of custody, from sentencing to incarceration to potential release. Collectively, the chapters aim to examine the experiences of older inmates, from courts through prisons and reentry, with individual chapters rigorously assessing factors that shape older inmates' daily routines and potential trajectories in correctional systems.

In Chapter 2, Kathleen Auerhahn critically examines how changes in sentencing strategies have increased the number and proportion of older inmates. Beginning with historical and conceptual analyses, she traces the evolution of sentencing reforms from an era that favored discretion in sentencing policy (indeterminate sentencing) to an era that favored dictation of the terms and conditions of sentencing policy (determinate sentencing), especially as applied to recidivists. Thereafter, using data from California, she empirically tracks and analyzes the growth in the state's population of older prisoners, and the relationship between the increase in California's older prisoner population and changes in sentencing policy related to the shift from indeterminate to determinate sentencing strategies. The chapter concludes with a review of some provocative policy suggestions, including implementation of geriatric release programs for older offenders who present little threat to public safety.

In Chapter 3, Margaret Leigey looks at the bio-psycho-social needs of older prisoners and policy implications aimed at addressing identified needs. She highlights both what is known and what is not known about older prisoners' needs, while simultaneously identifying a series of inconsistent findings and gaps in the published research to date. Her literature review provides insight into how the older prisoners' biological, psychological, and social needs differ from the needs of the younger inmates; moreover, she explores the current status of knowledge regarding special populations of older prisoners, including older women and older minorities in federal and state prisons. Finally, she concludes by advocating for the use of age-specific programs, policies, and procedures.

In Chapter 4, Ronald Aday and Jennifer Krabill critically analyze (using the developmental lens of gerontology) the fit between older inmates' bio-psycho-social needs and the services that are provided to them. To this end, they explore how correctional systems can promote the creation of humanistic prisons that creatively apply resources to structure the daily routines of aging inmates in ways that address their special needs. Models of successful aging are described and used as frameworks for evaluating the ways in which current modes of prison programming do, and do not (as is often the case), support aging inmates' psychosocial engagement and integration. Moreover, models of successful aging are used to describe the programming practices and approaches that correctional officials should consider using to promote the psychosocial engagement of aging inmates via productive and healthy daily routines. Finally, various components of gerontologically specialized programming (e.g., support groups and work opportunities) are described in depth, and a fully integrated best-practice model from Nevada (the True Grit program) is used to demonstrate the potential benefits that may be derived from providing a strong therapeutic social milieu for a diverse aging inmate population.

In Chapter 5, Jennifer Jolley, John Kerbs, and John Linder assess the treatment of older women in prison; given the paucity of research available on this topic, they provide both a brief overview of the best available research regarding their sociodemographic characteristics and their gender-specific needs, especially in relation to their physical and mental health needs. To avoid a redundant review of the literature on older women in prison as discussed in Chapter 3, the authors of Chapter 5 focus on methodological problems that undermine the results of most studies to date concerning older women in federal and state prisons. Thereafter, the authors make suggestions for potential modifications of research designs to improve the quality of research involving older women in prison, our base of knowledge regarding the needs of older women in prison, and the utility of this research to inform the development of policies, procedures, and programs to meet their needs. The chapter concludes by reviewing a heuristic model for quality of care as applied to health-care systems that serve older women in prison who require specialized treatment for serious and often multiple chronic conditions. The authors of this chapter demonstrate that this model, if utilized in the development of studies that examine and evaluate the delivery of health services to older women behind bars, could advance our understanding of the longitudinal aspects of their care. More specifically, this model examines the structures (buildings, equipment, and staff) that might serve their needs, the clinical processes (technical care and interpersonal relationships) involved in their treatment, and the short- and long-term outcomes of their care (changes in health status, the levels of functioning, symptom relief, and so on).

In Chapter 6, Naoki Kanaboshi analyzes case law and legislation that affects the handling of older inmates; legal liabilities and mandates are reviewed and specifically applied to the most pressing issues facing older prisoners (e.g., end-of-life care, accommodations for disabilities, right to refuse medications). In order to provide the reader with needed insights into the future of prisoners' rights for the aging prison population in the United States, this chapter serves as a constitutional primer that addresses five major issues: health care, conditions of confinement, protection from other prisoners, refusal of medical treatment, and statutory rights of prisoners. Specific legal analyses examine the role of the Eighth and Fourteenth Amendments, the Americans with Disabilities Act of 1990, and the Rehabilitation Act of 1973. This chapter demonstrates that the courts have provided strong protections to older inmates, especially those with disabilities, which suggests that policymakers and prison officials would be well advised to become aware of and fully compliant with the recent advancements in the rights of older disabled prisoners.

In Chapter 7, Anita Blowers, Jennifer Jolley, and John Kerbs present the foundational arguments of the age-segregation debate and assess whether it is more appropriate to mainstream older inmates into the general prison population or to provide them with age-segregated living arrangements. The authors place an emphasis on three key issues that those who advocate for the integration position and those who advocate for the segregation position build into their arguments: access to and utilization of quality medical and mental health services, maintenance of social order in prisons, and creation of age-appropriate social environments. Thus the authors assess each of these three points by summarizing the evidence presented from both the age-integration perspective and the age-segregation perspective. Finally, policy implications that stem from this debate are examined in detail.

In Chapter 8, John Kerbs and Jennifer Jolley examine the implications of the inverse relationship between age and crime; as offenders age, they are less likely to be rearrested, reconvicted, and reincarcerated. Thus, the authors suggest that the implication of warehousing aging offenders who are desisting from criminal activity is self-evident: the expensive and limited supply of prison beds in the United States is increasingly occupied with aging offenders who are at low risk of recidivism due to age-based desistance and other age-related factors, including health problems. That said, the authors seek to review three key issues: the empirical proof of age-based desistance across the life course; a theoretical explanation for age-graded declines in criminal behavior as theorized and empirically examined via Sampson and Laub's (2003) age-graded theory of informal social control; and policy and program suggestions as informed by the integration of empirical and theoretical aspects of age-based desistance from criminal behavior.

In Chapter 9, John Linder looks at end-of-life care as provided by disease-directed therapy (this includes efforts to cure or control life-threatening diseases or conditions), palliative care (these programs ameliorate patient distress and the relief of symptoms, regardless of whether the goals of treatment are curative or focused on comfort), and hospice care (these programs are reserved for terminally ill patients who decide to forego disease-directed interventions in favor of symptom management and a peaceful, natural death) for aging inmates. He argues that no issue will exert more strain on state and federal corrections systems in the next three decades than the aging of the inmate population and their required end-of-life care as they increasingly face life-limiting illness while incarcerated (morbidity) and (for many) inevitable death behind bars (mortality). He describes the medical conditions that will cause the most inmate morbidity and mortality for older inmates (typically those aged 55 and older), the different courses of treatment available for these illnesses, prisoners' entitlement to health care, and the cost and financing of that care. He also examines the facilities, policies, and programs for care that are currently available, versus those needed to deal with these diseases and deaths; moreover, he compares the end-of-life care available inside the prison system to that available in free society. Finally, his discussion focuses on health care disparities, treatment goals, and correlation between inmates' socioeconomic, ethnic, racial, and gender characteristics and probable treatment choices.

Because many older prisoners return to society, Kristie Blevins and Anita Blowers crafted Chapter 10 to include a comprehensive examination of reentry issues and options for older inmates. At present, most research on prisoner reentry tends to focus on younger releasees and age-neutral discussions that provide little insight into the age-specific issues facing older releasees. While such information is important, we must also explore issues relating to the successful reentry of older prisoners. Thus, the authors focus attention on the special needs (housing, employment, familial relationships, health-care issues) that older prisoners face during their reintegration back into society. First, the authors review issues that must be taken into account when designing and implementing reentry programs for older prisoners. Thereafter, they examine current reentry initiatives and programs for older prisoners and policy implications that need to be addressed to effectively manage their successful reintegration. Finally, the authors review the sociopolitical and policy-based obstacles that complicate the reentry of older federal and state prisoners into society.

Finally, in Chapter 11, John Kerbs and Jennifer Jolley examine the implications of this book in relation to the advancement of evidence-based programs for the aging US prison population. They begin by reviewing a framework for the development, implementation, and evaluation of effective correctional interventions. Based on this framework, they then propose multiple studies that are profoundly needed to advance the system's ability to work effectively and efficiently with older offenders in courts, prisons, and in free society thereafter for those who are released. While these studies are not exhaustive of all possible areas of inquiry, they do represent a modest and important first step in efforts to gain a better understanding of what works and what does not work with aging and older offenders and prisoners. Finally, the chapter concludes with comments about funding for such research, as such research will never materialize without adequate support from private foundations, state governments, and federal agencies like the US Department of Justice's Office of Justice Programs, which houses a myriad of funding opportunities as offered through related offices and bureaus therein.

Conclusion

The United States currently incarcerates more adults than any other country in the world (Porter, 2011), with federal and state prisons housing over 1.6 million inmates as of December 31, 2010 (Guerino, Harrison, and Sabol, 2012). It may also be the case that the United States incarcerates more older prisoners than any other country in the world, and perhaps more than all countries combined. Canada, for example, housed only about 2,900 older prisoners (aged 50 and older) in its federal penitentiaries in

July 2011 (representing about 19 percent of Canada's total federal population behind bars) (Sapers, 2011); moreover, many countries in the European Union house under a thousand older prisoners (e.g., Australia housed 656 prisoners aged 50 and older in 2009) (Turner and Trotter, 2010). To competently and humanely meet the needs of this expanding population (both in the United States and abroad), prison administrators and correctional officers would be well advised to use the best available information to inform their interventions, policies, procedures, and programs.

This book aims to provide a solid step toward this goal. Fortunately, there is a growing base of literature on older prisoners, who are no longer a "forgotten minority" as discussed by Ham in 1976. Today, older prisoners are more aptly characterized as a "memorable minority" who are poorly understood, often overlooked, and (as we shall see) vulnerable to a number of bio-psycho-social problems. They are becoming increasingly more challenging for the operational capacities of prisons nationwide. While most prisons are inherently designed for younger and relatively healthier offenders (Aday, 2003), the growing population of older prisoners is causing the United States to rethink the concept of care and custody to include the management of correctional nursing homes. Thus, because aging inmates become more vulnerable, unhealthy, and infirm over time, this book aims to provide insights into how best to meet their complex needs, both in prison and in the community after release.

With such insights, this book also aims to reframe the view of aging and older inmates so that they are seen as citizens who deserve an adequate and a humane standard of care and custody that is premised on a rights-based jurisprudence (philosophy of law). Most academics and policymakers do not view inmates as "citizens" in the typical sense, because the civil penalties imposed upon them effectively "deny felons the full rights of citizenship" (Uggen, Manza, and Thompson, 2006, p. 282)—the rights that are typically enjoyed by nonfelons outside of prison. The literature on the collateral consequences of felony convictions, on both incarcerated federal and state prisoners and released felons, is fairly extensive and covers how such convictions and prison placements can (depending on the jurisdiction involved) diminish or eliminate (temporarily or permanently) rights related to employment and licensure in specific occupations, eligibility for student grants and loans, possession of firearms, residency in the United States, jury service, marriage, parenting, eligibility for public assistance (such as food stamps), residency in public housing, holding of public office, and voting (Buckler and Travis, 2003; Ruddell and Winfree, 2006; Uggen, Manza, and Thompson, 2006).

Still, prisoners do have rights that have been affirmed in state and federal courts in the United States, including the Supreme Court. Thus, the book's title suggests the need to reconceptualize how we view older prisoners, from seeing them as a group of inmates who have (or deserve) diminished rights, to seeing them as a group of citizens who should still enjoy a rights-based jurisprudence, albeit modified based on the US Constitution, case law, and the statutes in any given jurisdiction. Thus, the contributors to the book will show that these aging prisoners are citizens with specific rights that need to be upheld and protected, both during their incarceration and after release for those who return to society. The "iron law of corrections" (Travis, 2005b) indicates that "with the exception of a very small percentage of inmates who actually die in custody, everybody else is released" (Ruddell and Winfree, 2006, p. 453). Thus, if as a society we fail to honor and shoulder the costs of adequate and humane care (including medical care) and custody, we may pay a heavy price related to successful legal claims against correctional officers, staff, and administrators. After the release of older prisoners, taxpayers also may find themselves shouldering health-care costs if these former inmates are in poor health and must rely too heavily on public insurance programs (Medicaid, Medicare, and Veterans Administration programs, etc), which is why Thompson noted that "the financial and public health impact of inadequate prison medical care cannot be ignored" (2010, p. 653).

In sum, to the extent that the number and proportion of older prisoners will continue to grow in the coming decades, we have an obligation, as a society, legally and otherwise, to meet the needs of these people. We cannot simply turn a blind eye to the graying of America's prisons. While we raise a number of concerns and document a plethora of disturbing findings in the extant literature, we also present feasible policy solutions to many of the issues that face federal and state inmates and the prisons that house them. To the extent that we honor and effectively address the needs of this special population, we will advance public health and public safety, but failure to do so will certainly result in adverse outcomes that are counter to such public interests.

2

Sentencing Policy and the Shaping of Prison Demographics

Kathleen Auerhahn

This chapter examines the role of criminal sentencing policy in generating populations of elderly offenders. Since the 1970s and continuing up to the present day, a great deal of sentencing policy reform has taken place in the United States. This chapter provides an examination of the ways in which the number and proportion of older inmates have increased in relation to changes in sentencing policy. Historical and conceptual analyses trace the evolution of sentencing reform across an era that favored discretion in sentencing policy (indeterminate sentencing) to an era that favored dictation of the terms and conditions of sentencing policy (determinate sentencing). Empirical analyses then track the growth in California's population of older inmates in relationship to changes in sentencing policy as California moved from indeterminate to determinate sentencing strategies.

The problem of aging inmates in United States prisons is one that has received an increasing amount of attention in recent years. Prisoners aged 50 and older are the fastest-growing segment of the prison population; in many states, the proportional representation of elderly prisoners doubled between 1992 and 2004 (Ahn-Redding, 2007; Williams, 2006). As the analysis of the extant literature and California's experience will show, relatively recent, highly publicized and politicized reforms such as habitual-offender or "three-strikes" laws, reforms promising "truth-in-sentencing," and the curtailment of parole release in many jurisdictions play a significant role in generating elderly prison populations. However, the origins of this crisis trace back four decades, to the 1970s. The long-term and systemic impact of sentencing reforms since then have shaped prison populations in complex and profound ways, bearing upon the effect of more recent trends and movements in sentencing policy reform. This chapter also discusses a number of demographic changes in California's prison population, including (1) the growth in the number of prisoners since the implementation of the state's Determinate Sentencing Law in 1976, (2) the increase in the number of prisoners aged 50 and older since 1977, (3) changes in the mean age of California's prison population since 1960, (4) changes over time in the percentage of California's prisoners aged 50 and older, and (5) changes over time in the percentage of newly admitted prisoners aged 50 and older in California.

Older prisoners fall into several distinct categories. These include career offenders, who are currently incarcerated as part of a pattern of multiple incarceration episodes and who have grown older both in and out of prison. Then there are the late-bloomers or first-timers, who were sentenced to prison at a relatively advanced age. Finally, there are the prisoners who were sentenced in their youth to life or similarly lengthy terms and who have aged in prison. Dunlop, Rothman, and Hirt (2001) report that among prisoners aged 55 and older in the United States, approximately 47 percent are career recidivists, 40 percent are first-timers, and a mere 13 percent are longtime inmates who have aged in prison. The distribution of offender types in the older prison population gives us some insight as to how sentencing reforms can play a powerful role in shaping this population. That more than 80 percent of prisoners aged 55 and older have been sentenced relatively recently (combined with stable or declining rates of offending in this population) indicates that recent sentencing reforms are heavily implicated in the growth of this segment of the prison population.

While admissions of older prisoners have increased dramatically since the 1990s, the rate at which older offenders commit crime has remained relatively constant or has declined (Federal Bureau of Investigation, 2003; Flynn, 2000; King and Mauer, 2001). However, older prisoners are disproportionately convicted of more serious offenses. Older prisoners are more likely to have been convicted of a violent offense than are younger prisoners, and older offenders who are sentenced to prison receive longer sentences, on average, than their younger counterparts (Martinez et al., 1999; Williams, 2006). However, recidivism rates for older offenders are quite low. A 1998 analysis reported that 45 percent of released prisoners between the ages of 18 and 29 were returned to prison within a year of release. The corresponding rate for released offenders aged 55 and older was 3.2 percent (Chiu, 2010; Coalition for Federal Sentencing Reform, 1998; see also Pastore and Maguire, 2010; Williams, 2006).

In this chapter, I first discuss the evolution of sentencing policy in the United States. While it is a misnomer to speak of "the US criminal justice system" (there are more accurately fifty state systems plus the federal system and the justice apparatus in the District of Columbia), there have been distinct movements or paradigms in criminal sentencing policy reform, showing evidence of consensus in this arena (see Auerhahn, 2003). Sentencing paradigms express policy goals, which in turn reflect beliefs about the causes of crime and the purpose of punishment. I then review national trends in the changing composition of prison populations and their relationship to sentencing reform.

Next, I turn to the empirical case of California. California is in many ways uniquely important to such an analysis. Despite declines in the prison population since 2000, California houses the largest state prison population in the nation (followed closely by Texas; Pastore and Maguire 2010). Despite an absolutely disastrous fiscal crisis—in no small part attributable to the massive expenditures on criminal justice—California has increased its prison population more than sixfold since 1980. This growth has been accompanied by an exponential increase in the number and rate of elderly prisoners housed in state correctional facilities; since 1980, the number of prisoners aged 50 and older has increased more than 3,500 percent (California Department of Corrections and Rehabilitation [CDCR], 2010). The proportional representation of prisoners aged 50 and older in the state's incarcerated population, currently 15.5 percent, has steadily increased since 1980.

In addition to examining trends in the growth of California's elderly prison population, the chapter also evaluates the effects of sentencing reform in the state with reference to the rationale underlying these reforms. In recent years, the primary goal of incarceration, as expressed in the nature and content of sentencing reform, has been social defense or incapacitation (i.e., removing offenders from society via imprisonment). As will be discussed, the promise of incarceration policy in California and elsewhere has been to protect the public from dangerous criminals. From the standpoint of policy evaluation and the goals of incarceration, the wisdom and efficaciousness of housing an ever-growing elderly prison population in light of this objective is questionable at best, particularly given what we know about the inverse relationship between age and dangerous criminal behavior. Because of the challenges associated with housing this population given the minimal public safety threat they present in the aggregate, sentencing policies that serve to increase the size of the elderly prison population deserve further scrutiny. The chapter concludes with a discussion of alternatives to the current state of affairs.

History of Criminal Sentencing Reform in the United States

The Rehabilitative Era

The first modern penitentiary, the Walnut Street Jail, was established in Philadelphia, Pennsylvania, in 1776. Based on the belief that the offender could be reformed through suffering, incarceration was merely a means to an end—the reform of the transgressor and ultimately their return to society (Wines, 1871). Shortly thereafter, indeterminate sentencing structures quickly swept through the nation. The central idea behind indeterminate sentences was that the offender was to be detained until such time as they were no longer a threat to society; the task of determining an offender's fitness to rejoin society fell to a panel of experts administering a parole system (Wines, 1871; Zalman, 1977–1978). Indeterminate sentencing as applied in the United States was not strictly indeterminate; most jurisdictions specified a maximum term, but the parole board could release prisoners at an earlier date if they were deemed to be reformed. Michigan was the first state to establish a system of indeterminate sentencing, in 1877. By 1915, twenty-five states had followed suit, and by 1922, there were only four states that did not have some form of indeterminate sentencing in place (Dershowitz, 1976; Miller, Dinitz, and Conrad, 1982).

A system of indeterminate sentencing was very well-suited to a paradigm based on the idea of rehabilitation and reformation of the offender. Sentencing judges had a great deal of discretion in handing down sentences, commonly with very long ranges. However, the real power in such a system lies in the hands of those who operate at the "back end" of the system. The actual length of time served by a convicted felon was ultimately determined by the parole board and sometimes supplemented by the input of experts such as psychologists, particularly in the latter half of the twentieth century, when actuarial risk-assessment tools came to be more and more ubiquitous.

The Demise of Rehabilitation: Searching for a Rationale

As the 1970s dawned, Americans became increasingly disenchanted with the rehabilitative vision of prisons. A number of causes of this have been identified, including the "radical loss of confidence in political and social institutions" (Allen, 1981, p. 18) fostered by the Vietnam War, the Watergate scandal, and increasing rates of crime. Critics on both the right and the left cited the lack of standardization and the uneven outcomes that resulted from the discretion of local release-granting authorities (Frankel, 1973; Morris, 1974; van den Haag, 1975; von Hirsch, 1976). Others questioned the ethics of the rehabilitative enterprise, claiming that it was essentially coercive, and as such antithetical to American ideals of self-determination and individual liberty (Kittrie, 1971; Mitford, 1973; Morris, 1974).

This discontent was buttressed by the widely held interpretation of the conclusions of a group of researchers tasked with the evaluation of a wide range of rehabilitative programs that "nothing works" for reducing recidivism (Lipton, Martinson, and Wilks 1975; Martinson, 1974). The rejection of rehabilitation as the primary purpose of criminal punishment was clearly articulated in a statement submitted by the Department of Justice during the congressional hearings concerning the Comprehensive Crime Control Act of 1983, which derisively dismissed the "outmoded nineteenth-century rehabilitative theory that has proved to be so faulty that it is no longer followed by the criminal justice system."

The next several decades brought a whirlwind of changes, as criminal justice authorities and experts endeavored to replace rehabilitation with a new paradigm. California, for example, has enacted over a thousand laws reforming criminal sentencing since 1976; more than 400 such bills were passed in the state legislature in the 1990s alone (Foote, 1993; Schrag, 1998). After holding nearly undisputed influence for almost 200 years, the rehabilitative ideal fell out of favor. What followed was a decisive move toward a different policy choice, albeit one lacking a coherent rationale. Unlike the indeterminate sentencing movement of the nineteenth and early twentieth centuries, which was guided by the reformers' utopian vision of rehabilitation, the initial shift in the 1970s toward determinate sentences appeared as more of a reaction to the perceived failure of the rehabilitative paradigm rather than the substitution of a new vision of the purpose of criminal punishment.

Despite the lack of a clear raison d'être, the shift away from indeterminate sentencing was as widely supported as the earlier movement toward it. Political liberals embraced determinate sentencing, in which an upper and lower term of incarceration was specified based on the conviction offense, as a means for reducing sentencing disparities (particularly as manifested along racial and geographic lines), and viewed the curtailing of discretion in the system as inherently favorable to justice (Hewitt and Clear, 1983; Kadish, 1978; von Hirsch and Hanrahan, 1981). Determinate sentencing also found support among conservatives, some of whom believed that it would increase the certainty of punishment, thus enhancing its deterrent effect (Wilson, 1975), while others embraced the more expressly punitive nature of determinate sentencing (van den Haag, 1975).

The move toward determinate sentencing reflected a new view about the causes of crime and the appropriate response to it. Criminal punishment under the rehabilitative paradigm was justified by the objective of "treatment," based on the belief that the causes of crime were something external to the individual, something that could be excised, changed, and reformed. The determinate sentence is oriented toward a different object. While the offender was paramount under indeterminate sentencing—the release decision being based on an individualized assessment of whether or not the individual had been rehabilitated—the new system of determinate sentencing focused not on the offender, but on the act. Individual offenders become irrelevant in this scheme; society demands punishment *for the act,* rather than punishment *of the offender.*

Deterrence quickly emerged as the supporting rationale for determinate sentencing frameworks. However, despite the profusion of research studies that emerged throughout the middle 1960s and into the 1970s, experts were generally in agreement that "arguing [in favor of] . . . a policy on the basis of the empirical evidence [of deterrent effects] is not yet justified because it offers a misleading impression of scientific validity" (Nagin, 1978, p. 136; see also Nagin, 1998).

Casting about for another rationale, US criminal justice took a punitive turn in the 1980s. Policy reforms such as mandatory minimum sentences reflected this retributive focus. That so many of these new sentences targeted drug offenses spoke to their retributive roots; the moral and symbolic character of harsh penalty structures for drug offenses was evidenced by their persistence, particularly in the absence of evidence that these penalties are effective in reducing either drug use or crime (Baum, 1996; Caulkins et al., 1997; Gordon, 1994; Harcourt, 2001). By 1994, every state had some form of mandatory sentencing in place. By the last decade of the twentieth century, social defense concerns had clearly won out in the search for a new rationale for the punishment of criminals. Given the empirical failures of both the rehabilitative and deterrence paradigms, incapacitation seemed the only remaining justification for the incarceration of criminals (Zimring and Hawkins, 1995). However, as Cohen (1983) pointed out, incapacitation, while effective, has its limits. While it would be theoretically possible to eliminate all crime by incarcerating an ever-larger segment of the population, that strategy is ultimately untenable. In the 1990s and beyond, sentencing policy reform was characterized by an emphasis on particularistic or targeted sentencing policies and practices that are grounded in the logic of selective incapacitation.

Selective Incapacitation: Targeted Sentencing

I have argued elsewhere (Auerhahn, 1999, 2003) that the idea of selective incapacitation has had a profound impact on the shaping of criminal justice policy and prison populations since the late twentieth century. The trend in sentencing reform during this period is frequently characterized as "getting tough on crime," but a deeper examination of the nature and content of sentencing reform—particularly in the post-1990 era—reveals that these policies are not *uniformly* tough; rather, sentencing policy and practice comes to be increasingly *targeted* or *particularistic* (Auerhahn, 2003). The idea of selective incapacitation has its origins in the findings of the Philadelphia cohort study conducted by Wolfgang, Figlio, and Sellin (1972). Following a cohort of boys born in the city of Philadelphia in 1945, these researchers discovered that a mere 6.3 percent of the cohort (representing 18 percent of those committing any criminal offenses) were responsible for 51.9 percent of all offenses committed by the cohort, a finding that was closely replicated in the Racine cohort study conducted by Shannon (1991). The 18 percent figure has also been closely approximated in studies of offending populations (Chaiken and Chaiken, 1984; Wright and Rossi, 1986).

The notion of selective incapacitation is a perfectly logical response to the empirical demonstration of the career criminal (also variously called "high-rate offenders" and "predators"). The idea is simple: since we know that a small fraction of the offenders are responsible for a large proportion of crime, then a strategy that targets these offenders and incapacitates them via incarceration would be the most efficient means of crime control, as well as the most efficient use of penal resources. The idea is often traced to Greenberg (1975; see also Avi-Itzhak and Shinnar, 1973; Shinnar and Shinnar, 1975), but the most comprehensive and influential statement on selective incapacitation is arguably a document produced by RAND Corporation researchers Greenwood and Abrahamse (1982). This report proposed the use of a predictive scale that could be used to prospectively identify high-rate offenders, and sentence these individuals to longer terms in prison. However, this extremely appealing notion is rendered of little use by the operational difficulties inherent in identifying these offenders (for more detailed treatment of these issues, see Auerhahn, 1999, 2006). Additionally, the idea of sentencing defendants convicted of similar crimes to punishments of differing severity on the basis of a prediction about their future behavior is at odds with the underlying principles of US criminal law (Dershowitz, 1973; Packer, 1968; von Hirsch, 1984).

The idea of selective incapacitation and the particularistic sentencing reforms it produces are of interest for the current analysis of the relationship of sentencing policy reform to the aging of prison populations for other reasons. As a way of circumventing the legal challenges of preventive detention and the problems inherent in predicting a low base-rate behavior (see Auerhahn, 1999, 2006), particularistic sentencing reforms that have their ideological origins in the idea of selective incapacitation, such as habitual-offender statutes, rely on the *retrospective* identification of so-called career criminals. Because it takes time to accumulate such a history, habitual-offender laws *by design* target older offenders. These statutes, sometimes labeled three-strikes laws, are the most obvious example of this type of policy reform. First implemented in the state of Washington in 1993, habitual-offender sentencing laws quickly swept the nation, with such laws in place in twenty-four states and the federal system by 1995

(Austin et al., 1999). These types of sentencing statutes provide for longer terms of incarceration for high-rate offenders. As a result of the difficulties in prospectively identifying high-rate offenders, habitual-offender statutes rely on a long conviction history to select defendants for longer sentences.

In addition to habitual-offender laws, two other relatively recent movements in criminal sentencing policy that have been influenced by the idea of selective incapacitation are implicated in generating elderly prison populations: truth-in-sentencing laws, and the curtailing of parole release.

Truth-in-Sentencing

The first truth-in-sentencing law was passed in the state of Washington in 1984 (Ditton and Wilson, 1999). Ten years later, the Violent Crime Control and Law Enforcement Act of 1994 contained provisions for incentive grants to states for prison construction, contingent on states' release policies being in compliance with minimum sentence-length requirements established in the act. As of 2013, forty-two states have some sort of truth-in-sentencing penalty structure in place, with the vast majority of these meeting or exceeding the federal requirement that prisoners convicted of certain types of offenses serve at least 85 percent of their minimum terms before becoming eligible for release (Ditton and Wilson, 1999). Truth-in-sentencing provisions generally target violent and serious offenses and have been associated with increased length of stay for affected prisoners (Ditton and Wilson, 1999).

Curtailing Parole Release

Although frequently identified as a relatively recent phenomenon, the demise of parole release began as part of the rejection of the rehabilitative paradigm in the 1970s (Petersilia, 1999). Parole release was an essential component of a system of indeterminate sentencing. California, Maine, and Indiana abolished or severely curtailed discretionary parole release in the 1970s. In 1987, parole was abolished in the federal system. By the end of the twentieth century, sixteen states had abolished or severely curtailed parole release for prisoners (Kuziemko, 2007; Petersilia, 1999). Currently, fewer than 25 percent of prisoners are released on discretionary parole (Glaze and Bonczar, 2009). When reviewing an analysis by Ditton and Wilson (1999) that revealed no significant differences in length of stay in prison between those released on discretionary parole and those released mandatorily, Petersilia concluded that "ending parole *by itself* appears to have had no real impact on time served" (1999, p. 495; emphasis added). However, the removal of parole release interacts with other recent sentencing reforms designed to increase the length of stay, such as habitual-offender and truth-in-sentencing laws.

Economic researcher Kuziemko (2007) identified other pathways by which the elimination of discretionary parole could contribute to the growth in prison populations. She notes that removing the possibility of early release eliminates incentives for behavioral compliance in prison, which could have the result of lengthening sentences as inmates are punished for institutional infractions. Similarly, the elimination of the possibility for early release can dampen voluntary participation in rehabilitative programming, which might result in relatively higher rates of recidivism. While analyzing the effects of targeted truth-in-sentencing reforms implemented in Georgia in 1998 that required prisoners convicted of certain offenses to serve 90 percent of their sentences prior to release eligibility, Kuziemko found that rates of disciplinary infractions increased, and participation in rehabilitative programming decreased for inmates affected by the reform. While Kuziemko did not directly analyze the effect of behavioral infractions on sentence length, her analysis did show a significant difference in the recidivism rates between the affected group and the nonaffected group, supporting the idea that if mandatory release or "maxing-out" is the only way a prisoner can expect to be released, "he doesn't really have to try and do anything to turn his life around" (*San Francisco Chronicle*, 2006, cited in Kuziemko 2007, p. 28).

The Aging Prison Population:
Two Eras of Sentencing Reform

There appear to be two distinct eras in the recent history of sentencing reform with respect to their impact on prison populations: the post-rehabilitative era (mid-1970s to 1990) and the targeted or particularistic era (1990–present). The early part of the post-rehabilitative period was defined by the rejection of indeterminate sentencing and the introduction of systems of determinate sentencing, later augmented with mandatory sentences and "enhancements," with each reform stacked upon the last. These reforms resulted in massive growth in the prison population and altered it in a variety of ways, including changing the distribution of conviction offenses in the prison population as well as beginning the trend of the aging of the prison population (Auerhahn, 2003; Blumstein and Beck, 1999). During this period, both commitments and length of stay increased (Blumstein and Beck, 1999).

During the targeted or particularistic era, beginning in 1990, sentencing reforms such as three-strikes and truth-in-sentencing have overwhelmingly reflected the logic of selective incapacitation. While the decline of parole release has spanned both the post-rehabilitative and particularistic eras, the effect of removing parole as a "safety valve" on prison populations undoubtedly interacts with the enactment of other reforms designed to increase length of stay, such as habitual-offender and truth-in-sentencing laws.

National Trends

In the United States as a whole, the effects of sentencing reform can be observed in the changes in the composition of prison populations. Noting the potentially misleading nature of a "national" analysis (Greenberg and West, 2001; Pew Center on the States 2010), given the near-universal influence of "movements" in sentencing reform, it is instructive to observe these trends in the aggregate before turning to a more detailed analysis of a single state.

There are two ways to grow a prison population. The first is by increasing the rate of commitments to prison; the other is by increasing the length of stay. In the early part of the post-rehabilitative era, both of these increased dramatically (Blumstein and Beck, 1999; Mauer, 2007). With very few exceptions, the shift toward determinate sentencing resulted in increased rates of prison commitments (Blumstein and Beck, 1999). It has been suggested that this was because judges were increasingly willing to incarcerate "marginal" defendants (i.e., those who might have been assigned a noncustodial sanction under the old system of indeterminate sentencing) once assured that a capricious parole board could not keep the offender incarcerated for an exceedingly lengthy term (Blumstein, 1983).

The causes of the increases in length of stay are more complex. Given the politicized nature of criminal justice issues, the near-exclusive reliance on incarceration naturally leads to "upping the ante," or increasing sentence severity across the board. Mauer, King, and Young (2004) suggest that the presence of the death penalty as a sentencing option in many states serves to further "ratchet up" noncapital penalties, as reflected in an increase in the use of life sentences. As incarceration comes to be seen as the presumptive sanction for so many crimes, the only way for legislators to appease constituencies' demands to "do something about the crime problem" is to increase the severity of punishment (Zimring, 1983). The effects of this can be seen in the proliferation of habitual-offender and truth-in-sentencing laws, which serve to lengthen sentences, rather than to target new types of offenders for incarceration.

The application of reforms to lengthen sentences emphasized during the targeted or particularistic era slowed the rate of growth in the prison population overall, but increased the rate of growth in the population of older prisoners (Pastore and Maguire, 2010; Pew Center on the States,

2010; Williams, 2006). While the general prison population more than doubled between 1990 and 2009, the elderly population grew at a much faster rate. Moreover, the rate of growth in the prison population slowed substantially between 2000 and 2008, increasing by only 10 percent. During the same period, the number of prisoners aged 55 and older in state and federal prisons grew by 75 percent (Beck and Harrison, 2001; Bureau of Justice Statistics, 2010; Sabol, West, and Cooper, 2009). In 1992, 5.7 percent of US prisoners were age 50 or older. By 2008, the proportional representation of older prisoners in state and federal prisons had climbed to 11 percent (Pastore and Maguire, 2010).

Increases in the length of stay during the targeted or particularistic era are more heavily implicated than are increases in commitments in both the growth and the aging of the prison population generally (Blumstein and Beck, 1999; Mauer, King, and Young, 2004; Mauer, 2007). Throughout the 1990s, the percentage of offenders failing to successfully complete parole held steady at approximately 60 percent nationwide (Hughes, Wilson, and Beck, 2001), resulting in large numbers of parolees being returned to prison. Blumstein and Beck (1999), in contrast to the earlier part of their analysis of the sources of growth in prison populations from 1980 to 1996, demonstrate that rates of parole revocations and new commitments to prison flattened substantially in the mid-1990s, and conclude that increases in length of stay are largely responsible for the growth in prison populations in recent years. Between 1990 and 1999, time served by offenders released from state prisons increased by seven months, on average, representing an increase of 32 percent in length of stay (Pastore and Maguire, 2010). The increased frequency of life sentences is a noteworthy factor in this trend. Between 1992 and 2003, the number of prisoners serving life sentences in US prisons increased by 83 percent; nearly one-third of these were sentenced to life terms without the possibility of parole (Mauer, King, and Young, 2004; Nellis and King, 2009).

The Case of California

California is in many ways ideal for an examination of the consequences of a sentencing regime that emphasizes selective incapacitation via the retrospective identification of habitual offenders.[1] California frequently exemplifies national trends, the most ready example being the state's three-strikes law, the most inclusive and widely applied such law in the nation (Austin et al., 1999; King and Mauer, 2001; California Legislative Analyst's Office, 2005).

California's prison population began to grow at an accelerated rate almost immediately following the passage of the state's Determinate Sentencing Law in 1976 (see Figure 2.1). As mentioned earlier, changes in the

Figure 2.1 California Prison Population, 1960–2009

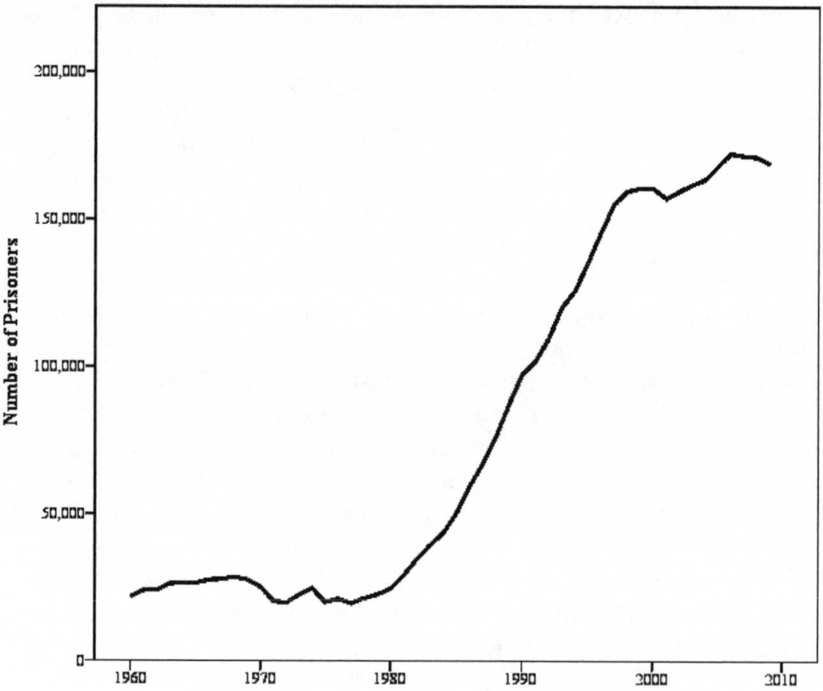

Source: California Department of Corrections and Rehabilitation, 2010.

size of prison populations are a function of the rate at which offenders are placed in prison and the length of stay. Both of these increased following the implementation of the 1976 law (Blumstein and Beck, 1999; Casper, Brereton, and Neal, 1983). The addition of the state's three-strikes and truth-in-sentencing laws further increased the length of stay for California prisoners (California Legislative Analyst's Office, 2005).

Consistent with national trends, California's older prison population is currently growing at a rate that far outpaces the rate of growth of the prison population generally. Between 1990 and 2005, the incarceration rate grew only 42 percent, from a rate of 380 per 100,000 adult residents to a rate of 539 per 100,000 adult residents. Over the same period, the incarceration rate for Californians aged 50 and older more than tripled, increasing from 59 to 185 per 100,000.[2] In 1998, California housed just over 9,200 prisoners aged 50 and older; yet by 2009, there were over 26,000 prisoners aged 50 and older in California prisons (see Figure 2.2).

Figure 2.2 California Prisoners Aged 50 and Older, 1977–2009

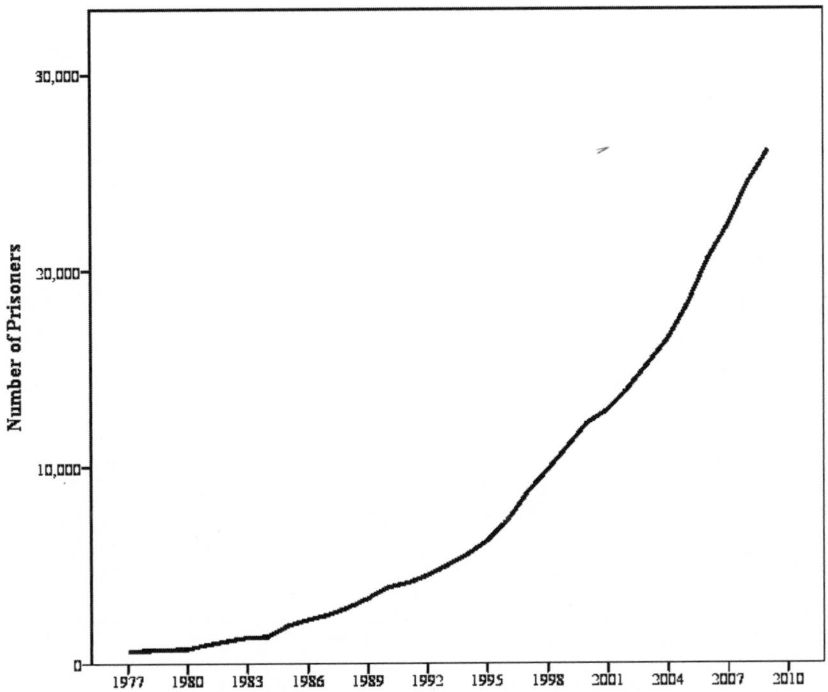

Source: California Department of Corrections and Rehabilitation, 2010.

Between 1976 and 2009, the mean age of California prisoners increased from 29 to 37 years (see Figure 2.3).[3] The differences in the two eras of sentencing reform are reflected in the growth curves tracing the various measures of the aging of the prison population. In the case of the mean age of prisoners in California state institutions, the difference can be seen in the rate of change before and after the 1990s. Between 1970 and 1990, the mean age of prisoners increased by a mere 3 percent. After 1990, the rate of increase accelerated substantially, registering an increase of 16 percent between 1990 and 2009. The proportional representation of older individuals in the prison population has increased dramatically as well since 1990 (see Figure 2.4). By 2009, an astonishing 15.5 percent of California prisoners were aged 50 and older.

The mean age of new admissions to prisons also increased during this period. The mean age of male offenders admitted to California state prisons in 2009 was 32 years (35 for females), up from 28 (and 30 for females)

Figure 2.3   Mean Age of California Prison Population, 1960–2009

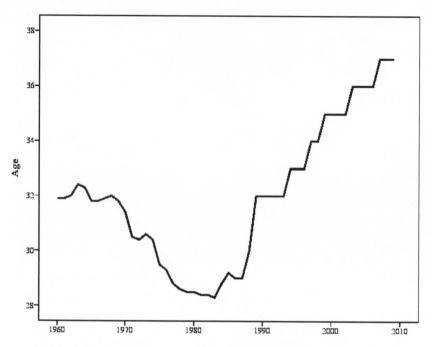

Source: California Department of Corrections and Rehabilitation, 2010.

in 1990. Echoing the other trends in the timing of growth-rate changes, the mean age of new male prison admissions increased at a rate of 1.2 months per year between 1970 and 1990; between 1990 and 1999, this rate of increase nearly quadrupled (Auerhahn, 2003). The percentage of new admissions for prisoners aged 50 and older also increased, from 3 percent in 1994 to nearly 10 percent in 2009 (see Figure 2.5).

Until quite recently, the majority of admissions to California prisons each year were offenders being returned from parole (Pastore and Maguire, 2010). In 2004, parole revocation accounted for 67 percent of all admissions to prison, an increase from 59 percent in 1990 (Bailey and Hayes, 2006). Some of the growth in this period may be attributable to increased levels of supervision for parolees with two or more "strikes" (California Legislative Analyst's Office, 2005); however, the California Department of Corrections and Rehabilitation has recently taken steps to actively reduce the rate at which low-risk parolees are returned to custody (CDCR, 2008; Pew Center on the States, 2010). Nevertheless, the mean age of individuals returned to prison from parole in California has increased steadily, climbing from 28 in 1990 to 36 in 2008.

Figure 2.4   Percentage of California Prison Population Aged 50 and Older, 1977–2009

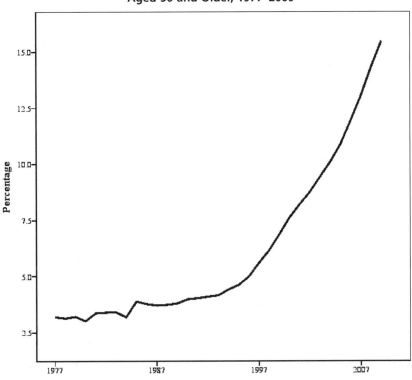

Source: California Department of Corrections and Rehabilitation, 2010.

California's three-strikes law has several features that differentiate it from habitual-offender statutes in other jurisdictions. The statutes implemented elsewhere were frequently symbolic in nature, in that they tended to replicate existing sentencing provisions for repeat offenders and, as such, were rarely invoked (Austin et al., 1999; Litvan, 1998). California's statutes, by contrast, were decidedly not symbolic in that nearly 50,000 offenders were sentenced under the provisions of the law just five years after the law's passage (California Legislative Analyst's Office, 1999). As of 2009, California prisons house over 34,000 second-strike and over 8,500 third-strike prisoners.

The provisions and structure of California's three-strikes statute account for these numbers. The statute provides for a doubling of the presumptive guideline sentence for a second-strike offense. Indeed, more than four times as many offenders are sentenced under the second-strike designation as under the third-striker designation. The third-strike feature of the law mandates a sentence of twenty-five years to life, or a tripling of the

Figure 2.5   Percentage of New California Prison Admissions Aged 50 and Older, 1994–2009

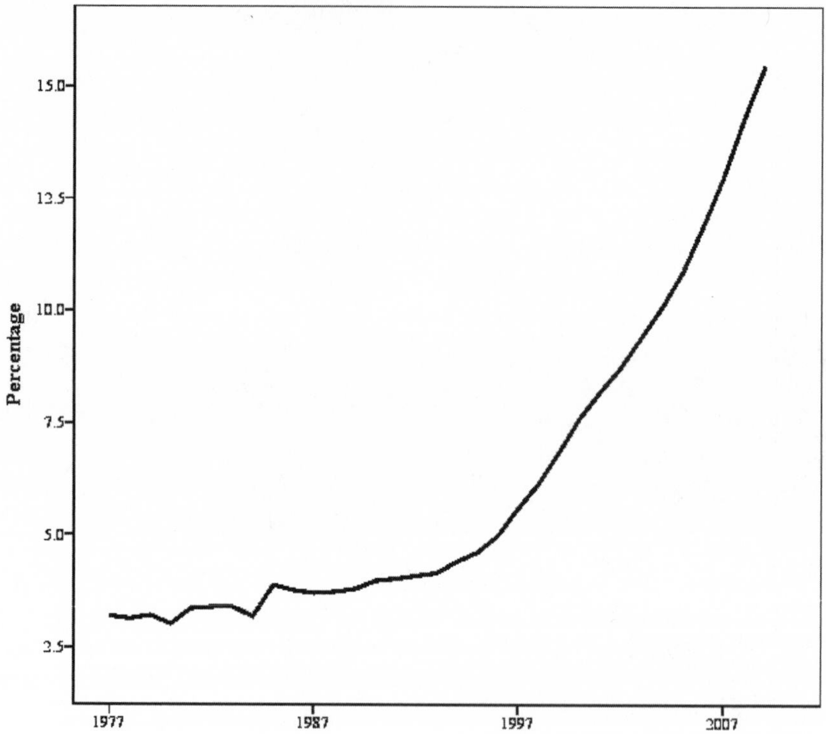

Source: California Department of Corrections and Rehabilitation, 2010.

presumptive sentence for the offense, whichever is longer. There is no "expiration date" on strikeable offenses, and if offenders are convicted of multiple offenses under the provisions of the statute, sentences must be served consecutively. Additionally, the law reduces the amount of "good time" credits from 50 percent to 20 percent for second- and third-strike sentenced prisoners (California Legislative Analyst's Office, 2005).

At first glance, it would seem that California's three-strikes statute merely replicated existing penalties. Prior to the passage of the three-strikes law, the state's sentencing guidelines prescribed a sentence of twenty years to life for a third violent conviction when the offender had two violent convictions resulting in incarceration, and life without parole for a fourth conviction for a violent felony (Austin et al., 1999). There are several key differences between this and the state's three-strikes law. The first is the definition of the "strike zone"—what triggers eligibility for sentencing under the law. The three-strikes law enumerates a list of "serious and violent" felonies that includes many common felonies like burglary and drug offenses. Another important difference is that both the second- and third-strike provisions are activated upon conviction for *any* felony, given one (or two) prior convictions for a "serious or violent" felony. The second-strike provision in the law also represents a significant departure from pre-existing law in that it moves the bar back such that the "habitual-offender" designation now subsumes those with only a single conviction for an offense enumerated among the highly inclusive list of "serious and violent" felonies.

The expected result of older prisoners "stacking up" in the third-striker population is evident. Age data on this population have been made available only from 2008, but in just two years, the proportion of third-strikers aged 50 and older increased by 16 percent, from 34 percent of the third-strike population in 2008 to 40 percent in 2010. As would be expected, older prisoners make up a smaller—but growing—proportion of second-strikers, rising from 13 percent to 15 percent between 2008 and 2010, representing a 15 percent rate of growth in just two years. Because the sentences imposed for third-strike-sentenced prisoners are substantially longer than those for second-strikers, it is likely that older offenders will not accumulate in the population of second-strikers to the degree that is apparent in the third-strike population.[4] However, the rate of growth in the proportional representation of older offenders among third-strike inmates and the twenty-five-year mandatory-minimum sentence associated with conviction under the statute, as well as the fact that the average third-strike admission is 36 years of age (King and Mauer, 2001; Austin et al., 1999), presages the continued aging and growth of the third-strike population in California prisons. (The earliest date for parole eligibility in this population is estimated to be 2019.) Relatedly, in California, the percentage of prisoners serving life sentences has doubled since 1990, with "lifers" now comprising 20 percent of the prison population (Bailey and Hayes, 2006; Mauer, King, and Young, 2004).

It should be noted that the California electorate has rejected several opportunities to reverse the course the state is currently on. Ballot measures that would have restricted the scope of the state's three-strikes law were proposed in 2002, 2004, and 2008. Of these, only the 2004 measure garnered enough signatures to qualify for the election, and it was ultimately rejected by voters.

Policy Recommendations

The aging of the prison population presents significant challenges for correctional systems, not the least of which are the costs associated with incarcerating older prisoners. The California Department of Corrections and Rehabilitation reports that the annual cost per inmate is approximately $49,000 (CDCR, 2010); older prisoners are estimated to be as much as three times more costly than the average inmate, due primarily to older prisoners' greater health-care needs and the high cost of health-care delivery in the prison setting (Coalition for Federal Sentencing Reform, 1998; Lamb-Mechanick and Nelson, 2000; California Legislative Analyst's Office, 2005; McDonald, 1999).

The aging of the prison population also serves to undermine the goals of sentencing and correctional policy, which has been dominated in recent years by public safety considerations and the idea of selective incapacitation. One of the most well-documented empirical regularities in the study of crime and criminal behavior is the inverse relationship between age and criminal activity, a phenomenon referred to as "aging out" of criminal behavior: rates of individual offending peak in the teenage years, and decline sharply thereafter, approaching zero by the fourth decade of life (Farrington, 1986; Piquero, Farrington, and Blumstein, 2007). The phenomenon of "aging out" is also demonstrated by the substantially lower recidivism rates recorded for older releasees (Coalition for Federal Sentencing Reform, 1998; see also Chiu, 2010; Pastore and Maguire, 2010; Williams, 2006).

The goal of selective incapacitation is to increase public safety by targeting the expensive resource of lengthy incarceration toward the most dangerous offenders. However, the relationship between age and criminal offending ultimately negates this premise. From the standpoint of incapacitation, the longer the time served, the "more likely it is that the individual would have terminated his criminal activity even if he were not in prison. In this sense additional prison time is wasted" (Blumstein, 1983, p. 245). Devoting an increasing proportion of scarce correctional resources to the housing of this population also limits our ability to more effectively use these resources to contain those offenders who actually do pose a greater threat to the community (Auerhahn, 2003).

For these reasons, the most sensible course of action from the standpoint of selective incapacitation (and the maximization of efficiency in general) would be to institute a program of geriatric release for older offenders who are deemed to present little threat to public safety. It should be noted that a policy of geriatric release would not necessarily relieve taxpayers of the responsibility of caring for these individuals. Many elderly prisoners, particularly those who have served extremely long terms prior to release, may not be able to support or care for themselves due to their age and infirmity. Even older releasees in comparatively better health may lack the skills (e.g., computer skills) needed to secure employment in today's labor market. Therefore, the release of elderly prisoners may result in the displacement of costs to other government agencies. However, some of these individuals may have family support systems that can assume some of the burden (financial and otherwise) of their care. Even for those requiring full-time care provided by the state, the costs of caring for such individuals outside of prison are substantially less than inside prison walls, due to the higher costs associated with the provision of health care in the prison environment. These costs range from an estimated $38,000 annually for assisted living (on average), to $72,000 per year for full-time nursing-home care (US Department of Health and Human Services, 2010).[5] When compared to the potential annual cost of nearly $150,000 to incarcerate an older prisoner who poses little to no threat to public safety, even if the state were forced to assume the entire cost of caring for these released prisoners, this is clearly the better option from a fiscal perspective.[6]

Fifteen states already have some mechanism by which to release older prisoners, whether based on age alone, length of time served, or the prisoner's medical condition—yet these provisions are barely used. Chiu (2010) reports that this is due in part to restrictive eligibility criteria—some of which intersect with existing sentencing structures. For example, Virginia's geriatric release program was established to work in tandem with truth-in-sentencing requirements. Eligible prisoners must be at least 60 years of age and must have served ten years of their sentence (or age 65, and having served five years), and may not have a conviction for a Class 1 felony (Chiu, 2010).[7] Other states' geriatric release provisions exclude prisoners who have been convicted for a violent or sex-related offense; many also exclude those who have been sentenced to life imprisonment. These restrictions explain the limited application of these provisions, as elderly offenders are disproportionately convicted of more serious offenses. Additionally, the increased use of life sentences further constrains the use of this mechanism to reduce the size of elderly prison populations. The "stacked" nature of sentencing policy reform should be considered when formulating release strategies for offenders who are likely to pose minimal threat to public safety, such that these strategies can achieve maximum benefit through release to community-based programs.

In addition to considering the release of older prisoners, greater consideration should be given to community-based or other alternative sanctions to slow the rate at which older offenders are sentenced to prison. Taking heed of the trends in the creation and movement of populations of older prisoners (the majority are career offenders and first-timers in prison), this population is growing in large part as the result of new commitments to prison, as compared to the relatively smaller impact of long-term sentenced offenders who are "aging in place." More thorough consideration of the public safety implications of sentencing older offenders to prison should inform this discussion to a greater degree than is currently in evidence.

Conclusion

As demonstrated throughout this book, elderly prisoners present a multitude of challenges for correctional systems. This chapter has shown that sentencing policy plays a significant role in shaping the composition of prison populations and is frequently far more salient than the rate or prevalence of criminal behavior.

Sentencing policies in the United States during the post-1970s period can arguably be defined by two trends: the massive expansion of the prison population and the concurrent aging of this population. Both of these trends are facilitated by an enormous amount of activity in the arena of sentencing policy reform—much of which reflects the evolution of goals and ideology of the enterprise of criminal punishment. Sentencing policy that deliberately targets relatively older offenders for lengthy terms of incarceration will generate an elderly prison population. This is problematic not only for reasons detailed elsewhere in this book, such as the elevated costs posed to correctional systems, but also from the standpoint of the criminal justice system achieving its goals. Sentencing reform based on the idea of selective incapacitation is successful if it actually achieves the incapacitation of dangerous offenders. Devoting an increasing proportion of scarce correctional resources to the housing of an ever-growing population of low-risk individuals undermines our ability to provide protection from those offenders who actually do threaten public safety (Auerhahn, 2003; Auerhahn and McGuire, 2010). For reasons relating to such wide-ranging concerns of fiscal responsibility, conformity to evidence-based practices in criminal justice, humane treatment of prisoners (see, e.g., Crawley 2005; Crawley and Sparks 2005b), and logical and efficient use of expensive resources, it is imperative that we take steps to slow or reverse current trends with respect to the aging of the prison population.

Notes

1. Unless otherwise indicated, data are from the California Department of Corrections and Rehabilitation (CDCR, 2010).
2. Calculated from figures provided by Bailey and Hayes (2006) and CDCR (2010).
3. Data are for male prisoners. In nearly all years of the analysis, the average age of female prisoners is about one year older than the average age of male prisoners.
4. Furthermore, Austin et al. (1999) report that the majority of second-strike cases are sentenced at the low end of the range in California's sentencing guidelines.
5. In California, the cost for full-time nursing-home care is estimated at close to $87,000 annually (US Department of Health and Human Services, 2010).

6. Some older prisoners would undoubtedly be kept in prison on public safety or other grounds. In California, for example, it seems extremely unlikely that Sirhan Sirhan and Charles Manson—both of whose sentences were commuted from death to life imprisonment in the wake of the *Furman* ruling—will ever be released from prison. Additionally, while selective incapacitation is the dominant consideration in contemporary sentencing reform, it is not the only goal of incarceration. Others have noted that, among adult offenders, age is not relevant to considerations of blameworthiness and deservedness of punishment, and that to base the quanta of punishment on age threatens ideals of equal justice under a system of offense-oriented sentencing (Porcella, 2007).

7. In Virginia, Class 1 felonies include rape, kidnapping, and certain kinds of aggravated murder and sexual assault, and are punishable by death or life imprisonment.

3

Bio-Psycho-Social Needs

Margaret E. Leigey

Institutions, and their physical layouts, policies, and procedures, are not commonly designed with the needs of older inmates in mind. This group has been described as a forgotten and marginalized population (Krajick, 1979; Moore, 1989; Morton and Anderson, 1982; Vito and Wilson, 1985; Crawley, 2005). However, with the number of inmates aged 50 and older climbing to almost 250,000 in the United States as of 2010 (Guerino, Harrison, and Sabol, 2012), it is vital that the needs of this group be identified, prepared for, and accommodated. From a humanitarian perspective, older inmates should be treated with dignity. That said, prison offers a meager existence for all inmates; but for older inmates, the contemporary prison experience poses additional hardships (Crawley, 2005; Kerbs, 2000b).

If humanitarian reasons do not encourage an increased focus on the aging prison population, financial incentives also exist. For example, the implementation of preventive prison health-care programs such as routine health checkups and exercise programs have long been advocated to bolster the health of older inmates and to lower prison health-care costs (Aday, 2003; Aday and Krabill, 2011; McCarthy, 1983). Prevention and early treatment of illnesses are more cost-effective than treating diseases in advanced stages. To illustrate, Morton provides the following example: "Early treatment of elevated blood pressure is far more efficient than maintaining the victim of a massive stroke" (1992, p. 18). Moreover, as the annual costs of incarcerating older inmates are estimated to be double or triple (approximately $60,000 to $70,000) that of younger inmates (approximately $20,000 to $30,000) (Abramsky, 2004; Adams, 1995; Aday, 2003; Beiser, 1999; Dubler, 1998; Florida Corrections Commissions, 2001;

Ornduff, 1996; Smyer, Gragert, and LaMere, 1997), the proliferation of preventive health care could lead to substantial savings in the health-care arena for correctional administrators. The delivery of programming that is appropriately matched to older inmates' bio-psycho-social needs could also assist corrections departments in reducing the threat of litigation and the attendant financial liability associated with litigation that challenges the conditions of older prisoners' confinement. Certain areas of prison life are particularly vulnerable to litigation and include age-based discrimination in prison programming, institutional noncompliance with the Americans with Disabilities Act, staff failure to protect older inmates from victimization, and inadequate medical treatment (Goetting, 1985; Ham, 1980; Kerbs, 2000b; Kerbs and Jolley, 2009b).

For these reasons, correctional practitioners should prioritize a focused response to the needs of older prisoners. To advance this goal, this chapter examines the biological, psychological, and social needs of older inmates and the policy implications derived from them. This growing body of literature is hampered by inconsistent findings and gaps in knowledge, since the extant "research has relied heavily upon nonrandom, small, and otherwise potentially unrepresentative samples" (Kerbs, 2000b, p. 220). Despite these limitations, a review of the literature provides insight into the correctional experiences of aging inmates and potential responses to the aging prison population in the United States.

The Biological Needs of Older Inmates

Defining "Older" Inmates

When defining the age at which an inmate is considered to be "older," it is important to remember that there may be a substantial divergence between an individual's chronological age and his or her physiological age, where physiological age is a reflection of the individual's overall physical and mental health, as well as his or her overall level of functioning (Flynn, 1992). Moreover, the gap between chronological and physiological age is particularly pronounced for older inmates, and variation in the gap between inmates' chronological and physiological ages has contributed to the heterogeneity in the older inmate population. The age criterion most commonly used by researchers and correctional administrators when defining older inmates is 50 years (Lemieux, Dyeson, and Castiglione, 2002). Obviously, age 50 is substantially younger than age 65, a common age of retirement and the age at which full social security benefits can be received without penalty. A commonly used guideline is that aging inmates are ten to fifteen years older in physiological years than their chronological ages (Abramsky, 2004; Aday, 1994b; Mitka, 2004).

The rationale for the discrepancy between physiological and chronological aging is that inmates have had more physically and mentally taxing lives than nonincarcerated individuals (Anno et al., 2004; Kratcoski and Pownall, 1989). Preincarceration health risks that could accelerate the process of aging include chronic drug, alcohol, and tobacco use (Anno et al., 2004; Chaneles, 1987; Kratcoski and Pownall, 1989; Mitka, 2004), sexual promiscuity (Anno et al., 2004; Chaneles, 1987), poor diet (Kratcoski and Pownall, 1989), and limited access to medical care prior to incarceration (Anno et al., 2004; Mitka, 2004). In addition, the stress of confinement is believed to hasten the aging process (Anno et al., 2004; Smyer Gragert, and LaMere, 1997). When drafting prison policy for older inmates in the areas of housing and work assignments, program development, and treatment availability, the recognition of accelerated aging and the consideration of physiological age could be more helpful than the reliance on chronological age exclusively.

The Physical Health of Older Inmates

Older inmates experience the same types of medical conditions and chronic illnesses as do older individuals outside of prison (Morton and Anderson, 1982). Nonetheless, there is evidence to suggest that older male and female inmates are in worse health than older individuals outside prison, in part because higher proportions of older inmates have chronic illnesses that affect all major systems of the body (e.g., respiratory, pulmonary, and nervous systems) (Aday and Krabill, 2011; Fazel et al., 2001). For example, in a national study based on a stratified two-stage probability sample of male and female inmates, about 60 percent of older state and federal prisoners (aged 45 and older) reported having a medical problem (Maruschak, 2008). Similarly, in two different studies that relied on convenience samples with a limited number of older male prisoners (n = approximately 40 per study), drawn from a small number of state prison facilities (Moore, 1989; Vega and Silverman, 1988), 80 percent of older inmates reported having chronic illness. Furthermore, older inmates are generally affected by more than one chronic health condition. The average number of chronic health conditions per older inmate has ranged from three to five, respectively, in two studies that utilized convenience samples of older male prisoners, one in a facility in the southeastern United States (Aday, 1994a; n = 25), and one in a Pennsylvania facility (Loeb and Steffensmeier, 2006; n = 51).

As compared to their younger counterparts, older inmates suffer from a greater number and severity of health ailments. According to the Bureau of Justice Statistics, state inmates aged 45 and older, as compared to state inmates aged 35 to 44, were more likely to report a current medical problem (50.0 percent versus 68.5 percent, respectively), dental problem (54.8 percent versus 60.3 percent), hearing impairment (7.2 percent versus 13.4 percent), vision impairment (10.3 percent versus 19.4 percent), or mobility impairment (2.5 percent versus 6.1 percent) (Maruschak, 2008). Additionally, state inmates aged 45 and older, again as compared to state inmates aged 35 to 44, were more likely to have the chronic health conditions of arthritis (17.4 percent versus 32.6 percent, respectively) and hypertension (15.4 percent versus 30.6 percent) (Maruschak, 2008).

Despite consistent findings from various studies in which relatively high proportions of older inmates reported having one or more chronic medical conditions, findings from studies that measure older inmates' assessments of their health statuses have been inconsistent. For example, findings from Colsher et al. (1992) and Loeb and Steffensmeier (2006) indicate that a majority of older inmates, 64.7 percent and 70.6 percent, respectively, described their current health status as positive, yet 64 percent of respondents in Deaton, Aday, and Wahidin's (2009–2010) sample described their health as either fair or poor. Finally, some studies have found that older inmates reported their health as declining or worsening (Aday, 1994a; Colsher et al., 1992; Marquart, Merianos, and Doucet, 2000; McCarthy, 1983), while others claimed that their health stayed the same or even improved during incarceration (Loeb and Steffensmeier, 2006). One important factor that could account for the inconsistency in older inmates' self-assessment of their health is the high degree to which study findings are influenced and constrained by the unique characteristics of each study's sample. For example, these studies are typically based on snowball or convenience samples of inmates (Marquart, Merianos, and Doucet, 2000; McCarthy, 1983) who are all male (Colsher et al., 1992; Marquart, Merianos, and Doucet, 2000) or all female (Deaton, Aday, and Wahidin, 2009–2010), who are from a limited number of prisons (Colsher et al., 1992; Deaton, Aday, and Wahidin, 2009–2010; Marquart, Merianos, and Doucet, 2000), or who are from a limited number of states (Colsher et al., 1992; Deaton, Aday, and Wahidin, 2009–2010; Marquart, Merianos, and Doucet, 2000). Another important factor that clouds this debate is physical health at the time of confinement. Some older inmates may have had limited access to health care prior to being incarcerated, or they may have been unaware of preexisting medical conditions. As such, they may inaccurately blame the prison environment for causing or contributing to their health conditions (Marquart, Merianos, and Doucet, 2000).

Beyond having to cope with the symptoms and deficits typically associated with a range of medical conditions, older inmates must also experience the aging process and related chronic health conditions within "total institutions" that are removed from the outside world (Goffman, 1961, p. 4). Poor health can negatively affect the ability of older inmates to perform daily activities in the institution, including getting in and out of a bed or a wheelchair, bathing, using the toilet, and dressing (Abramsky, 2004; Aday, 2003; Aday and Krabill, 2011; Anderson and Hilliard, 2005). Limited mobility may also make it difficult for older inmates to move around the institution, deterring visits to the dining hall, library, and infirmary, and limiting participation in prison programs. Vision problems, such as blindness, cataracts, glaucoma, and near-sightedness (Anno et al., 2004; Krajick, 1979; Marquart, Merianos, and Doucet, 2000) can negatively affect the ability of older inmates to safely navigate the prison, watch television, and read letters, magazines, and books. Hearing impairment is also common among older inmates (Anno et al., 2004; Colsher et al., 1992), which could make interacting with others more challenging, such as when having conversations with other inmates and when communicating with family members or friends during visits, and could make it more difficult for these inmates to hear orders from correctional staff. Colsher et al. (1992) and Marquart, Merianos, and Doucet (2000) noted that only a small proportion of older inmates reported having a full set of teeth, 3 percent and 24 percent, respectively. As a result, the diets of older inmates could be limited and deficient of proper nutrition (Strupp and Willmott, 2005). The caloric intake of older inmates could be further limited if they are not given sufficient time to consume their meals (Strupp and Willmott, 2005). Finally, not only do the current health problems of older inmates need to be addressed, but correctional administrators should also anticipate that as inmates continue to age in prison, their health problems will become increasingly serious and potentially debilitating. For instance, Colsher et al. (1992) noted that inmates aged 60 and older were significantly more likely to be incontinent ($p < 0.01$) and hearing-impaired ($p < 0.05$) than inmates aged 59 and younger.

An examination of prison mortality rates using individual inmate death records provides another perspective from which the health of older inmates can be assessed. A direct relationship exists between age and the prison mortality rate. From 2001 to 2004, male and female prisoners aged 45 and older comprised about 14 percent of the prison population across the fifty states; however, they accounted for 67 percent of all inmate deaths (Mumola, 2007). This overrepresentation is even more pronounced for elderly inmates; while inmates aged 65 and older accounted for 1 percent of state prisoners in 2001 to 2004, they accounted for 15 percent of deaths (Mumola, 2007). In fact, the mortality rate for male and female inmates aged 55 and older in state prisons is three times greater than the rate for inmates aged 45 to 54, and eleven times greater than the rate for inmates aged 35 to 44 (Mumola, 2005). The leading causes of death among older inmates during this time period were heart disease, cancer, liver disease, and respiratory illness (Mumola, 2007). While the correlation between mortality and age makes intuitive sense, the short life expectancy of older inmates is a matter of concern. At Angola Prison in Louisiana between 1996 and 2001, the mean age of inmate mortality for natural causes was 51 (Cain and Fontenot, 2001).

The Physical Health of Older Female and Minority Inmates

The needs of older female and minority inmates have received even less attention than those of older inmates in general. The limited research that has been conducted on older female inmates indicates that they perceive their health to be worse compared to their older male counterparts. For example, in a study with a nonrandom sample of 442 male and female inmates (aged 50 to 84) in eight federal prisons from three states (Florida, Ohio, and Pennsylvania), Kratcoski and Babb (1990) found that 47 percent of the surveyed older women described their health in negative terms, compared to only 25 percent of the older men.

The findings of two recent studies are consistent with this research. First, a multistate study confirms older female inmates' negative self-assessments of their physical health. Aday and Krabill (2011), in their study of 327 older female inmates from a nonrandom sample across five southeastern states (Arkansas, Georgia, Kentucky, Mississippi, and Tennessee), found that 42 percent of respondents rated their health as fair and 23 percent as poor. Moreover, a sizable percentage perceived their health to be declining, with 47 percent of the sample reporting that their health was worse at the time of survey than it was two years prior. The most common chronic illnesses reported by older female inmates were arthritis (61 percent), hypertension (52 percent), stomach/intestinal ulcers (30 percent), emphysema/asthma (28 percent), menopause problems (27 percent), heart condition (26 percent), and diabetes (21 percent).

Second, Leigey and Hodge (2012), in a study based on a stratified two-stage national probability sample of 997 male and 142 female inmates (aged 50 and older), found significant gender differences in the physical health of the older inmate population. Specifically, they found that older female inmates were significantly more likely than older male inmates to report suffering from arthritis (58.3 percent versus 39.7 percent, respectively; $p < 0.001$) and asthma (20.9 percent versus 14.1 percent; $p < 0.05$) during their lifetimes. In addition, co-morbidity was another significant difference, as older female inmates reported a slightly higher average number of chronic health conditions as compared to older male inmates (3.0 versus 2.5; $p < 0.01$).

There is also a paucity of research related to older nonwhite inmates. One of the few studies that included a racially and ethnically heterogeneous sample (i.e., a disproportionate random stratified sample) of older male and female inmates was conducted by Haugebrook et al. (2010). They examined the medical records of 114 inmates aged 55 and older in New Jersey prisons. The study revealed no significant racial or ethnic difference in the medical issues of the older inmate population, as roughly half of Caucasian inmates (54.2 percent), Latino/Latina inmates (50.0 percent), and African American inmates (47.3 percent) reported a medical issue. However, comparisons between the groups were not reported for important dimensions of health, such as the incidence of a specific condition, the severity of the medical issue, and the degree of impairment for any specific condition.

Environmental Issues and Health in Prison

Living in prisons that are totally removed from the outside world may contribute to or exacerbate the physical and mental health conditions of older inmates. The features of confinement—the noise, distance between buildings, temperature, dampness, limited privacy, and so forth—may take a greater toll on older inmates by increasing or aggravating their health conditions (Aday, 1994b; Ham, 1980; Krajick, 1979; Marquart, Merianos, and Doucet, 2000; Morton, 1992; Morton and Anderson, 1982; Strupp and Willmott, 2005; Vito and Wilson, 1985; Wilson and Vito, 1986). The serious overcrowding of institutions (West, Sabol, and Greenman, 2010) can further compound environmental issues by diminishing the already minimal amount of privacy that inmates have and increasing the contraction of communicable diseases such as pneumonia, tuberculosis, and influenza (Aday, 2003; Smyer, Gragert, and LaMere, 1997).

Using a convenience sample of 120 older female inmates incarcerated in California (aged 55 and older), Strupp and Willmott (2005) revealed the special challenges that older inmates face when negotiating the prison environment. At least half of the sample rated the following activities as being very difficult: getting in and out of a top bunk (58 percent), dropping to the ground when alarms sound (57 percent), and removing clothes during a strip search (50 percent). Over half of the older female inmates reported having fallen in the previous year, which they attributed in part to limited access to handrails. Falling is a common issue among older inmates, regardless of gender. In a nonrandom sample of 25 male inmates in a mid-Atlantic state, all of whom were older than 50 and had served at least fifteen years of a sentence of life without the possibility of parole, Leigey (2007) found that older male inmates also reported having fallen as they attempted to climb up to or down from their top bunks. Furthermore, respondents in this study noted that some older inmates were so fearful of falling that they slept on the floor of their cells. Clearly, the physical and mental well-being of older inmates can be adversely affected if they are forced to sleep on concrete flooring. As such, one logical policy implication would be to modify the prison environment and existing prison protocol to ease the burdens of confinement for older inmates by installing handrails and assigning inmates to lower bunks to prevent falls.

Correctional Health-Care Utilization

Older inmates rely on correctional health care to treat acute and chronic medical conditions, and their collective need for health care is great. Special aids and equipment (e.g., dentures, glasses, hearing aids, canes, walkers, and wheelchairs) are necessary to assist them in their daily lives (Aday and Krabill, 2011; Marquart, Merianos, and Doucet, 2000). Medications are needed to care for or alleviate physical conditions. More invasive care, such as dialysis or surgery, is common in treating the physical health needs of older inmates (Aday, 1994a). For example, 22 percent of state and 23 percent of federal inmates aged 45 and older reported having had a surgical procedure while incarcerated (Maruschak, 2008). Largely because of greater health-care expenditures, the cost of incarcerating older inmates is about three times higher than that for younger inmates (Adams, 1995; Beiser, 1999; Florida Corrections Commissions, 2001; Ornduff, 1996; Smyer, Gragert, and LaMere, 1997), with estimates ranging from $60,000 to $70,000 per year for older inmates as compared to $20,000 to $30,000 per year for younger inmates (Abramsky, 2004; Aday, 2003; Beiser, 1999; Dubler, 1998).

While most previous research suggests that older inmates are overrepresented in health-care consumption when compared to younger inmates (Anderson and Hilliard, 2005; Chaiklin, 1998; Lemieux, Dyeson, and Castiglione, 2002), chronic health condition is an individual-level variable that has also been found to influence the utilization of medical services. Falter (1999) found that in addition to sentence length and age, the most important predictors of medical encounters in a six-month period in prisons totally removed from the outside world were hypertension, heart disease, diabetes, and chronic obstructive pulmonary disease. Moreover, a constellation of institutional-level factors, such as prison environment, housing considerations, and availability of specialized programming, "also influence the extent to which older inmates consume services" (Lemieux, Dyeson, and Castiglione, 2002, p. 448).

As documented earlier, many older inmates have legitimate medical problems; however, some may request medical treatment for nonmedical reasons, such as boredom or a need for social interaction or attention, as a means to miss work, or because of a preoccupation with a medical condition (Marquart, Merianos, and Doucet, 2000). To deter frivolous requests for medical attention, some institutions have implemented co-payments, ranging from two to fifteen dollars, for infirmary visits (Mara and McKenna, 2000). Older inmates report that these co-pays create an additional obstacle for them to receive medical treatment (Aday and Krabill, 2011; Strupp and Willmott, 2005).

In sum, it is apparent that older inmates rely on prison medical services to treat a broad range of physical health conditions. However, based on their reports, it does not appear that prison health care is meeting their needs. Older inmates have described prison-based health care as "'frightening,' 'terrible,' and 'worthless'" (Leigey, 2007, p. 321). Specific complaints include delays in seeing doctors and specialists and in receiving medications, the limited services provided at the prison, and the perception that health-care staff do not have older inmates' best interests in mind or are insensitive to their needs (Aday, 1994a; Aday and Krabill, 2011; Dubler, 1998; Leigey, 2007; McCarthy, 1983; Strupp and Willmott, 2005; Wilson and Vito, 1986).

The Psychological Needs of Older Inmates

Just as age affects the varying biological needs of older inmates, it also affects their psychological needs. Empirical research focused on the mental health of older inmates has been sparse (Caverley, 2006), resulting in two unfortunate outcomes. First, it is difficult to know the prevalence rates of specific mental health illnesses. In a study by James and Glaze (2006) that used a two-stage national probability sample of male and female inmates drawn from state and federal facilities, older state inmates (aged 55 and older) were slightly more likely to report a mental problem as compared to older federal inmates (39.6 percent versus 36.1 percent, respectively). However, national rates of particular mental conditions or disorders among the aging prison population are not known. Second, the limited available research on the mental health of older inmates has produced conflicting characterizations. Based on one account, older inmates, compared to older people outside prison, are at a greater risk of mental health disorders, including depression, anxiety, and antisocial personality disorder (Koenig et al., 1995). Using a convenience sample of 95 older male inmates (aged 50 and older) from one federal prison, this same study found that the one-month prevalence of depression was approximately fifty times higher for older inmates as compared with nonincarcerated older people. Other studies have revealed that worry, loneliness, and malaise are commonly experienced by older inmates. For instance, in a convenience sample of 248 male and female inmates (aged 52 to 82) in a state prison in Florida (McCarthy, 1983), it was found that about one-half of the older inmates reported that they often worried (49.6 percent) and felt lonely (57 percent); additionally, more than one-third indicated that they felt unhappy (34.7 percent), and about one-fourth rated their current life satisfaction as poor (25.4 percent).

In contrast, other studies have found that mental impairment is not highly prevalent among older inmates. In a population-based sample of 360 older male and female inmates (aged 50 to 96) from a state prison in Utah (Caverley, 2006), it was found that, with the exception of schizophrenia, the prevalence of mental illness was roughly the same for incarcerated and nonincarcerated older people. In fact, some research suggests that older inmates are in better mental health than younger inmates. According to the Bureau of Justice Statistics study by James and Glaze (2006), older inmates had the lowest incidence of mental health problems as compared to their younger counterparts (mental health problems were measured by a clinical diagnosis, treatment by a mental health professional, or presence of symptoms of a mental disorder based on standard criteria [from the American Psychiatric Association's *Diagnostic and Statistical Manual* IV] in the twelve months prior to the interview). In this study, 39.6 percent of older state inmates (those aged 55 and older) reported a mental health problem, as compared to 51.3 percent of inmates aged 45 to 54, 55.9 percent of inmates aged 25 to 34, and 62.6 percent of inmates aged 24 and younger. Other studies have found that younger inmates are more likely to report feeling lonely (Gallagher, 1990), depressed (Teller and Howell, 1981), or anxious (MacKenzie, 1987) as compared to older inmates.

While more research is needed to provide conclusive answers as to whether older inmates have greater mental health issues than younger inmates or than older people outside prison, older inmates do suffer from a range of mental health issues, including depression, schizophrenia, bipolar disorder, anxiety, posttraumatic stress disorder, Alzheimer's disease, dementia, memory decline, and confusion (Abramsky, 2004; Caverley, 2006; Reimer, 2008). Similar to the ways in which incarceration poses additional challenges for physically impaired older inmates, standard institutional rules and policies may be ill-suited for mentally impaired older inmates. For example, older inmates may not be able to comprehend instructions given by correctional officers and thus they may unknowingly violate prison rules. An example can be found in Hassine's book *Life Without Parole* (2009). Hassine recounts the experience of an older inmate who was transferred to the special-needs unit following his diagnosis of Alzheimer's disease; however, the inmate had difficulty remembering the change in his housing assignment and would return to his previous cell. He was issued a disciplinary citation "for being in an unauthorized area" (p. 263) and subsequently placed in solitary confinement as punishment.

The Mental Health of Older
Female Inmates and Minority Inmates

Gender and race/ethnicity are two important factors that affect the self-assessment of mental health and incidence of mental health disorders in the aging prison population. Older female inmates have been reported as being more likely to rate worry and depression as their "most persistent health problems" as compared to older male inmates (Kratcoski and Babb, 1990, p. 276). More recently, Leigey and Hodge (2012) have found that older female inmates are significantly more likely than older male inmates to report mental health problems across two time periods: in their lifetimes and in the prior year. They have found that older female inmates, when reporting a mental health diagnosis across their lifetimes, are significantly more likely than their aging male counterparts to note a diagnosis for a depressive disorder (28.3 percent versus 14.4 percent, respectively; $p < 0.001$), a bipolar disorder (13.8 percent versus 6.0 percent; $p < 0.001$), a posttraumatic stress disorder (12.4 percent versus 6.2 percent; $p < 0.01$), and an anxiety disorder (12.3 percent versus 5.0 percent; $p < 0.001$). Furthermore, a significant difference in self-harm has been found by Leigey and Hodge, with 23 percent of older female inmates reporting at least one suicide attempt in their lifetimes as compared to 8 percent of older male inmates ($p < 0.001$).

Leigey and Hodge (2012) found several statistically significant gender differences in older inmates' evaluations of their mental health in the previous year. Older female inmates reported experiencing an average of five mental health conditions as compared to an average of three for older male inmates ($p < 0.001$). More specifically, as compared to older male inmates, older female inmates were significantly more likely to report that they moved or talked more slowly than normal (23.3 percent versus 42.0 percent, respectively; $p < 0.001$), to report feeling that no one cared about them (28.4 percent versus 40.6 percent; $p < 0.01$), to report a change in sleeping habits (28.8 percent versus 39.1 percent; $p < 0.05$), to report experiencing a decline in overall functioning (27.8 percent versus 38.0

percent; $p < 0.05$), and to report feeling numb or empty inside (26.1 percent versus 37.0 percent; $p < 0.01$).

Depression is the most commonly referenced mental health issue in the literature on aging female inmates, and previous studies have reported that about one-half of older female inmates experience this mental health condition. Aday and Krabill (2011) found that 46 percent of their sample of older female inmates met the clinical diagnosis of depression. Other studies of older female inmates also find similar estimates. Strupp and Willmott (2005) found that 43 percent of their sample of older female inmates reported experiencing symptoms indicative of depression, such as prolonged periods of sadness. In addition, Aday and Nation (2001) found that 43 percent of older female inmates reported depression as a chronic mental health issue (cited in Aday, 2003).

It is important to note that discrepancies can exist between the inmate's perception of mental health and an evaluation based on a formal screening. For example, upon administering the Hopkins Symptoms Self-Report Inventory to older female inmates, Aday and Krabill (2011) found that 46 percent of the sample were classified as highly or severely depressed. However, when the same respondents were asked to rate their mental health, 25 percent of the sample rated their mental health as excellent, 33 percent as good, 33 percent as fair, and 8.7 percent as poor. This finding underscores the need for correctional staff to verify older inmates' self-reports with formal instruments when conducting mental health screenings.

Only one study could be identified that investigated the relationship between mental health and race/ethnicity. In this study, Haugebrook et al. (2010) noted that one-third of the total sample of male and female inmates reported a mental health issue. Perhaps even more illuminating is the significant difference revealed in the bivariate analysis of the relationship between mental health and race/ethnicity ($p < 0.05$), with 49 percent of Caucasians in the sample reporting a mental health issue as compared to 29.1 percent of African Americans and 27.8 percent of Latino/Latinas.

Treatment Needs of Older Inmates

In addition to these mental health concerns and conditions, prison mental health programming should address the ways in which the trauma and stress in the older inmates' preincarceration lives affect their present treatment needs. Previous lifetime estimates indicate that older inmates on average have experienced at least three traumatic or stressful life events, such as abuse, loss of employment, and death of a loved one (Haugebrook et al., 2010). Furthermore, almost one-third (29.8 percent) of older inmates report experiencing trauma in both childhood and later in adulthood (Haugebrook et al., 2010). Particularly with abuse, female inmates have experienced more extensive histories than their male counterparts (Leigey and Reed, 2010). National estimates based on a two-stage stratified probability sample of male and female inmates in state prisons indicated that 43 percent of female inmates and 12 percent of male inmates reported being physically or sexually abused prior to incarceration (Snell and Morton, 1994). Thus, it is expected that counseling for abuse survivors is especially needed among older female prisoners.

Offense-related characteristics (to include the presence of drug and drug-related offenses) also provide insight into the treatment needs of older inmates. Substance abuse, particularly alcohol, is a common issue for both older male and older female inmates (Aday and Nation, 2001, cited in Aday, 2003; Arndt, Turvey, and Flaum, 2002; Gallagher, 1990; Lemieux, Dyeson, and Castiglione, 2002; Wilson and Vito, 1986). Haugebrook et al. (2010) found that 81 percent of their total sample reported a substance abuse issue, with older African American inmates (81.8 percent) and older Caucasian inmates (85.4 percent) reporting greater rates of substance abuse than older Latino/Latina inmates (66.7 percent). In addition, Lemieux, Dyeson, and Castiglione (2002) have reported that a disproportionate number of older inmates are sex offenders or violent offenders; as such, offense-targeted therapy would be of utility when rehabilitating older inmates.

However, previous research indicates that the mental health care needs of older inmates are more likely to go untreated compared to their physical health care needs (Arndt, Turvey, and Flaum, 2002; Fazel et al., 2004; Koenig et al., 1995). Leigey and Hodge (2012) also found a discernable treatment gap, with the number of older inmates who report a mental health problem exceeding the number of older inmates who report receiving treatment for a mental health problem. This gap can be explained by lack of training of correctional staff, lack of age-specific treatment programming in prisons, and the stigma surrounding mental health issues. If correctional staff do not receive the necessary training to detect symptoms of mental health illnesses, they will remain unable to refer older inmates to mental health staff for treatment (Aday, 1994b). Alternatively, older inmates may be reluctant to seek mental health treatment because of the stigma surrounding mental health conditions in prison (Leigey, 2007), or because there are a limited number of age-specific treatment programs available to them (Lemieux, Dyeson, and Castiglione, 2002). Kerbs has commented that prison programs should address "chronic illness, death and dying, depression, grief, institutional dependence, isolation, loss, and other concerns pressing older inmates" (2000b, p. 222).

Living in Prison: Accelerator or
Inhibitor of Psychological Aspects of Aging?

As noted earlier, correctional health-care staff report that aging inmates are roughly ten to fifteen years older physiologically than chronologically (Abramsky, 2004; Aday, 1994b; Mitka, 2004). However, a different picture emerges when older inmates report their perceptions of aging in prison. In previous studies, older inmates reported that confinement has insulated them from growing old (Leigey, 2007; Reed and Glamser, 1979; Silfen et al., 1977; Wilson and Vito, 1986). These older inmates may feel younger than their chronological ages because "prisoners are not exposed to heavy industry, hard labor, or heavy drinking. They eat well, rest often, and have ready access to medical care. This is unlikely to be the case among lower and working class men on the outside" (Reed and Glamser, 1979, p. 358).

Yet when inmates were dichotomized into middle-age (ages 30 to 59) and older-age (ages 60 and older) groups, results indicate that middle-aged inmates were more likely to espouse the belief that confinement had slowed their aging process, while older inmates were more likely to report that incarceration had hastened their aging process (Gillespie and Galliher, 1972). Further studies are needed to determine if this differing perception of aging can be replicated across different samples of middle-aged and older inmates.

Undoubtedly, health status is an important factor that influences the perception of aging. According to Goetting (1983), an inverse relationship exists between health and perceived age. In other words, older inmates in better health are more likely to report feeling younger than their chronological ages, while inmates in worse health are more likely to report feeling older than their chronological ages. Loeb and Steffensmeier (2006) uncovered a significant direct relationship between self-efficacy (i.e., confidence in managing health at the time of the study) and perceived health status ($p < 0.01$). Finally, Allen et al. (2008) found that a favorable perception of health is inversely associated with anxiety ($p < 0.07$) and depression ($p < 0.05$). These findings highlight the interdependence of physical and mental well-being for older inmates.

The Concerns of Older Inmates

The status of older inmates in the prison social system. It is difficult to make generalizations about the status that older inmates maintain in the prison social system. Goetting (1983, 1985) contends that younger inmates treat older inmates with respect and deference. In contrast, other research suggests that older inmates believe that younger inmates fail to provide them with the level of respect that they feel they deserve or that they previously possessed (Hunt et al., 1993; Leigey, 2007). A variety of factors could influence an older inmate's status, including the offense for which he or she is incarcerated (e.g., sex offense), the inmate's demeanor, race/ethnicity, and sexual orientation, and whether he or she is an informant (Kerbs and Jolley, 2007; Leigey, 2007). According to the reports of older inmates, higher status is afforded to inmates who have been incarcerated for long periods of time and to those older inmates with reputations for violent behavior or who demonstrate a continued willingness to use violence (Leigey, 2007).

Fear of victimization. Although previous research has found an inverse correlation between age and violent victimization (Bowker, 1982; Wooldredge, 1994), older inmates have reported all types of victimization, including psychological, property, physical, and sexual. Of these four types of victimization, psychological victimization, which includes such acts as threats and insults, is the type most commonly experienced by older inmates (Kerbs and Jolley, 2007). Older inmates report being targeted for victimization because they often have more possessions and financial resources than younger inmates (Vito and Wilson, 1985; Wilson and Vito, 1986). Another explanation is that aggressors perceive a lower likelihood of retaliation from older inmates (Marquart, Merianos, and Doucet, 2000). Although the level of serious violence is lower in female prisons than in male prisons (Wolff et al., 2007), older female inmates report feeling uneasy when interacting with younger inmates (Aday and Krabill, 2011) and are more likely than older male inmates to report feeling fearful or unsafe (Kratcoski and Babb, 1990).

A discrepancy exists in the older inmate literature on fear of victimization by younger inmates. While some previous research suggested that older inmates were not overly fearful of victimization (Kratcoski and Pownall, 1989; Leigey, 2007; MacKenzie, 1987; Silfen et al., 1977), other research has reported the opposite, noting that older inmates had serious safety concerns (Bergman and Amir, 1973; Mara and McKenna, 2000; Rodstein, 1975). Still other studies have found that older inmates in segregated units were more likely to feel unsafe as compared to older inmates in the general population (Wilson and Vito, 1986), while some studies have produced contrary findings (Kerbs and Jolley, 2007; Marquart, Merianos, and Doucet, 2000).

The fear of victimization can have a debilitating effect on mental well-being (McCorkle, 1993) and could severely limit the daily activities of older inmates. For instance, while Wilson and Vito (1986) did not document the actual incidence of victimization among older inmates, they found that the fear of victimization profoundly shaped the lives of respondents residing in a geriatric unit. Older inmates made calculated efforts to prevent victimization, including remaining in their unit, traveling in pairs, and avoiding areas of the institution that they perceived as being less secure (e.g., the prison yard). Wilson and Vito's study demonstrates how fear has the related negative consequences of further isolation and deprivation in the lives of older inmates.

Dying in prison. Older inmates have expressed concern with growing old (Strupp and Willmott, 2005), becoming seriously ill (Deaton, Aday, and Wahidin, 2009–2010), and dying while incarcerated (Aday and Krabill, 2011; Crawley and Sparks, 2006; Wilson and Vito, 1986). Deaton, Aday, and Wahidin (2009–2010) found significant inverse relationships between death anxiety and self-reported assessments of physical health ($p < 0.01$) and mental health ($p < 0.01$). They also found significant positive relationships between death anxiety and age ($p < 0.01$), general anxiety ($p < 0.01$), number of health problems ($p < 0.01$), and social activity ($p < 0.01$). In particular, older inmates are concerned that if they do become seriously ill, they will receive inadequate medical care (Aday and Krabill, 2011; Deaton, Aday, and Wahidin, 2009–2010; Strupp and Willmott, 2005; Wilson and Vito, 1986). They also report that a social stigma exists for inmates who die in prison (Deaton, Aday, and Wahidin, 2009–2010; Leigey, 2007; Wilson and Vito, 1986) and claim that their lives would be a failure or a waste if they were to die in prison (Deaton, Aday, and Wahidin, 2009–2010). Another concern is the irreverent manner in which their bodies will be treated while they are dying (e.g., being handcuffed to a bed before or after they are dead) (Aday, 1994a). Older inmates are also concerned that dying in prison would be a lonely death, without their loved ones (Aday, 2003; Deaton, Aday, and Wahidin, 2009–2010; Wilson and Vito, 1986). In order to manage their death anxieties, older inmates use the coping strategies of acceptance, avoidance, and denial (Aday, 1994a; Aday and Krabill, 2011; Deaton, Aday, and Wahidin, 2009–2010).

That said, not all older inmates are fearful of dying in prison. In fact, some older inmates look forward to death, because it offers an escape from their present lives (Crawley and Sparks, 2006; Deaton, Aday, and Wahidin, 2009–2010; Leigey, 2007). As Aday explains, "Some inmates viewed death more like a friend that would take them away from their horrible life in prison" (2003, p. 129). However, it appears that these older inmates are passively anticipating the end of their lives as opposed to actively pursuing an end through suicide. Although older inmates have reported contemplating suicide, especially in the early stages of confinement (Aday, 1994a), it is uncommon for older inmates to commit suicide (Mumola, 2005).

The Social Needs of Older Inmates

Adjustment to Prison

Adjustment to prison is an individualized process (Leigey, 2007). Some older inmates have described their initial experience of prison as a shock (Aday, 2003; Crawley and Sparks, 2006; Leigey, 2007). Other older inmates have found that their expectations of prison were worse than their actual experiences (Wilson and Vito, 1986). In addition, previous research has found that older inmates are well-adjusted (Gallagher, 1990) and that they adjust to confinement more easily than do younger inmates (Teller and Howell, 1981). Other research, though, suggests that older inmates only give the appearance of being well-adjusted, as they are more likely to internalize anger and stress and are less likely to outwardly display signs of a negative mental affect (Vega and Silverman, 1988). Among older inmates, certain factors have been found to be directly or indirectly related to adjustment to confined life: contact with family, level of education, and health status (Sabath and Cowles, 1988). Aging inmates who have greater contact with family, who have less education, and who are in better health report smoother adjustments to prison (Sabath and Cowles, 1988).

Relationships with Outside Contacts

Regardless of the length of time a person has been incarcerated, confinement is accompanied by a reduction in contact with family and friends. Similar to other inmate groups, older inmates miss their loved ones (Wilson and Vito, 1986). However, separation from loved ones may be even more salient for older inmates, as they perceive having less time available to be with relatives (Wilson and Vito, 1986). While confined, older inmates (like other inmates) rely on their outside contacts for emotional and financial support (Chaneles, 1987; Strupp and Willmott, 2005). Over time, however, it may be increasingly difficult for both older male inmates (Leigey, 2007) and older female inmates (Strupp and Willmott, 2005) to maintain these relationships.

Inmates can communicate with their family members and friends through letter-writing, telephone calls, and visitations. The face-to-face interaction and the ability to have physical contact with loved ones are unique features of visitation. Visits are important to the mental well-being of inmates, as previous research has revealed a positive association between inmate morale and communication with family (Sabath and Cowles, 1988). Despite the benefits of visitation, the bulk of previous research indicates that older inmates do not frequently receive visitors (Aday, 1994a; Colsher et al., 1992; Goetting, 1984; Leigey, 2007; Morton and Anderson,

1982; Reed and Glamser, 1979; Wilson and Vito, 1986). For instance, in his sample of twenty-five older male inmates, Aday (1994a) found that only two older inmates received a visit at least once per week, five reported a visit at least once a month, and eleven never received visits.

Several explanations can be offered to account for the low likelihood of older inmates receiving visits. Relationships with family could become strained as a result of the nature of the offense, in particular if the victim is a relative (Aday, 1994a, 1994b). The distance to the institution may make it difficult for family members to regularly visit (Aday, 1994a; Aday and Krabill, 2011; Vega and Silverman, 1988). Relatives could have died or they may be limited in their ability to travel due to advanced age or poor health (Aday, 1994a, 1994b, 2003; Aday and Krabill, 2011; Leigey, 2007; Vega and Silverman, 1988). Institutional restrictions on visitors, or the features of the prison, such as noise or uncomfortable seating, could further deter visitors (Leigey, 2007; Strupp and Willmott, 2005). Moreover, the expense of travel or the inability to take time off work or arrange for child care could also prevent regular visits.

Despite evidence of limited visitation, some older inmates may not report experiencing dissatisfaction with their social networks. For example, seventeen of the twenty-five inmates interviewed by Aday (1994a) reported satisfaction with their relationships with family members. Among older female inmates, Aday and Krabill (2011) found that 54 percent of respondents were very satisfied and 26 percent were fairly satisfied with their relationships with relatives. Furthermore, older inmates are able to have more regular communication with their families through letters and telephone calls (Aday and Krabill, 2011; Goetting, 1984; Leigey, 2007). For instance, Vega and Silverman (1988) found that 57 percent of older inmates did not receive visits from family members, but that 90 percent of the sample communicated with relatives by telephone or mail. That said, impediments do exist to maintaining frequent communication by mail or phone. Letter-writing is difficult for inmates or family members who are unable to read or write (Aday, 1994a, 2003), and older prisoners generally have lower levels of education as compared to younger prisoners (Kerbs, 2000b). Both letter-writing and speaking on the phone could be difficult for older inmates who are physically or mentally impaired. The expenses of communication, such as purchasing stationary and stamps, may be too costly for older inmates who are indigent and without paying jobs inside prison or without external incomes from friends and families. In addition, older inmates have reported that they do not want to burden their families with the expense of collect telephone calls and, as a result, do not call their families as often as they desire to (Aday and Krabill, 2011; Leigey, 2007; Strupp and Willmott, 2005).

Older Female Inmates and
Relationships with Outside Contacts

While studies show that older inmates in general have limited access to visitation, Kratcoski and Babb (1990) found that older female inmates have an even lower likelihood of visitation than their older male counterparts, with 54 percent of older female inmates reporting never receiving visits as compared to 25 percent of older male inmates. Based on research conducted with a convenience sample of 256 male and female inmates in Kansas, Mississippi, and New Mexico (Bond, Thompson, and Malloy, 2005), it was found that older female inmates were less likely to receive visits and less likely to communicate by mail and telephone with their loved ones as compared to older male inmates. In this study, the mean number of visits in the previous month was less than one (0.88) for older female inmates and three for older male inmates. Additionally, the mean number of phone calls was two for older female inmates and five for older male inmates. Finally, the mean number of pieces of received mail was six for older female inmates compared to twelve for older male inmates.

One explanation offered to account for the gender difference in communication with the outside world is that the relationships of older female inmates could be more fractured or tenuous, as evidenced by the finding that older female inmates are significantly less likely to be married than older male inmates, 37 percent versus 51 percent, respectively ($p < 0.01$) (Kratcoski and Babb, 1990). However, recent research is more optimistic. In Strupp and Willmott's sample (2005), one-third of older female inmates reported receiving a visit at least once each month, though 13 percent of the sample had not received a visit in the prior five years. Visitation for older female relatives may be made even more difficult given that there are fewer female prison institutions compared to male institutions, and consequently, family members may have to travel a greater distance to see older female relatives as compared to older male relatives (Aday and Krabill, 2011).

Relationships Inside Prisons

Inmate to inmate. While it would make sense for older male inmates to develop friendships in prisons as substitutes for the diminished communication with outside contacts, most of the empirical evidence does not support this line of reasoning. Instead, it appears that they form few close attachments while incarcerated (Aday, 1994a; Gallagher, 1990; Kratcoski and Pownall, 1989; Reed and Glamser, 1979; Wilson and Vito, 1986). Older inmates may be distrustful of other inmates (Vega and Silverman, 1988) or believe that the formation of friendships would make them vulnerable, since friendships are seen as a sign of weakness in the prison community (Reed and Glamser, 1979). Although not extensively developed, friendships with other inmates do offer benefits. Older male inmates have reported that they are able to discuss personal topics with friends (Aday, 1994a), ask for and offer advice (Leigey, 2007), and provide protection from victimization (Leigey, 2007).

Some older inmates report that they have befriended younger inmates. These older inmates act as paternal figures (Bergman and Amir, 1973; Leigey, 2007; Rodstein, 1975) or maternal figures (Aday and Krabill, 2011) to younger inmates and assist new inmates as they become acclimated to prison life (Leigey, 2007). Intergenerational relationships provide older inmates with the opportunity to act in a parental role, which they are limited in doing with their own children. Younger inmates, in turn, assist them with daily activities (Leigey, 2007; Silfen et al., 1977) and offer protection from aggressive inmates (Leigey, 2007). However, challenges to the development of intergenerational friendships exist. Older inmates may feel as though they have little in common with younger inmates (Leigey, 2007) or that younger inmates are disrespectful toward them (Hunt et al., 1993; Leigey, 2007). They may also resent younger inmates, as older inmates blame the misbehavior of younger inmates for increasingly restrictive institutional rules (Kerbs and Jolley, 2007; Leigey, 2007; Wilson and Vito, 1986).

Inmate relationships in female prisons. Older female inmates describe the formation of friendships that resemble those described in the literature on female inmates as "'fictive' or 'affiliated' kin" (Aday and Krabill, 2011, p. 105). In the most detailed examination of older female friendships to date, Aday and Krabill (2011) found that these friendships, which are most often formed with their age peers, provide emotional support, companionship, and assistance in daily activities or during times of illness. However, even within these close relationships, the extent to which older female inmates disclose personal or sensitive information is limited. For example, the researchers found that prison conditions, prison staff, or positive aspects of life were frequent topics of conversation among friends; conversely, the inmate's health, her finances, or any topics that were associated with feelings of shame, anger, or sadness, were less commonly shared.

In their interactions with other inmates more broadly, older female inmates (as compared to older male inmates) were significantly more likely to have negative opinions of other inmates (Kratcoski and Babb, 1990). For example, when asked to describe other prisoners, 20 percent of older female inmates used the adjectives "friendly" and "helpful," in comparison to 25 percent of older male inmates who used these adjectives; furthermore, 13 percent of older female inmates used the adjectives "aggressive" and "violent," in comparison to 2 percent of older male inmates who used these adjectives ($p < 0.01$) (Kratcoski and Babb, 1990). Older female inmates were also more likely than their older male counterparts to report having little to no interaction with younger inmates (Kratcoski and Babb, 1990). Intergenerational tension remains a problem, as reported recently by older female inmates incarcerated in prisons in the western United States (Strupp and Willmott, 2005) and in the southern states (Aday and Krabill, 2011).

Relationships between older inmates and prison staff. Older inmates' relationships with prison staff have been characterized using a variety of conflicting descriptors. Earlier studies include reports from staff members who contended that older inmates were demanding and dependent upon them, and required greater assistance and attention than did their younger counterparts (Bergman and Amir, 1973; Kratcoski and Babb, 1990; Kratcoski and Pownall, 1989). Alternatively, other accounts of older inmates suggest that they do not cause problems, and serve their time quietly, and are consequently overlooked by prison staff (Krajick, 1979; Morton and Anderson, 1982; Vega and Silverman, 1988; Wiegand and Burger, 1979).

Hostility has not been commonly reported in the relationships between older inmates and prison staff. Instead, previous research suggests that older inmates are more likely to report conflict with other inmates than staff (MacKenzie, 1987; Vega and Silverman, 1988). The lack of conflict between older inmates and staff could be explained as a result of the low likelihood of older inmates violating prison rules (Goetting, 1984; Leigey, 2007; Morton and Anderson, 1982; Wilson and Vito, 1986).

While staff-on-inmate physical abuse is not a commonly reported issue, older inmate reports of verbal abuse have been documented (Aday and Krabill, 2011). Strupp and Willmott (2005) found that 62 percent of the older women in their study reported having been verbally abused by staff, with 12 percent reporting having been physically abused by staff. Additional research is needed to examine the effect that staff-on-inmate abuse has on the mental and physical well-being of older female and male inmates. Moreover, this finding underscores the need to create guidelines and training designed to assist staff members in developing greater awareness of and sensitivity to the needs of older inmates.

Participation in Prison Programming

An examination of the daily activities of older inmates not only provides an understanding of older inmates' isolation from prison programs and services, but also serves as evidence of the need for age-specific programming and activities. Thus the chapter now turns to issues pertaining to work assignments, educational and vocational programs, religion, and recreational activities.

Work assignment. Marquart, Merianos, and Doucet (2000) noted that 76 percent of older male inmates who participated in their study and who resided in the general prison population had work assignments. In comparison to that study of older male inmates, Aday and Krabill (2011), in studying older female inmates, found that approximately half of their sample (49.6 percent) reported having a work assignment. Work provides several important intrinsic and extrinsic benefits. A work assignment provides structure to an inmate's daily routine (Marquart, Merianos, and Doucet, 2000) and also serves to increase physical activity and to reduce boredom (Aday, 2003; Reed and Glamser, 1979). In addition, paid work assignments provide inmates with the funds to purchase items at the commissary (Aday and Krabill, 2011). For inmates who are estranged from their relatives, the money they earn through their work assignments is often the only revenue available to them (Leigey, 2007). While work could improve the physical and mental health of older inmates, work assignments may be limited, especially in special-needs or geriatric facilities (Aday, 2003; Krajick, 1979; Marquart, Merianos, and Doucet, 2000). In addition, certain work assignments such as laundry, janitorial, kitchen, or yard work, may be too physically demanding for older inmates (Strupp and Willmott, 2005). Because of the benefits of work, it is recommended that prisons implement work assignments that take into consideration the health of older inmates so that those with varying levels of health problems can be employed (Kratcoski and Pownall, 1989).

Educational and vocational programs. Although educational and vocational programs are available in prisons, they are usually not designed to meet the needs and preferences of older inmates (Goetting, 1985; Krajick, 1979; Vega and Silverman, 1988; Vito and Wilson, 1985; Wilson and Vito, 1986). The involvement of older inmates in classes is limited (Sabath and Cowles, 1988; Wilson and Vito, 1986), despite the fact that previous research notes that older inmates have greater educational deficiencies than younger inmates (Goetting, 1984). Illiterate older inmates may be reluctant to ask for help or to participate in a class in which their illiteracy could be discovered (Krajick, 1979). In addition, older inmates could believe that there is little practical value in attending educational classes or learning new vocational skills (Goetting, 1983, 1985; Leigey, 2007; Wiegand and Burger, 1979). This perception may be more likely for those older inmates who do not anticipate being released (Flynn, 1992). Ageism may also be an explanation for limited involvement. Previous research has shown that prison staff may discourage older inmates from participating in educational and vocational courses in order to increase the access of younger and short-term inmates to limited programming opportunities (Goetting, 1983, 1985; Leigey, 2007; Wiegand and Burger, 1979). In an effort to increase older inmates' utilization of programming, correctional administrators should consider developing educational courses that are suitable for this population's stage in the life course (Kerbs, 2000b; Vito and Wilson, 1985; Wiegand and Burger, 1979).

Religion. According to Koenig (1995), 92 percent of ninety-six older male inmates (aged 50 and older) from one federal prison reported having a religious affiliation at the time of the study. Older inmates are less likely to engage in formal religious activity such as attending church services; instead, they are more likely to practice their religions through praying and the reading of religious texts (Aday, 1994a; Koenig, 1995; Reed and Glamser, 1979). Furthermore, Koenig (1995) examined the relationship between mental health and religion, and found religion to be a central coping mechanism among the older inmate population. Approximately one-third reported that religion was the most important mechanism that helped them cope with incarceration. In addition, depression scores were lower for respondents who reported a religious affiliation (Koenig, 1995). More recently, Deaton, Aday, and Wahidin (2009–2010) noted an inverse relationship between religious activity and death anxiety. However, Allen et al. (2008) found a positive correlation between religiosity and depression. In explaining their results, the authors contended: "It may be that depressed inmates attempt to cope with their negative emotional state by turning" to religion (p. 696). In other words, religion does not cause or contribute to depression; instead, depressed inmates turn to religion as a coping mechanism.

Recreational activities. Recreational and leisure activities also generally have positive effects on the physical and mental health of inmates (Bintz, 1974; Buckaloo, Krug, and Nelson, 2009). However, older inmates may be reluctant to participate in competitive sport programs with younger inmates (Goetting, 1985; Wilson and Vito, 1986). Interviews with prison staff indicate that aging female inmates have lower rates of participation in activities as compared to aging male inmates (Kratcoski and Babb, 1990). As a result of the lack of recreational programs that are designed specifically for older men and women in prison (Aday, 1994a; Wilson and Vito, 1986), older inmates may not receive enough physical exercise. In fact, in Leigey and Hodge's (2012) study, only about one-half (48.0 percent) of older male inmates and one-third (33.8 percent) of older female inmates reported exercising in the prior twenty-four hours. Rather than participating in activities that require physical exertion, older inmates engage in mostly sedentary leisure activities, including watching television, reading, listening to the radio, playing cards, or socializing with other inmates (Aday, 2003; Aday and Krabill, 2011; Goetting, 1984; Marquart, Merianos, and Doucet, 2000; Sabath and Cowles, 1988). The creation and implementation of recreational activities that take into consideration the abilities of older inmates (e.g., board games, chess, shuffleboard, and separate gym times) could increase their physical and social activity (Kratcoski and Babb, 1990; Vito and Wilson, 1985; Wilson and Vito, 1986).

In relation to group-based activities, clubs and organizations provide inmates with the opportunity to socialize with others. Depending on the study, the involvement of older inmates has been described as either widespread (Reed and Glamser, 1979) or limited (Sabath and Cowles, 1988; Wilson and Vito, 1986). One explanation for the discrepancy is that the level of older inmates' participation is dependent upon the number of accessible social clubs and organizations, which varies between institutions (Leigey, 2007).

Conclusion

In 1984, Goetting noted that the public was not accustomed to thinking of aging individuals as prison inmates. The same perception of inmates persists today. However, in this case, perception is not reality. The number of older male and female inmates in prisons today is sizable, and most of them have at least one chronic ailment. Unless significant changes occur in sentencing and correctional practices in the United States, their numbers will continue to grow. As has been outlined in this chapter, the biological, psychological, and social needs of the older inmate population are different than the needs of younger inmates, demonstrating the necessity of age-specific programs, policies, and procedures.

A certain level of discomfort is expected with confinement; however, incarceration is fraught with additional challenges and burdens for older inmates. Since their needs are not generally taken into consideration in the design of the prison, or in its policies and programming, confinement is more punitive for older inmates as compared to younger inmates. While correctional administrators will continue to face obstacles as they accommodate the needs of the aging prison population in the United States, especially in times of budget constraints, humanitarian and financial incentives exist for considering the needs of older inmates and for ending the marginalization of this population.

Finally, in an effort to better understand the correctional experiences of older inmates, it is essential to improve the rigor of future studies. As noted earlier in this chapter, previous research on older inmates has been hindered by unrepresentative samples (Kerbs, 2000b). Moving forward, researchers should strive to increase the generalizability of their findings by using larger random samples in order to obtain a more accurate picture of the bio-psycho-social needs of the aging inmate population.

4

Social Programming and Activities

Ronald H. Aday and Jennifer J. Krabill

It is now common knowledge that the number of geriatric inmates in the United States has been rising steadily since the 1980s, both in absolute terms and as a proportion of state and federal prison populations. As the number of aging inmates continues to escalate during the coming decades, creating supportive social and physical environments will be crucial determinants for developing a well-adjusted graying prison population (Aday, 2003; Cain and Fontenot, 2001; Harrison, 2006; Thivierge-Rikard and Thompson, 2007). Nonetheless, the growth of the aging population has coincided with deteriorating conditions of confinement influenced by overcrowded living conditions and the rising costs of health care (Reimer, 2008). Additionally, correctional systems are struggling to treat a range of health conditions that normally accompany aging while also facing challenges in creating suitable social environments necessary for geriatric inmates.

A greater understanding of this often "forgotten" population is essential for the creation of policies and programs that are cost-efficient and effective in meeting the special needs of older inmates. To date, correctional systems have neither anticipated nor responded adequately to the challenge of providing age-appropriate programming for the growing population of long-term inmates (Sterns et al., 2008) as well as those entering prison for the first time late in life (Yates and Gillespie, 2000). A number of researchers have suggested that the diversity of older offenders must be recognized and incorporated into the range of rehabilitative programs within US correctional systems (Aday, 2003; Kratcoski, 2000; Mara, 2002). For example, some older inmates who are ideal candidates to return to

69

society will need reentry-focused programs that are effective in supporting a successful transition. Other aging inmates will need a prison environment that protects them as they continue to age and eventually die in custody. It must be understood that aging inmates have a reduced ability to cope, and that correctional administrators face complex challenges in accommodating older inmates' diverse array of specialized needs in a typical prison setting.

Many things are important for understanding how individuals cope with the prison experience in later life. Chronic offenders and other long-term inmates are more likely to know what to expect in prison because they have served a considerable amount of time behind bars. Other older offenders, the ones imprisoned for a serious crime late in life, are often ill-prepared to successfully adjust to prison life (Aday, 2003). Regardless of their respective pathways to prison adjustment, it has been noted that one of the dominant challenges for inmates is how they are able to structure their time (Toch, 2006). The availability of prison programs may spell the difference in whether the older inmate suffers disorganization and withdrawal or manages to cope and avoid such damage to self (Wright, 1993). As inmates "age in place," correctional officials should be increasingly aware of the need to tailor the various programs and levels of activity required by each program to meet the special needs of aging inmates. Considerable evidence suggests that the availability of prison activities such as work, adult education, religious activities, social and recreational opportunities, and other interpersonal interactions is important to facilitating the adaptation process to prison (Aday, 2003; Jiang and Winfree, 2006; Wooldredge, 1998).

This chapter addresses the ways in which correctional systems can promote the creation of a humanistic social environment by investing available resources in activities that creatively structure the daily routines of longer-term aging inmates. Models of successful aging are described and used as frameworks for evaluating the ways in which current modes and levels of prison programming do, and do not (as is often the case), support aging inmates' psychosocial engagement and integration. Moreover, models of successful aging are used to describe the programming practices and approaches that correctional officials should consider using to promote the psychosocial engagement and integration of aging inmates while helping them to establish productive and healthy daily routines. In particular, the person-environment and activity perspectives introduced in this chapter have been recognized as two approaches that have influenced successful community-based living environments for the elderly outside prison. Finally, various components of gerontologically specialized programming (e.g., support groups and work opportunities) are described in depth, and a fully integrated best-practice model from Nevada is used to demonstrate the potential benefits that can be derived from providing a strong therapeutic social milieu for a diverse aging inmate population.

Aging and Prison Adaptation

The assumption that the process of aging occurs in context has become an important feature of bio-psycho-social models of aging. Since the late 1970s, gerontologists have sought to understand the effects of environmental settings on older people as well as the ways in which to optimize living environments for aging individuals (Kahana, 1982). More recently, similar concerns have emerged in the field of corrections as the consequence of "aging in place" among older prisoners receiving greater attention (Hooyman and Kiyak, 2011). Aging in prison does not occur in a vacuum, but rather aging takes place in a correctional social context that includes individual prisoners' needs and resources, attachment to their surroundings and patterns of activities, and their relationships with others (Harrison, 2006; Aday and Krabill, 2011). Environmental psychologists have pointed out that maintaining a good fit between individual characteristics and one's environment is conducive to positive adjustments late in life (Allman, Sawyer, and Roseman, 2006; Crowe et al., 2008).

Person-Environment Perspective

The person-environment perspective is a useful lens through which the effects of incarceration on older offenders can be examined (Gibbs, 1991; Stedman, 2002; Wahl and Oswald, 2010). Congruent with this perspective is an examination of the ways in which interactions among physiological, psychological, and social changes associated with the aging process affect older offenders (Hooyman and Kiyak, 2011; Lawton, 1983). The person-environment perspective assumes that the environment is not static, but must change continually to accommodate the evolving needs of the older individual. Environment press (a concept taken from the competence model) refers to the demands that the social and physical environments make on the individual to adapt, respond, or change. Integrating concepts from the person-environment perspective and the competence model, the environment-press model focuses on the elements of human behavior and the need to develop a better fit between the individual's needs and their environment (Hooyman and Kiyak, 2011). The environment-press model has been adopted by a variety of disciplines to include, for example, architects who may be interested in developing ways to make prison environments more accessible for aging inmates with disabilities (Moore, 1989).

Adaptation in prison implies a process in which the older offender adjusts to the following prison-based conditions: physical conditions of the prison, including stairs, crowding, and walking a considerable distance to and from meals; social dynamics of prison life, including interactions with younger inmates, prison crowding, and noise; and psychological demands of prison life, including the need to develop specialized problem-solving and mental coping abilities (Aday, 2003; Toch, 2006). For example, social engagement may decline as an inmate's level of contact with their loved ones outside prison declines over time, thus creating a devastating emotional impact. To deal with this pain and perceived rejection by the outside world, many inmates begin to identify with the prison subculture, which provides a new reference group, social relationships, and rationalizations that help neutralize feelings of isolation and rejection (Jiang and Winfree, 2006; Krabill and Aday, 2005). Many older inmates adapt to environmental pressures by forming social support networks with other inmates who are simultaneously living with similar deprivations and anxieties.

According to the person-environment perspective, an individual is more likely to be better-adjusted in an environment that is congruent with their physical, cognitive, and emotional needs and abilities. In its broadest sense, this perspective presumes that the level of press (or demand) that the environment imposes on an individual will greatly influence the given individual's competence (as defined by behavior and affect). It has long been acknowledged that elders require and even benefit from a slightly greater press or demand for adaptation from their external environments; such slightly increased environmental press helps elders to remain active, alert, engaged, and stimulated (Hooyman and Kiyak, 2011). If there are too few environmental challenges for the older adult, the likelihood of boredom, apathy, and idleness increases. An environment that is too strenuous, however, results in a range of other unintended negative consequences, including anxiety as the most frequently occurring negative outcome. As Toch noted, inmates often feel that a significant amount of continuous activity is crucial to their survival in prison: "Activity can serve a number of purposes in coping with the environment beyond those of ameliorating redundancy. It can be a release for feelings, can distract attention from pain, or can keep the mind from being concerned with unpleasant thoughts or memories. Transcending survival needs, activities can provide goals, fulfillment, or scope for creativity" (2006, p. 28). The "eventlessness" of prison life over the life cycle can be a significant stressor for many inmates (Cowles, 1990, p. 17). The person-environment perspective calls for increased *relevant social stimulation* as a means of helping the elder return to an optimum state of equilibrium following a period of extreme idleness (Kahana, 1982). Relevant social stimulation involves inmates in new activities and further opportunities for growth.

In many institutions, however, geriatric offenders are exposed to excessively high levels of demand—an event that undeniably results in adverse outcomes for the entire prison community (Yates and Gillespie, 2000). Such press is considered by many elders to be unnecessarily overwhelming in facilities, dormitories, or units where they must face overcrowding, noise, and abrasive interactions on an ongoing (and often daily) basis (Kerbs and Jolley, 2007; Marquart, Merianos, and Doucet, 2000). Older inmates are often unable to cope with the fast pace of a regular mainstream prison environment. The new elderly offender can feel particularly vulnerable coming into an unfamiliar environment late in life without adequate prison experience and coping skills. For example, without sufficient opportunities to establish niches to which they can retreat for much-needed privacy and solitude, aging prisoners run increased risks of overstimulation or too much environmental stress (Toch, 2006).

In relation to environmental concerns, acknowledgement of older offenders' sentence lengths is essential to facilitating optimum adaptation and adjustment. Specifically, the need for predictability, stability, and structure rises dramatically over time (Aday, 2003). Long-termers and lifers will encounter a range of circumstances beyond their immediate personal control and will therefore require the highest level of support from their environments. For example, the belief that a person can accurately predict and therefore prevent obstacles, such as the possibility of parole denials, deteriorating health, or even the death of loved ones, can be extremely anxiety-provoking for inmates. The combined challenge of having to negotiate a largely demanding prison environment with severely limited opportunities for personal control can be a tremendous threat to aging prisoners' self-esteem and self-worth.

Activity Perspective

In a similar fashion to the person-environment perspective presented above, the activity perspective also argues that people adjust best to late life when they maintain high levels of activity that are similar to those that are considered normal for middle-aged individuals (Lemon, Bengtson, and Peterson, 1972; Longino and Kart, 1982). The activity perspective is a highly accepted framework in communities of older adults outside prison, and assumes that both frequency of participation in activities and levels of intimacy are essential for life satisfaction. Toch (2006) identifies activity as a release of energy serving to stabilize the "economy" of the body and mind. Proponents of the activity perspective contend that levels of activity will not deteriorate as the individual ages if the following conditions are met: the elder is in reasonably good health, the elder has access to a variety of stimulating pursuits that they find interesting, and the elder has access to others who support their participation in long-standing pastimes (Aday, 2003). Within a prison context, the activity perspective would support age-based policies and programs that develop new roles and activities for older adults and help to encourage social integration. To some extent, this perspective is consistent with the value placed on work, individual responsibility, and productivity (Powell, 2006).

A contemporary version of the activity perspective has been extended by Rowe and Kahn's (1997) conceptualization of "successful aging." They identified three key components of successful aging: a low risk of disease and disease-related disability, a maintenance of high levels of mental and physical functioning, and an active engagement with life. According to Rowe and Kahn, remaining active proves to be beneficial in a wide range of spheres in later life, including healthy aging. It has been argued that productive activities such as exercise can be psychologically and physically beneficial by slowing functional decline (Clark, Long, and Schiffman, 1999). In particular, as Toch has so aptly stated, "engaging in meaningful and engrossing activities can be oases for psychological nurturance; they may become salient, positive features of an otherwise negative experience" (2006, p. 32). Activity plays an important role in the lives of older people because it is commonly recognized that age-based deterioration in physical and mental processes significantly decreases when individuals remain active and engaged in their social environments. Cunninghis (1989) identified five key ways in which participation in activities programming has met the psychosocial needs of older people who reside in institutions: (1) the promotion of group membership and companionship, (2) the promotion of self-determination and independent action, (3) assistance in achieving status and accumulating life experience, (4) the provision of opportunities to serve others and feel useful, and (5) the provision of opportunities to be a part of the larger community in which one lives. Ideally, older inmates' psychosocial engagement and social integration should be promoted through the delivery of prison programming that is multifaceted; activities should stimulate and challenge inmates cognitively and physically. Any programming directed toward the older inmate should also be effective in helping the inmate to bypass or successfully cope with a full range of negative bio-psycho-social outcomes that are common among older inmates, including isolation, dependency, helplessness, institutionalization, apathy, lowered sensory input, and atrophy.

Programs, Activities, and Applications

While people maintain diverse preferences for how they age, social theory is considered a useful tool for understanding the ongoing interchange between older individuals and their social and physical environments. Theory can also be helpful in guiding prison programming, in providing practical interventions, and even in developing opportunities that optimize the aging experience in restrictive prison environments. Regardless of older inmates' characteristics or diverse coping styles, both the person-environment perspective and the activity perspective stress the importance of designing social environments that offer elderly individuals structured opportunities for activity and engagement. For example, for some geriatric inmates as they become frail and vulnerable, the person-environment perspective suggests that we should create a variety of programs and activities along a continuum that will permit aging prisoners to adapt more successfully. Furthermore, the demands of meeting the heterogeneous needs of elderly inmates with chronic illnesses (Potter et al., 2007) and the gender-based differences in inmates' processes of adaptation and support-seeking (Jiang and Winfree, 2006) have created a need for multidisciplinary programming. Correctional programming that is influenced by a collaboration across disciplines is better-suited to the complex task of reorienting the prison environment to meet the diverse psychosocial needs of an aging inmate population.

Increasing numbers of states are beginning to explicitly target the special programming and therapeutic needs of elderly inmates (Gaydon and Miller, 2007; Harrison, 2006; Sterns et al., 2008). Prison officials are now concerned with the growing number of middle-aged prisoners who are coming into the system as first-time offenders and the increasing number of medically and cognitively challenged inmates who have a variety of end-of-life issues (Sterns et al., 2008). Since 1985, numerous states have had no choice but to build special-needs facilities or secure nursing homes to accommodate the increasing number of geriatric inmates. A little over half of the states now provide geriatric accommodations, including selected clustering, dedicated units, free-standing prisons, and dedicated and secure nursing-home facilities (Abner, 2006; Aday, 2003; Sterns et al., 2008).

Although states differ markedly in terms of the breadth and depth of geriatric activities provided to aging inmates (Lemieux, Dyeson, and Castiglione, 2002), researchers have estimated that approximately thirty states currently provide at least some form of structured recreational programming specifically targeted to geriatric inmates (Aday, 2003; Anno et al., 2004). Numerous states are beginning to hire psychologists, social workers, or other such professionals who specialize in geriatrics, which has promoted significant advancements in the quality of programs that are designed to assist older inmates in coping with the various biological, psychological, and social changes that accompany the aging process. Popular activities that correctional administrators are being encouraged to adopt for use with geriatric offenders include age-appropriate work and educational opportunities, religious activities, assorted leisure pursuits (arts, crafts, gardening, woodworking), group work activities, and individual psychotherapy. Described here are geriatric-specific programs and activities that correctional officials should consider implementing in an effort to support the well-being of aging inmates.

Creative Work Assignments

Cain and Fontenot (2001) have noted that realizing the importance of providing meaningful work opportunities to inmates and allowing them to positively and creatively express themselves constitute a crucial factor in managing aging and long-term inmates. Moreover, Litwin and Shiovitz-Ezra (2006) have stressed that the activity perspective provides the opportunity for positive feedback on role performance, which leads to enhanced self-esteem and personal well-being. Work as an activity provides a variety of important functions in the prison setting, especially for aging inmates serving long sentences. In particular, many aging prisoners have been influenced by the value of hard work earlier in their lives, and they view the respect one obtains through hard work as an important source of identity and social recognition. Moreover, work in a prison environment helps to determine interaction guidelines and patterns of association. For example, according to Marquart, Merianos, and Doucet (2000), work assignments provide older inmates with the opportunity to interact with peers of varying ages. Participating in work activities also provides older inmates with the opportunity to remain in similar routines while encouraging them to remain engaged and physically active. In this regard, work can be considered a "wellness" activity, since older inmates have to walk to work and in some cases participate in physically demanding labor. Maintaining a structured routine can serve as a stimulating experience for older inmates while perhaps slowing down age-related mental and physical decline.

However, according to Stephan and Karberg (2003), only about 50 percent of the population of inmates who are eligible for and able to work actually spend a portion of their sentences engaged in work assignments. Inmates have generally found a dearth of work opportunities in prison (Aday, 2003; Caes, 1990), and the big challenge is finding suitable work opportunities for eligible and interested inmates. The inability to match interested inmates with suitable work opportunities frequently leads to forced disengagement. Finding suitable work assignments for older prisoners poses significant challenges for correctional officials. Older inmates housed in the general prison population typically have a much greater opportunity for prison employment as compared to inmates living in special-needs facilities (Aday, 2003). Some fortunate older inmates may work in a variety of cottage industries, which provide not only a legitimate community contribution, but also a significant income for prisoners. In some selective cases, inmates may earn up to two dollars per hour for contract prison labor. In contrast, work assignments associated with daily prison upkeep and operation may pay only ten to twenty-five cents per hour. Moreover, some states offer no compensation whatsoever for inmate labor (Aday, 2003; Aday and Krabill, 2011).

Encouraging the geriatric offender to adopt and maintain vocational skills or behaviors often entails recognizing that, for many of these individuals, prison employment will be regarded outside of prison as the equivalent of holding a career. Able-bodied elders could potentially be assigned a series of tasks that are integral to sustaining the prison facility's daily operations. Aging male and female inmates may seek refuge in completing tasks in the areas of kitchen, laundry, and janitorial services. Additional practical duties to which older offenders have been assigned with remarkably high success rates include landscaping, carpentry, and miscellaneous types of repair work (Aday, 2003). Moreover, elder inmates who possess an eye to detail and talents in the areas of bookkeeping, clerical work, and prison libraries are in a position to make valued contributions to the daily operations of a prison facility. According to older persons who have actively assumed roles and responsibilities in such areas, work is often regarded as a welcome escape from various institutional stressors that are routinely found in their living and sleeping areas (Aday and Krabill, 2011). Moreover, the practice of maintaining a prison job can be a tremendous boost to the offenders' sense of self-esteem (Aday, 2003).

Consideration of work assignments, however, raises numerous questions for correctional officials regarding the most effective approaches for providing such assignments to all inmates who desire and would benefit from them. Involvement in work assignments can prove to be challenging for those who have started to experience physical decline, including reduced strength and stamina; these individuals depend on a correctional administrator's sense of age-based equity in relationship to the overall fairness in the distribution of work assignments. Occasionally, correctional administrators may be able to create new and innovative positions that can be staffed by elderly inmates whose physical decline necessitates a sedentary lifestyle. Individuals who have grown old in the system and who have already made full use of the more traditional types of prison labor may need options for retirement as well as incentives to increase their levels of participation in other less strenuous activities in exchange for work-type credit (Harrison, 2006; Sterns et al., 2008).

Long-term offenders, in particular, may benefit substantially from motivation to engage in tasks such as assisting their fellow offenders with legal research, letter writing, or similar tasks that do not require continuous engagement in physically demanding manual labor such as pushing heavy mops all day or committing lengthy hours to work in the kitchen (Cowles, 1990; Aday, 2006). Work options that do not require continuous engagement in physically demanding manual labor will undeniably become more important in the coming years, as older inmates are vulnerable to falls and injuries while they are performing work-related duties (Williams et al., 2006) but are still very focused on being included and valued in the everyday social milieu. In fact, the most important consideration in determining program assignments for older inmates revolves around their physical limitations (Anno et al., 2004). Issues such as reduced physical strength, hearing and vision loss, and the inability to stand for long periods typically affect the type of work assignment that may be appropriate. Hence, prison administrators should consider more individualized programming that reflects various levels of functioning.

The older inmate population is frequently characterized as one with diverse interests and abilities; moreover, as just noted, older inmates experience a strong desire to occupy meaningful social roles while they contend with a series of physical limitations that restrict their work assignment options. Rather than placing an emphasis solely on vocational activities, individualized programming along a continuum of levels of functioning should also include structured opportunities for cottage industry or part-time work as well as volunteer activities within the institution (Anderson and McGehee, 1991; Rosefield, 1993). For example, older inmates should be encouraged to volunteer their talents to sit bedside with other inmates nearing the end of life and to provide companionship to the terminally ill; such activity provides older inmates with the opportunity to feel needed while making a lasting contribution to other inmates in the larger prison community (Hoffman and Dickinson, 2011; Wright and Bronstein, 2007). Additionally, individualized programming along a continuum of levels of functioning should include structured opportunities for recreational activities such as gardening, woodworking, ceramics, and other craft activities (Anderson and McGehee, 1991; Rosefield, 1993). In keeping with the person-environment and activity perspectives on successful aging discussed earlier, older inmates should be encouraged to stay physically active and mentally alert for as long as possible.

Fostering Reciprocal Exchanges

Informal activities such as social ties have long been a measure of engagement identified as an important correlate of successful aging (Litwin and Shiovitz-Ezra, 2006). Yet creating an effective social milieu is likely to be one of the most challenging tasks that prison administrators will negotiate when preparing to manage a growing geriatric prison population. In part, the successful management of an aging prison population rests on the creation of a milieu that fosters older inmates' overall social integration. Successful integration among a group of supportive inmates increases feelings of safety and helps to increase older inmates' overall level of social activity. In recent years, prison administrators with limited funding have been pressed with the ever-growing burden of deciding how to assist older inmates in creating niches for themselves. The creation of a supportive climate where offenders feel as if they are assisted in maintaining an optimum level of stress benefits the institution (and inmates alike), as it restores the inmates' faith in the system, and supports rehabilitative goals and ideals.

Research conducted in a variety of environments including prisons has highlighted the positive influence that social attachments (emotional support and exchanges) can have on the psychological well-being of those choosing to socially engage with others (Aday and Krabill, 2011; House, Umberson, and Landis, 1988; Jiang and Winfree, 2006; Krabill and Aday, 2005; Wilson and Spink, 2006). Social relationships function as a supportive network and sustain one's social identity (Stevens and Van Tilburg, 2000). Research has also found that even the perception that a support network is available has been linked to improved mental health (Cohen, Gottlieb, and Underwood, 2001; Liang, Krause, and Bennett, 2001). Friends who provide an individual with a supportive network can mediate the negative effects of problematic or stressful life experiences (Stevens and Van Tilburg, 2000). Even within the criminal justice system, where administrators maintain a position that the primary purpose of confinement is to punish (not coddle) offenders, interest is being placed on providing prisoners with assistance in preserving their social connections to the maximum extent possible (Aday and Krabill, 2011).

Limited research tends to support the notion that female prisoners, as compared to male prisoners, seek more social support activities both within and outside of prisons (Pollock, 2002). Based on recent findings from Aday and Krabill's (2011) five-state study of 327 older women in prisons, Table 4.1 shows the degree to which older female inmates provided each other with assistance. It is evident from inmate responses that an active support network was an important element in the creation of a humanizing prison environment; moreover, the older female inmates' relationships proved to be quite beneficial for the majority of them. Although many of the older female inmates received constant support from their family circles on the outside, inside connections were apparently also very important. Most women (82 percent) reported that they had a supportive

Table 4.1 Measures of Inmate Support Among Older Female Offenders, 2006 (*n* = 327)

Support Indicators	Percentage
Perceived support network	
I frequently provide some type of assistance to a fellow inmate	83.8
There are fellow inmates here who share my interests and concerns	82.0
I have fellow inmates here I can depend on whenever I need them	78.9
The friends I have made here are very important to me	77.6
There is always someone I can talk to about my day-to-day problems	71.4
My relationships with fellow inmates provide me a sense of well-being	69.5
I have fellow inmates I can confide in about my personal problems	64.8
I can call on my friends whenever I need them	64.6
There are plenty of people I can rely on in case of trouble	51.0
I feel personally responsible for the well-being of my fellow inmates	43.1
Assistance received from prison friends	
Other inmates have been there to console me when I'm upset	74.2
My friends here frequently listen to my problems	71.0
I have received emotional support from my friends	63.4
Other inmates have cared for me when I'm ill or assisted with my daily needs	56.6
I frequently receive advice or help in making personal decisions	52.7
I have received gifts from some of my prison friends	51.6
My friends here provide me with companionship	45.2

Source: Aday and Krabill, 2011.

network, in this case defined as someone who shared their interests and concerns. Approximately three out of four inmates in this large sample indicated that the friends they had made in prison were very important to them; additionally, over 80 percent of the older female inmates stated that they frequently provided some type of assistance to a fellow inmate.

Although friends are considered to be an invaluable resource to whom older adults can turn for assistance during times of need, supportive relations are not always easily established within the prison environment. As discussed extensively in the literature (Bond, Thompson, and Malloy, 2005), aging prisoners are extraordinarily cautious about entering into relations with their fellow offenders; furthermore, aging inmates are extremely cautious about engaging in any meaningful degree of self-disclosure with the very individuals with whom they are in close proximity on a daily basis. Efforts at helping older inmates develop and strengthen relationships inside prison are most effective when emphasizing the strategy of socializing with a narrow range of potentially supportive peers, including those who share key defining characteristics such as age, race/ethnicity, housing assignments, and participation in educational, vocational, and recreational activities (Aday, 2003; Aday and Krabill, 2011).

Since social support is considered to be a primary contributor to successful aging, efforts should be made to promote and support the use of inmate peers when appropriate. Correctional officials are beginning to explore the advantages of identifying, recruiting, training, and supervising younger inmates to assume responsibilities for working with persons of advanced age, thus freeing correctional staff for more pressing tasks (Sterns et al., 2008). With budget cuts and rising caseloads, correctional staff are increasingly limited in their ability to assist older inmates with the completion of activities of daily living, which include such personal care tasks as eating, dressing, and getting in or out of a bed or a chair (Anno et al., 2004). Thus, correctional officials are working to identify alternative sources of support for older inmates. For example, fellow offenders can be depended upon to help geriatric inmates with a number of important tasks such as "pod" cleaning, laundry, transportation to meals, sick calls, pushing wheelchairs, letter writing, and immediate communication with staff members when the need for an intervention arises. Carefully designed and implemented prisoner assistance programs have the potential to transform the entire prison community by facilitating the development of a collective culture that values empathy and compassion among inmates (Wright and Bronstein, 2007).

Although willingness to engage in reciprocal exchanges is imperative to the well-being of older offenders, most elders will acknowledge that the benefits of reciprocal exchanges are maximized when accompanied by boundaries defining the degree of support that is acceptable to give or receive. As Leigey (2007) highlighted in her research conducted with older men who were serving sentences of life without parole, the provision of too much assistance may discourage older inmates from seeking or receiving guidance from trained professionals; furthermore, the provision of too much assistance may foster a sense of dependency on individuals who may not have the time, patience, skills, or desire to provide continued support. This, in return, not only affects the quality of life experienced by younger offenders who volunteer services, but also interferes with the older inmate's ability to achieve personal growth.

Benefits of Religious Activities

Although religious education and programming have always been offered to prisoners (Johnson, Larson, and Pitts, 1997), a variety of more recent factors have influenced the reemergence of religious programming in correctional systems today. These factors include such issues as the growth of the restorative justice movement grounded in biblical teachings, the growth of faith-based prisons, and the constitutional right to practice any religion in a prison setting (O'Connor and Duncan, 2008). Currently, almost every prison in the United States has a chaplain responsible for assisting inmates with the practice and expression of their faith. Numerous studies have found that religious involvement is one of the most common activities for structuring prison life (Kerley, Allison, and Graham, 2006; O'Connor, 2004; O'Connor and Duncan, 2008). This is particularly the case for female prisoners, who, as compared to male prisoners, report higher rates of religious participation (Levitt and Loper, 2009).

The development of social programming to accommodate members of a graying prison population should include consideration of individuals' religious or spiritual needs. Numerous studies have recently proliferated to document a strong positive correlation between older adults' levels of religiosity and positive physical and mental health outcomes (Crowther et al., 2002; Koenig, McCullough, and Larson, 2001). For example, inmates frequently discover that religious beliefs and activities provide them with the following positive outcomes: meaning for incomprehensible life events by increasing self-efficacy (Thomas and Zaitzow, 2006), enhanced life satisfaction (Clear et al., 2000), ways of dealing with excessive idle time (Crawley and Sparks, 2005a), delays in emotional deterioration (Bishop and Merten, 2011), and reduction in fear, depression, and death anxiety (Deaton, Aday, and Wahidin, 2009–2010).

Opportunities for engagement in pursuits such as prayer, reading scriptures, meditation, and participation in faith-based support groups can prove advantageous to older prisoners who are experiencing problems that would otherwise prove to be insurmountable. Involvement in such religious and spiritual activities buffers stress following significant life events such as identity crises, a history of victimization, deteriorating health, loss of loved ones, and reduced social networks (Koenig, George, and Siegler, 1988; Crowther et al., 2002; Turesky and Schultz, 2010). It is in times of crisis that the general principles behind religious or spiritual belief systems translate into actions that individuals can use to seek support while transitioning from a time of crisis to a period of greater stability (Pargament, 1990). Losses, specifically those that are permanent and involve a loss of personal control, can be spiritual turning points during which lifers begin to receive strength from more frequent religious participation (Fiori, Hays, and Meador, 2004).

The value that older adults receive from engaging in religious lifestyles is most effectively understood by viewing the practice of religious activities within the context of the prison environment. In environments where older inmates may be otherwise inclined to ruminate over their personal circumstances, opportunities for immersion in religious activities can be highly welcomed, fulfilling, and inspiring; moreover, immersion in religious activity can help older inmates develop the patience and hope that are necessary for thriving in times of adversity. The prison context is extremely stressful, and older inmates may use religion as a coping mechanism when dealing with a profound range of stressors, including being stripped of their identities, being separated from society, enduring undesirable living conditions, experiencing a lack of autonomy in decisionmaking, suffering from boredom with daily routines, experiencing problems relating to staff and peers, and experiencing insecurities about dying in prison (Branco, 2007; Choi, Ransom, and Wyllie, 2008; Deaton, Aday, and Wahidin, 2009–2010; Fletcher, 2004). In fact, research comparing religiosity among older adults across various contexts suggests that imprisoned elders may actually draw more comfort from participation in religious activity during crises compared to elders outside prison (Fry, 2000).

The Value of Groups

Working with the elderly in groups can serve as a valuable tool in creating a social milieu that is conducive to enhancing the self-esteem of those who participate. Group-based programming is supported by both the activity perspective and Rowe and Kahn's (1997) components of successful aging. Specifically, group-based programming is designed to help participants preserve their cognitive and mental faculties while staving off the potential adverse effects of institutionalization (Haber, 2006; Pitkala et al., 2004). Jiang and Winfree (2006) identified a variety of both informal and formal social support groups that are important to the overall well-being of those in incarcerated settings. Informally, inmates may create Bible clubs, other religious groups, music groups, writing groups, educational groups, recreational groups, prisoner counseling groups, and other self-improvement groups. Formally, prison staff or community volunteers may develop and conduct organized groups in correctional settings for the purpose of enhancing socialization skills and creating a supportive environment (Stojkovic and Lovell, 1997). Group members learn from each other and feel reassured when they hear fellow group members sharing similar fears and concerns (Masters, 1994). According to Jacobs and Spadaro (2003), inmates are often distrustful of prison staff, but they may willingly listen to their peers in a group setting. The use of groups can be ideal in overcoming loneliness, dealing with guilt or grief issues, and, in general, facilitating positive personal changes and self-actualization (Toch, 2006). Toseland (1995, pp. 18–19) has identified numerous benefits of group participation, which

- Provides feelings of belonging and affiliation while helping older adults to overcome social isolation and loneliness.

- Helps to validate and affirm the experiences of older adults.
- Provides older adults the opportunity to share and to learn new information.
- Provides older adults with unique opportunities for interpersonal learning.
- Offers older adults the opportunity to resolve problems with the help and support of fellow group members.

There are three basic categories of older adults for whom groups are particularly beneficial: older adults who are socially isolated, older adults who have interpersonal problems, and older adults who need assistance in identifying and participating in new social roles. Older inmates who are transitioning into prison for the first time as well as those who are coping with the effects of long-term imprisonment can benefit greatly from participating in groups that are well matched to their various psychosocial needs. Groups centered around reminiscing and life review, the provision of support, creating opportunities for recreation, grief counseling, and psychotherapy have been used productively in working with aging inmates in selective correctional settings (Aday, 2006).

Support Groups

In nearly any setting, participation in support groups is considered to be a highly valued activity that elders can turn to when coping with the stressors of advanced age. Membership in support groups presents numerous opportunities for sharing concerns across a wide range of themes. Elders warmly welcome opportunities to become involved in support groups that invite them to explore topics centered around the management of specific emotional and physical issues such as abuse histories, anger problems, or chronic illnesses; moreover, elders welcome the opportunity to explore topics that are stigmatized within the community at large. In fact, support groups are typically regarded as the perfect method for assisting aging inmates in working through problems such as alcoholism, desertion by families, age changes, and major depression. Moreover, support groups provide aging inmates with opportunities to share and work through personal experiences among a closed circle of peers.

In support groups, members are bonded together by the knowledge that they share similar concerns that are often not well understood by untrained prison staff. For example, the Golden Girls Behind Bars support group, which is designated for female inmates aged 55 years and older, meets monthly at the California Prison for Women in Corona to discuss the issues that its members face on a routine basis (Sundaram, 2009). Many in

the group are lifers, convicted of crimes ranging from drug-related offenses to kidnapping for ransom and murder. Others are serving life sentences for nonviolent offenses under the state's three-strikes law. Topics
frequently addressed include health issues, since many of the women suffer from heart disease, osteoporosis, arthritis, diabetes, and asthma and
other lung diseases. A large number of the participants joined the support
group to seek assistance with depression. That said, support groups need
not be limited to the discussion of extremely sensitive or crisis-based issues. Instead, older adult populations may establish and participate in thematic support groups designed for the purpose of discussing topics such as
family visits or legal issues. Aday (2003) identified a variety of beneficial
support-group topics, including personal development (e.g., loneliness and
isolation, fears and desires about the future, maintaining independence,
and changes in energy level), daily life issues (e.g., learning to live in
prison, prison stress and conflict, staff-inmate relations, chronic illness),
family and social relationships, parenting from prison, and family conflicts.

Grief and Death Education Groups

Given the continuously increasing number of long-term inmates in the US
prison system, including many who are serving life sentences, dying in
prison is becoming a more common event (Deaton, Aday, and Wahidin,
2009–2010). To many inmates, dying in prison is one of the most dreaded
fears of incarceration (Aday, 2005–2006; Byock, 2002). In addition to fears
associated with dying in prison, inmates will also experience a number of
losses, including loss of freedom, loss of self and of past life, loss of
health, loss of family relationships, and loss of prison friends and acquain-
tances. It has been noted that each loss is cumulative in nature and each is
accompanied by complex and confusing emotional reactions (Stevenson
and McCutchen, 2006). In any setting where loss is likely to occur, the
severity and enormity of the loss can trigger a grieving process that elicits
feelings of shock, confusion, disorientation, anxiety, anger and rage, and
occasionally even guilt (Worden, 2008).

Glamser and Cabana (2003) articulated that healthy, open discussions
of death alleviate some of the tension, ease the depression, and help individuals understand that death is a normal phase of life. Unfortunately, there
is evidence of minimal discussion about death in institutions (Deaton,
Aday, and Wahidin, 2009–2010; Junior, 2003) and especially in formalized
group settings. That said, the Ohio Department of Rehabilitation and Correction does offer a special grief group program called Life Beyond Loss
(Taft and Wilkinson, 1999). This particular program familiarizes older offenders with the issues of death, dying, and significant loss. Using the work

of Kubler-Ross (1969) and other resource material, this program explores the grieving process as inmates deal with the loss of family members and friends, the loss of physical health, and the reality of their own eventual death. Grief groups are also commonly employed at various prisons that offer hospice services, including the Louisiana State Prison at Angola, where approximately 90 percent of inmates are expected to die while incarcerated (Cain and Fontenot, 2001).

Aday and Shahan (1995) described a structured death education program for institutionalized elders that would be most appropriate in a prison setting. The program included a series of group sessions involving an open discussion of different topics related to issues of death and dying. Visual aids, exercises, poetry, and other materials were utilized throughout the sessions. Group sessions focused on multiple topics: (1) fears related to coming into or residing in an institutional setting (participants focused on lack of adequate health-care services and fears of institutionalization); (2) previous experiences with death (participants discussed experiences both outside and inside the institution); (3) fantasizing about one's own funeral (participants stressed different values and opinions about attending funerals); (4) preparation for one's own death (participants made prearrangements for death that addressed issues regarding burial plots, wills, funeral plans, body disposal, and epitaphs); (5) reading and writing obituaries (participants raised specific issues about how to express life achievements and quality of life); (6) euthanasia, living wills, and suicide (participants discussed their values and opinions regarding whether life in an institutional setting is worth living); and (7) fears about loved ones, finality, and closure (participants expressed fears regarding how others will respond to their deaths).

As the number of inmates who will die in prison increases, programs such as the one just described will be needed to assist inmates with numerous end-of-life issues. When working with those older offenders who have experienced the loss of loved ones, care must be taken to ensure that the inmates receive sufficient time and space to bring closure to their relationships. As compared with individuals grieving outside prison, inmates generally feel more restricted when expressing their emotions and working through the grieving process (Harner, Hertz, and Evangelista, 2010). Thus, therapeutic programming provides an important social environment wherein inmates can feel safe and receive encouragement as they engage in self-expression. Moreover, therapeutic programming is now being directed toward assisting inmates who are striving to overcome the deaths of supportive individuals (other individuals besides spouses, partners, and family members) outside prison; such programming helps inmates express their farewells to the dying or deceased. Finally, care should always be taken to permit offenders to speak openly, honestly, and candidly about their past interactions with the deceased individual.

Reminiscence Groups

Reminiscence groups have also proven to be highly popular and effective in working with aging prisoners (Aday, 2003, 2006). Both outside and inside prison, reminiscence has been shown to serve a number of invaluable functions. Several popularly reported advantages associated with elder involvement in reminiscence include coming to terms with prior unfortunate life circumstances, preserving memories of loved ones with whom they may no longer have contact, reaffirming their identities, developing ego integrity while placing their lives within a context of meaningful activities, and preparing for death as one approaches the final phases of life (Webster and Gould, 2007; Webster, Bohlmeijer, and Westerhof, 2010). Reminiscence groups are commonly used to help individuals cope with goals that have yet to be fully realized; furthermore, reminiscence groups are commonly used to help individuals find value in positive events while coming to terms with events that are less than favorable (Lo Gerfo, 1980–1981; Haber, 2006).

As with other activity groups, reminiscence groups are structured in a manner that will most likely maximize participants' opportunities for self-disclosure. Suitable topics may be inspired by cherished memories from childhood experiences to which nearly every group member would be able to relate. Themes such as favorite holidays, playmates, toys, pets, and school experiences have all been identified as ideal foundations upon which group work of this nature can be built. Favorite holidays, for example, can be a helpful topic when working with older adults, because this theme can stimulate discussions of Christmas, Hanukkah, Kwanzaa, Ramadan, and associated family rituals, gift exchanges, meals, and so on. Even elders who have mild to moderate cognitive impairments can benefit immeasurably from engagement in activities of this nature when warmly encouraged to reminisce without being pressured to recall specific aspects of their lives that may have long since left their memories. Including props such as music, pictures, or other illustrative materials can also foster socialization and stimulate areas of consciousness that are unlikely to be ordinarily available within the context of everyday living in the institutional environment (Toseland, 1995).

A Best-Practice Illustration

Florida, Ohio, Pennsylvania, Alabama, Georgia, Virginia, and Louisiana are a handful of states that have offered more ambitious programming primarily for older male offenders. However, one of the most comprehensive best-practice models ideally suited to the person-environment perspective of aging is the structured senior living program called True Grit at the Northern Nevada Correctional Center (Harrison, 2006). This program was initially established for older men in 2004 as a response to the unique needs of an increasing number of vulnerable elderly inmates. Along with Nevada's Division of Aging Services, the senior living program was designed to enhance physical health (by means of various recreational and physical therapy activities), mental health (by using group and individual therapy along with self-help modalities), and spiritual health (by coordinating with the prison chaplain and volunteers). In the True Grit program, 160 male participants aged 55 and older are housed together in a separate unit and are assigned activities and modalities based on individual levels of competence. Using a case-management approach, each inmate is assigned daily tasks that fall within an optimum range bound between their individual capabilities and the demands of each activity. Given the large number of participants who are considered terminal lifers, this program has excelled in assisting men in preparing themselves physically, mentally, spiritually, and emotionally for end-of-life realities.

One of the most critical components responsible for the success of the True Grit program is the highly structured participation requirements (Harrison and Benedetti, 2009). Within the context of a social model that prioritizes activity and accountability, each True Grit participant must sign a contract when entering the program; by signing the contract, participants agree to complete all of their assigned daily tasks, such as maintaining personal hygiene, keeping their personal living areas clean, and participating in a range of recreational tasks that emphasize the use of a variety of physical and cognitive skills. Table 4.2 describes a cross-section of various True Grit activities that use participation in music, art, crafts, and sports (to name a few modalities) to stimulate a variety of physical and mental competencies. The goal of the True Grit program is to offer a minimum of ten activities on a weekly basis. Regardless of their physical abilities, inmates are encouraged to compete to the fullest extent possible, whether participation includes playing softball or basketball in a wheelchair, making latch-hook rugs to keep arthritic fingers nimble, working on puzzles, attending education classes, participating in music therapy, or walking 10,000 steps daily (Harrison, 2006).

The True Grit program serves as a model program and helps to lead the way as correctional systems work to accommodate the special needs of aging inmates. Geriatrically informed activities and programs that are designed to meet the needs of elderly inmates provide members of this vulnerable population with a reason to rise each day. Rather than sit stagnant on benches or on beds, inmates who have access to specialized programming can find a greater purpose in life behind bars. The True Grit program

Table 4.2 True Grit: Structured Senior Living Program

Therapeutic Activities

Life-skills training: This training helps participants increase interpersonal and social skills that are important for successful daily living, whether the participating elderly inmates remain in prison or reintegrate into society. Such activities and skills include meal planning on a budget, nutrition, microwave cooking, decisionmaking, time management, goal setting, victimization prevention (elder abuse, identify theft, and telephone and Internet scams), financial planning, and acquiring or reacquiring necessary identification documents.

Music appreciation: A comprehensive collection of cassette tapes and compact discs are provided so that participants can enjoy jazz, big band, rock and roll, country and western, contemporary, and classical music. Several music groups provide a variety of activities and opportunities for social engagement. A twenty-man ensemble performs weekly, and doo-wop, rock, country, and spiritual music groups frequently practice and entertain fellow inmates.

Art appreciation: Led by a talented retired art teacher from a nearby college, art appreciation emphasizes drawing with pencils, charcoal, and pastels, and painting with acrylics and oils. Participants use art as a creative medium to improve mobility and foster self-expression, regardless of their infirmities.

Beading: Beading enhances cognitive function and improves manual dexterity. Participants learn how to create beaded jewelry, wrist- and headbands, decorative beaded art objects, and other unique items.

Puzzles and games: Active participation in puzzles and games provides cognitive therapy, while enhancing problem-solving and coping skills. Many of these activities are designed to stimulate areas of the brain damaged by dementia and Alzheimer's disease, while also offering opportunities for socialization and fun.

Crafts: As a means of enhancing and maintaining physical dexterity for those with arthritis, this program provides participants with materials for latch-hooking rugs, crocheting afghans, and creating needlepoint art. Several dozen men work regularly on individual projects in this voluntary diversion-therapy activity.

Physical fitness: The physical fitness program includes an assortment of weekly aerobic exercise opportunities, games, and activities such as weight training, stretching, volleyball, tennis, wheelchair softball, horseshoes, Ping-Pong, basketball, billiards, and walking.

Pet therapy: With the assistance of the local-area Delta Society, two or three therapy dogs make monthly visits to the prison, providing True Grit participants (many of whom are serving life sentences) with companionship and the opportunity to bond with animals.

Writing groups: Assists participants who will live their remaining years in prison by providing them with the opportunity (through reflective writing in memoirs and chapters) to prepare for end-of-life related issues (mental, spiritual, and emotional), and the physical aspects of death and dying.

Source: Harrison, 2006.

includes a continuum of activities designed to meet the bio-psycho-social needs of a heterogeneous population; thus, older inmates have the opportunity to engage in the kind of age- and health-specific activities that might be found at a local senior center (Harrison, 2006). While this program has been replicated recently at the Nevada Prison for Women, other programs for elderly women, such as Aunt Jane's Storybook (wherein inmates write an age-appropriate book and personal message to a young relative) and Older Resourceful Women (wherein inmates make quilts and other knitted and embroidered items for needy families), have long histories of success in the Ohio Prison for Women (Aday, 2006).

Future Challenges

With correctional personnel wielding considerable power over access to coveted resources and a limited number of open program slots, evidence of ageism has repeatedly been observed and reported throughout mainstream prison facilities (Aday, 2003). Very frequently, administration and staff members systematically exclude persons of advanced age from participation in social programming and activities, thus subjecting them to passivity and dependency well before they may be physiologically or psychologically prepared to withdraw and isolate themselves from productive activity (Wahidin, 2004). In many cases, this may occur due to the fact that personnel assigned to a prison unit have a very limited interest in older adults, insufficient training in responding to the programmatic needs of this population, and minimal (if any) incentives for investing in older inmates' social care. In many institutions it has become an almost routine practice for correctional personnel to overlook the programming needs of elders who may earnestly desire involvement in constructive, productive pursuits, while favoring younger inmates who will be engaged in different developmental tasks following their reintegration into society. For example, younger favored inmates are focused on preparing for such tasks as working and childbearing upon release from prison. In an era where resources for specialized programming are extremely limited, the True Grit program offers a potential solution by providing gerontologically informed programmatic elements that may be implemented at a limited cost depending on the availability of interested prisons and volunteers.

As repeatedly illustrated, older inmates are significantly less likely than members of other age groups to express an interest in formal structured activities (Santos, 2003; Zamble, 1992), and many older people will need more encouragement to become involved in recreational and social activities (Aday, 2006). Correctional officials who are preparing for the growth of this population will discover that aging prisoners appear to be highly satisfied when occupying their time in more solitary pursuits. Of course, many older inmates suffer from infirmities or disabilities that influence their opportunities for involvement in the prison community (Aday, 2003). Because such conditions can restrict social interactions and limit work or recreational opportunities, inmates who suffer from infirmities or disabilities may pass the time by engaging in more passive activities. It is not uncommon to find geriatric inmates spending their leisure time reading, writing, watching television, or listening to the radio; likewise, it is not uncommon to find geriatric inmates conversing informally with a select group of like-minded peers as they swap stories and talk about mutually shared interests (Aday and Krabill, 2011; Aday, 1994b). Even attempts to entice or encourage them to expand their horizons by joining existing groups may be met with a sense of reservation. Such reservation may be particularly true for older men or women who are serving long-term sentences and have been incarcerated for most of their adult years. Older lifers are especially likely to remove themselves from formal opportunities, as they may have already made extensive use of the available resources earlier in their sentence (Leigey, 2007).

Geriatrically informed programming that is designed to meet the unique needs of older inmates can provide great benefits to inmates and their families as well as correctional health-care providers. This is especially true if older inmates adopt and display healthy aging practices. Moreover, engaging in age-specific activities within the institution can be beneficial to the mental health of older inmates. Participating in reminiscence therapy and other support activities has proven successful in helping inmates to cope with incarceration (Aday and Krabill, 2011). Social interaction and assistance among fellow elderly inmates can reduce feelings of loneliness and the negative effects of institutionalization (Harrison and Benedetti, 2009). As the number of elderly inmates continues to grow, it will not only become justifiable but also increasingly necessary to implement gerontologically specialized programs. Furthermore, the provision of such specialized programming should be considered within the age-segregation debate, as older inmates generally prefer to reside in age-segregated environments, which are likely to be quieter and more conducive to developing social relationships (Aday, 2003; Aday and Krabill, 2011).

If inmates are to age successfully in the prison environment, a case-management approach should be utilized in order to coordinate the care of inmates. Inmates should be comprehensively assessed to initially determine their functional and cognitive limitations and strengths, personal interests, and existing supports. Follow-up assessments should be used to monitor the ongoing fit between older inmates and the demands of their environment. Furthermore, services and prison environments should be altered as inmates' health care and social needs change. Particular attention should be paid to older inmates' mental health needs and issues, including dementia, victimization, and grief reactions to loss, as these mental health needs contribute to the older offender's overall level of competency and resulting need for a more supportive environment. Careful monitoring can also make it more feasible for older inmates to be placed in the least-restrictive prison environment, thus preventing many of the negative outcomes associated with institutionalization and victimization therein. A therapeutic approach that honors personal dignity and gears programming toward meeting individualized needs can offer an elderly prisoner improved physical and mental health as well as an improved sense of purpose and direction.

5

Women and Issues of Care

Jennifer M. Jolley, John J. Kerbs, and John F. Linder

Back in the 1970s, the United States often overlooked the needs of small and largely invisible (from a numerical standpoint) groups of prisoners. At that time, older inmates in general were identified by Ham (1976) as one such group that was so small in number and proportion within US prisons that he named them the "forgotten minority." The vast majority of this largely invisible group (about 95 percent) comprised older males, but older women in prison did (and still do) constitute about 5 percent of all older inmates in the United States (Guerino, Harrison, and Sabol, 2012). Thus, while older inmates of all ages are generally no longer an overlooked minority in prisons, due to their rapid growth in number and proportion as discussed in Chapter 1, one could argue that older women have become the new "forgotten minority" within federal and state correctional facilities.

Demographically speaking, older women (aged 50 and older) in US prisons represented around 5.5 percent of all older inmates as of 2010 (Guerino, Harrison, and Sabol, 2012). As compared to younger inmates in general and older male inmates in particular, older women in prison appear to have distinct health-care needs (Aday and Krabill, 2011). Still, despite specific calls for age- and gender-specific health-care services and programming (Aday, 2003; Aday and Krabill, 2011), there is no clear delineation regarding what such services and programs should actually look like, because the literature on older women's needs is exceedingly thin and methodologically compromised. Thus, in an effort to clarify such issues, this chapter uses a quality-of-care model for exploring their health-care needs and efforts to identify whether their needs are being met. To be sure, these issues are of great importance to taxpayers, given the potential costs associated with quality care in correctional facilities; additionally, these issues have legal implications that impinge on the quality of life that older women experience in prison and in society after their release.

This chapter begins with a review of the main findings from studies that have examined older women in relation to their physical and mental health needs. The main needs of older women are clearly identified and the gender differences between older men and older women are briefly highlighted. This review also documents the strengths and limitations of this research; by critiquing the methodological designs of these key studies, the chapter tries to pinpoint needed methodological improvements for future research so that results can more competently inform policies, programming, and procedures that affect older women in US prisons. Next, the chapter reviews a heuristic model for tracking the quality of care that women receive in correctional settings in order to gain a more advanced understanding of what women need and how their needs might be best addressed. While most studies to date are largely descriptive of health problems, this model (if applied to correctional health-care services for older women) could advance our understanding of how women are processed through correctional health-care systems and how short- and long-term outcomes are affected by such processing. The chapter concludes by examining the policy implications of such research, with an emphasis on the need to critically examine the relationship between morbidity and mortality rates for older women, identify the predictors of morbidity and mortality rates for older women in prison, and extend research from prison-based studies to reentry studies for older women who leave correctional facilities.

Background on the Physical and Mental Health of Older Women in Prison

To date, there are primarily four main sources of data on older women in prison that are consistently used for analyses aimed at documenting their physical and mental health problems and some of their experiences in relation to accessing care. The first data source, at the national level, originated from the Bureau of Justice Statistics, which released the 2004 Survey of Inmates in State and Federal Correctional Facilities. The data from this survey are based on a probability sample that can be generalized to the larger population of federal and state inmates in the United States (see, e.g., Leigey and Hodge, 2012; Maruschak, 2008). Second, at the state level, the Texas Department of Criminal Justice has released data on the total census of prisoners who were incarcerated for any duration between 2006 and 2007 (see, e.g., Harzke et al., 2010). Third, the California Department of Corrections and Rehabilitation has also released data, from a random sample of male and female inmates aged 55 and older and from a sample of inmates of all ages who came from medical units (see, e.g., Hill et al., 2006). Finally, although based on a convenience sample, Aday and Krabill (2011) examined one of the largest samples of older inmates, comprising 327 older women from prisons in five southern states. These four sources of data have provided some of the best information to date on older inmates' physical and mental health, but each data source also has limitations relative to our understanding of gender-based differences in the physical and mental health of older women in federal and state prisons.

Beginning with data from national surveys, the Bureau of Justice Statistics (part of the US Department of Justice) has yet to publish analyses on the intersection of age and gender, or age and race/ethnicity, as applied to the physical and mental health problems reported by older federal and state prisoners (see, e.g., Maruschak, 2008). What is known for gender-based and age-based comparisons for federal and state prisoners is reproduced from research by Maruschak (2008) in Table 5.1. Using national data from the 2004 Survey of Inmates in State and Federal Correctional Facilities, Maruschak found that women in federal and state prisons were generally more likely than men to report one or more of fourteen medical problems (i.e., arthritis, asthma, cancer, diabetes, heart problems, hypertension, kidney problems, liver problems, paralysis, stroke, hepatitis, HIV, sexually transmitted diseases, and tuberculosis); moreover, older federal and state prisoners (aged 45 and older) generally reported more health problems than younger inmates (aged 44 and younger). Not surprisingly, Maruschak's research also found that women in federal and state facilities were more likely than men to report impairments. Nonetheless, Maruschak's 2008 study did not provide us with an understanding of the self-reported health or mental health problems for women across various age groups, for racial/ethnic minorities across various age groups, or for women from differing racial/ethnic backgrounds across different age groups.

Based on Maruschak's (2008) analysis, the top five medical problems reported by women (regardless of age) in state prisons were arthritis (24.5 percent reported this condition), asthma (19.2 percent), hypertension (16.8 percent), hepatitis (9.5 percent), and heart problems (9.0 percent). For women in federal prisons, the top five medical problems were similar: arthritis (23.8 percent), hypertension (20.7 percent), asthma (13.7 percent), heart problems (10.0 percent), and (in a tie for fifth place) diabetes (6.9 percent) and kidney problems (6.9 percent). Using the same database as Maruschak (2008), Leigey and Hodge (2012) employed bivariate analyses to look for the potential presence of gender differences among older men

Table 5.1 Medical Problems Reported by Prison Inmates, by Gender and Age, 2004 (percentages)

Medical Problem	All Inmates	Gender		Age			
		Male	Female	24 and Younger	25–34	35–44	45 and Older
State inmates							
Arthritis	15.3	14.6	24.5	5.4	8.6	17.4	32.6
Asthma	9.1	8.4	19.2	10.1	9.1	8.3	9.6
Cancer	0.9	0.8	2.4	0.1	0.3	0.6	2.8
Diabetes	4.0	3.9	5.5	0.4	1.5	4.1	11.3
Heart problems	6.1	5.9	9.0	2.7	4.1	5.7	13.3
Hypertension	13.8	13.6	16.8	3.4	8.0	15.4	30.6
Kidney problems	3.2	2.9	6.9	1.5	2.2	3.6	5.7
Liver problems	1.1	1.1	1.3	0.1	0.4	1.4	2.9
Paralysis	1.4	1.4	1.4	0.5	1.0	1.8	2.4
Stroke	2.6	2.5	3.7	1.3	1.7	3.1	4.6
Hepatitis	5.3	5.0	9.5	0.9	2.4	6.8	11.7
HIV	1.6	1.6	1.9	0.3	0.8	2.5	2.6
Sexually transmitted disease (other than HIV)	0.8	0.7	2.0	0.6	0.7	1.1	0.7
Tuberculosis	9.4	9.6	6.1	4.0	6.5	11.5	15.8
Federal inmates							
Arthritis	12.4	11.5	23.8	3.8	5.7	10.8	28.3
Asthma	7.2	6.7	13.7	10.5	5.5	7.9	7.8
Cancer	0.6	0.6	1.0	0.0	0.1	0.4	2.0
Diabetes	5.1	5.0	6.9	0.7	2.0	4.2	12.9
Heart problems	6.0	5.7	10.0	2.2	3.9	4.4	12.8
Hypertension	13.2	12.6	20.7	2.1	7.5	11.5	28.4
Kidney problems	3.1	2.8	6.9	1.8	2.1	2.7	5.5
Liver problems	1.1	1.1	1.1	0.0	0.3	1.2	2.9
Paralysis	1.6	1.6	1.5	0.2	1.6	1.3	2.6
Stroke	1.7	1.6	2.9	0.1	1.1	1.5	3.7
Hepatitis	4.2	4.2	4.5	0.0	1.9	5.6	7.9
HIV	1.0	1.0	1.4	0.7	0.4	1.9	1.1
Sexually transmitted disease (other than HIV)	0.4	0.4	0.4	0.5	0.5	0.5	0.2
Tuberculosis	7.1	7.2	6.2	2.7	5.7	8.0	10.1

Source: Maruschak, 2008.

($n = 997$) and women ($n = 142$) aged 50 and older who had served at least one year in prison prior to participating in the 2004 Survey of Inmates in State and Federal Correctional Facilities. As compared to older men in state and federal prisons, older women in prison reported a larger number of physical health conditions and mental health disorders since their admission to prison, in the previous year in prison, and over their lifetimes. The top five medical problems reported by women (aged 50 and older) in federal and state prisons were arthritis (98.8 percent reported this condition), diabetes (91.3 percent), high blood pressure (90.9 percent), heart disease (83.8 percent), and asthma (69.0 percent). While the rates reported by Leigey and Hodge (2012) are much higher than the rates reported by Maruschak (2008), the higher rates may be related to the ways in which the former authors censored the data (i.e., they only included respondents who had served a year or more in prison, meaning that all respondents had ample opportunity to be assessed by correctional health-care systems).

Interestingly, there is a lot of overlap between the most commonly reported conditions that women noted in Maruschak's (2008) study, in the study by Leigey and Hodge (2012), in other state-level studies from Texas (see, e.g., Harzke et al., 2010) and California (see, e.g., Hill et al., 2006), and in many of the other studies listed in Table 5.2. To avoid a redundant review of the most prevalent chronic-care conditions that older women report in prison (i.e., arthritis, diabetes, hypertension, vascular disease, and chronic obstructive pulmonary disease and asthma), it is suggested that readers review the larger constellation of results from past studies regarding the bio-psycho-social issues facing women of all ages in prison, including older women, as documented by Margaret Leigey in Chapter 3. Leigey generally finds that older women in prison, as compared to their incarcerated male counterparts, are more likely to

- Perceive their health as relatively worse.
- Report higher rates of arthritis and asthma in their lifetimes.
- Report a higher average number of chronic health conditions.
- Report more mental health problems in the previous year and in their lifetimes.
- Report diagnoses for depression, bipolar disorders, posttraumatic stress disorder, and anxiety disorder.
- Report worry and depression as their most persistent health problem.
- Report prior suicide attempts.
- Report receiving fewer visits, pieces of mail, and phone calls.

That said, the remainder of this section is devoted to a broader discussion of the implications of these and other findings for the provision of specialty

Table 5.2 Comparison of Studies That Examine Physical and Mental Health Problems of Older Women in Prison

Study	Sample	Number of Facilities	Number of Female Prisoners	Physical and Self-Report and Mental Health Measures	Official Data	Comparison Groups
1. Kratcoski and Babb (1990)	Convenience sample	8 Federal 7 State	86 women 356 men	Physical and mental health	Self-report only	Males ages 50 to 84
2. Fogel (1993)	Not specified	Not specified	55 women (ages 17 to 59)	Physical and mental health	Self-report only	None
3. Jordan et al. (1996)	Census and random sample	Not specified	805 women (ages 18 to 64)	Mental health only	Clinical assessments	No males; Women in community
4. Baillargeon et al. (2000)	Population-based study	Not specified	170,215 men and women (ages 18 to 50+)	Physical and mental health	Official data via clinical assessments	Males ages 50 and older
5. Conklin, Lincoln, and Tuthill (2000)	Convenience sample	1 state	116 women 1,082 men	Physical and mental health	Self-report only	Males (ages not specified)
6. Regan, Alderson, and Regan (2002)	Population-based study	All state facilities in Tennessee	82 women 562 men (ages 55+)	Mental health only	Official records only	Males ages 55 and older
7. Caverley (2006)	Population-based study	1 prison in Utah	42 women 318 men	Mental health only	Official records only	Males ages 50 to 96
8. Hill et al. (2006)	Stratified random sample	11 prisons in California	~ 642 inmates (~ 9% female)	Physical and mental health	Official record and survey data from correctional officers	Males ages 55 and older
9. James and Glaze (2006)	Stratified random sample	274 state 39 federal	15,915 men and women	Mental health only	Self-report only	No gender comparisons by age groups

(continues)

Table 5.2 continued

Study	Sample	Number of Facilities	Number of Female Prisoners	Physical and Self-Report and Mental Health Measures	Official Data	Comparison Groups
10. Williams et al. (2006)	Convenience sample	Not specified	120 women	Activities of daily living Physical health problems	Self-report only	No males
11. Maruschak (2008)	National probability sample	287 state 39 federal	14,499 inmates (all ages)	Physical and mental health	Self-report only	Gender comparisons
12. Baillargeon et al. (2009)	Cohort population	All 116 state facilities in Texas	79,211 inmates (all ages)	Mental health only	Official records only	Males ages 16 to 50+
13. Binswanger, Krueger, and Steiner (2009)	Probability sample	287 state 40 federal	14,373 inmates (ages 18 to 65)	Physical health only	Self-report only	Males ages 18 to 65
14. Harzke et al. (2010)	Population-based study	All state facilities in Texas	23,530 women 210,501 men (ages 18 to 64)	Physical health only	Official records only	Males ages 55 to 64
15. Haugebrook et al. (2010)	Random sample	Not specified (New Jersey)	9 women 105 men (ages 55+)	Physical and mental health	Official records only	None
16. Aday and Krabill (2011)	Convenience sample	7 prisons total in Arkansas, Minnesota, Tennessee, and Georgia	327 women (ages 50 to 77)	Physical and mental health	Self-report only	None
17. Leigey and Hodge (2012)	National probability sample	Not available	142 women 997 men	Physical and mental health	Self-report only	Males ages 50 and older

care and for the advancement of needed methodological improvements in research that examines the health and mental health needs and care of aging women in prison.

In terms of implications for the provision of specialty care, the most prevalent conditions just noted suggest that there is a need for enhanced access to both chronic-care clinics and specialized medical personnel. The management of these conditions can be complex. Dependent on the severity of arthritis (for example), rheumatologists may be required for assessments, diagnoses, and treatment. Diabetics may require intermittent or consistent access to skilled medical doctors who specialize in endocrinology. Prisoners with cardiovascular disease may require access to cardiologists. Finally, asthmatics may require access to pulmonologists for assessments and the coordination of their care.

In terms of needed methodological improvements for studies that examine the medical and treatment needs of older women in prison, most of the prior studies to date have methodological flaws that limit our ability to identify who needs what type of care and what type of access to specialized medical personnel. In short, we need better studies to statistically document the prevalence and severity of various conditions among older inmates in general and among incarcerated older women in particular. That said, this base of research often suffers from methodological limitations (see Table 5.2 for key studies that examine older women in prison) that block our ability to competently inform the development of programs and services.

For example, the first methodological point of concern is the overreliance on convenience samples, purposive samples, and other such "nonprobability" samples. Studies that use nonprobability sampling designs rely on samples that are not fully representative of the sampled population, which means that the results are not generalizable due to the potential presence of sampling biases (a threat to a given study's external validity) (Frankfort-Nachmias and Nachmias, 2000). While studies with nonprobability sampling methodologies are often cited and even reviewed throughout this book (see, e.g., Kratcoski and Babb, 1990; Fogel, 1993; Conklin, Lincoln, and Tuthill, 2000; Williams et al., 2006; Aday and Krabill, 2011), the inability to generalize such results undermines the utility of such studies for the development of policies, procedures, and programs.

Small samples represent yet another methodological point of concern. The primary problem with small samples is related to sampling error: as sample size decreases, sampling error increases (Frankfort-Nachmias and Nachmias, 2000). When sample sizes decrease and sampling error subsequently increases, estimated prevalence rates can become inaccurate and vary widely. Moreover, small samples can limit a study's statistical power:

as sample size decreases, the statistical power of any given analysis decreases and the risk of "Type II error" (false negative) increases in studies that engage in hypothesis testing with the intent of identifying (among other things) the potential presence of between-group differences. Regrettably, many studies noted in Table 5.2 and elsewhere in this book only examined data from samples with few older women (often fewer than 150 older women, and some studies had samples with fewer than 50 older women) (see, e.g., Kratcoski and Babb, 1990; Fogel, 1993; Conklin, Lincoln, and Tuthill, 2000; Regan, Alderson, and Regan, 2002; Caverley, 2006; Hill et al., 2006; Williams et al., 2006; Haugebrook et al., 2010; Leigey and Hodge, 2012). For example, the often-cited study by Kratcoski and Babb (1990) regarding the physical and mental health of older prisoners only examined data from a convenience sample of 86 women.

The use of multiple data sources, including self-report data from prisoners and official records from prison systems, can be of help when it comes to expanding our understanding of the physical and mental health needs of older women in prison. While we have a few studies that use either self-report data or official records, we have a dearth of research that includes both data sources (see Table 5.2). Even though self-report data can provide insights into the prisoners' perspectives about their own health, mental health, and experiences with correctional health-care systems, official records based on (among other things) clinical assessments can provide evidence of completed assessments, confirmed diagnoses, implemented treatment strategies, and the frequency, duration, and quality of follow-up care (to mention but a few things). Generally speaking, it helps to have both self-report and official data because each provides a different perspective on treatment needs, service provision, and health outcomes; moreover, using both forms of data can enhance the application of findings for potential reforms of the health-care system (Donabedian, 1980, 1988, 2005).

Another methodological limitation in the research stems from studies that examine gender-based differences without regard for age. If we are to really understand how and why older women are different from older men in prison, we need studies that provide age-based comparison among younger and older men and women so that we can better understand both within- and between-group differences. Only a few studies do this (Kratcoski and Babb, 1990; Baillargeon et al., 2000; Regan, Alderson, and Regan, 2002; Caverley, 2006; Hill et al., 2006; Harzke et al., 2010; Leigey and Hodge, 2012), and even fewer employ analyses that control for one or more important covariates such as age, gender, race, education, employment status at time of arrest, birthplace, marital status, and alcohol and drug consumption (Baillargeon et al., 2000, 2009; Binswanger, Krueger, and Steiner, 2009; Harzke et al., 2010; James and Glaze, 2006). Such additional covariates should be included in future studies given their potential effects on the relative risk of reporting, or being diagnosed with, physical and mental health problems.

The final methodological limitation is related to the overreliance on cross-sectional data. While cross-sectional analyses provide us with a good snapshot of information at a given time, they lack the capacity to track the developmental trajectories of chronic conditions and the developmental course of potential treatment (i.e., assessment, diagnosis, intervention/ treatment, and follow-up), including the role of treatment in short- and long-term outcomes for physical and mental health problems. Only one of the studies in Table 5.2 included longitudinal data (Fogel, 1993), but this study only examined 55 women (aged 17 to 59) from a convenience sample of prisoners, which impeded the generalizability of results.

In sum, most studies that examine the physical and mental health of older women in prison are methodologically limited to the point of undermining the capacity of their findings to inform policies, procedures, and programs at the state and federal levels. Future studies, whenever possible, should use large probability samples of older male and female prisoners (aged 50 and older) with oversampling (as needed) for older women; this will increase the statistical power of all analyses and decrease the risk of a Type II error while allowing for both within- and between-group comparisons that rest on more than just a handful of older women. Such an approach to sampling would help advance a generation of findings that are both generalizable and (thus) useful for policy forums at the state and federal levels. There is also a serious need for the collection of longitudinal data to understand the developmental trajectories of care as evidenced by (over time) the types of care provided (preventive, acute, chronic, and palliative/hospice care), the functions of care as provided over time (assessment, diagnosis, treatment, and follow-up), the course of technical treatment, and the short- and long-term outcomes of care (e.g., symptom relief, changes in the levels of functioning, and changes in health status relative to diagnoses). Finally, self-report survey data from inmates should be collected along with official data from clinical records to allow for the validation of self-reported conditions with official records, while providing a complete picture of older women's experiences within correctional health-care systems.

A Heuristic Model for Tracking Quality of Care for Women in Prison: Future Directions

Although quality of care as a concept is not something that has been extensively examined in the correctional context, it has been examined on many levels in society. Indeed, there are many models that were developed to measure the quality of medical care and related components; that said, in this section, we adapt one such model as originally developed by Donabedian (1980, 1988, 2005) and refined by others (see, e.g., Campbell, Roland, and Buetow, 2000; Campbell et al., 1998). Our goal in this section is to initially describe the basic components as conceptualized for society outside prison and then adapt the components into a framework that can be used to study the quality of medical care in correctional environments. As the reader will see, this model will be both clinically relevant and practically useful for the tracking of services and the related outcomes of medical care in prisons for older inmates in general and older women in particular.

For studies of society outside the prison context, this framework has three main components (structure, process, and outcomes) as conceptualized by Donabedian (1980, 1988, 2005) and as later refined by Campbell, Roland, and Buetow (2000). These three components conjoin to create a complex and multidimensional pathway that people take to access healthcare services (Campbell and Roland, 1996; Rogers, Hassell, and Nicholaas, 1999). Hence, in society outside prison, the delivery of health care and related outcomes can be viewed as a progressive set of steps that begins with the very structures (organizational and otherwise) that define systems of care. S*tructural aspects of care* include the physical characteristics of health-care facilities (buildings and equipment) and the characteristics of staff (personnel) who provide care therein. Taken together, these structural aspects constitute the building blocks of care that either increase or decrease the chances of receiving services and quality care (Donabedian, 1980, 1988, 2005; Campbell, Roland, and Buetow, 2000).

Of course, buildings, equipment, and personnel have implications for the *processes of care,* which by definition "involve interactions between users and the health care structure . . . what is done to or with users" (Campbell, Roland, and Buetow, 2000, p. 1613). The scholarly literature to date suggests that "processes" can be broken down into two components: (1) technical interventions, whereby clinical medicine and techniques are applied to clients, patients, and users; and (2) interpersonal interactions between clients and health-care personnel, which are defined by the psychosocial skills and interpersonal skills that personnel employ with their patients (Donabedian, 1980; Campbell, Roland, and Buetow, 2000). Technical interventions should be efficient and effective at producing desired health outcomes, while interpersonal interactions should be based on sound communication skills, a capacity to build trusting relationships between personnel and patients (which is not easy in prisons), the development of understanding and empathy with patients, and the use of humanism, sensitivity, and responsiveness to patients (Blumenthal, 1996; Campbell, Roland, and Buetow, 2000; Carmel and Glick, 1996).

Finally, *outcomes* are the consequence of structures and processes that combine to form a resulting change, with regard to either the functional status of the patient or the relief of symptoms (or both); such outcomes are often defined by patients' self-reported satisfaction with outcomes and documented changes in functional status via self-report or clinical evaluations. For care outside the prison setting, Campbell, Roland, and Buetow (2000) use these concepts to define their systems-based model for accessing care, as shown in Figure 5.1. This model of care includes a series of reciprocal feedback loops wherein structure can affect process, which in turn (not surprisingly) affects outcomes, but outcomes also directly and indirectly affect process and structure.

While this model makes intuitive sense for the care of citizens outside prison, one must ask if it makes sense for older women within prison. We believe that it does, albeit with significant modifications as seen in Figure 5.2, which represents a highly altered version of Donabedian's (1980, 1988, 2005) work. These modifications reflect the reality of correctional health care for prisoners, including older women with chronic-care needs. As with the original model shown in Figure 5.1, Figure 5.2 also examines the three main issues of structure, process, and outcome. That said, there is much more detail in Figure 5.2 that is specific to the daily operations of correctional health-care systems. This model depicts health-related outcomes as a function of variables that include, but are not limited to, the

Figure 5.1 System-Based Model for Assessing Medical Care

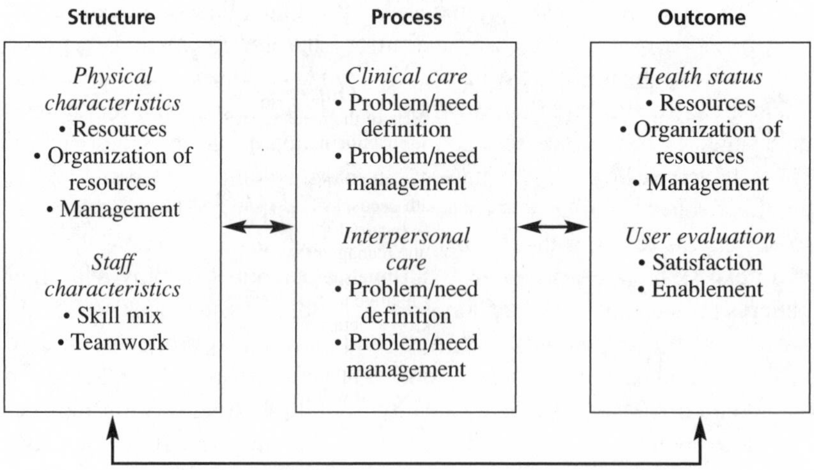

Structure	Process	Outcome
Physical characteristics • Resources • Organization of resources • Management *Staff characteristics* • Skill mix • Teamwork	*Clinical care* • Problem/need definition • Problem/need management *Interpersonal care* • Problem/need definition • Problem/need management	*Health status* • Resources • Organization of resources • Management *User evaluation* • Satisfaction • Enablement

Source: Campbell, Roland, and Buetow, 2000.

Figure 5.2 Adaptation of Donabedian's "Structure, Process, Outcome" Quality-of-Care Model for Older Female Inmates

Regional Location
Northeast, West, Midwest, South

↓

Community Location
With variation in the community's level of urbanization and the distribution of community-based providers, equipment, and clinical-care settings.

↓

Structure

• Levels of privatization and specialty-care centralization
• Inmate population size and needs
• Facility's custodial and health functions
• Security level

Characteristics of the correctional service delivery system that influence access to care within a given facility.

  • Component 1: Physical and temporal availability of clinical providers, equipment, and settings.
  • Component 2: Affordability of care.
  • Component 3: Administrative availability of care through the application of service utilization management techniques.

↓

Process

• Age
• Race
• Literacy
• Language skills
• Income/assets
• Trauma history
• Preexisting diagnosis

Characteristics of the services an inmate receives in relationship to their specific medical and mental health needs; process comprises the inmate's acess to applied clinical knowledge, judgment, and skill (i.e., technical care) and the interpersonal relationship between the clinical provider and the inmate. Evaluation of process is further conditioned on measuring the effectiveness of technical care and the acceptability of the care to the inmate.

  • Component 1: Access to effective technical care that conforms to evidence-based practices that are associated with desired health outcomes.
  • Component 2: Inmate's experience of the technical processes of care.

↓

Outcome
Characteristics of the effects of the medical and mental health care on the inmate's health status and functioning.

  • Component 1: Inmate's response to treatment relative to identified health needs, such as changes in clinical signs and symptoms, risk factors for illness, and knowledge and behaviors necessary for the management of a chronic condition.
  • Component 2: Inmate's level of functioning, such as changes in functioning relative to ADLs, PADLs, safety, and fit with housing, work, and dietary assignments.
  • Component 3: Inmate's satisfaction with care and related outcomes, such as compliance with treatment plan, engagement in follow-up care, and willingness to request care in the future.

Sources: Donabedian, 1980, 1988, 2005.

individual level. Thus, beyond looking at the effects of, for example, a person's sociodemographic background at the individual level on health outcomes, the model also includes effects that may stem from the correctional facility, the community that surrounds the correctional facility, and the region that surrounds both the community and facility.

The utility of this multilevel model is quickly appreciated when one looks at the reality of correctional health-care systems, their limitations, and their potential reliance on community-based medical services outside of any given prison. Because correctional health-care systems can often include interplay between health-care services offered from inside the prison system and those offered from the outside when prison-based health-care systems alone are not adequate to handle serious medical needs (Anno, 2001, 2004a; Kerbs, 2000a, 2000b), the top part of Figure 5.2 situates any given prison's health-care system within regional and community locations. These additional levels in the model are important given that variation in urbanization can influence the distribution of and access to community-based providers, equipment, and clinical care settings outside prison. Generally speaking, prisons tend to be located in remote or rural communities (Aday, 2003; Anno, 2001, 2004a; Young and Reviere, 2006), and this is especially true of prisons that house women (Aday, 2003; Young and Reviere, 2006); consequently, women are often far removed from mainstream medical services (e.g., specialists in obstetrics and gynecology) that are often more available in urban areas. Indeed, the more remote a prison's location is in the rural United States, the more difficult it becomes to staff the prison with medical specialists or find such specialists within close proximity to a given correctional facility (Anno, 2001, 2004a). Thus, our modification of Donabedian's framework includes the location of a prison because this affects access to medical personnel and community-based facilities.

Moving to the concept of structure as defined by characteristics of the correctional service delivery system (buildings, personnel, and equipment) that influence access to care within a given prison, we suggest that there are three structural components to care that need to be examined relative to older women's access to correctional health-care services: (1) the physical and temporal availability of clinical providers, equipment, and settings; (2) affordability of care, including the potential presence of co-payments for treatment; and (3) the administrative availability of care through the application of service utilization management techniques (Anno, 2001, 2004a; see also Robbins, 1999; Siever, 2005).

With regard to physical availability of structures, we believe that it is important to highlight the dated nature of prisons that often house women and the medical facilities that serve them. To be sure, older women in prison appear to have more chronic health problems than older men, as discussed earlier (Aday, 2003; Aday and Krabill, 2011), and one would hope that these older women would be given access to the most updated and fully equipped facilities available for the treatment of chronic conditions. Although information on this topic is limited, studies and correctional experts suggest that only a small number of prisons that hold women are compliant with the standards as established in the Americans with Disabilities Act (ADA) of 1990 (Loeb and AbuDagga, 2006). As of 2003, there were about 108 prisons that housed women, and only 28 percent ($n = 30$) were opened after 1990, which is when the ADA was passed (American Correctional Association, 2003); additionally, about one in five was opened prior to 1950, and four facilities were opened prior to 1900 (Young and Reviere, 2006), which does not bode well for compliance with ADA standards and the provision of quality of medical care in dated facilities. Moreover, older women in prison, as compared to older men, do not appear to have equal access to geriatric units and alternative living arrangements, purportedly because they represent an exceedingly small and thus neglected proportion of older inmates (Loeb and AbuDagga, 2006; Kratcoski and Babb, 1990).

As noted in Figure 5.2, there are also certain factors (shown on the left side of the figure) that undoubtedly affect structural characteristics and access to care. For example, a prison's security level can affect staffing considerations, space considerations, and a prisoner's ability to physically access care both inside and outside of a given prison, such as for off-site care in the latter case (Anno, 2001). Facilities with higher security classifications can slow a prisoner's access to different sections of a prison, including medical facilities; moreover, if off-site treatment is required for prisoners with higher security classifications, which suggest greater potential threats to public safety, then a larger number of correctional officers may be needed to safely escort shackled prisoners to community-based treatment for outsourced services (Kerbs and Jolley, 2009a, 2009b).

Beyond a prison's security level, other factors can affect the structural components of health-care systems (e.g., the facility's mix of custodial and health-care functions, the size and needs of the prison population served by a given structure, and the levels of privatization and specialty-care centralization). Of these factors, we are particularly concerned about the role of privatization and how it affects the structural components of care. We highlight this factor because of recent research that has found a positive association between the proportion of privatized medical personnel in a given prison and inmate mortality rates; as the proportion of privatized staff increases, so do inmate mortality rates (Bedard and Frech, 2007). Additionally, the literature has found that some prisons with privatized care tend to privilege profits over quality of care (Robbins, 1999) and inappropriately provide financial incentives to medical personnel who are willing to operate medical units with inadequate staffing and facilities (Siever, 2005).

Moving to the concept of process in Figure 5.2 , we highlight two important components that need to be examined. The first component measures access to effective technical care that conforms to evidence-based practices, which should be statistically associated with desirable health outcomes; the second component measures prisoners' experiences with the processes of care via interpersonal interactions between patients and clinicians (Donabedian, 1988, 2005).

With regard to technical care, Aday and Krabill examined qualitative data from 327 incarcerated women (aged 50 and older) in five states, and noted the following: "For many aging prisoners, it was a very common occurrence to fear or mistrust the medical care provided in what they perceived to be a highly defective system" (2011, p. 64). Additionally, Aday and Krabill (2011) noted that some of the older women in prison reported "a lack of appropriate medical response," including lack of access to appropriate medications and the use of improperly administered medications. That said, this study did not provide quantitative summaries of the incidence or prevalence of inappropriate medical responses as experienced by older women in state prisons.

In qualitative and quantitative studies by Ammar and Weaver (2005) and Young (1998, 1999, 2000), the results generally suggest that the interpersonal interactions between women (of all ages) in prison and clinicians are problematic. For example, Ammar and Weaver interviewed a total of fifty-six women in two Ohio prisons (the median age of the purposively sampled respondents was 40, but only four women in the sample were aged 55 and older) and found that many women in prison "complained of a lack of compassion coming from medical staff" (2005, p. 84), a finding that is congruent with other qualitative studies of women in prison and their perceptions of medical personnel (see, e.g., Fisher and Hatton 2010; Magee et al., 2005).

Young (1999) examined qualitative data from fifteen interviews with women who were admitted to a single prison in the state of Washington between September 1, 1995, and April 30, 1996, and who were still incarcerated at the time of the sample draw and collection of medical records in mid-August 1996 (thus the research design included a four-month study period). This study examined health-service use and perceptions of care among white and nonwhite women in prison. A larger proportion of white women (100 percent) as compared to nonwhite women (83 percent) perceived their care to be inadequate on one or more occasions; conversely, 89 percent of white women in prison, but only 50 percent of nonwhite women, reported one or more experiences with adequate care. Interestingly,

100 percent of both groups reported one or more experiences with non-empathetic treatment (e.g., no respect or courtesy shown to the prisoner); conversely, 89 percent of white women reported receiving empathetic treatment on one or more occasions, compared to only 33 percent of non-white women. Thus there appear to be large differences between groups with respect to their perceptions of interpersonal care in prison; that said, Young's study did not link perceptions of care to specific types of technical care (e.g., prevention, acute care, or chronic-care services), to specific conditions with specific symptoms or levels of functioning, or to health outcomes.

In another study, Young (2000) used the same sample of fifteen women as examined in the 1999 study to look at additional measures of perceived care. In terms of technical care, Young found that 87 percent of the sample described receiving partial care, 67 percent described receiving no care or delayed care, and 53 percent reported misdirected care, in that they did not receive the care they needed (they received something else). Conversely, 47 percent described receiving thorough or responsive care, and 40 percent described receiving immediate care. In terms of interpersonal care, 67 percent of the women felt that they were not treated in an individual manner and that services were not responsibly targeted to their individual needs and preferences. Moreover, 53 percent felt disregarded in that they were not treated with respect, concern, or dignity; and 27 percent reported being treated with abruptness. Only 40 percent reported receiving treatment by a clinician who took a personal interest in them or provided treatment that they considered respectful and courteous. Finally, only 20 percent experienced clinical interactions wherein the treating professional listened and answered their questions.

In sum, it is clear that process studies are needed that specifically compare younger inmates with older inmates in a way that allows the results to distinguish between younger and older men and women, and between different racial/ethnic groups. Additionally, there are no well-designed studies that assess the quality of technical care received by older inmates relative to the optimal (i.e., evidence-based) care that they should be receiving. Specific emphasis should be placed on those processes that are empirically supported and professionally regarded as the standard of care that older women should be receiving per their diagnosed conditions, but such processes also should take into account their symptom severity and their levels of functioning. Some studies provide very crude measures of episodic care and the frequency of episodic care among women of all ages in general, but findings are never tied to specific conditions, symptom severity, or levels of functioning (see, e.g., Hyde, Brumfield, and Nagel, 2000; Young, 1998).

Factors that affect the process of care (technical care and interpersonal interactions) include the prisoner's age, race, literacy, language skills, income/assets, trauma histories, pre-existing diagnoses, and so on (shown on the left side of Figure 5.2). The importance of these factors should not be underestimated. For example, a prisoner's income and assets can play a role in accessing medical personnel and technical care, because a majority of states permit the collection of co-pays from prisoners for health-care services (Anno, 2001), which can potentially slow or block access to needed care (see also Fisher and Hatton, 2010; Magee et al., 2005). Although incarcerated women (regardless of age) use health services at a higher rate than their male counterparts, with about a third of all women compared to about one in ten male inmates accessing health services daily (Bloom, Owen, and Covington, 2003; Lewis, 2006), we do not know about the corresponding rates of use for older men and women aged 50 and older; that said, qualitative research by Aday and Krabill (2011) has suggested that older women's access to health-care services may be blocked in some states by co-pays, thus reducing their access to needed care. Additionally, literacy can also play a role in accessing technical care, given that many states operate "kite" systems wherein prisoners are required to submit written requests for services (Anno, 2004a, 2004b). Given that older inmates tend to have lower levels of education as compared to younger inmates (Goetting, 1984; Kerbs, 2000a), the former may have more trouble than the latter in accessing technical care that is premised on written requests.

Finally, moving to the concept of outcome, as defined in Figure 5.2 by the characteristics of the effects of medical and mental health care on the inmate's health status and functioning, we see the need to study three components: (1) a prisoner's response to treatment relative to their identified health problem and changes in their clinical signs, symptoms, risk factors, and knowledge of behaviors needed to manage their condition; (2) a prisoner's level of functioning as defined by their capacity to complete acts of daily living and prison acts of daily living (dropping to the floor for alarms, standing for periods of time for head counts, moving to and from the dining hall for meals, hearing orders from correctional officers and staff in general, and getting in and out of bed to include top bunks as needed); and (3) a prisoner's level of satisfaction with care and related outcomes.

In sum, this model provides a sound conceptual framework to critically examine the outcomes that stem from correctional health-care services. Because older women in prison have more chronic conditions than older men, as discussed earlier, the application of this model to older women in prison could provide us with a better understanding of their complicated care as they pass through certain structures and processes that hopefully lead to desirable health outcomes (e.g., positive changes in health status and functioning) for their multiple chronic conditions. Although we know very little about the effects of multiple chronic conditions in the world outside prison (Vogeli et al., 2007), we know even less when it comes to the role of treatment for multiple chronic conditions relative to various outcomes, including the functional status of women who have such complicated medical needs. In the world outside prison, we know that people who have more chronic conditions become more functionally impaired, and at a quicker rate, than do people who have fewer chronic conditions (Vogeli et al., 2007); moreover, the level of disability associated with having multiple chronic conditions appears to be far worse than the levels of disability that might be expected from having any individual chronic condition alone, perhaps because people who have multiple chronic conditions are less likely to receive optimal care, even in the world outside prison (see, e.g., Vogeli et al., 2007). Thus, we suggest that future prison-based research should critically examine the role of chronic-care clinics for the health conditions that older women experience, to determine if such clinics are capable of providing technical care that improves health outcomes relative to both the conditions and the functional status of older women with multiple conditions.

Conclusion

Despite our best efforts to understand and improve the delivery of quality physical and mental health services for older women in federal and state prisons, some of these women will inevitably die behind bars. Given the serious nature of the most prevalent health problems reported by older women in prison (e.g., arthritis, asthma, diabetes, heart problems, and hypertension) and the fact that these women often reside in dated facilities that may be poorly equipped to address their health-care and disability needs, it is important to look at mortality rates in the prison setting. Regardless of gender, prisoners aged 55 and older represented an increasing percentage of all deaths in custody between 2001 (33.8 percent) and 2009 (47.7 percent) (Noonan and Carson, 2011). For women prisoners (of all ages), the rate of deaths in custody increased from 129 to 160 deaths per 100,000 women between 2001 and 2009 (Noonan and Carson, 2011), but the Bureau of Justice Statistics has yet to release the death rates for women of various age groups and/or the rates for women from varying racial/ethnic backgrounds who fall into differing age groups. Hence, we need more research to fill this knowledge gap and develop a better understanding of the predictors of mortality rates for older women in prison.

There is also a need for more longitudinal research that examines the potential link between the provision of correctional health-care services and both the morbidity and the mortality rates of older women from various racial/ethnic groups. We suggest that such longitudinal research utilize a quality-of-care framework as outlined in this chapter. Given the emergent literature on health disparities relative to diseases and health-care utilization patterns between men and women and between whites and nonwhites in the world outside prison (see, e.g., Dunlop et al., 2002; Gorman and Read, 2006; McGlynn et al., 2003), one must ask whether such disparities also exist within the prison setting, especially among older women who have multiple chronic health conditions. Donabedian's framework (1988, 2005), as modified and depicted in this chapter, would serve as a solid platform for conceptualizing research questions and informing analyses that examine predictors from multiple levels, including the individual level, the institutional level, the community level, and the regional level. Without multilevel research designs that examine longitudinal data, there will continue to be voids in our basic knowledge regarding the predictors of morbidity and mortality for older women behind bars.

For those older women in prison who survive their incarceration and return to society, we still have a long way to go when it comes to understanding their morbidity and mortality upon release. Reentry into society is undoubtedly complex for most prisoners, but we believe that reentry is particularly difficult for older women who have multiple chronic health conditions. In order for prison- and community-based correctional systems to more fully understand the relationships between the health profiles and the reentry experiences of these older women, we will need to move beyond the data collected by the Bureau of Justice Statistics. Indeed, we will need to collect data regarding the health of released prisoners, including older men and women, who should be included in cross-sectional and longitudinal surveys that are national in scope (i.e., surveys of free citizens) but outside of the purview of Bureau of Justice Statistics surveys, the latter of which focus primarily on institutionalized individuals (Ahalt et al., 2012). Nationally representative health datasets of free citizens often lack the variables needed to identify the incarceration histories of survey respondents, but these datasets, if they were to include such variables (current and prior incarceration status), could serve as valuable resources for tracking those who reenter society after a period of incarceration (Ahalt et al., 2012). Such variables would help to advance our understanding of the short- and long-term effects of incarceration, and of treatment received during incarceration, on the health of released women, including older women.

Federal and state prisons have a long way to go when it comes to understanding the correctional health-care experiences of older women—the new "forgotten" minority. That said, there is much to learn from this medically complicated group, and the time has come to pay more attention to their needs and treatment, both behind bars and within society after release.

6

Prisoners' Rights and the Law

Naoki Kanaboshi

The way of the transgressor is hard. The way of the captured and imprisoned transgressor is especially hard. In addition to being hanged, beheaded, drawn-and-quartered, immolated by fire, impaled, crucified, and otherwise killed by sundry other nefarious techniques, prisoners have also been held alive within pits, cages, dungeons, cells, torture chambers, ships, barbed-wire enclosures, and a miscellany of other reprehensible settings. Prisons have never been intended to be easy or pleasant, but there is no doubt that historically prisoners have been horribly mistreated and abused in a myriad of ways. "The mood and temper of the public in regard to the treatment of crime and criminals is one of the most unfailing tests of the civilisation of any country" (Churchill, 1910).

The treatment of prisoners of the United States, at both the federal and state levels, has come a long way since the founders outlawed "cruel and unusual punishment" by means of the Eighth Amendment to the US Constitution. The interpretation of that phrase has changed a great deal since the enactment of the Bill of Rights. In general, the plight of prisoners in the United States has gradually been mitigated—especially since the mid–twentieth century. Now to a large extent, it is required that prisoners be treated as humanely and decently as is practical within the prison societal structure.

One of the most significant improvements of late pertains to the handling and treatment of older prisoners. As this chapter will show, the courts in the United States have made it clear to the administrators of prison systems that this particular category of prisoners must be provided with special attention commensurate with ordinary and reasonable needs of aging

113

human beings. Older prisoners are different than younger prisoners, and they must therefore be treated differently. The special needs and concerns of aging prisoners have been addressed in detail by the courts in several cases. The US Congress has also enacted statutes that have relevance to the main legal issues pertaining especially to older prisoners.

While lawfully incarcerated, prisoners retain several constitutional rights (*Procunier v. Martinez,* 1974; *Wolff v. McDonnell,* 1974). They also retain some statutory rights (see, e.g., *Pennsylvania Department of Corrections v. Yeskey,* 1998 [regarding Title II of the Americans with Disabilities Act of 1990]; see also the Religious Land Use and Institutionalized Persons Act of 2000). This chapter focuses on rights that are particularly important to older prisoners as well as the emergent national discussion concerning the care and custody of older prisoners by prison administrators who are charged with meeting these prisoners' special needs, including physical and psychological health, disabilities, safety, and victimization related to predatory conduct by younger prisoners (regarding inmate-on-inmate victimization, see generally Aday, 2003; Kerbs and Jolley, 2007). As currently interpreted, the US Constitution requires that the federal and state governments provide care, protection, and assistance to these prisoners. Additionally, the Americans with Disabilities Act (ADA) of 1990 and the Rehabilitation Act of 1973 prohibit discrimination against older prisoners based on disabilities. These statutes also require that prison officials provide reasonable accommodations for prisoners with disabilities. Thus it behooves policymakers, correctional administrators, and prison staff to become well acquainted with all of these mandates and prohibitions.

In order to provide the reader with needed insights into the future of prisoners' rights for the aging prison population in the United States, this chapter begins with a constitutional primer, and then addresses five major issues: health care, conditions of confinement, protection from other prisoners, refusal of medical treatment, and statutory rights of prisoners.

A Primer on Constitutional Protections for Prisoners

Age, Disability, and Constitutional Equal Protection

The Equal Protection Clause of the US Constitution, which is part of the Fourteenth Amendment, states that "no State shall . . . deny to any person within its jurisdiction the equal protection of the laws." The US Supreme Court has determined that this clause also applies to the federal government via the Due Process Clause of the Fifth Amendment (*Bolling v. Sharpe,* 1954). One might imagine that the clause would provide a natural fit with the advancement of equal justice for older prisoners, including those who are sick and disabled. However, the Equal Protection Clause plays a very limited role with regard to the prevention of discrimination based on age or disability. Both racial and gender discrimination are unconstitutional unless the government can show strong justification to do so (see, e.g., *Korematsu v. United States*, 1944 [race]; *Craig v. Boren*, 1976 [gender]). However, age and disability-based discrimination are constitutional, unless the government's action is irrational or ill-motivated, thus representing arbitrary or groundless discrimination (*Massachusetts Board of Retirement v. Murgia*, 1976; *City of Cleburne v. Cleburne Living Center, Inc.*, 1985). It is thus unlikely that courts will intervene to stop prisons' discrimination based on age or disability (for examples of lower court cases, see *Taylor v. Ortiz*, 2010 [age]; *Miller v. Hinton*, 2008 [disability]). This is not to say that prisons are immune from legal challenges to age- or disability-based discrimination. Successful challenges to discrimination based on age or disability will likely need to be based on rationales other than the Equal Protection Clause.

Prisoners' Constitutional Rights in General

Prisoners retain additional constitutional rights that extend beyond equal protection issues. As the US Supreme Court has said, "There is no iron curtain drawn between the Constitution and the prisons of this country" (*Wolff v. McDonnell*, 1974). The constitutional rights of prisoners as recognized by the Supreme Court include First Amendment rights (see *Jones v. North Carolina Prisoners' Labor Union, Inc.*, 1977 [freedom of association]; *Turner v. Safley*, 1987 [right to correspond]; *Thornburgh v. Abbott*, 1989 [right to access reading materials]; *O'Lone v. Estate of Shabazz*, 1989 [freedom of religion]). The Supreme Court also has recognized the rights of prisoners to access the courts (*Johnson v. Avery*, 1969), and to marry (*Turner v. Safley*, 1987). However, the Court has held that prisoners' constitutional rights are significantly limited compared with those of free individuals. For example, the Court has upheld prisons' reasonable restrictions on inmates' First Amendment rights for the purpose of prison security or prisoner rehabilitation (e.g., *Turner v. Safley*, 1987; *O'Lone v. Estate of Shabazz*, 1989).

Prisoners' Rights Under the Eighth Amendment

Beyond the aforementioned rights, prisoners have other constitutional rights that free members of the public do not. For example, to avoid violations of the Eighth Amendment's prohibition against "cruel and unusual punishment," prisons must provide all inmates with "the minimal civilized measure of life's necessities" (*Rhodes v. Chapman,* 1981). Medical care for serious medical problems is also required (*Estelle v. Gamble,* 1976). Prisons must also make reasonable efforts to protect prisoners from violence perpetrated by other prisoners (*Farmer v. Brennan,* 1994). The Eighth Amendment is thus especially important to older prisoners, because they tend to have more health problems than younger prisoners, and they are more likely to be victimized than are younger inmates. If their conditions of incarceration are inhumane or their medical care is inadequate, then prison administrators will likely be held to be in violation of the Eighth Amendment. That can result in major problems for the institution.

Constitutional issues regarding medical care for health problems. The Eighth Amendment prohibits "cruel and unusual punishment." This ban applies to how the death penalty is implemented (see, e.g., *Furman v. Georgia,* 1972; *Kennedy v. Louisiana,* 2008). The Eighth Amendment also applies to the medical care of inmates. Because of age-related declines in health across the normal human life-span, older prisoners require a disproportionate amount of health-care services, including care for chronic health conditions such as arthritis, cardiovascular disease, pulmonary disorders, neurological diseases, vision problems, and hearing problems (see Aday, 2003; Kerbs, 2000b; generally Maruschak and Beck, 2001). In light of these typical problems of older prisoners, the Eighth Amendment mandates that prison officials have a duty to provide care and assistance for them.

The US Supreme Court held in *Estelle v. Gamble* (1976) that a prison official's "deliberate indifference to serious medical needs of prisoners" constitutes a violation of the Eighth Amendment's prohibition against cruel and unusual punishment (p. 104). Although the general public does not have a constitutional right to health care, *Estelle* clarified that prisoners have the right to treatment for serious medical needs because "an inmate must rely on prison authorities to treat his medical needs; if the authorities fail to do so, those needs will not be met" (p. 103). "A prison that deprives prisoners of basic sustenance, including adequate medical care, is incompatible with the concept of human dignity and has no place in civilized society" (*Brown v. Plata,* 2011, p. 1928).

However, the courts have held that Eighth Amendment violations regarding health care can happen only in limited circumstances involving the simultaneous presence of two conditions: serious medical needs, and a prison official's deliberate indifference to such needs. With regard to the former, the prisoner's medical needs must be of a "serious" nature. But a federal appellate court stated that "[a] medical condition need not be life-threatening to be serious" (*Gayton v. McCoy,* 2010, p. 620). According to another federal court's explanation, a "serious" medical need is a condition "that has been diagnosed by a physician as mandating treatment or one that is so obvious that even a lay person would easily recognize the necessity for a doctor's attention" (*Hill v. Dekalb Regional Youth Detention Center,* 1994, p. 1187). Additionally, "an injury that a reasonable doctor or patient would find important and worthy of comment or treatment; the presence of a medical condition that significantly affects an individual's daily activities; or the existence of chronic and substantial pain are examples of indications that a prisoner has a 'serious' need for medical treatment" (*McGuckin v. Smith* 1992, p. 1059–1060). Deliberate indifference to serious medical needs is considered present when a prison official "knows that inmates face a substantial risk of serious harm and disregards that risk by failing to take reasonable measures to abate it" (*Estelle v. Gamble,* 1976, pp. 105–106). The disregard of substantial risks is comparable to the concept of recklessness commonly used in criminal law (*Farmer v. Brennan,* 1994; Model Penal Code § 2.02(2)(c)). Medical neglect caused by an accident or by simple negligence is not considered sufficient for an Eighth Amendment violation concerning "deliberate indifference" (see, e.g., *Estelle v. Gamble,* 1976; *Lindsey v. McGinnis,* 1994 [a federal appellate court found that a prison physician's treatment decisions for a 70-year-old prisoner, even if they were in fact incorrect, constituted at most negligence and not deliberate indifference]).

Most recently, in *Brown v. Plata* (2011), the US Supreme Court held that the conditions of confinement in California's prisons violated the Eighth Amendment on multiple levels. With regard to insufficient medical care, the Court stated:

> Prisoners in California with serious mental illness do not receive minimal, adequate care. Because of a shortage of treatment beds, suicidal inmates may be held for prolonged periods in telephone-booth sized cages without toilets. . . . A psychiatric expert reported observing an inmate who had been held in such a cage for nearly 24 hours, standing in a pool of his own urine, unresponsive and nearly catatonic. . . . Wait times for mental health care range as high as 12 months. . . . Prisoners suffering from physical illness also receive severely deficient care. . . . [E]xtreme departures from the standard of care were widespread, . . . and the proportion of possibly preventable or preventable deaths was extremely high. . . . Many more prisoners, suffering from severe but not life-threatening conditions, experience prolonged illness and unnecessary pain. (pp. 1924–1926)

Lower-court cases regarding older prisoners (aged 50 and older) also have held that when prison officials knowingly or recklessly fail to treat older prisoners' serious medical needs, they violate their Eighth Amendment rights. For example, *Hayes v. Snyder* (2008) relates to an inmate who was in his 50s and suffered from testicular cysts. Despite the prisoner's repeated complaint of extreme pain, the physician refused to refer him to a specialist or to provide him with prescription-strength painkillers. The court held that the prisoner's assertion, if proven in trial, would violate the Eighth Amendment. In the case of *Guzman v. Cockrell* (2011), the court held that a prisoner, who was older than 55, made a sufficient deliberate-indifference claim with regard to two factors: his injury and suffering caused by falling from an upper-bunk bed without a ladder, and a lack of medical personal available between 6 P.M. and 6 A.M. In *Brown v. Englander* (2010), the court held that a 72-year-old prisoner successfully made a deliberate-indifference claim with regard to the prison's failure to arrange for surgery to correct his perforated lumbar disks, its failure to provide sufficient painkillers given his medical records, which showed the necessity of surgery and his repeated complaints of extreme pain. In *Woods v. Goord* (2002), the court held that the plaintiff, an inmate in his 50s who had been diagnosed with rheumatoid arthritis, degenerative joint disease, and leukemia, made a sufficient deliberate-indifference claim in that the prison physicians repeatedly failed to implement specialists' recommendations regarding further appointments, physical therapy, and surgery.

Accordingly, any knowing or reckless disregard of the serious medical needs of older prisoners will very likely be determined to be a violation of the Eighth Amendment. Such a ruling would create serious problems for the offending prison official. Older prisoners have special needs regarding age-related medical vulnerabilities compared to the needs of younger prisoners.

Constitutional issues regarding conditions of confinement. Prisons must provide inmates with not only medical care, but also "adequate food, clothing, shelter . . . and . . . [protection] from violence at the hands of other prisoners" (*Farmer v. Brennan,* 1994, p. 833). To determine the adequacy of conditions of confinement, courts consider both the overall correctional environment and the particular needs of individual prisoners. Thus, for example, even when the overall prison condition is adequate for most inmates, a constitutional violation may be considered to occur when prison officials put an older inmate into inhumane conditions by failing to provide special accommodations for adequate nutrition (which can be needed for older prisoners who have special dietary requirements) (see Marquart, Merianos, and Doucet, 2000), or failing to provide reasonably sanitary conditions.

Other cases have further expanded our understanding of under what circumstances conditions of confinement may be deemed to violate the Eighth Amendment. For example, in *Hutto v. Finney* (1978), the US Supreme Court described unconstitutional prison conditions as follows:

> Confinement in punitive isolation was for an indeterminate period of
> time. An average of 4, and sometimes as many as 10 or 11, prisoners

were crowded into windowless 8' × 10' cells containing no furniture other than a source of water and a toilet that could only be flushed from outside the cell. At night the prisoners were given mattresses to spread on the floor. Although some prisoners suffered from infectious diseases such as hepatitis and venereal disease, mattresses were removed and jumbled together each morning, then returned to the cells at random in the evening. Prisoners in isolation received fewer than 1,000 calories a day; their meals consisted primarily of 4-inch squares of "grue," a substance created by mashing meat, potatoes, oleo, syrup, vegetables, eggs, and seasoning into a paste and baking the mixture in a pan. (pp. 682–683)

In *Goodman v. Georgia* (2006), a prisoner with disabilities argued that his conditions of confinement violated the Americans with Disabilities Act of 1990. Without deciding the merits of the case, the Supreme Court remanded it to the lower courts. In its opinion, the Court said that the alleged condition, if proven at trial, may well violate the Eighth Amendment. The Court summarized the prisoner's allegation as follows:

Among his more serious allegations, he claimed that he was confined for 23-to-24 hours per day in a 12-by-3-foot cell in which he could not turn his wheelchair around. He alleged that the lack of accessible facilities rendered him unable to use the toilet and shower without assistance, which was often denied. On multiple occasions, he asserted, he had injured himself in attempting to transfer from his wheelchair to the shower or toilet on his own, and, on several other occasions, he had been forced to sit in his own feces and urine while prison officials refused to assist him in cleaning up the waste. He also claimed that he had been denied physical therapy and medical treatment, and denied access to virtually all prison programs and services on account of his disability. (p. 155)

Thus, if prisons fail to provide adequate accommodations for older inmates who have disabilities by subjecting the inmates to these kinds of inhumane conditions, the administrators of those prisons will likely be held to be in violation of the Eighth Amendment. Data from the Bureau of Justice Statistics suggests that a legal crisis may be forthcoming when it comes to elders with physical disabilities behind bars. In short, a substantial percentage of surveyed state prisoners (25.2 percent) and federal prisoners (21.9 percent) aged 45 and older reported that they had physical impairments (Maruschak and Beck, 2001). This suggests that a significant proportion of aging prisoners will likely be deemed to have standing to seek legal remedies if their respective facilities fail to provide adequate accommodations for them.

Constitutional issues regarding protection from other prisoners.
The ban on "cruel and unusual punishment" has been found to apply to issues concerning the safety and victimization of prisoners. The US Supreme

Court, in *Farmer v. Brennan* (1994), declared that prisons have a constitutional duty "to protect prisoners from violence at the hands of other prisoners" (p. 833) or "to ensure reasonable safety" (p. 844). In the *Farmer* case, a male transgender prisoner with "feminine characteristics" asserted that he had been beaten and raped by other inmates; additionally, he argued that officials failed to protect him from these assaults, and that this failure amounted to deliberate indifference. While the Court did not answer whether the officials' conduct in this case actually amounted to deliberate indifference (the Court remanded the case to a lower court to decide this issue), the Court did confirm that it is a prison official's duty to protect prisoners from such harm and to ensure their safety. The clear implication of *Farmer* as applied to older prisoners is that if a prison official is aware that an older prisoner is at significant risk of victimization at the hands of other prisoners, then the Eighth Amendment requires that the official take reasonable measures to secure the prisoner's safety. In light of the fact that older prisoners suffer psychological, economic, physical, and sexual inmate-on-inmate victimization at the hands of younger prisoners (see generally DeLuca, 1998; Kerbs and Jolley, 2007), the implications of *Farmer* are substantial. In short, failure to take reasonable measures to protect older prisoners will likely result in significant liabilities for prison officials.

Constitutional and Legal Issues
Regarding the Right to Refuse Medical Treatment

What rights do older inmates have with regard to medical treatment decisions? In the context of mentally competent people who are not imprisoned, it is well established that patients have a constitutional right to decide whether or not they will consent to medical treatment. This right covers the relationship between free individuals and the government when the government seeks to provide or impose medical interventions. For example, in *Cruzan v. Director, Missouri Department of Health* (1990), the US Supreme Court recognized that "a competent person has a constitutionally protected liberty interest in refusing unwanted medical treatment" (p. 278).

Prisoners also have a right to refuse medical treatment, including psychiatric treatment, although this right can be overridden by prison authorities. In *Washington v. Harper* (1990), the Supreme Court recognized that a prisoner has "a significant liberty interest in avoiding the unwanted administration of antipsychotic drugs under the Due Process Clause of the Fourteenth Amendment" (pp. 221–222; see also *Riggins v. Nevada,* 1992; *Sell v. United States,* 2003 [in these cases, the Court recognized that a criminal defendant has a constitutionally protected interest in avoiding forced medication]). In *Washington v. Harper,* a prisoner with a diagnosed manic-depressive disorder refused antipsychotic medication, but he was not found to be mentally incompetent. While the Court found that prisoners retain a constitutional right to refuse antipsychotic medication, the Court upheld the involuntary administration of medications in this case, for reasons noted later.

As with several other constitutional rights of prisoners, such as First Amendment rights or the right to marry, the Constitution has been interpreted to allow prison officials to restrict these rights as long as restrictions are *reasonable* (the so-called *Turner* test). Prison officials do not need to demonstrate, for example, that the restriction is the minimum means necessary to achieve prison safety and discipline (see *Turner v. Safley,* 1987). In the *Washington v. Harper* case, the Court held that if the inmate poses a danger to himself or to others *and* if the forced medication serves a prisoner's medical interests, then the restriction will be considered reasonable, regardless of whether or not the prisoner is deemed incompetent. Accordingly, though significantly curtailed, prisoners do retain the right to refuse medical treatment. Moreover, some federal appellate courts have recognized inmates' constitutional right to make informed consent regarding medications (*Benson v. Terhune,* 2002; *White v. Napoleon,* 1990).

Beyond prisoners' curtailed right to refuse antipsychotic medications, it is also important to examine prisoners' rights to refuse life-sustaining treatment. This will undoubtedly be one of the main issues facing the graying prison population in the immediate future. The US Supreme Court has not ruled on this issue, but at least one state supreme court has recognized such a right. In *Thor v. Superior Court* (1993), the highest court of California held that prisoners have a right to refuse life-sustaining medical treatment under state law. In this case, the inmate suffered as a quadriplegic after he fell off a wall; thereafter, he refused food and medication. The California supreme court also found that his right to refuse treatment outweighed the state's interests to impose treatment. The court did not apply the *Turner* rational-basis test, but instead applied the same test that is applicable to a free person's refusal of life-sustaining medical treatment. This test balances the four legitimate interests that the government retains (preserving life, preventing suicide, maintaining the integrity of the medical profession, and protecting innocent third parties) vis-à-vis the right of a person to refuse treatment (see also *In re Conroy,* 1985; *Superintendent of Belchertown State School v. Saikewicz,* 1977 [these state court cases also considered the same governmental interests]). As for the state's interest in the preservation of life, the California supreme court found that this governmental interest does not surpass an inmate's right of refusal if medical treatment for the prisoner is at best palliative and does not improve his or her condition. Moreover, the court held that the government's interest in the prevention of suicide does not outweigh a prisoner's right of refusal, since refusal of life-sustaining treatment is not suicide when the treatment would just prolong life and would not cure the disease or injury. The court also held that the state's interest in preserving medical integrity does not justify forced treatment, because medical integrity is served by physicians advising patients fully so that patients can decide for themselves whether or not to undergo treatments. Finally, the court held that the government's interest in protecting third parties is not strong in the case of prisoners, because refusal of the treatment does not adversely affect public health or minor children's welfare. In *Thor*, the state also argued that the prison has a duty to provide life-sustaining treatment to an inmate based on the holdings of *Estelle v. Gamble* (1976). The court answered that this duty is discharged by the inmate's refusal (waiver) of the right to treatment. The California supreme court therefore denied the prison physician's request to impose involuntary medication on the prisoner. Thus, competent older prisoners in California have the right to refuse life-sustaining treatment and medications.

Only time will tell if the US Supreme Court will rule on this issue, on which it has remained silent as of 2011 (but see *Pitre v. Cain*, 2010 [Justice Sotomayor, in dissenting from denial of certiorari, argued that the Court should accept the appeal of the case involving a prison inmate's right to refuse HIV medication]). Thus, for now, it is up to each state to determine if prison rules and policies will permit or deny prisoners the right to refuse life-sustaining treatment and medication. As the prison populations continue to age, these end-of-life debates will likely be addressed further by the courts.

Statutory Rights of Older Prisoners

Americans with Disabilities Act

Pragmatically speaking, it is difficult to say with certainty how far prison officials must go toward meeting the needs of older inmates who have disabilities. This section of the chapter examines the role of the Americans with Disabilities Act of 1990 pertaining to the aging prison population. The section begins by providing a brief background on the ADA and the four titles within the act. Then the applicability or inapplicability of each title to the plight of older prisoners with disabilities is discussed. The validity of the ADA under Section 5 of the Fourteenth Amendment is then reviewed, including a discussion of the possibility of denial of monetary damages being awarded to prisoners, even if prisons violate their rights.

These issues are significant given that as prisoners age they become more and more likely to have a broad variety of disabilities (Maruschak and Beck, 2001).

A brief review of the ADA. The Americans with Disabilities Act is a federal statute, passed by Congress in 1990 with an explicit purpose: "to provide a clear and comprehensive national mandate for the elimination of discrimination against individuals with disabilities" (42 U.S.C. § 12101(b) (1)). This landmark legislation heralded the advancement of benefits for persons with disabilities, but eight years would pass before it was clearly established that the ADA is also applicable to prisoners. In 1998, the US Supreme Court ruled that certain portions of the ADA are applicable to prisoners (*Pennsylvania Department of Corrections v. Yeskey*, 1998). Federal regulations have also stated that the ADA is applicable to prisons (28 C.F.R. §§ 35.151(k), 35.152).

To fully understand the ADA as applied to prisoners, it is essential to first understand the four key titles within the act and their application to free persons with disabilities. Title I of the ADA prohibits employment discrimination against people with disabilities. It prohibits discrimination "against a qualified individual on the basis of disability in regard to job application procedures, the hiring, advancement, or discharge of employees, employee compensation, job training, and other terms, conditions, and privileges of employment" (42 U.S.C. § 12112(a)). This prohibition applies to nearly all employers except for the federal government and private membership clubs. As discussed later in this chapter, however, Title I has been considered generally inapplicable to prison laborers.

Title II of the ADA prohibits discrimination with regard to access to services provided by public entities. It provides that "no qualified individual with a disability shall, by reason of such disability, be excluded from participation in or be denied the benefits of the services, programs, or activities of a public entity, or be subjected to discrimination by any such entity" (§ 12132). "Public entity" includes "any State or local government" (§ 12131(1)(A)). It also includes "any department, agency, special purpose district, or other instrumentality of a State or States or local government" (§ 12131(1)(B)). Title II is considered to be applicable to prisoners. Additionally, prison laborers, while not covered by Title I, can be covered by Title II. One federal appellate court recently held that Title II is inapplicable to inmates in private prisons (*Edison v. Douberly*, 2010). However, a new 2010 federal regulation provides that Title II does apply to state-level private prisons (28 C.F.R. § 35.152(a)).

Title III requires that public facilities operated by private entities provide "reasonable accommodation" to people with disabilities. It also requires that, as a general rule, "no individual shall be discriminated against on the basis of disability in the full and equal enjoyment of the goods, services, facilities, privileges, advantages, or accommodations of any place of public accommodation" (42 U.S.C. § 12182(a)). Because Title III focuses on private entities, this provision is generally considered inapplicable to prisons, most of which are state-funded and state-operated. But some prisons are operated privately with state funds, and some commentators say that these facilities may be covered under Title III (Columbia Human Rights Law Review, 2011, p. 760). Finally, Title IV involves telecommunication access for people with hearing or speech disabilities. This title arguably applies to prisons, but only a few cases have been litigated under this provision.

Inapplicability of Title I to prisons. There are a number of statutes that protect older free individuals from employment discrimination. These include the Age Discrimination in Employment Acts of 1967 and 1975, Section 188 of the Workforce Investment Act of 1998, and Title I of the Americans with Disabilities Act of 1990. Title I of the ADA prohibits discrimination against people with disabilities "in regard to job application procedures, the hiring, advancement, or discharge of employees, employee compensation, job training, and other terms, conditions, and privileges of employment" (42 U.S.C. § 12111(8)). The Age Discrimination in Employment Act of 1975 prohibits similar practices (see 29 U.S.C. § 623(a)) against those aged 40 and older. Despite the protections that these statutes provide for free citizens, the courts have repeatedly found that prison laborers are not employed in a legal sense. Thus these statutes are considered inapplicable to inmates, because inmates are not seen as employees. The denial of the "employment" status of prison laborers has often been based on the lack of regular market or economic relationships between inmates and the prisons that "hire" them (see Zatz, 2008). Additionally, unlike employment, "prison labor does not fit a paradigm of discrete, financially motivated market transactions that are independent of any other relationship between the parties" (Zatz, 2008, p. 882).

Federal appellate court cases have mirrored this logic. For example, in the case of *Williams v. Meese* (1991), the plaintiff was a federal prisoner who argued that he was denied a prison job assignment because of his age and disability. He claimed, among other things, that this denial violated the Age Discrimination in Employment Act of 1975. The court rejected this claim because he was not found to be in an employment relationship with the defendants (the government and prison officials). The court noted: "Although his relationship with defendants may contain some elements commonly present in an employment relationship, it arises from plaintiff's having been convicted and sentenced to imprisonment in the defendants' correctional institution" (p. 997).

In another case (*Hale v. Arizona*, 1993), a federal appellate court held that the Fair Labor Standards Act of 1938 was not applicable to the labor of prisoners, because they were "working for a prison, in a program structured by the prison pursuant to state law requiring prisoners to work at hard labor" (p. 1393). Relying on this reasoning, a federal district court recently held that Title I of the ADA does not apply to the labor of prisoners, even when they are working for a private corporation (*Castle v. Eurofresh* [*Eurofresh* I], 2010 [the defendant corporation had contracted with the state for prisoner labor]). In this case, the court argued that because the Arizona law required prisoners to work and because it was the prison that was structuring inmates' labor, there was no "employment" relationship that was covered by Title I.

However, because prison labor can be categorized as "services, programs, or activities of a public entity" in Title II, it is covered by Title II (see *Castle v. Eurofresh* [*Eurofresh* II], 2010). Title II is considered to be applicable to prisons.

Applicability of Title II to prisons. Contrary to the inapplicability of the ADA's Title I to prisons, Title II does apply to prisoners, as held in *Pennsylvania Department of Corrections v. Yeskey* (1998). In this US Supreme Court case, a prisoner with a documented history of hypertension was denied entrance to a motivational boot camp that could have resulted in his parole within six months of admission to the camp. The Court held that the term "public entity" includes state prisons. The Pennsylvania Department of Corrections argued that prison does not offer any "benefits" by its nature. The state posited that Title II was thus inapplicable to prison programs; but the Court flatly rejected this argument, stating that "Modern prisons provide inmates with many recreational 'activities,' medical 'services,' and educational and vocational 'programs,' all of which at least theoretically 'benefit' the prisoners" (p. 210).

An overview of Title II requirements. Title II of the ADA prohibits discrimination against a "qualified individual with disability." The ADA defines a "qualified individual" as "an individual who meets the essential eligibility requirements for the receipt of services or the participation in programs or activities provided by a public entity" (42 U.S.C. § 12131(2)). The term "disability" is defined as "a physical or mental impairment that substantially limits one or more of the major life activities of such individuals," which can include a prisoner having "a record of such an impairment" or "being regarded as having such impairment" (§ 12102(1)).

In order to supersede these US Supreme Court rulings, Congress has recently passed new statutory provisions, in the ADA Amendment Act of 2008, to revive a broader definition of disability. The purposes of this act include "reinstating a broad scope of protection to be available under the ADA" (42 U.S.C. § 12101(b)). Also, the 2008 act explicitly requires that the "definition of disability . . . shall be construed in favor of broad coverage of individuals . . . to the maximum extent permitted by the terms of [the ADA as amended]" (§ 12102(4)(A)). Congress legislated several important modifications to the then-existing case law by passing the ADA Amendment Act. Two of the most important of them are that the act disallows courts from considering mitigating measures when making disability determinations, except for "ordinary eyeglasses and contact lenses" (§ 12102(4)(E)(i)); and that the act provides detailed examples of what is meant by substantial limitations in "major life activities" by including nonvolitional bodily functions. These functions include, but are not to be limited to, the immune system, normal cell growth, digestive processes, and processes involving bowels, bladder, nervous system, respiration, endocrine, and circulatory systems (see § 12102(2); see also Long, 2008, p. 223). This new provision is intended to overturn the Court's narrow reading in *Toyota Motor Manufacturing, Kentucky, Inc. v. Williams* (2002), which narrowly interpreted "major life activities."

Title II's integration mandate for people with and without disabilities. As mentioned, the dictates of Title II of the ADA require that prisoners with disabilities have access to and be allowed to participate in prison programs and other prison activities. Moreover, prisons, as a public entity, are prohibited from engaging in "discrimination" based on disability. The federal regulations require that the public entity "administer services, programs, and activities in the most integrated setting appropriate to the needs of qualified individuals with disabilities" (28 C.F.R. § 35.130(d)). Consistent with this regulation, the US Supreme Court has also declared for nonprisoners that the ADA prohibits unjustifiable segregation; according to the Court, "institutional placement of persons who can handle and benefit from community settings perpetuates unwarranted assumptions that persons so isolated are incapable or unworthy of participating in community life" (*Olmstead v. L.C.*, 1999, p. 600). Hence, such segregation "severely diminishes the everyday life activities of individuals, including . . . social contacts, work options, economic independence, educational advancement, and cultural enrichment" (p. 601).

The new 2010 federal regulations provide an integration requirement in prisons. These regulations require prisons to ensure that prisoners with disabilities "are housed in the most integrated setting appropriate to the needs of the individuals" (28 C.F.R. § 35.152(2)). The regulations prohibit prisons from placing inmates with disabilities "in inappropriate security classifications because no accessible cells or beds are available" (§ 35.152 (2)(i)). Inmates with disabilities may not be placed in medical areas "unless they are actually receiving medical care or treatment" (§ 35.152(2) (ii)). The regulations also require that even when segregation is allowed, the segregated facility must offer the same programs as those offered to the general prison population (§ 35.152(2)(iii)). Furthermore, the facility must not be so distant that it deprives prisoners of visitation with family members (§ 35.152(2)(iv)).

One can expect that the *Olmstead* case and the new 2010 regulations will have significant positive implications for beneficial integration of older prisoners with disabilities; but this will depend on future court interpretations involving inmates with disabilities. But because older prisoners have an average of three chronic health conditions (Kerbs, 2000b), the relevant section 35.152(2)(ii) might be interpreted by the courts as allowing mandatory segregation of older prisoners with disabilities—many of whom will need ongoing medical care, treatment, and monitoring by qualified medical personnel and specialists.

Title II cases in prisons. There are several lower-court cases that have held that prisoners have made valid claims of violation of Title II of the ADA. For example, in the case of *Love v. Westville Correction Center* (1996), a federal appellate court held that the prison violated the ADA when an inmate with quadriplegia was not allowed to access various facilities and educational and religious programs. In a federal district-court case, *Schmidt v. Odell* (1999), an inmate whose legs had been amputated below the knee claimed that the jail officials did not provide a required wheelchair or shower chair, which forced him to crawl or slide around on the floor. The court held that this was a violation of Title II.

In *Flynn v. Doyle* (2009), another federal district court found, among others things, that Title II violations can occur under the following conditions: denial or substantial delay in accommodating inmates who have hearing- and vision-related disabilities; separation of dining rooms for inmates who have mobility-related disabilities; and lack of wheelchair-accessible paths. In accord with the federal regulations (28 C.F.R. §§ 35.150– 151), the court held that facilities altered after the implementation date of the ADA must be "readily accessible to and usable" by prisoners with disabilities. Moreover, for an existing facility, "when viewed in its entirety," the services or programs must be accessible and usable (*Flynn v. Doyle,* 2009, pp. 879–880).

In *Purcell v. Pennsylvania Department of Corrections* (2006), a prisoner who had been diagnosed as having multiple psychological disorders claimed, among other things, that the prison violated Title II by refusing to circulate to the officers a memorandum about his Tourette-syndrome diagnosis. The district court suggested that such refusals may violate Title II of the ADA. In *King v. CDCR* (2007), a federal district court held that the confiscation of a cane from an inmate, which effectively resulted in denial of breakfast and church services for three months, violated Title II of the ADA. In *Kutrip v. City of St. Louis* (2009), the federal appellate court reversed a district court's decision that there was no violation of Title II when a jail did not offer the inmate a handicap-accessible shower facility. In *Phipps v. Sheriff of Cook County* (2009), a district court held that a prison's failure to provide wheelchair-accessible toilets, sinks, and shower facilities could violate Title II.

Validity of the ADA as Section 5 legislation. Even though the courts have clarified that Title II applies to prisons, it has recently become apparent that it will be difficult for a prisoner to obtain monetary damage awards for ADA violations in prison. The Constitution may be interpreted to prohibit the granting of such damages with regard to at least some form of Title II violations. The restriction against lawsuits against the state is provided by the Eleventh Amendment. It states: "The Judicial power of the United States shall not be construed to extend to any suit in law or equity, commenced or prosecuted against one of the United States by Citizens of another State, or by Citizens or Subjects of any Foreign State." Under this principle of "sovereign immunity" as declared in this amendment, states are immune from individuals' suits for damages. Though the text of the amendment states "Citizens of another State," the Court has interpreted that the Eleventh Amendment also applies to suits by its own citizens (see *Board of Trustees of the University of Alabama v. Garrett,* 2001).

However, Congress has a limited power to nullify this sovereign immunity and thus allow individuals to file lawsuits against states for monetary damages. This limited power of Congress is provided by Section 5 of the Fourteenth Amendment. Under this section, Congress may, by statute, abrogate sovereign immunity in order to "enforce" individuals' constitutional rights against states. The ADA nullifies sovereign immunity as follows:

> A State shall not be immune under the eleventh amendment to the Constitution of the United States from an action in Federal or State court of competent jurisdiction for a violation of this chapter. In any action against a State for a violation of the requirements of this chapter, remedies (including remedies both at law and in equity) are available for such a violation to the same extent as such remedies are available for such a violation in an action against any public or private entity other than a State. (42 U.S.C. §12202)

The central issue now is whether or not Title II is a statute that "enforces" existing constitutional rights. If an individual sues under Title II because of a state's Title II violation that also constitutes a constitutional violation, then Title II is clearly being used to "enforce" constitutional rights. For example, if a prison's lack of wheelchair-accessible cells causes inhumane living conditions to wheelchair users (as previously discussed in relation to the case of *Goodman v. Georgia* [2006]), then prison officials are violating both Title II and the Eighth Amendment. If this inmate files a suit claiming a Title II violation, courts will be very likely to consider that Title II is being used to "enforce" the Eighth Amendment. On the other hand, if an individual is using the ADA to challenge a state's conduct that violates the ADA while not violating any constitutional right, then it is possible that the courts might consider that the ADA is creating a new statutory right and not "enforcing" an existing constitutional right. In this situation, such a suit against a state could be barred. For example, if a wheelchair-using inmate is only claiming denial of access to some recreational programs because of inaccessible paths, without validly claiming a violation of the Eighth Amendment (participation in recreational programs is hardly a constitutional right), then the case would be much more difficult to sustain because the inmate would not be able to claim that Title II is "enforcing" a constitutional right.

If the legislative nullification of sovereign immunity is given for the purpose of something more than the enforcement of constitutional rights, then nullification of sovereign immunity is invalid and the immunity stands. The Supreme Court has clarified that valid Fourteenth Amendment Section 5 legislation must "enforce" a constitutional right and be a "congruent and proportional" response to the "pattern of discrimination by the States" (*Board of Trustees of the University of Alabama v. Garrett,* 2001, p. 374).

For example, in the aforementioned *Garrett* case, the US Supreme Court did not rule on Title II, but it did hold that Title I of the ADA failed the "congruence and proportionality" test; thus the Court did not consider Title I to be valid Section 5 legislation as it applied to state employers. Now that Title I suits for monetary damages against states are barred by the Court, a new question surfaces: Can individuals sue states for monetary damages in Title II cases? A clear answer to this question is essential to discussions regarding prison settings, because the defendants are state government entities in Title II cases. But the Court has not yet directly addressed this question. However, this issue was mentioned in *Tennessee v. Lane* (2004) and *United States v. Georgia* (2006). In *Lane,* the plaintiffs, individuals with paraplegia, argued that inaccessibility of the second floor of the state courthouse violated Title II of the ADA. The state argued that nullification of sovereign immunity by the ADA was invalid with regard to Title II suits, like Title I suits, and thus that state courthouses could not be sued by individuals. In response, the Court gave a limited answer by holding that for Title II cases, as applied to barriers that block access to courts, the nullification is valid because a person's lack of access to the courtroom violates both Title II of the ADA *and* the constitutional right of access to courts.

Even if Title II were declared invalid Section 5 legislation and lawsuits against states based on Title II were barred by the Eleventh Amendment's principle of sovereign immunity, plaintiffs would still have one remaining avenue for addressing their concerns under Title II: plaintiffs may be able to sue state officials for injunctive relief—that is, they may be able to obtain a court order requiring the removal of a Title II violation. In this regard, the Supreme Court has stated that even when an action for monetary damage is barred by sovereign immunity, an individual can still sue state officials for injunctive relief (see, e.g., *Board of Trustees of the University of Alabama v. Garrett,* 2001; *Ex parte Young,* 1908). For example, if a prison fails to provide a handicap-accessible cell, and if prisoners are barred from filing lawsuits due to sovereign immunity, a prisoner may nonetheless seek an injunction for specific performance from a court to mandate a remedy for the situation.

There is, however, a substantial barrier to achieving such successful injunctive relief, namely the prisoner's release from prison or transfer to another prison, which halts all such litigation by the dismissal of the case. Whereas a lawsuit for monetary awards seeks a retrospective remedy and targets the government's past wrongdoing (or wrong inaction), injunctive relief is about the government's rectification of current problems aside from monetary compensation. In other words, prison administrators can block a prisoner plaintiff from success with an injunctive relief filing by releasing the prisoner or transferring the prisoner to another facility. Once released or transferred, the (former) prisoner's case is usually dismissed. To correct for the limitations of individual prisoners filing for injunctive relief, there is the possibility of filing a class-action suit for injunctive relief among similarly situated inmates under the Federal Rule of Civil Procedure (§ 23(b)(2)) (see, e.g., *Armstrong v. Wilson,* 1997; *Flynn v. Doyle,* 2009).

It is quite possible that the US Supreme Court might eventually hold that Title II of the ADA is not a valid Section 5 legislation. This would foreclose the possibility of monetary damages for violations of Title II. Even if that occurs, an injunctive relief could still be available, as long as the inmate with disability stays in the same condition in the same institution, or if inmates in the similar circumstance in the same institution successfully become recognized as class-action plaintiffs. Despite such possible limitations, however, the ADA nonetheless gives strong protections to older inmates with disabilities. The equal protection benefits provided by the ADA keep it substantially applicable in prisons. As we have seen, the lower courts in Title II cases have held that a prison's denial of equal access to services and programs, or of auxiliary devices, to inmates with disabilities, violates the ADA.

Section 504 of the Rehabilitation Act

The ADA was based on Section 504 of the Rehabilitation Act of 1973, which prohibited recipients of federal funds from discriminating against individuals with disabilities. If prisoner plaintiffs are not successful in using the ADA to obtain monetary damages or injunctive relief, they may nonetheless be able to pursue damages and injunctive relief under the Rehabilitation Act. Along with Title II of the ADA, Section 504 of the Rehabilitation Act also protects prisoners from discrimination based on disabilities. The purpose of the Rehabilitation Act is primarily to provide rehabilitation services by establishing and enforcing barrier-free constructions. Section 504 provides the following mandate that prohibits discrimination against people with disabilities: "No otherwise qualified individual with a disability in the United States . . . shall, solely by reason of her or his disability, be excluded from the participation in, be denied the benefits of, or be subjected to discrimination under any program or activity receiving Federal financial assistance or under any program or activity conducted by any Executive agency" (29 U.S.C. § 794(a)). Title II of the ADA's comprehensive protection from discrimination goes beyond the Rehabilitation Act's level of protections. However, unlike the ADA, the Rehabilitation Act may be able to avoid issues of sovereign immunity. Whereas the ADA automatically applies to all states, the Rehabilitation Act applies only to those states and their agencies that choose to accept federal funds. When states take federal money, they waive their sovereign immunity. Of course, states are free to reject the Rehabilitation Act by refusing to accept federal funds. Unlike the ADA, which was enacted pursuant to Section 5 of the Fourteenth Amendment, the Rehabilitation Act applies to states based on the spending clause of Article I, Section 8 of the Constitution. Thus, the Rehabilitation Act does not face the same constitutional restrictions as does the ADA. The courts have recognized that the Rehabilitation Act is applicable to prisons (see *Bonner v. Lewis,* 1988; *Yeskey v. Pennsylvania Department of Corrections,* 1997). Hence the Rehabilitation Act appears to provide a platform for further advancement of rights for older prisoners with disabilities. Also, prisoner plaintiffs might possibly be allowed to file suits against states for monetary damages or injunctive relief via simultaneous claims that utilize both the ADA and the Rehabilitation Act jointly.

Conclusion

As we have seen, the Eighth Amendment to the US Constitution requires adequate medical care for older inmates. It also requires that older prisoners' living conditions must not be inhumane and that prisoners must be protected from predatory conduct by other prisoners. A prison official's deliberate indifference to an inmate's serious medical or security needs, or to inhumane prison conditions, violates the strictures of the Eighth Amendment. We have also seen that at least competent prisoners, including older inmates, have, at least to some extent, the right to refuse medical treatment.

The courts have given strong protections, under the ADA and the Rehabilitation Act, to older inmates with disabilities. Given the growing population of aging inmates in prisons, policymakers and prison officials should be aware of recent advancements in the rights of older prisoners with disabilities.

7

The Age-Segregation Debate

Anita N. Blowers, Jennifer M. Jolley,
and John J. Kerbs

According to the Bureau of Justice Statistics, there were 1.61 million federal and state prisoners with a sentence of one year or longer at the end of 2010 (Guerino, Harrison, and Sabol, 2012), with about 246,000 inmates aged 50 and older and nearly 1.4 million inmates under age 50. While it may seem surprising that age 50 serves as the defining line between younger and older inmates, most correctional researchers and state-level departments of corrections have adopted age 50 as the chronological starting point for defining older inmates (Aday, 2003, 1999). In fact, inmates typically experience a process of accelerated aging wherein their physiological age surpasses their chronological age by approximately twelve years (Anno et al., 2004; Shimkus, 2004). This process of accelerated aging occurs as a result of high-risk lifestyles and limited access to health care prior to incarceration (Kerbs, 2000b; Shimkus, 2004) and is further compounded by the strain of incarceration (Gal, 2002). Thus, a 50-year-old inmate is likely to be physiologically similar to a 62-year-old individual living as a free citizen.

In addition to experiencing a physiological process of accelerated aging, older inmates are also one of the fastest-growing special-needs populations in the US correctional system (Cox and Lawrence, 2010; Sterns et al., 2008; Thivierge-Rikard and Thompson, 2007). The number of prisoners aged 50 and older grew by about 450 percent between 1991 and 2008 (Camp and Camp, 1991; West and Sabol, 2009). Moreover, it is estimated that one-third of US prisoners will be 50 years of age and older in 2030 (Enders, Paterniti, and Meyers, 2005; Smyer and Burbank, 2009; Williams et al., 2006). Though the number of inmates aged 50 and older is rapidly increasing on an annual basis, the total prison population still includes a very large number of inmates under the age of 50. In short, mandatory sentencing policies such as three-strikes and truth-in-sentencing laws have led to an increase in both the number of persons entering prisons and the number of inmates who will grow old in prison while serving life sentences with and without the possibility of parole (Benekos and Merlo, 1995; Turner et al., 1995). The increased numbers of people in prison, combined with increased numbers of inmates who have longer sentences, have created a stacking effect: those with longer sentences remain in prison, as more people are added to the total, straining the capacity in facilities throughout the United States (Kerbs and Jolley, 2009a; Sterns et al., 2008).

This stacking effect has led to a unique drain on the already limited resources within the US correctional system, wherein prison administrators are simultaneously pressured to "develop and modify programs and strategies focused on the special challenges of the aging inmates" (Cox and Lawrence, 2010, p. 53) while delivering services to meet the needs of younger inmates. As noted earlier, inmates of all ages are typically exposed to a number of risk factors prior to incarceration that increase their likelihood of poor physical and mental health outcomes, including poverty, low levels of education, drug and alcohol abuse, and restricted access to health care, particularly at a young age (Anno et al., 2004; Gal, 2002; Hill et al., 2006; Sterns et al., 2008; Williams and Abraldes. Thus, younger and older inmates alike may require access to competent medical and mental health care. However, older inmates are even more likely to require access to a costly, complex, and specialized set of medical and mental health services due to the high prevalence of chronic diseases, terminal illnesses, functional impairments, and serious psychiatric disorders among inmates aged 50 and older (Maruschak, 2008; Maruschak and Beck, 2001).

The challenges of allocating limited resources to the care and custody of both younger and older inmates in a system that was designed for a population of younger inmates has sparked much debate among academics, policymakers, and prison administrators. Assessment of correctional policies, practices, and facilities has generated two positions on how best to simultaneously meet the needs of younger and older inmates. The first position advocates for the continued integration of younger and older inmates into the same correctional facilities. The second position advocates for the segregation of older inmates from younger inmates. For both positions, the integration position and the segregation position, advocates build their arguments around three key points: access to and utilization of quality medical and mental health services, maintenance of social order in prisons, and creation of age-appropriate social environments. This chapter assesses each of these three points by summarizing the evidence from both positions, the age-integration perspective and the age-segregation perspective. For each of the three points, the chapter also presents research findings on the needs of older inmates and the fit between their functional limitations and the formal and informal expectations they are expected to fulfill while negotiating the daily challenges of prison life.

Access to and Utilization of Quality Medical and Mental Health Services

As noted earlier, inmates who are chronologically 50 years of age are more likely to physiologically resemble nonincarcerated individuals who are 62 years of age (Anno et al., 2004; Shimkus, 2004). Poor outcomes related to the process of accelerated aging experienced by inmates have been documented by studies that compare the physiological status of older inmates with that of similarly aged individuals living as free citizens. On average, older inmates have more chronic diseases as compared to older free adults outside prison (Anno et al., 2004; Colsher et al., 1992; Curtin, 2007; Fazel et al., 2001; Williams and Abraldes, 2007); additionally, older inmates are more likely to spend a longer time in bed recovering from injury or illness compared to their counterparts outside prison (Curtin, 2007). Other research findings describe the substantial distribution of adverse medical conditions across aging inmates, including the distribution of a wide range of chronic diseases across a large proportion of older inmates. For example, researchers who surveyed inmates aged 45 and older in state and federal correctional facilitates found that 68 percent of the inmates reported having some type of physical or mental health problem (Haugebrook et al., 2010; Maruschak, 2008). Another study, published in the *Journal of the American Medical Association,* found that inmates aged 55 and older have an average of three chronic medical conditions, and that up to 20 percent of the inmates have a mental illness (Mitka, 2004). Loeb and AbuDagga (2006) found that a wide range of chronic medical conditions affect older inmates, including sensory deficits such as vision and hearing problems, arthritis, back problems, hypertension, cardiovascular conditions, psychiatric conditions, respiratory diseases, endocrine disorders, substance abuse, and cognitive disorders such as dementia. Further expanding this list of chronic diseases are the extensive dental and periodontal needs that older inmates have, as noted by Aday (2003).

The degenerative effects of these and other chronic medical conditions are particularly pronounced for older prisoners because co-morbidities are found in approximately 85 percent of older inmates (Loeb and AbuDagga, 2006; Loeb, Steffensmeier, and Myco 2007); as the number of chronic medical conditions climbs to three or more for most older prisoners (Loeb and AbuDagga, 2006; Loeb, Steffensmeier, and Myco 2007), the likelihood of functional impairment also increases, making it substantially more difficult for older inmates to negotiate daily life (Smyer and Burbank, 2009). Functional impairments experienced by older inmates may also occur in relationship to mental health disturbances. An increasing number of people outside prison are not only suffering from mental disorders, but also entering the US correctional system (Adams and Ferrandino, 2008; Aday, 2003; Fellner, 2008; Hill et al., 2006; Williams, 2007). For example, in 1983, 6.4 percent of inmates in jails and prisons were documented as having a serious mental illness, but in 1996 through 1997, 16 percent of inmates in jails and prisons were documented as having a serious mental illness (Torrey et al., 2010). Thus, in less than 15 years, the percentage of seriously mentally ill prisoners almost tripled. In fact, there are currently more mentally ill individuals housed in correctional facilities than in mental hospitals and institutions in the United States (Williams et al., 2006).

One particular mental health disorder that is likely to be associated with older inmates is dementia. While some older prisoners may arrive in prison with cognitive impairments, others will develop such impairments after incarceration (Williams and Abraldes, 2007). The rate of new cases of dementia outside prison is projected to double in the next four decades, and the rate of new cases of dementia within the US correctional system is expected to be two to three times greater than the rate outside prison (Wilson and Barboza, 2010). A complicating factor that is likely to impede a timely diagnosis of dementia for older inmates is the strict regimentation of daily prison life; such regimentation tends to hinder a detection of mild cognitive impairment and early-stage dementia, making it more likely that an appropriate diagnosis for older inmates with dementia will not occur until the problem reaches more advanced stages (Sterns et al., 2008). Further complications can also occur in relation to co-morbidities; and as noted above, most older inmates have three or more chronic health conditions. A high prevalence of co-occurring disorders among older inmates with dementia is also the case. In fact, older prisoners with dementia have, on average, two or three additional medical conditions (Wilson and Barboza, 2010). Even with state-of-the-art health care, most prisoners with dementia will eventually need nursing care twenty-four hours a day in protected units. As Wilson and Barboza noted, "the correctional system is already the largest provider of mental health services in the country. Very soon, we may also become the largest provider of skilled nursing and dementia services" (2010, p. 14).

Older inmates who must contend with the degenerative effects of multiple chronic diseases face significant challenges in negotiating even basic tasks, including the five basic activities of daily living: bathing, eating, toileting, dressing, and transferring (Williams et al., 2006). A range of medical services, assistive devices, and environmental accommodations are needed to bridge the lack of fit that occurs when an individual with altered physical and mental capacities can no longer perform required daily tasks. This lack of fit, referred to as functional impairment, can be prominent for older inmates as they struggle to perform daily tasks with deteriorating physical and mental dexterity in an environment that was generally designed for young and healthy inmates who have no functional limitations (Williams et al., 2006). For example, inmates with mobility impairment are likely to require aids such as canes, walkers, or wheelchairs (Anno et al., 2004; Hill et al., 2006). Frail inmates and epileptics will require assignments to bottom bunks. To avoid the need to climb stairs, older prisoners with heart disease and respiratory problems should be housed in first-floor cells. Even older prisoners without mobility impairments could benefit from additional supervision and assistance in situations that involve, for example, a risk of falling, as is the case when older prisoners are required to walk while being handcuffed (Hill et al., 2006). Certain chronic-care patients, including those with respiratory problems, also need special placements, in this case in nonsmoking cells or units; moreover, prisoners with certain spinal cord injuries must be assigned to air-conditioned units and prisons. It is especially important that correctional staff make accommodations when responding to cognitively impaired prisoners who have a diminished ability to comprehend and remember. Correctional staff need to be sensitive to the fact that these prisoners will have difficulty following multistep directions and may lack the capacity to follow some of the basic behavioral expectations that are part of the normal prison routine (Adams and Ferrandino, 2008; Fellner, 2007; Williams and Abraldes, 2007; Wilson and Barboza, 2010).

Given the fact that chronic diseases are progressive, many older inmates will experience increasing levels of functional impairment, and a number of older inmates with chronic diseases will also reach a terminal stage while in prison (Quinn, 2009). For instance, 97 percent of all prisoners in the state penitentiary in Angola (Louisiana) will eventually die in prison. In Texas, more than 100 prisoners die behind bars each year. Nationally, the US Justice Department has estimated that about 4,000 prisoners died behind bars in 2002. Most of these inmates are elderly (Williams, 2007). Treating terminally ill inmates is difficult at best; they tend to cycle in and out of infirmaries and hospitals, and they are usually isolated from their friends and families during a time when access to social support is critical. Needless to say, these inmates need a high standard of medical care that extends far beyond that which is typically provided to the general inmate population (Aday, 2003). In short, the prison health-care system was not designed to provide sophisticated and intensive care to large numbers of chronically ill and elderly inmates.

From a medical perspective, a majority of older inmates need a combination of health-care services, assistive devices (e.g., walkers, wheelchairs, hearing aids, and breathing aids), and accommodations (e.g., bathroom handrails); furthermore, rulings issued by the Supreme Court and various lower courts have consistently held that inmates retain the right to basic medical care (Commission on Safety and Abuse in America's Prisons, 2006; Curtin, 2007; Mitka, 2004; Quinn, 2009). Nonetheless, medical need and a constitutional right to health care have not proven to be sufficiently powerful factors in increasing the number of older inmates who are given access to adequate medical care (Aday, 2003; Anno et al., 2004; California Department of Corrections and Rehabilitation, 2006; Commission on Safety and Abuse in America's Prisons, 2006; Curtin, 2007; Greifinger, 2007; Hill et al., 2006; Kerbs and Jolley, 2009b; Quinn, 2009; Williams, 2007). In terms of service delivery, US prisons still have a long way to go in ensuring that inmates have access to and opportunities for the appropriate utilization of cost-effective and quality medical care.

The Commission on Safety and Abuse in America's Prisons (2006) identified several systemic barriers that prevent inmates from receiving quality health care, and as expected, the inadequate funding of prison health-care systems is a significant barrier. In fact, it is generally estimated that the current cost of providing housing, programming, and medical care to older inmates is two to three times the cost of providing housing, programming, and medical care to younger inmates (Aday, 2003; Anno et al., 2004; Hill et al., 2006; Moore and Unwin, 2002; Price, 2006; Zimbardo, 1994). Even if costs are shifted to the individual inmate, lack of funding still functions as a powerful barrier in part because inmates are not entitled to receive medical coverage through Medicare and Medicaid. Even when prisons charge inmates a required co-payment, as some are currently doing, it does not appear that inmates are receiving quality health-care services or adequate access to such services. Furthermore, the provision of quality medical care to inmates has been compromised by the failure to consistently screen for infectious diseases, and the failure to strategically build collaborative partnerships between correctional facilities and community-based health-care providers.

One of the three main points addressed in the age-segregation debate is related to older inmates' access to and their appropriate utilization of quality medical and mental health services. Within this context, both the proponents of the age-integration perspective and the proponents of the age-segregation perspective have cases to make. Both perspectives lend critical insights into options that might best advance different aspects of care; therefore, both perspectives should be viewed as useful in relation to this debate.

Arguing for the Age-Integration Perspective

Proponents of the age-integration perspective argue for the integration or mainstreaming of elderly inmates with prisoners of all ages in the general prison population as a way of ensuring that older prisoners have equal access to existing prison programs, services, and activities. Advocates for mainstreaming point to the importance of complying with the requirements set forth in two key pieces of federal legislation: the Rehabilitation Act of 1973 and the Americans with Disabilities Act of 1990. These pieces of legislation define, protect, and promote the right of equal access to facilities, programs, services, and activities for disabled persons. While older prisoners are not necessarily disabled, they are far more likely (as compared to younger inmates) to be disabled, to become disabled, or to develop conditions that require special accommodations (Fazel et al., 2001; Williams et al., 2006, 2009). Thus, disability legislation becomes important in determining if older prisoners' rights are being violated. Furthermore, disability legislation provides an important framework for assessing the specific ways in which age-integration versus age-segregation approaches could support or compromise disabled inmates' equal access to existing programming, burden the correctional system with liability should disabled inmates' right to equal access be compromised, and increase the degree to which the correctional system would be required to provide accommodations to promote equal access to existing programming.

In terms of providing for equal access to all existing programming, the Rehabilitation Act requires that both the federal government and programs receiving federal funding cease discriminatory practices toward disabled persons. Specifically, as per Section 504 of the Rehabilitation Act: "No otherwise qualified individual with handicaps in the United States . . . shall, solely by reason of his handicap, be excluded from the participation in, be denied the benefits of, or be subjected to discrimination under any program or activity receiving Federal financial assistance" (29 U.S.C. § 794(a)). Building from the Rehabilitation Act of 1973, the Americans with Disabilities Act (ADA) of 1990 not only recognizes an unprecedented right of access on behalf of disabled Americans (Robbins, 1996), but also provides characteristically broad coverage of physical and mental disabilities. Furthermore, the ADA provides disabled inmates with equal access to facilities, participation in programs and proceedings, and accommodations within a facility (Paz, 2007). Examples of the ways in which the ADA has been applied in prison settings to promote disabled inmates' right to equal access include

- Increased access to and use of the prison dining hall and library (after declaring that use of these facilities constituted an activity).
- Participation of hearing-impaired inmates in prison counseling sessions, administrative and disciplinary hearings, and medical treatment and diagnosis by providing an interpreter.
- Access of visually-disabled inmates to the same reading and educational opportunities offered to fully sighted inmates through provision of recording devices and large-print materials.
- Access of mobility-impaired inmates to and use of facility-based programming and activities through provision of wheelchairs and other assistive devices (Paz, 2007; Robbins, 1996).

In short, advocates for mainstreaming are therefore concerned that if elderly inmates were to be housed in separate units or facilities, the segregated inmates would be placed in unsuitable settings that are not program-rich (Anno et al., 2004; Curtin, 2007; Florida House of Representatives, 1999), and therefore would be denied equal access to the same programs, services, and activities that are already provided to inmates in the general prison population. Furthermore, advocates for mainstreaming are concerned that building separate, more specialized facilities for older inmates may open the door for prisoner litigation, because inmates may perceive differences between the facilities and programming as unfair (Curtin, 2007). Finally, it should be noted that advocates for mainstreaming do not discuss the quantity, quality, and cost-effectiveness of existing programs, services, and activities. In sum, the argument for an age-integration perspective rests on the notion of promoting equal access to programming.

Arguing for the Age-Segregation Perspective

Proponents of the age-segregation perspective argue for the custody and care of elderly inmates within separate units or facilities as a way of ensuring that older prisoners have access to medical and mental health services that are cost-effective and high-quality (i.e., tailored to specifically meet the medical and mental health needs of older inmates). As noted earlier, a high proportion of older inmates suffer from multiple chronic diseases, serious psychiatric disorders such as dementia, functional limitations, and terminal illnesses (Loeb and AbuDagga, 2006; Loeb, Steffensmeier, and Myco, 2007; Maruschak, 2008; Maruschak and Beck, 2001; Mitka, 2004; Quinn, 2009; Smyer and Burbank, 2009; Williams and Abraldes, 2007;

Wilson and Barboza, 2010). At the same time, the US correctional system is not designed to provide the kind of medical and mental health services, assistive devices, and accommodations that constitute both a necessary and a sufficient standard of care for a group of inmates beset with serious medical needs (Aday, 2003; Anno et al., 2004; California Department of Corrections and Rehabilitation, 2006; Commission on Safety and Abuse in America's Prisons, 2006; Curtin, 2007; Greifinger, 2007; Hill et al., 2006; Kerbs and Jolley, 2009b; Quinn, 2009; Williams, 2007). It is this lack of fit between older inmates and the US correctional system—in which older inmates are not provided access to quality care that is effective in meeting their serious medical needs—that is central to the argument espoused by proponents of the age-segregation perspective.

In short, age-segregation proponents cite the ruling of the US Supreme Court in *Estelle v. Gamble* (1976), wherein the failure of a prison to provide a community standard of care (i.e., services that would otherwise be available in the community) to meet an inmate's serious medical needs, constitutes a violation of the Eighth Amendment's prohibition against "cruel and unusual punishment." Thus, due to the prison's control over an inmate's body, it is incumbent upon the prison to provide medical care that is capable of addressing serious medical needs; and as noted by Williams et al. (2006), elderly inmates' extensive need for adaptive services supports a very plausible rationale for separate facilities. Given the degree to which existing correctional facilities would need to be adapted to meet the medical and mental health needs of a growing population of aging inmates, age-segregation advocates argue that creating specialized units or facilities for the care and custody of older inmates is the optimal solution. Specialized age-segregated units and facilities would create specific opportunities for the cost-effective provision of quality medical and mental health services that are capable of addressing the unique physiological and psychological needs of elderly inmates, and the provision of assistive devices and accommodations that are capable of remediating the unique functional limitations experienced by older inmates.

Providing cost-effective medical and mental health care. According to a National Institute of Corrections report (Anno et al., 2004), the per capita cost of incarcerating an elderly inmate is more than twice the cost of incarcerating the average inmate in the general population, with approximately $60,000 to $70,000 spent per year per elderly inmate as compared to $27,000 per year for a younger inmate. The substantially higher cost of housing an elderly inmate is due in large part to older inmates' greater health-care needs, including hospitalization, medications, diagnostic tests, and skilled nursing care. Correctional health-care spending in general increased by 27 percent from 1997 to 2001 (Anno et al., 2004; Shimkus, 2004); furthermore, it is generally accepted that health-care expenditures for elderly inmates are disproportionately responsible for overall increases in correctional medical spending (Curtin, 2007). Beyond the cost of providing direct medical care to inmates, increases in correctional spending can also be attributed to custodial costs, as correctional officers must accompany inmates receiving medical services that are not available within the prison health-care system and are therefore outsourced to clinics, practices, and hospitals outside the prison system (Hill et al., 2006). In short, the cost of incarcerating older inmates will only continue to increase as the number of older inmates grows and as the adequacy of the prison health-care system improves. Ironically, "with increased care comes increased duration of treatment for inmates, i.e. the better the treatment the inmate receives, the longer that inmate will live, and the longer the prison system will have to care for him or her" (Williams, 2006, p. 29). Thus with the improvement of preventive health services, inmates will live longer, thereby increasing both the number of elderly prisoners as well as their length of stay in prison (Aday, 2003; Curtin, 2007; Williams, 2007).

If left unchecked, the rising cost of providing health care to inmates in general and to elderly inmates in particular will exceed annual correctional budgets. Consider, for example that correctional medical-care spending in recent years doubled in California (Curtin, 2007). Additionally, Vitiello and Kelso (2004) performed some rough calculations and found that the cost of incarcerating elderly inmates will not only continue to increase over time, but will also exceed California's total correctional budget. Specifically, the calculations assumed that the cost of maintaining older prisoners in California would rise modestly to around $87,500 per year. When this figure is multiplied by the projected number of older prisoners aged 60 and older, the anticipated housing costs for these older prisoners in 2025 will exceed $4 billion—about equivalent to what California spent in 2002 to maintain its entire Department of Corrections and Rehabilitation (Vitiello and Kelso, 2004).

North Carolina, Wisconsin, and Virginia present additional evidence of the soaring cost of providing health care to inmates and the disproportionate amount of spending being directed to the medical needs of older inmates. For example, in a 2006 report published by the North Carolina Department of Correction (Division of Prisons), it was noted that health-care expenditures for all inmates amounted to $583 million across three years; and looking specifically at the 2004–2005 fiscal year, health-care expenditures for all inmates totaled over $88 million. Although inmates aged 50 and older constituted about 10 percent of the total inmate population as of 2005, 28 percent of the total health-care expenditures for the 2004–2005 fiscal year (nearly $25 million) was accounted for by inmates aged 50 and older (Price, 2006). In terms of outsourcing medical care during the 2004–2005 fiscal year, over $53 million was spent on external medical care; external medical care for inmates aged 50 and older accounted for the largest proportion of the total amount spent on outsourced medical care (over $18 million, or 34 percent). Additionally, the average annual cost of health-care expenditures (i.e., dental, medical, mental health, and pharmaceutical expenditures) for inmates aged 50 and older ($7,159) was nearly four times the average cost of health-care expenditures for inmates younger than 50 ($1,919) (Price, 2006). Dramatic increases in health-care expenditures for inmates in general and for older inmates in particular have also been documented for prisoners in Virginia and Wisconsin (Curtin, 2007; Johnson, 2008).

Costs related to the delivery of specialized health-care services to older inmates are on a steep upward climb in part because of the growing number of older inmates and the degree to which these inmates have serious and complex medical needs. However, the way in which health-care services are delivered in the US correctional system also contributes to the rising costs of medical expenditures for older inmates. Hence it is important to understand how the duplication and fragmentation of health-care services across many different facilities form a structural barrier to containing these skyrocketing costs (Anno et al., 2004). The duplication of specialized medical and mental health services, in addition to the duplicative distribution of assistive devices and accommodations, occurs because the entire population of aging inmates is spread across many different US facilities. Thus, costs increase in part because prison-specific medical and mental health service delivery systems, along with the physical layout of the facilities themselves, must be adapted to meet the needs of the particular group of older inmates located within each facility. The fragmentation of services occurs in tandem with the duplication of services because it is not feasible to adapt and extend the capabilities of each and every prison-based health-care service delivery system that serves a group of older inmates (Anno et al., 2004). The increasing medical and mental health needs of older inmates require that prisons contract with community-based providers for the delivery of subspecialty care, inpatient procedures, and rehabilitative services within each facility. Thus, expensive outsourced health care is duplicated across a myriad of facilities that are not equipped to provide the range of services that older inmates need. The contracting of similar services across a number of different prison facilities is driving up the overall cost of older inmates' health care because arrangements must be made to transport and secure inmates who must temporarily leave the prison to receive medical services in the community (Kerbs, 2000a).

Advocates for the age-segregation perspective argue that centralizing the custody and care of older inmates within specialized facilities or units would eliminate the costs incurred by the duplication and fragmentation of service delivery across multiple poorly equipped facilities (Anno et al., 2004). Centralizing the custody and care of older inmates within a designated number of facilities or wings would give correctional administrators greater control over the planning and evaluation of specialized service delivery systems for older inmates. Instead of patching together clusters of geriatric-specific services and accommodations across a large number of prison facilities for a relatively small number of older inmates per facility, limited resources could be directed toward a concentration of older inmates for maximum effect. Thus, only a limited number of facilities would need to be retrofitted with accommodations or constructed with physical layouts that are designed to support the activities of older inmates who have a variety of functional limitations (Williams and Abraldes, 2007). Furthermore, only a limited number of prison-based health-care service delivery systems would need to be adapted and extended in order to meet older inmates' diverse and specialized health-care needs.

Ultimately, consolidation of the older inmate population among a limited number of designated facilities or units facilitates a more cost-effective manner of providing health-care services to the entire inmate population. Specialized services for geriatric and medically compromised inmates would be provided only in facilities where they are needed and consistently utilized, while a more basic range of health-care services would be provided in facilities that house younger inmates. In short, cost savings will be realized because the medical needs and utilization patterns of the majority of inmates housed in a given facility would determine the distribution of prison health-care services across facilities. Furthermore, the volume of outsourced medical care could be reduced and cost savings realized by strategically increasing the prison-based health-care system's capacity to meet the needs of older inmates (Aday, 2003; Anno et al., 2004; Curtin, 2007; Kerbs and Jolley, 2009b).

Not surprisingly, some states have identified significant cost savings associated with age segregation. Virginia, for example, runs a separate facility designed to meet the age- and medically-specific needs of a population of geriatric and terminally ill inmates (Johnson, 2008). The average annual cost of housing an inmate in this specialized facility is $22,299 and is only slightly higher than the average annual cost of housing an inmate in Virginia's other prisons ($21,079). In fact, this specialized facility has one of the lowest overall medical expense budgets out of the entire Virginia correctional system. Furthermore, the Virginia Department of Corrections found that it is able to provide a more cost-effective approach to preventing, diagnosing, and managing inmates' diseases as compared to the services provided by the private sector. More specifically, in 2006 the average yearly cost per inmate housed in a correctional nursing home with on-site hospital care was far lower ($25,395) than the average yearly cost for private nursing homes without hospital care ($56,940 to $66,430) (Johnson, 2008).

Providing access to quality medical and mental health care. Despite steep increases in correctional health-care budgets, prison systems are still failing to provide adequate medical and mental health care to meet inmates' needs (Aday, 2003; Anno et al., 2004; California Department of Corrections and Rehabilitation, 2006; Commission on Safety and Abuse in America's Prisons, 2006; Curtin 2007; Hill et al., 2006; Kerbs and Jolley, 2009b; Williams, 2007; Williams et al., 2006). For example, control over the provision of health-care services to inmates in the California correctional system has been transferred to a federal judge. Moreover, the inadequacy of medical care in the California correctional system as recently as 2005 had reached a point where one prisoner was dying needlessly from medical malpractice or neglect every six to seven days (Commission on Safety and Abuse in America's Prisons, 2006).

While age-segregation advocates argue for a cost-effective approach to the custody and care of older inmates, they also argue for providing older inmates with access to and appropriate utilization of quality medical and mental health services. One critical area that is addressed by age-segregation advocates is the lack of correctional and medical staff who are specifically trained in gerontology and the provision of geriatric medicine (Anno et al., 2004). Thus, age-segregation supporters suggest that the few correctional and medical staff who are trained in gerontology and geriatric medicine should be concentrated in a limited number of age-segregated facilities to improve the quality of care that is delivered to older inmates. Moreover, strategic recruitment and retention efforts could be used to populate specialized facilities with staff members who would receive ongoing and advanced training in gerontology, chronic disease, and the comprehensive delivery of bio-psycho-social services (Aday, 2003; Anno et al., 2004; Hill et al., 2006; Sterns et al., 2008). Even correctional officers could be trained to observe and report changes in inmates' physiological, mental, and social status, which could assist medical staff in orienting the delivery of older inmates' health care toward a more preventive approach to treatment (Hill et al., 2006; Sterns et al., 2008). Furthermore, equipping prison staff with a vocabulary of aging could improve the overall quality of health-care delivery in specialized units by helping medical staff to more effectively tailor the available resources to the distribution of inmates' medical and mental health needs. Interestingly, the focus that age-segregation advocates place on the delivery of quality medical care to older inmates is well supported by the Commission on Safety and Abuse in America's Prisons (2006), which suggested that correctional systems should enhance the delivery of custodial and care-based services by staffing facilities with correctional officers who are trained in health-care.

The Maintenance of Social Order in Prison

Although correctional administrators, prison staff, and correctional officers try to achieve a number of goals when running prisons (e.g., the provision of rehabilitative and recreational programming), the maintenance of social order in prison is of primary concern. More specifically, prison administrators are profoundly concerned with their efforts to run orderly, safe, and secure prison facilities characterized by a well-behaved prison population that follows the rules, regulations, policies, and procedures. That said, studies from the 1970s confirmed that aging inmates rarely victimize other inmates; indeed, they are exceedingly well-behaved compared to their younger counterparts, and they are less likely to violate prison rules and less prone to try to escape (see Rubenstein, 1982, 1984). For example, Goetting found that "a significantly lower proportion of the elderly inmates had been found guilty of breaking prison rules during their current incarceration than had their younger counterparts (16.47% compared with 48.10%)" (1984, p. 19). Other researchers have also found similar results when studying age-graded differences in the proportions of younger and older inmates who have received disciplinary reports for violating prison rules (see, e.g., Wilson and Vito, 1986). Finally, research has shown that only a very small proportion of older prisoners (about 9.5 percent) are responsible for "serious" disciplinary problems in prison (McShane and Williams, 1990).

Aging inmates appear to be so well-behaved that they may have a stabilizing or calming effect on younger inmates (Aday, 2003); that is, a heterogeneous prison population of young and old inmates together could be viewed as optimal because older prisoners may reduce the likelihood of riots initiated by younger inmates (Krajick, 1979; Vito and Wilson, 1985). The argument is that older inmates can serve as important role models for younger, more volatile prisoners (Aday, 2003). Unfortunately, most of the research examining the impact older inmates have on younger inmates has involved prisoners between the ages of 35 and 50 (Johnson, 1988; Ornduff, 1996; Rikard and Rosenburg, 2007). Moreover, as the age and physical disparities widen between younger and more elderly inmates, the calming influence is likely to dissipate (Curtin, 2007). For example, Rikard and Rosenburg suggest that "senior inmates are no longer viewed by more junior inmates, relatively unquestioningly, as wiser and more steeped in prison culture, and thus older inmates are no longer guaranteed the respect and protection historically mandated by the [prisoner code]" (2007, p. 157). Thus it is not clear whether the stabilizing effect holds true for the oldest of the old in prison, but some studies have confirmed the presence of this purported calming effect. For example, when prison administrators make conscious efforts to increase the mean age of inmates in a prison by transferring younger inmates to other prisons, they have documented decreases in violence in the former facility (Mabli et al., 1979).

Even though the presence of older prisoners may calm younger prisoners, older prisoners may have their own difficulties when it comes to following prison rules and regulations. For example, inmates with cognitive impairment cannot be expected to remember or follow multistep directions (Wilson and Barboza, 2010). The challenge is that prisons operate with a hierarchical, militaristic approach of strict obedience to policies and procedures that govern all behaviors. Thus, violating prison rules leads to punishment, but the logic of punishment and deterrence falters if prisoners do not consistently and meaningfully control their behavior due to untreated mental impairments (i.e., either mental illness or organic brain damage) (Fellner, 2008). Hence, correctional administrators have to balance the maintenance of order while trying to avoid the punishment of certain prisoners for behavior that is beyond their control due to mental illness or organic brain damage that blocks their ability to clearly understand the rules or understand that rules have been violated (Adams and Ferrandino, 2008).

As inmates with mental and cognitive impairments age, they are also more likely to have greater difficulties socializing with inmates; furthermore, such deficits in socializing can have harmful consequences, including victimization and "acting out" behavior (Adams and Ferrandino, 2008; Fellner, 2008). One study found that inmates with mental illness, as compared to inmates without mental illness, were nearly one and a half times more likely to be injured and three times more likely to be sexually assaulted during their incarceration (Delgado and Humm-Delgado, 2009). As Fellner stated, "prison authorities confronting persons with serious mental disorders keep trying to fit these square pegs into the round holes of standard prison policies and procedures. Not surprisingly, the effort fails" (2008, p. 1080). For mentally ill inmates, assimilation into the prison culture can be harmful and they may need to be sheltered to keep them safe (Adams and Ferrandino, 2008; Fellner, 2008).

Even older inmates who do not have mental and cognitive impairments can have trouble assimilating safely into mainstream prison culture. Some older inmates, for example, experience problems related to inmate-on-inmate victimization, fear of victimization, and perceived risk of victimization (Kerbs and Jolley, 2007). In comparison to younger inmates, older inmates tend to report higher levels of anxiety and nervousness, and an inmate's perception of the risk of abuse may intensify as the inmate ages and becomes more physically and emotionally frail (Aday, 2003). The following example illustrates the tensions these older inmates often feel. Elmore Elliot, a 64-year-old prisoner in a New Hampshire facility, pled guilty to manslaughter in the early 1990s. After four hospital visits, two bypass surgeries, and the installation of a pacemaker, he spoke to an interviewer about his day-to-day experience. "It's like living in a minefield, when you're my age, in a place like this," Elliot said. "You don't know what you're going to step on next, whether it's going to blow up in your face" ("The Price of Punishment," 2000, at 00:52). Similarly, Jonathan Turley, legal scholar and noted expert on older prisoners, states: "We all know grandparents who complain they're afraid of walking at night because of crime. Imagine being geriatric in a neighborhood where everyone is certifiably violent" (Jonathan Turly, cited in Gubler and Petersilia, 2006, p. 6).

Kerbs and Jolley (2009a), in their review of the literature, suggest that the sociocultural environment in prison provides some explanation as to why older inmates perceive higher risks of victimization. Similar to the elderly outside the prison system, older inmates may find that they no longer get the respect they once received when they were younger. Aging inmates may experience a loss of social status as they find themselves assigned to a lower rung within the prison culture's hierarchy; thus, they may be at significant risk of victimization by younger, more aggressive inmates. For example, Kerbs and Jolley (2007) found that significant proportions of older prisoners reported being psychologically victimized (e.g., approximately 25 percent reported being threatened with fake punches), economically victimized (e.g., approximately 28 percent had things in their cells stolen by other inmates), physically attacked and assaulted (approximately 11 percent), and sexually harassed (e.g., approximately 11 percent were the target of unwanted verbal comments, groping, staring, touching, or grabbing); moreover, younger prisoners were often identified as the perpetrators of this victimization. Such victimization is also compounded by the fact that many older inmates are sex offenders, and generally inmates with this type of criminal background are more likely to be disrespected by their fellow inmates, regardless of their age (Flynn, 1998, 2000; Kerbs and Jolley, 2007, 2009a, 2009b).

Arguing for the Age-Integration Perspective

For all of these considerations related to social order, policymakers should consider whether or not the best interests of the older inmate are more likely to be advanced in age-integrated or age-segregated settings. Proponents of age-integrated settings typically suggest that the mixing of younger and older inmates will help to maintain social order by calming younger inmates. While the calming effect of older prisoners on younger prisoners may exist, some suggest that the quantitative evaluations of this purported effect may be methodologically flawed (Kerbs and Jolley, 2009b), rendering this finding suspect.

Arguing for the Age-Segregation Perspective

The majority of the evidence related to social order appears to support the use of age-segregated units and facilities that are dedicated to older prisoners. New approaches are needed for responding to older inmates who have mental and cognitive impairments (Adams and Ferrandino, 2008; Fellner, 2007; Williams and Abraldes, 2007; Wilson and Barboza, 2010). Correctional administrators must be creative in developing and maintaining disciplinary systems that keep order amid the cognitive confusion and emotional problems presented by older and chronically ill inmates (Anno et al., 2004). The use of separate facilities for older inmates who have mental and cognitive problems may provide more opportunities to establish special milieus that can allow inmates with mental health issues to function more effectively and in a manner that reduces their risk of victimization by other (especially younger) inmates. The use of dedicated facilities also enables prison officials to account for different levels of cognitive ability when designing disciplinary and work policies (Curtin 2007; Aday, 2003).

Those who advocate for dedicated facilities for older inmates also argue that this type of arrangement enhances inmate safety for older prisoners, many of whom feel vulnerable to the intimidating and predatory behavior of younger inmates, and many of whom are victimized by younger inmates when mainstreamed into age-integrated facilities (Aday, 2003; Curtin, 2007; Florida House of Representatives, 1999; Kerbs and Jolley, 2007; Ornduff, 1996; Rikard and Rosenburg, 2007; Stojkovic, 2007; Vega and Silverman, 1988). Indeed, older prisoners should not be used as a potential calming agent when there is little evidence to support the assumption that older inmates are capable of assisting correctional officers and staff in maintaining social order. Correctional officers and staff (not inmates) are charged with and equipped for the responsibility of maintaining social order; hence it seems inappropriate to saddle aging inmates with the dubious responsibility of calming aggressive younger inmates in age-integrated settings.

The Creation of Age-Appropriate Environments

This chapter has defined the fit between inmates and the prison facility in relationship to the degree to which medical services, assistive devices, and accommodations are provided to support the treatment of inmates' serious medical needs as well as their daily levels of functioning. Thus, the fit between inmates and the prison facility has been targeted to a specific discussion of the ways in which the prison environment influences the health of inmates, including their ability to engage in daily self-care. In this section, the fit between inmates and the prison facility is examined more broadly to include a discussion of the ways in which daily conditions of confinement influence older prisoners' general sense of well-being and engagement in age-appropriate activities. Daily conditions of confinement include a broad range of physical circumstances, correctional expectations, and programming options. By imposing a broad range of conditions on inmates, the prison environment substantially influences the degree to which inmates feel comfortable (or uncomfortable) in their daily surroundings, and the degree to which they are (or are not) stimulated by opportunities for physical, mental, and social engagement.

In the discussion that follows, a broad range of information is provided regarding the ways in which the daily conditions of confinement differentially influence older inmates' general sense of well-being and engagement in age-appropriate activities as compared to younger inmates. Specifically, as individuals age, their biological, psychological, and social capacities and needs change. Routine conditions of confinement in a correctional system that was primarily designed for a population of young inmates do not fit well with older inmates' changing bio-psycho-social status.

In terms of the daily physical conditions of the typical prison facility, limited temperature control, lack of adequate lighting, loud noises, and crowded facilities present problems for older inmates (Aday, 2003). Older inmates generally have difficulty coping with the typical routines of the prison day and feel more agitated when they cannot escape from the continuous noise and distracting activities of other inmates. They tend to be uncomfortable in large groups and need more privacy and time alone (Aday, 2003; Crawley and Sparks, 2006; Sterns et al., 2008). Furthermore, older inmates may struggle in completing routine tasks and in attending correctional programming within the context of the typical prison facility's layout and the inflexibility of the normal prison routine. For example, older inmates may not be given sufficient time to complete activities or to get to and from specific locations such as the dining hall. Engaging in basic acts of eating and bathing becomes difficult when older prisoners must climb stairs while carrying food trays and take showers in slippery tiled cubicles. Even the act of obtaining prescribed medication can be challenging for older inmates when they must stand in line for sustained periods of time—even up to one hour—while waiting to receive the medication. An older inmate may hesitate to participate in programming if there is no close access to a toilet or if there is insufficient time to walk to the location, complete the activity, and return within the expected amount of time (Crawley, 2005; Hill et al., 2006). In fact, the requirements of prison life are such that the five basic activities of daily living (bathing, eating, toileting, dressing, and transferring) (Williams et al., 2006) are complicated by the five following prison activities of daily living (dropping to the floor for alarms, standing for head count, getting to the dining hall for meals, hearing orders from staff, and climbing on and off the top bunk when needed). Completion of these prison activities can become increasingly challenging for aging inmates and even result in injuries as aging inmates navigate changes in their strength, endurance, balance, flexibility, hearing, and eyesight (Williams et al., 2006; Williams and Abraldes, 2007).

In terms of correctional expectations and programming options, even caring correctional staff may display "institutional thoughtlessness" (Crawley, 2005) as they fail to adjust the ways in which they interact with older inmates to include addressing older inmates' age-specific psychosocial needs. Generally speaking, older inmates need more orderly conditions, emotional feedback, and familial support as compared with younger prisoners (Aday, 2003; Crawley and Sparks, 2006; Sterns et al., 2008). At the same time, older inmates find it progressively harder to maintain ties with their families as the years go by; moreover, inmates who must come to terms with the fact that they will die in prison often experience increased anger and depression and a higher risk of suicide (Anno et al., 2004). Few older inmates participate in correctional programs and activities that involve interaction with other prisoners; as a result, the elderly tend to become idle (Aday, 2003; Crawley, 2005; Crawley and Sparks, 2006; Gal, 2002; Gubler and Petersilia, 2006; Hill et al., 2006; Smyer and Burbank, 2009).

As one expert noted, "the present modality of 'warehousing' these inmates with minimal programming or activities intensifies day-to-day management concerns and significantly contributes to the general decline in the individual, which escalates [the] daily cost of institutional and health care" (Florida House of Representatives, 1999, p. 23). Older inmates do not typically have access to structured routine activities that are geared toward providing them with opportunities for physical, mental, and social engagement that are in line with their changing capacities and needs. Moreover, programming is not currently geared toward the provision of practical and age-appropriate activities that help older inmates to maximize their level of functioning (Aday, 2003; Crawley, 2005; Crawley and Sparks, 2006; Florida House of Representatives, 1999; Gal, 2002; Gubler and Petersilia, 2006; Hill et al., 2006; Smyer and Burbank, 2009).

Arguing for the Age-Integration Perspective

Proponents of the age-integration perspective note that some older inmates have indicated that they find it more enjoyable to be living among an age-diverse population of inmates. Similar to sentiments expressed by elders outside the prison system who eschew placement in a facility designated for elderly individuals, some older inmates may find it demoralizing to be forced to move to a separate facility set aside for the custody and care of older inmates. Living in a separate prison that only houses older inmates could contribute to feelings of depression for some older prisoners and their fear of being perceived as old, weak, and helpless (Aday, 2003). A lack of contact with younger inmates may also reinforce a sense of isolation and may make adjustment upon release more difficult (Curtin, 2007). Age-integration advocates also raise concerns regarding the potential likelihood that placing elderly inmates in a limited number of separate facilities will reduce opportunities for interaction between elderly inmates and their friends and family. Should the facilities designated for the custody and care of older inmates be located in areas that increase the distance friends and family must travel in order to engage in regular visits, older inmates will be less likely to access social networks that are important to their psychological adjustment in prison, and important to their preparation for reintegration into general society upon release from prison (Aday, 2003; Curtin, 2007).

Arguing for the Age-Segregation Perspective

Proponents of the age-segregation perspective argue that specialized facilities provide a unique opportunity for the creation of an age-friendly environment that is likely to benefit older inmates (Aday, 2003; Thivierge-Rikard and Thompson, 2007). Although studies have generally shown that most elderly inmates react well to living in age-integrated environments (Williams et al., 2006), older prisoners often prefer to live in age-segregated environments, because these environments are likely to be quieter and more conducive to developing social relationships. Sharing an environment that is populated with inmates of the same age group increases opportunities for social interaction and in turn may help to reduce older inmates' loneliness while increasing their self-respect (Aday, 2003; Gubler and Petersilia, 2006; Vitiello and Kelso, 2004). That said, most prisons do not have adequate programming for aging inmates and for those serving long-term sentences (Aday, 2003; Crawley and Sparks, 2006; Gubler and Petersilia, 2006; Sterns et al., 2008).

Housing older inmates together may make it easier for correctional administrators to design work assignment policies, rehabilitation programming, and recreational activities that are specifically tailored to meet the needs of aging inmates while taking into account their varying levels of ability (Aday 2003; Curtin, 2007). Specifically tailoring a range of policies and programming for inmates who are housed in a limited number of facilities is more practical than creating specialized programming for inmates who are housed in small numbers across a wide range of facilities. Furthermore, consolidating older prisoners among a few facilities provides correctional staff and administrators with increased access to a special-needs population that is defined by the ways in which older inmates are different from younger inmates (i.e., between-group variation), as well as by the ways in which older inmates differ among themselves (i.e., within-group variation). Thus, success in tailoring policies and programming to meet the diverse needs of a special population of inmates depends on the extent to which administrators and staff members can assess the needs of older inmates and then provide a range of policies and programs that measurably improve their physical, mental, and social functioning. Age-appropriate policies and programming should be used to promote an age-relevant process of rehabilitation, one that capitalizes on older inmates' increased need for social interconnectedness while adjusting for their physiological and psychological changes. Moreover, to the extent that policies and programming are effective in creating an age-friendly environment, older inmates' engagement in work, rehabilitation, and recreational opportunities will increase.

In response to the age-based needs of older inmates, the Ohio Department of Rehabilitation and Correction collaborated with the Ohio Department of Aging to develop a training program that is open to all prison staff interested in learning about the ways in which older inmates' functional limitations affect their ability to comply with standard correctional practices. Prison staff who attend this training program, called Try Another Way, participate in exercises that give them the opportunity to experience common functional limitations that occur with an accelerated aging process and the presence of chronic medical disorders. For example, staff members experience the difficulties associated with loss of mobility and eyesight as well as difficulty in completing basic activities due to loss of coordination, physical strength, and fine motor control (Moore and Unwin, 2002). Moreover, the Ohio Department of Rehabilitation and Correction has established a specialized set of programs that promote older inmates' physical, mental, and social functioning. In a 2002 report titled "Ohio's Older Inmates," it was noted that 90.7 percent of the state's older inmate population was housed within a single prison, the Hocking Correction Facility, so that older inmates would benefit from an environment that was "safe and secure . . . with quality programming for our aging population so they may, upon their return to society, be productive citizens" (Moore and Unwin, 2002, p. 39).

General programming offered through the Ohio Department of Rehabilitation and Correction is designed around two goals: to assist inmates in adjusting to prison life by helping them to engage in a personally based process of rehabilitation, and to prepare inmates for successful release back into society by focusing on living a productive life in the community. Specialized programming for older inmates in the Hocking Correction Facility supplements and extends the purpose of the Ohio Department of Rehabilitation and Correction's general programming by tailoring additional activities to meet older inmates' unique needs. Overall, the range of specialized programming that is offered to older inmates is extensive and is designed to (1) support physical and mental functioning within the context of accelerated aging and common medical disorders, (2) support social connectedness, and (3) facilitate personal growth through knowledge and skills acquisition in relationship to negotiating the process of aging (for a complete list of all age-specific programs and services offered by the Hocking Correction Facility, see Moore and Unwin, 2002). In sum, though there are indeed examples of exceptional prison programs and services for older inmates, they are typically available in age-segregated facilities that are designed to operate in a developmentally and age-appropriate manner.

The Age-Segregation Debate: Policy Implications

As the older inmate population grows larger, it will be increasingly important for correctional officials to develop and test best-practice methods for meeting the special needs of a complex and vulnerable group of inmates. This chapter has presented an overview of the issues that need to be addressed when dealing with an aging population and questioning whether it is best to mainstream older inmates into the general prison population or segregate them away from the younger population. States are only now beginning to experiment with alternatives in response to this debate.

According to a national survey on facilities and services for older prisoners (Sterns et al., 2008), most states do not provide dedicated facilities exclusively for older prisoners. Of the forty-one states that responded to this survey, thirteen (32 percent) reported having units dedicated to older prisoners, six (15 percent) reported having prison facilities dedicated to older prisoners, nine (22 percent) reported having secure medical facilities dedicated to older prisoners, five (12 percent) reported having secure nursing homes dedicated to older prisoners, and eight (20 percent) reported having hospice care dedicated to older prisoners. In total, the number of dedicated facilities across all states was very small (eighty), and they collectively housed a very small number (9,192) of older inmates. It should also be noted that states differed in how they defined and operationalized what "dedicated" means; thus it is somewhat difficult to make clear sense of between-state practices (Sterns et al., 2008). Further, there is no uniform policy at the state or federal level, and there is little consensus among scholars with regard to the use of age-based segregation or integration (Aday, 2003; Kerbs and Jolley, 2009b; Rikard and Rosenberg, 2007; Thivierge-Rikard and Thompson, 2007).

While some jurisdictions are moving forward by developing specialized programs and services for older inmates, studies to date have yet to provide an accurate cost-benefit analysis to determine which housing arrangements are most effective and efficient. Moreover, a review of the scholarly literature on state-based practices documents that correctional policies and procedures for older prisoners are still in their infancy (Price, 2006). As Thivierge-Rikard and Thompson (2007) argue, research on the efficacy of age-segregated versus age-integrated living arrangements is still in its formative stage. Most of the current evidence tends to be anecdotal and does not adequately determine a true cause-and-effect relationship. Moreover, what works in one state may not be as effective in another. Thus, we must be cautious in making any definitive assessments about whether one housing arrangement is better than another.

Rather than taking a uniform stance on one housing model over another, it seems more appropriate to provide a tiered approach. The fact of the matter is that there is no one type of older inmate, because older inmates are a very diverse group; thus, it is impossible to identify "the" services that all older inmates will need (Shimkus, 2004). The pertinent question should not be which housing method is better. Rather, correctional administrators need to provide a mechanism for implementing individualized responses based on each inmate's needs. Housing arrangements should be based on need and not age (Hill et al., 2006; Shimkus, 2004). Thus, Hill and his colleagues (2006) recommend that correctional administrators focus on developing a continuum of specialized units and support programs that can provide inmates with the least-restrictive level of care needed. For some older prisoners, this may mean being mainstreamed with younger inmates; for others, housing in separate and specialized facilities (e.g., correctional nursing homes) may be required to meet their unique needs, especially when they may benefit from a more protected location (Williams et al., 2006). Clearly, inmates with serious physical and mental health impairments would be candidates for segregated housing, while older inmates in good health may prefer to and be able to safely live in the general population. However, the automatic segregation of older inmates who have certain chronic diseases should not be allowed, given that some diseases may be manageable in age-integrated settings (Stojkovic, 2007).

If such a tiered approach is used for housing older inmates, then more sophisticated classification and screening instruments and policies will be needed. Although the early and accurate identification of elderly inmates' complex needs is critically important, current prison classification and screening instruments were not designed (generally speaking) for use with older inmates (Anno et al., 2004; Shimkus, 2004), making appropriate placement more complicated. Thus, future research will be needed to develop valid and reliable screening instruments for older inmates.

Most important, prison systems must begin to employ gerontological theory and research to inform correctional staff on how best to accommodate the needs of aging inmates (Stojkovic, 2007; Thivierge-Rikard and Thompson, 2007). Given the unique biological, psychological, and social issues affecting aging inmates, correctional administrators will need to strike a balance between treatment and control; moreover, correctional administrators will need to develop management principles that promote the implementation of evidence-based interventions, keeping in mind that what works with younger inmates may not be applicable to aging inmates. Managing the special needs of elderly, chronically ill, and terminally ill inmates behind bars is indeed challenging, but all prison systems must face this task. Meeting this task requires a multidisciplinary approach that encourages collaboration and coordination among correctional staff, parole officers, community organizations, health-care providers, and gerontologists (Stojkovic, 2007; Thivierege-Rikard and Thompson, 2007; Williams and Abraldes, 2007). Anything less is certainly a violation of a commitment to rehabilitation and may be a violation of the letter and the spirit of US Supreme Court decisions and legislative mandates requiring that prisoners be provided access to a range of necessary medical services, assistive devices, accommodations, and programming opportunities.

8

The Implications of Age-Graded Desistance

John J. Kerbs and Jennifer M. Jolley

Criminologists have a long history of examining the correlates of criminal behavior and the propensity (i.e., the likelihood) of individuals to commit crime. One such correlate is age, which has been found to be consistently and inversely related to criminal behavior; thus as age increases, criminal behavior decreases across the life-course (Piquero, Farrington, and Blumstein, 2003). This age-based desistance in criminal activity (*desistance* is hereby defined as a dynamic process whereby an offender slows and eventually ceases participation in criminal activity) has been extensively studied from both empirical and theoretical standpoints (Brame, Bushway, and Patternoster, 2003; Bushway et al., 2001), but empirical and theoretical aspects of desistance have yet to be conjoined to fully inform policies and programs for federal and state prisoners in the United States. This chapter seeks to take a modest step toward examining how the United States might infuse the science and theory of age-based desistance with policy and program development, because as Gottfredson once said, "the general decline in offending with age is ubiquitous—or so nearly so that there is much to be risked by ignoring it" (2005, p. 52).

The importance of informing policies and programs with an integrated understanding of empirical and theoretical aspects of age-based desistance should not be underestimated given the long-standing efforts in the United States to selectively incapacitate serious and purportedly persistent ("chronic") offenders, *regardless of age,* via long-term prison sentences with reduced or eliminated access to early-release mechanisms such as parole (for advanced discussions of such sentencing strategies, see Benekos and Merlo, 1995; Ditton and Wilson, 1999; Turner et al., 1995). Such sentences have effectively increased the average length of stay in prison (Kerbs and Jolley, 2009a, 2009b), with over 20 percent of all federal and state inmates in the United States serving prison sentences for twenty or more years (Camp, 2003) and about 9.5 percent of all inmates serving life sentences (Nellis and King, 2009). Nonetheless, such sentences may not be a good financial investment of our correctional dollars if purportedly "serious" and "chronic" offenders do eventually desist from criminal behavior as they age across their life-spans. As this chapter shows, desistance is indeed the case, as we have conclusive evidence to document how "even the most hardened offender is not a persistent offender in the true sense of the term, and all offenders eventually desist albeit at different rates and ages" (Laub and Sampson, 2003, p. 194).

The implications of warehousing aging offenders who are desisting from criminal activity are self-evident. Our expensive and limited supply of prison beds is increasingly being occupied with aging offenders who are at low risk of recidivism due to age-based desistance and other age-related factors, including health problems as covered elsewhere in this book (see Chapters 2, 3, and 7 for expanded discussions of these age-related topics). That said, this chapter seeks to review three key issues: (1) the empirical proof of age-based desistance across the life-course; (2) a theoretical explanation for age-graded declines in criminal behavior as theorized and empirically examined via Sampson and Laub's (2003) age-graded theory of informal social control; and (3) policy and program suggestions as informed by the integration of empirical and theoretical aspects of age-based desistance from criminal behavior.

Empirical Age-Based Indicators of Desistance for Offenders and Prisoners

Empirical evidence documenting the inverse relationship between age and crime (i.e., as age increases, criminal behavior decreases) can be traced back to studies from the early 1800s. For example, Quetelet (1831) examined data from the late 1820s for crimes against persons and property in France; interestingly, he found that age was substantively and inversely related to the propensity for criminal activity—i.e., the likelihood of engaging in criminal acts peaks in the late teens through the mid-twenties and then declines thereafter). Since the 1800s, the methodological design and statistical rigor of studies that examine the association between age and crime have improved, but findings that document the presence of age-based desistance in criminal activity have largely been a constant throughout two centuries of inquiry (Piquero, Farrington, and Blumstein, 2003).

These findings have been so consistent throughout the research that Sampson and Laub noted the following: "Crime declines with age sooner or later for all offender groups, whether identified prospectively according to a multitude of childhood and adolescent risk factors, or retrospectively based on latent-class models of trajectories" (2003, p. 555).

When examining age-based aspects of criminal desistance, one could easily become overwhelmed by the seemingly endless number of studies and findings published over the past two centuries (see, e.g., Laub and Sampson, 2003; Sampson and Laub, 1993). To simplify the collective results of the research to date, the discussion in this chapter will focus on topics that are directly pertinent to the sentencing of older offenders, the care and custody of older prisoners, and the release of older inmates. For example, it may help the courts to more effectively sentence persisting offenders to prison and desisting offenders to community-based alternatives or to shorter prison stays if there are different ages of desistance that are identifiable for different crime types. Such information may also help to focus prison-based programming and postrelease interventions on desisting prisoners who might be most likely to benefit from such programs and interventions.

Interestingly, the quantitative research to date has identified an average age of desistance. By examining data from a sample of delinquent boys who were followed to age 70, Sampson and Laub (2003) identified age 37 as the average age of desistance (i.e., the average age for the last arrest) for all official arrest records. They also discovered that the lowest average age of desistance occurred for property crimes (age 26) followed by violent and sex crimes (age 31) and alcohol and drug crimes (age 37). Given that older prisoners are (by definition) aged 50 and older, most older prisoners have a high probability of being in the process of desisting from criminal behavior, which bodes well for their potential sentencing to shortened lengths of stay in prison or to community-based alternatives to prison (Kerbs and Jolley, 2009a, 2009b).

To the extent that desistance from most crimes tends to begin somewhere between 26 and 37 years of age, one would expect that older citizens outside the prison system would have very low arrest rates and be responsible for a very small proportion of all arrests in the United States (Sampson and Laub, 2003). Recent research has confirmed older citizens' low level of criminal activity as measured by arrest rates in a pooled series of cross-sectional studies. Using cross-sectional data from the Federal Bureau of Investigation's Uniform Crime Reports (UCR), Feldmeyer and Steffensmeier (2007) found that arrest rates for citizens aged 55 and older either declined or remained stable between 1980 and 2004 for most UCR offense categories.

As shown in Table 8.1, arrest rates per 100,000 citizens aged 55 and older in 2004 were very low for their top six offenses: drug violations (37.0 per 100,000), larceny-theft (44.9), public drunkenness (45.8), simple assaults (52.7), driving under the influence (118.2), and other offenses excluding traffic offenses (165.2) (Feldmeyer and Steffensmeier, 2007). The percentage profiles for each offense in Table 8.1 represent the proportion of all elderly arrests in 2004 for any given offense category; thus, the aggregate of all six percentage profiles indicates that these six offenses collectively represented 78.6 percent of all reported arrests for older citizens aged 55 and older in 2004. Finally, Table 8.1 contains information on the proportion of elderly involvement in various crime categories (i.e., the proportionate age involvement rates), which is defined as elderly citizens' proportional contribution to arrests in a given crime category *relative to other age groups;* in short, all proportionate age involvement rates for the top six offenses by the elderly were under 7 percent, which means that older citizens made up less than 7 percent of all arrests in their six highest categories for offending as defined by their arrest rates. Moreover, looking at all twenty-seven offenses examined in this study (i.e., eight Type I offenses or UCR index crimes, and nineteen Type II offenses), not one of the

Table 8.1 Arrest Rates, Proportionate Age Involvement, and Percentage Profiles for the Elderly (Aged 55 and Older), 2004

Top Six Offenses	Elderly Arrest Rate[a]	Elderly Proportional Age Involvement[b]	Elderly Percentage Profile[c]
Other excluding traffic violation[d]	165.2	3.5	28.0
Driving under the influence of alcohol	118.2	6.5	20.0
Simple assault	52.7	3.3	8.9
Public drunkenness	45.8	6.7	7.8
Larceny-theft	44.9	3.0	7.6
Drug violation	37.0	1.8	6.3

Source: Feldmeyer and Steffensmeier, 2007, p. 313.

Notes: To add stability to these figures, arrest rates, proportionate age involvement rates, and percentage profiles are calculated using averages for 2003–2004.

a. Rates per 100,000 population are adjusted for age composition. The population base for elderly arrest rates includes ages 55 to 74.

b. For any given offense, the elderly proportionate age involvement is calculated by dividing the summed arrest rates for the 55+ age groups (55–59, 60–64, 65+), by the summed arrest rates for all age groups (10–14, 15–19, . . . , 65+), and then multiplying that result by 100.

c. The percentage profile reflects the percentage of all elderly arrests in 2004 that are for each specific offense category.

d. This category includes other alcohol-related crimes, crimes of mischief, and ordinance violations. In other words, these are generally minor offenses.

twenty-seven rates for proportionate age involvement rose above 9 percent. Thus, older citizens were responsible for no more than 9 percent of all arrests in any given offense category in 2004, which is a clear indictor of the inverse relationship between age and crime in society. As far as the most serious crimes that include homicide, a recent study by Feldmeyer and Steffensmeier (2012) found that the proportionate age involvement for elderly offenders (aged 55 to 74) who commit homicide did not increase (or decrease) over time from 1985 to 2009. Not surprisingly, elder homicides accounted for a small proportion of all homicides (less than 5 percent) between 1985 and 2009.

Once incarcerated, aging prisoners also tend to desist from poor behavior while in the general prison population. More specifically, there is an inverse association between age and prison misconduct as measured by the presence of disciplinary reports for prison-rule violations. As age increases, prison misconduct has been found to decrease across a variety of studies that have controlled for a number of confounding variables, including both offender and facility characteristics (see, e.g., Cooper and Werner, 1990; Craddock, 1996; Cunningham and Sorensen, 2007; Goetting and Howsen, 1986; Ireland, 2000; Light, 1991; Wooldredge, 1991, 1994; Wooldredge, Griffin, and Pratt, 2001). Similar to Sampson and Laub's (2003) identification of the average ages of desistance (defined as the average age at the time of the last arrest) for property, violent/sex, and alcohol/drug crimes as falling between the mid-20s and the mid-30s, it would appear as if desistance from prison misconduct also begins (dependent upon the study) in the late 20s (DeLisi, 2003) or mid 30s (Cunningham and Sorensen, 2007). Moreover, there appears to be a significant and inverse association between age and disciplinary reports for violence; with each additional year in age, the number of violent acts for any given prisoner seems to decrease by more than 5 percent (Sorensen and Cunningham, 2010). Not surprisingly, under 10 percent of all older inmates present serious disciplinary problems (McShane and Williams, 1990), which may be due, in part, to the process of desistance among older inmates and the fact that older prisoners, as compared to younger inmates, are more likely to use passive and avoidant coping strategies to secure their safety, and are less likely to use aggressive strategies to secure their safety (McCorkle, 1992). Given that older prisoners are less likely to violate prison rules and more likely to engage in passive and avoidant coping strategies to secure their safety, they appear to represent model inmates (from a behavioral standpoint at least) for potential placement in prison-based rehabilitative programs.

Although good behavior among older prisoners behind bars is an indication of desistance, one must ask if this good behavior continues after release from prison. This is a particularly salient issue for older prisoners because of their criminogenic backgrounds as defined by their modal sentencing offenses, which include violent and sex offenses for older male prisoners (Aday, 1994a; Flynn, 1998, 2000; Kerbs, 2000a) and violent and drug offenses for older female prisoners (Aday and Krabill, 2011; Kerbs, 2000a). Given the nature of these dominant sentencing offenses for older men and women behind bars, their release could potentially pose significant threats to public safety. Nonetheless, the age-based process of desistance from criminal activity is clearly visible when one looks at the recidivism rates for older released prisoners (Bureau of Justice Statistics, 2011; Langan and Levin, 2002; Langan, Schmitt, and Durose, 2003).

In the tables that follow, data from the Bureau of Justice Statistics clearly document age-graded declines in recidivism as defined by the rates of rearrest, reconviction, and reincarceration for a cohort of male and female prisoners from fifteen states who were released in 1994 and tracked for three consecutive years thereafter. Table 8.2 contains the results of Langan and Levin's (2002) analysis of the Bureau of Justice Statistics data and related recidivism rates, which clearly decreased as age increased for this cohort of released prisoners. Dramatic differences can be seen in the proportions of recidivating inmates aged 18 to 24 as compared to those aged 45 and older for rearrest rates (75.4 percent versus 45.3 percent, respectively), reconviction rates (52.0 percent versus 29.7 percent), and reincarceration rates (52.0 percent versus 40.9 percent) within three years. Hence, the good behavior that many older prisoners display while in prison also extends to free society upon release.

As a point of clarification, the rates in Table 8.2 are not specific to any given offense category or offender group. Consequently, it is important to determine if similar age-based reductions in recidivism are present for the modal sentencing-offense categories that bring older men and older women into prison (violent and sex offenses versus violent and drug offenses, respectively). As compared with the findings in Table 8.2, Table 8.3 illustrates

Table 8.2 Three-Year Recidivism Rates for 1994-Released Prisoners, All Sentencing Offenses Combined (percentages)

Age at Release	Rearrested	Reconvicted	Returned to Prison
18–24	75.4	52.0	52.0
25–29	70.5	50.1	52.5
30–34	68.8	48.8	54.8
35–39	66.2	46.3	52.0
40–44	58.4	38.0	50.0
45+	45.3	29.7	40.9

Source: Langan and Levin, 2002.

Table 8.3 Three-Year Recidivism Rates for 1994-Released Male Prisoners with Convictions for Violent Offenses (percentages)

Age at Release	Rearrested	Reconvicted	Returned to Prison
< 21	81.6	57.6	35.5
21–25	72.5	46.9	27.2
26–30	69.1	48.4	23.8
31–35	65.0	42.7	23.1
36–40	61.9	39.9	20.7
> 40	46.4	29.2	12.1

Source: Bureau of Justice Statistics, 2011.

similar age-based reductions in recidivism for men who were sent to prison for violent offenses and released in 1994. Again, dramatic differences in recidivism rates can be seen for the proportions of younger prisoners who were under 21 years old as compared to those who were over 40 years of age for rearrest rates (81.6 percent versus 46.4 percent, respectively), reconviction rates (57.6 percent versus 29.2 percent), and reincarceration rates (35.5 percent versus 12.1 percent) within three years.

As shown in Table 8.4, the same inverse relationship between age and recidivism also exists for men in prison who were convicted of sex offenses and subsequently released in 1994. Despite the serious nature of this sentencing offense, large age-based decreases in recidivism rates are visible for released sex offenders. Thus, the recidivism rates were far higher for younger prisoners who were under 21 years old as compared to those who were over 40 years of age for rearrest rates (65.1 percent versus 27.4 percent, respectively), reconviction rates (46.2 percent versus 13.8 percent), and reincarceration rates (26.5 percent versus 6.8 percent) within three years.

Of course, not all male sex offenders are the same, given wide differences in offense patterns (i.e., rapists versus sexual assaulters) and victim preferences (i.e., adults versus children). These variations suggest the need for additional clarification regarding the potential presence of age-based desistance for all types of sex offenders, including rapists, sexual assaulters, child molesters, and statutory rapists. That said, Table 8.5 summarizes the results of a study that examined the Bureau of Justice Statistics data regarding rearrest rates for convicted male sex offenders released in 1994 (Langan, Schmitt, and Durose, 2003). Again, the results clearly demonstrate that age-based reductions in recidivism rates for rearrest are present for men convicted of rape, sexual assault, child molestation, and statutory rape. Of these four groups, statutory rapists had the greatest age-graded reduction in rearrest rates, which decreased from 70.0 percent for statutory

Table 8.4 **Three-Year Recidivism Rates for 1994-Released Male Prisoners with Convictions for Sex Offenses (percentages)**

Age at Release	Rearrested	Reconvicted	Returned to Prison
< 21	65.1	46.2	26.5
21–25	57.4	35.1	19.7
26–30	54.4	33.5	17.1
31–35	45.8	25.4	12.5
36–40	40.9	24.3	11.5
> 40	27.4	13.8	6.8

Source: Bureau of Justice Statistics, 2011.

Table 8.5 **Three-Year Rearrest Rates for 1994-Released Male Prisoners with Convictions for Sex Offenses (percentages)**

Age at Release	All Sex Offenders	Rapists	Sexual Assaulters	Child Molesters	Statutory Rapists
18–24	59.8	58.6	60.2	59.6	70.0
25–29	54.2	53.8	54.3	51.4	56.4
30–34	48.8	52.6	46.7	46.5	47.7
35–39	41.4	46.1	38.9	38.0	37.9
40–44	34.7	41.2	31.6	28.0	44.4
45+	23.5	23.0	23.7	23.8	23.8

Source: Langan, Schmitt, and Durose, 2003.

rapists aged 18 and 24, to 23.8 percent for those aged 45 and older (i.e., a 66.0 percent reduction). The respective reductions in rearrest rates for prisoners in the youngest versus oldest age group were also substantive for rapists (60.75 percent reduction), sexual assaulters (a 60.63 percent reduction), and child molesters (a 60.07 percent reduction).

As for women, the age-based rates of recidivism for their modal sentencing-offense categories are a bit more complicated than those of their male counterparts, but age-based reductions in recidivism are still visible among women released from prison. The results in Table 8.6 summarize the age-based reductions in recidivism rates for women with violent convictions who were released in 1994 and tracked for three years. With regard to the rates for rearrest, they rise from those under age 21 (35.1 percent) to those between ages 26 and 30 (63.2 percent); thereafter, the rates decline to a low of 25.4 percent for those over the age of 40. With regard to the percentage of women with violent convictions who were reconvicted, their rates peak between the ages of 26 and 30 at 41.1 percent; thereafter, they reach a low of 11.1 percent for those over age 40. Finally, the proportion of women who are returned to prison within three years of release is very low (only 2.4 percent) for those released after age 40.

Table 8.6 Three-Year Recidivism Rates for 1994-Released Female Prisoners with Convictions for Violent Offenses (percentages)

Age at Release	Rearrested	Reconvicted	Returned to Prison
< 21	35.1	29.0	19.6
21–25	56.0	34.8	22.5
26–30	63.2	41.1	15.9
31–35	56.6	35.9	11.0
36–40	34.1	27.6	14.9
> 40	25.4	11.1	2.4

Source: Bureau of Justice Statistics, 2011.

Interestingly, for all types of recidivism noted in Table 8.6, the rates for women who are over age 40 are always lower than the corresponding rates for men who are over age 40 in Table 8.3. Thus, these analyses clearly indicate that women have lower rates of recidivism than men. Such findings are congruent with the extant literature, which suggests that "recidivism data uniformly indicate that women are less likely to reoffend than men" (Kruttschnitt and Gartner, 2003, p. 44). Quantitative research has confirmed that recidivism among women is inversely associated with age, but it is also positively associated with unstable family histories, substance abuse, mental health problems, unstable employment, and prior offending (Kruttschnitt and Gartner, 2003). Qualitative research has found that women's lower rate of recidivism might be attributed to their formation of attachments and bonds to prosocial (conventional) people who sustain and reinforce crime-free living (Baskin and Sommers, 1998; Kruttschnitt and Gartner, 2003; Maruna, 2001; Shover, 1996).

Finally, Table 8.7 shows the recidivism rates for female prisoners with drug convictions for their sentencing offense. Again, their rates of recidivism tend to decline toward the end of the age brackets (i.e., for those 36 to 40, and those over age 40), but there is some fluctuation in the age-based rates of recidivism for women who are returned to prison.

In sum, for male and female prisoners who are 50 years of age and older, these tables demonstrate the undeniable inverse association between age and criminal behavior, whether defined by arrest, rearrest, reconviction, or reincarceration rates. The next section of this chapter uses criminological theory to explain why age is inversely related to criminal behavior and what mechanisms explain this negative relationship. To the extent that the theoretically derived and scientifically tested explanations for desistance can be identified, they can be applied to the development of programs and policies that promote the successful rehabilitation of aging prisoners and the advancement of public safety via the stabilization and release of older desisting offenders into free society.

Table 8.7 Three-Year Recidivism Rates for 1994-Released Female Prisoners with Convictions for Drug Offenses (percentages)

Age at Release	Rearrested	Reconvicted	Returned to Prison
< 21	75.3	46.3	2.4
21–25	49.9	37.5	14.0
26–30	65.3	44.8	19.9
31–35	65.3	50.0	22.7
36–40	56.5	33.9	14.3
> 40	48.4	32.6	18.9

Source: Bureau of Justice Statistics, 2011.

Using Theory to Explain Age-Graded Desistance from Criminal Behavior

Explaining age-graded aspects of desistance from criminal behavior across the life-course implicates the need for a theory of crime and delinquency that is capable of explaining both persistence in and desistance from criminal behavior over the life-span. One of the more empirically tested theories has been Sampson and Laub's age-graded theory of informal social control, which has been retrospectively and prospectively studied using longitudinal data from offenders and nonoffenders who were tracked from childhood through age 70 (see, e.g., Sampson and Laub, 1993; Laub and Sampson, 2003; Laub, Sampson, and Sweeten, 2008).

This age-graded theory of informal social control posits that the probability of criminal behavior increases when an individual's bonds to prosocial society are weakened, damaged, or totally broken (Sampson and Laub, 1993); conversely, strengthening social bonds between people and prosocial institutions decreases the probability of criminal behavior. During adolescence, the most important (primary) social bonds occur between children and their parents, their schools, and their peers. As children and adolescents age into adulthood, the primary bonds shift to those between adults and their spouses, their educations, their jobs, and their communities. Accordingly, adults progress through paths in their life-spans that involve "a sequence of culturally-defined, age-graded roles and social transitions" (Laub, Sampson, and Sweeten, 2008, p. 314) that are predominantly related to family, school, and work.

Three concepts are fundamental to understanding this theory (Laub, Sampson, and Sweeten, 2008). First, a person's life-course is embedded within *trajectories,* defined as long-term behavioral patterns related to a person's work life (i.e., paid employment), family life (marriage), parenthood, criminal behavior, and so forth. Second, within these long-term behavioral patterns that characterize trajectories, people experience short-term events or *transitions*—for example, starting a new job, getting married, having a child, getting arrested, being sent to jail, being incarcerated in a state or federal prison, and so forth. Third, some transitions serve as *turning points* when they alter or modify a person's long-term trajectory. For example, finding a great job or wonderful intimate partner can lead an offender to change his or her life, friends, routine activities, and associates from anti-social to prosocial in nature.

Ultimately, this theory joins a person's social history with the social structure that surrounds them to explain their persistence or desistance in criminal behavior (Laub and Sampson, 2003; Sampson and Laub, 2005). Age-graded informal systems of social control as applied to adults (e.g., spouses, educational systems, employment, enlistment in the military, etc.) can act as systems of restraint that shape good behavior and extinguish bad behavior. Thus, empirically identified ingredients for desistance include, among other things, a good marriage or relationship with an intimate part-ner and legitimate employment, which facilitate a knifing-off process wherein individuals' lives are socially reordered from a context of criminal opportunities to a context of prosocial activities. More specifically, the mechanisms underlying relationships between social bonds (e.g., marriage and employment) and desistance have been identified via quantitative and qualitative research. They include informal monitoring, prosocial ties to law-abiding people, social support for conventional activities and routines, the imposition of normative expectations, informal social control, and so-cial sanctions (Laub and Sampson, 2003; Sampson and Laub, 2005).

Aging modifies the bonds of intimate relationships and employment, and identity transformation occurs in association with aging and the con-text of social bonds (Laub, Sampson, and Sweeten, 2008; Sampson and Laub, 2005). As people age, for example, they have more time to develop "social capital" within the contexts of their social networks at home, at work, and in their communities. Lin defined social capital as an "invest-ment and use of imbedded resources in social relations for expected re-turns" (2000, p. 786). Broadly defined, social capital stems from interper-sonal trust (i.e., a reciprocal and earned trust) between people that allows them to achieve certain goals, objectives, and benefits (e.g., good life out-comes) within their social context (Coleman, 1988; Bourdieu, 1986; Sav-age and Kanazawa, 2002). By "going straight" via participation in prosocial relations at home, at work, and in the community, offenders can develop social capital that ultimately builds a "respectability package" to facilitate the acquisition of good outcomes in life (Laub, Sampson, and Sweeten, 2008). The concept of social capital is central to age-graded informal social control, since offenders who develop "respectability packages" tend to avoid criminal behavior because it might jeopardize their social capital and related returns on their social investment in prosocial society (Laub and Sampson, 2003).

While marriage, education, and employment can lead to desistance in the trajectories of offenders, Sampson and Laub are quick to note that marriage per se and employment per se are not necessarily (for example) going to help people desist from a life of crime (Laub, Sampson, and Sweeten, 2008). The quantitative and qualitative research on such matters indicates that quality marriages (not just any marriage—see, e.g., Laub, Nagin, and Sampson, 1998; Sampson and Laub, 1990) and good jobs (not just any employment opportunity—see, e.g., Shover, 1996; Sampson and Laub, 1990) are necessary to promote desistance (Laub, Sampson, and Sweeten, 2008).

With regard to the difference between marriage per se and good marriages (the latter being defined by generally good conjugal relations, family cohesiveness, and general attachment to spouse), it appears that just being married (as compared to not being married) may actually be positively associated with crime over time (i.e., longer marriages can actually increase criminal behavior); nonetheless, good marriages significantly decrease crime over time and this decrease intensifies over the life course (Laub, Nagin, and Sampson, 1998). Interestingly, the benefits of marriage as a preventive factor in the etiology of crime appear to be significantly stronger for men than women, perhaps because men are more likely to marry women who have less deviant histories, which creates more of a conventional (crime-free) lifestyle for men (King, Massoglia, and Macmillan, 2007). Additionally, some research shows that marriage can increase criminal behavior among men who marry delinquent women (Osborn and West, 1979; Ouimet and LeBlanc, 1996; Shavit and Rattner, 1988). In sum, the majority of research on this topic suggests that the underlying strength and quality of bonds within intimate relationships (broadly speaking) help to promote desistance (see, e.g., Laub, Nagin, and Sampson, 1998; Laub and Sampson, 2003; Sampson and Laub, 1990, 1993; Sampson, Laub, and Wimer, 2006; Theobald and Farrington, 2011).

Employment is also important for desistance from criminal behavior in adulthood. Attachment to good jobs appears to be inversely related to criminal behavior when employment is characterized by stability of work history over time (i.e., the time employed at a current job or previous job), work habits (i.e., how reliable offenders are at the job and frequency of absences), and one's level of commitment to occupational goals (i.e., level of commitment expressed regarding work, educational, and economic aspirations) (Sampson and Laub, 1990). The timing of employment also matters when it comes to the strengthening of social bonds that assist with desistance from crime. For example, Uggen (2000) found that assignment to supported work programs decreased criminal behavior for those over age 26, but not for those at or under age 26.

The mechanisms within these informal social bonds that facilitate desistance from criminal behavior include (to varying degrees) the provision of supervision and monitoring, social support for prosocial activities, changes in routine activities to include prosocial activities, and opportunities to transform identities from criminal to law-abiding in nature. Thus, these social bonds with various age-graded institutions of informal social control (e.g., employment and marriage) "reorder situational inducements to crime [in the short term] while in the long term they enhance commitments to conformity" (Laub, Sampson, and Sweeten, 2008, p. 324).

If this theory is accurate, it should be applicable to all offenders, including prisoners who are fortunate enough to maintain contact with spouses, family members, and friends outside prison; in theory, such contact should promote rule-abiding behavior in prison and law-abiding behavior after release from prison. This is indeed the case. Research has found an inverse relationship between contact with family and friends and both the rates of inmates' disciplinary infractions in prison and recidivism after release (Christian, Mellow, and Thomas, 2006; Bales and Mears, 2008).

One of the methodologically stronger studies from the recent past (Bales and Mears, 2008) examined recidivism data from 7,000 prisoners who were released from the Florida Department of Corrections between 2001 and 2002 and tracked for twenty-four months. The findings indicated that visitation from family and friends both reduced and delayed recidivism. Moreover, the frequency of visitation was inversely associated with recidivism (more visits resulted in decreased recidivism). Interestingly, while marital status alone did not affect recidivism rates, the greatest reduction in recidivism was observed for prisoners who received visits from spouses as compared to those who did not receive such visits. Also, visits from a plethora of outside contacts (i.e., significant others, relatives, and friends) were all associated with decreased recidivism. Accordingly, as compared to those inmates who did not receive visits, those who did were 30.7 percent less likely to recidivate, and each additional visit reduced the odds of recidivism by 3.8 percent. Thus, significant reductions in recidivism might be achieved by means of multiple visits (e.g., ten visits could decrease the odds of recidivism by almost 40 percent).

Such evidence has not gone unnoticed by state-level departments of corrections. In a survey by the National Institute of Corrections (2002), 78 percent of surveyed departments of corrections had policies or programs to facilitate the maintenance of contact between prisoners and their families. As discussed in the next section of this chapter, such policies and programs should be encouraged because the benefits of visitation for prisoners are numerous, including social support from friends and family; the provision of material and emotional assistance before and after release; the facilitation of access to housing and money; and assistance with the acquisition of jobs, counseling services, and other needed resources (Bales and Mears, 2008; Christian, Mellow, and Thomas, 2006; Hairston, 1988; Jiang and Winfree, 2006).

Policies and Programs That Promote Desistance from Criminal Behavior

As noted previously, age-based desistance from criminal behavior has been empirically verified. Moreover, Sampson and Laub's age-graded theory of informal social control also provides a scientifically tested understanding of why offenders desist from criminal activities. Despite our theoretical and empirical understandings of the undeniable inverse relationship between age and criminal behavior, our court-based and corrections-based policies and procedures tend to be developed without a sound understanding of the science and theory of desistance. Thus this chapter concludes with suggestions for programs and policies that are congruent with the current literature on criminal desistance over the life-span of offenders.

Court Reforms

The solution to America's graying prison population will depend, in part, on the implementation of court systems that understand the developmental and correctional differences between younger and older offenders. Thus, state and federal court systems should consider the creation of "elder courts" that focus on the implementation of a therapeutic jurisprudence as applied to criminal prosecutions for older offenders (aged 50 and older) who are charged with felonies (Abrams, 1984; Gaydon and Miller, 2007; Rothman and Dunlop, 2006). To date, elder courts typically focus on non-violent and mental health cases at the exclusion of offenses involving violence or sex (Rothman and Dunlop, 2006). That said, there is a need for more elder courts with trained personnel who are capable of processing *all* offenses with an understanding of age-graded desistance, gerontology, community-health and mental-health issues, risk assessment, and effective correctional supervision and treatment, including programming for older violent and sex offenders both outside and inside prison. Such courts should facilitate desistance by helping all older offenders to form, maintain, and strengthen social ties to informal networks of social control that promote engagement in prosocial lifestyles and routine activities with spouses, intimate significant others, family members, employers, community centers, and the like.

Sentencing Reforms

Federal and state sentencing strategies need to be reformed. To date, almost 10 percent of all prisoners are serving life sentences (i.e., life sentences with or without parole) and over 20 percent of all prisoners are serving sentences of twenty or more years (Camp, 2003; Nellis and King, 2009). While many of these prisoners start their sentences as younger high-risk offenders, they can quickly advance into age brackets that are characterized by good behavior in prison and relatively low rates of recidivism after release, as discussed in this chapter. To advance public safety, the time has come to implement statutorily-mandated age-graded reductions in the duration of prison sentences so that prisons do not end up holding high-cost (i.e., medically intensive) offenders with little to no risk of recidivism due to advanced age and age-related health problems that render older and infirm inmates harmless to society.

When sentencing an older offender, either in elder courts or in regular criminal courts, judges should implement sanctions that tailor correctional responses based on the offender's prior criminal history, their present offense, and their age. For older recidivists with convictions for violent and sex offenses, incarceration appears to be appropriate, but sentences should be age-graded based on a scientific understanding of desistance and an actuarial consideration of a prisoner's expected life-span. Thus, reduced prison sentences for older recidivists could be justified using an age-based argument as follows: (1) an offender's age can become so advanced that recidivism and the potential comprising of public safety would be unlikely; (2) although sentence severity should be proportional to the gravity of the crime, older offenders as compared to younger offenders are losing (on average) a greater proportion of their remaining years of life for each year in prison, which makes longer prison sentences disproportionately retributive and thus potentially inappropriate in such situations; and (3) regardless of offense severity, even a short sentence could equate to a life sentence for the oldest of offenders, which raises additional concerns regarding the potential for disproportionately retributive sanctions as experienced by aging inmates (James, 1992). For older offenders who are incarcerated for the first time after age 50, alternatives to prison may be appropriate, even for more serious violent and sex offenses, if community-based supervision is intensified. For example, the supervision of older offenders in home confinement, halfway houses, and other institutional settings outside of prison (e.g., nursing homes) could be enhanced with global-positioning technology (i.e., electronic monitoring devices) to advance public safety.

Prison-Based Reforms

If prisons are to capitalize on older prisoners' age-graded desistance, they should consider tailoring correctional environments to the bio-psychosocial and criminological needs of America's aging inmate population. In short, prison systems should consider the benefits of age-segregated units and prisons that provide older inmates with wider access to prosocial lifestyles and routine activities so that these inmates do not have to compete for resources that may otherwise be controlled by younger inmates (Kerbs and Jolley, 2009a, 2009b). Within such facilities, "therapeutic communities" could be developed to address older inmates' criminogenic treatment needs and to support the facilitation of their desistance by helping them to form, maintain, and strengthen social ties to informal networks of social control (both inside and outside of prison) that promote engagement in prosocial lifestyles and routine activities. As discussed earlier, aging prisoners do have serious treatment needs given that their modal sentencing-offense categories include violent and sex offenses for aging men behind bars and violent and drug offenses for aging women in prison (Aday, 1994a; Flynn, 1998, 2000; Kerbs, 2000a). Therapeutic communities should be developed to address such criminological needs, and not just bio-psychosocial needs, which should also be treated in a context that promotes desistance. Fortunately, there are isolated examples of such comprehensive programs, including the structured senior living program called True Grit at the Northern Nevada Correctional Center (Harrison, 2006; Harrison and Benedetti). Similar programs should be considered for adaptation and implementation in other states and in the Federal Bureau of Prisons.

Programs That Facilitate Communication
Between Older Prisoners and the Free Society

Whenever possible, prison programs and policies should facilitate the maintenance of mail- and phone-based communication and in-person visitation between prisoners and their supports outside prison, including spouses, intimate partners, family members, friends, potential employers, and community-based support networks in general. The scholarly literature clearly demonstrates the benefits of such contact for the advancement of rule- and law-abiding behavior both inside of prison and after release (Christian, Mellow, and Thomas, 2006; Bales and Mears, 2008). Since the vast majority of states and the Federal Bureau of Prisons already have programs and policies to support the maintenance of such contacts (National Institute of Corrections, 2002), we suggest that all states aggressively support the initiation and maintenance of contacts between prisoners and free society. These contacts can assist soon-to-be-released prisoners with access to outside money, housing, and help with the acquisition of jobs, counseling services, and other needed resources (Bales and Mears, 2008; Christian, Mellow, and Thomas, 2006; Hairston, 1988; Jiang and Winfree, 2006).

Given that many older prisoners are often located in rural (i.e., isolated) facilities or in facilities that are far away from family members and loved ones, video- and voice-based conferencing (also known as virtual visitation) through the Internet might well provide an alternative and affordable approach to the creation of and maintenance of contacts between older prisoners and the outside world (Pennsylvania Prison Society, 2012). Research has found that visitation can be prohibitively expensive and logistically difficult to arrange for spouses, intimate partners, family members, and friends who want to maintain contact with offenders during their incarceration (Christian, Mellow, and Thomas, 2006), but virtual visitation through the Internet has been used successfully as an affordable alternative to in-residence visits (Pennsylvania Prison Society, 2012).

We suggest that in-residence and virtual visitation programs should be funded, implemented, and evaluated to determine if they can improve the level of contact that older inmates have with people outside prison, the psychosocial well-being of older prisoners, and the rates of recidivism for older prisoners. Such programs will potentially face many barriers, because older inmates report a low frequency of visitation (Aday, 1994b; Colsher et al., 1992; Leigey, 2007; Wilson and Vito, 1986), and older women in prison experience even lower levels of mail- and phone-based communication and in-residence visitation as compared to older men in prison (Bond, Thompson, and Malloy, 2005; Kratcoski and Babb, 1990). Many prisoners (especially older prisoners) have diminished access to visitation because of travel difficulties that stem from the advanced age, disability, poor health, and financial problems of family and friends (Aday, 1994a, 1994b, 2003; Aday and Krabill, 2011; Leigey, 2007; Pennsylvania Prison Society, 2012). Hence, although virtual visitation may provide needed solutions to overcome some of these barriers, additional innovations will also be needed in order to strengthen communications between some aging inmates and the outside world.

Parole Reforms

Federal and state correctional strategies pertaining to older prisoners need to be reformed on multiple levels. For example, age-based parole is an option that all states should consider. By definition, age-based parole allows prisoners who reach a certain age (e.g., 60 or 70) to request a parole hearing, regardless of the original sentencing statutes that initiated any given offender's incarceration (American Civil Liberties Union, 2012). Such parole systems should not automatically result in release, but they should provide parole boards with the opportunity to considering the merits of a prisoner's release based on a thorough review of a given prisoner's current offense, time served to date, behavior in prison, efforts to engage in rehabilitative programming, and risk of recidivism as assessed via validated instruments. Although there is always the temptation to restrict parole eligibility by excluding violent and sex offenders from such release programs, such aging offenders (as noted earlier) have very low rates of recidivism relative to the rates of younger inmates. Thus, states should avoid placing offense-based restrictions on such programs if they want to advance public safety via the release of the most low-risk offenders in any given pool of aging inmates.

Medical parole programs (also known as compassionate-release programs) represent another release option that should be available in all states. The scholarly literature clearly documents that older prisoners experience a disproportionate number of illnesses that are associated with advanced age and can decrease their risk of harm to society (Kerbs, 2000b; Lundstrom, 1994). Thus, while advanced age alone may not be adequate to justify potential release, age-graded declines in health could be considered in tandem with age-graded declines in the potential risk of recidivism to justify potential release, especially when eroded health renders prisoners harmless to public safety. Again, as with the need to avoid offense-based restrictions to age-based parole, we suggest that offense-based restrictions also be lifted from medical parole programs. Additionally, some states restrict medical parole to prisoners with terminal illnesses that are expected to result in death within six to twelve months, but such programs should also be available to prisoners with nonterminal illnesses when appropriate (i.e., when their illnesses remove any threat to public safety, regardless of life expectancy).

Finally, family-based parole should be utilized aggressively when possible. Although this model of parole was originally designed for juvenile offenders being released from secure forms of confinement, this approach to community-based supervision can also be used with older parolees. By definition, family-based parole requires that parole officers broker services to offenders and establish enduring prosocial relationships between offenders and members of their immediate families, neighborhoods, and communities to support positive behavioral changes (Gavazzi et al., 2003). Such social networks are established to "leverage" law-abiding behavior and discourage illegal activities (Rhine, Neff, and Natalucci-Persichetti, 1998). Clearly, in special situations involving older prisoners who have victimized one or more family members, the establishment of social networks therein may not be possible, feasible, or advisable. Similar restrictions may also apply to situations involving victims in the community who may not want to have future contact with offenders. Nonetheless, in such situations, parole officers can help support the development of connections between older parolees and prosocial members of community-based organizations, including senior-citizen centers.

In closing, while around 80 percent of all states have early-release options via parole (i.e., early-release options based on the discretionary decisions of parole boards) or via postrelease supervision (i.e., early-release dates identified by judges at the time of sentencing), the federal government abolished parole as an option for the Federal Bureau of Prisons in 1984 (American Civil Liberties Union, 2012). That said, the federal government would be well-advised to follow the wisdom of most states, which do support the implementation of early-release options where appropriate. Moreover, both the states and the Federal Bureau of Prisons would benefit from one or more of the parole options noted here (i.e., age-based, medical, and family parole), but each option will require rigorous evaluations to identify programmatic strengths and to correct for potential weaknesses in each model of parole as applied to America's aging prison population.

Conclusion

By 2030, about one-third of all prisoners in the United States will be 55 years of age and older (Enders, Paterniti, and Meyers, 2005; Williams et al., 2006). As discussed at the start of this chapter, this rapid growth in the number and proportion of aging prisoners in the United States is due, in part, to the predominant use of sentencing statutes that emphasize longer sentences, regardless of age, for both younger and older inmates, and the reduction of options for early release via restricted or eliminated access to (among other things) parole. Given the inverse relationship between age and criminal behavior, it is clear that the United States is paying an unnecessarily high price to increasingly warehouse a large number of aging offenders who, relative to younger prisoners, are far less likely to be rearrested, reconvicted, and reincarcerated. To be sure, the US approach to the selective incapacitation of purportedly "serious" and "chronic" offenders has become so inflexible that the country has undermined public safety via the retention of low-risk inmates who have been empirically shown to desist (on average) from further criminal behavior.

Gottfredson (2005) was correct when he said that "there is much to be risked" when we ignore the science and theory of age-graded desistance. This oversight has compromised public safety, but options for reform are available and should be pursued if we are to properly allocate our correctional dollars to the advancement (not the demise) of our safety. In the parlance of Sampson and Laub's age-graded theory of informal social control, scientifically and theoretically informed programs and policies can provide offenders with *transitions* (short-term events) that can serve as *turning points* to promote desistance from criminal behavior in the life-course *trajectories* of aging offenders who are trying to lead law-abiding lives in free society.

9

Health Issues and End-of-Life Care

John F. Linder

No issue will exert more strain on state and federal corrections systems in the United States in the next three decades than the aging of the inmate population. Without significant changes in existing laws and policy, this aging population will continue to grow in size; increasing numbers of inmates will confront life-limiting illness while incarcerated (morbidity) and inevitably more inmates will die behind bars (mortality).

This chapter describes the primary medical conditions that exacerbate inmate morbidity and mortality for older inmates (typically aged 55 and older), the different courses of treatment available for these illnesses, prisoners' entitlement to health care, and the cost and financing of that care. An examination of the facilities, policies, and programs for care currently available versus those needed to deal with these diseases and deaths as the older inmate population swells is included, as well as a comparison of the type and quality of end-of-life care available in free society and in prisons. Additionally, the discussion of health care for older inmates focuses on health-care disparities, treatment goals, and the correlation between inmates' socioeconomic, ethnic/racial, and gender characteristics and probable treatment choices.

Finally, much of this chapter focuses on the three core options for end-of-life care. First, this chapter contains an expanded discussion of *disease-directed therapy,* which includes efforts to cure or control life-threatening diseases or conditions. Second, this chapter examines *hospice care,* which is a multidisciplinary team-based approach reserved for terminally ill patients who decide to forego disease-directed interventions in favor of symptom management and a peaceful, natural death. Finally, the third option, *palliative care,* forms a bridge between the two prior options by emphasizing a multidisciplinary team approach to the amelioration of distress and the relief of symptoms, regardless of whether the goals of treatment are curative or focused on comfort. Palliative care also involves ongoing discussion and evaluation of the goals of treatment and the consistency of those goals with an individual's specific disease stage and disease progression.

Sociodemographics and the Prison Population's Health

Age, Race, and Gender

The international inmate population has grown dramatically in the past three decades ("World Prison Brief: Entire World," 2010). That said, more inmates are incarcerated for life, and longer sentences have also been applied to the majority of inmates who will be released at some point; this has been described as "sentence inflation" (Prison Reform Trust, 2007), which appears to be a somewhat global phenomenon. Consequently, aging prisoners in the United States (aged 55 and older) form the fastest-growing segment of the prison population (Cummings, 1999; Mara, 2002; Mitka, 2004; West, Sabol, and Greenman, 2010; Yorston, 2006). The statistics used to characterize the inmate population reflect this evolving reality. The Bureau of Justice Statistics, part of the US Department of Justice, publishes annual and periodic reports on the number and health status of inmates in US prisons and jails that show this evolution. The oldest age group was once 45 and older (Maruschak and Beck, 2001), then it became 50 or 55 and older (Gilliard and Beck, 1998), and now it is usually 65 and older (Sabol, West, and Cooper, 2009; West and Sabol, 2008; West, Sabol, and Greenman, 2010).

The racial composition of the US inmate population is not a perfect reflection of the nation's overall population; a disproportionately high number of inmates belong to racial or ethnic minority groups (Pettit and Western, 2004). Poverty, limited education, and illiteracy are likewise overrepresented. Table 9.1 illustrates the racial discrepancies between the prison population and the general population in the United States.

In relation to gender, women in the United States and abroad compose only 7.0–8.8 percent of the incarcerated population (Walmsley, 2006; West, Sabol, and Greenman, 2010; "World Prison Brief: Female Prisoners," 2010), though they have been among the fastest-growing subpopulations, until 2008–2009 (West, Sabol, and Greenman, 2010). Although the gender-specific needs of aging female inmates are dealt with in earlier chapters (see, for example, Chapters 1, 3, and 5), this chapter examines end-of-life issues for older prisones from various sociodemographic groups.

Table 9.1   Racial Discrepancies Between the General Population and the Prison Population, 1980–2009 (percentages, with numbers of individuals in parentheses)

	General Population, 2009	State and Federal Prison Population			
		1980[1]	1990[2]	2000	2009
White	79.6	52.3	35.6	35.6	34.2
	(244,298,000)	(165,400)		(471,000)	(530,200)
Black	12.9	46.5	44.5	46.2	38.2
	(39,641,000)	(146,900)		(610,300)	(591,700)
Hispanic[3]	15.8	—	17.4	16.4	20.7
	(48,419,000)			(216,900)	(321,000)
Asian, Indigenous, and all other[4]	7.5	1.2	2.5	1.8	6.9
	(23,068,000)	(3,674)		(23,000)	(106,860)
Total	100	100	100	100	100
	(307,007,000)	(315,974)		(1,321,200)	(1,548,700)

Sources: Beck and Gilliard, 1995; Beck and Harrison, 2001; US Census Bureau, 2011; West, Sabol, and Greenman, 2010.

Notes: 1. For 1980, the white and black categories included undisclosed percentages of individuals of Hispanic ethnicity; the 1990 figures suggest that most Hispanics were included as white in the 1980 data.

2. Reported as percentages only (in the *Prisoners in 2000* narrative), based on inmates with sentences of longer than one year.

3. Persons of Hispanic origin may be any race and do not count toward the 100% total.

4. These categories are not reported separately in the Bureau of Justice Statistics annual reports on prisoners; American Indian, Alaska Native, Native Hawaiian, Pacific Islander, and all others are combined.

Inmate Morbidity

Inmates are sicker than age-matched peers in free society; in general, it is estimated that inmates experience health problems that are typical of non-incarcerated individuals who are seven to fifteen years older (Aday, 1994a; Fazel et al., 2001; Linder and Meyers, 2007; "End-of-Life Care in Corrections," 2008–2009; *Promoting Inmate Rehabilitation,* 2007; Stand Up for What's Right and Just, 2009); ten years is the most commonly cited number. Aging inmates show an increase in significant medical problems (Maruschak and Beck, 2001). This increased morbidity as compared to age-matched peers in free society is well-documented in official reports (Anno, 2004a; Anno et al., 2004; Maruschak and Beck, 2001; Thigpen and Hunter, 1998) and in the professional literature (Clear, Rose, and Ryder, 2001; Linder and Meyers, 2009; Sheu et al., 2002; Stephenson et al., 2005).

Many factors prior to incarceration affect inmate health, including poverty, lack of access to health services, childhood trauma and abuse, substance abuse and chemical dependency, lack of employment opportunities, environmental hazards such as violence and inadequate or unsafe housing, overcrowded living conditions, homelessness, limited access to fresh and wholesome foods, unhealthy diet, undiagnosed or untreated mental illness, undiagnosed or untreated disabilities, poor literacy and health literacy, employment discrimination, and (for many inmates) both historical and contemporary racial discrimination (Cowdrey, 2006; Dubler, 1998; Falter, 1999; Freudenberg, 2001; Gibbons and Katzenbach, 2006; Harris, Hek, and Condon, 2006; Haugebrook et al., 2010).

Prison itself also adversely affects overall inmate health (Marquart and Merianos, 1997). One indicator of the cumulative impact of prison on health is the significantly higher death rates for prisoners serving longer terms; according to a Bureau of Justice Statistics population-based study that included all deaths reported in the years 2001–2004 under the Death in Custody Reporting Act of 2000, inmates who had served ten or more years in prison had a death rate triple that of matched inmates who had served less than five years in prison (Mumola, 2007).

The literature on health disparities in the Unites States confirms that ethnic minorities and the socioeconomically disadvantaged have decreased access to routine health care, are less likely to have a primary-care physician overseeing their care, and are less likely to be screened regularly for health problems like hypertension, cardiovascular disease, diabetes, hepatitis, HIV/AIDS, and cancer (Barr, 2008; Cooper and Kaufman, 1998; Gravlee, 2009; Kaufman, 2008). The result is often lifelong degradation of health-related quality of life and increased risk of being diagnosed with more advanced serious illness. The Surveillance Epidemiology and End Results (SEER) database (Kohler et al., 2011; Ries et al., 2007; National Cancer Institute, 2010) and the disparities literature (Do et al., 2008; Osborn et al., 2010; Philips et al., 2011) clearly document that ethnic minorities (as compared to whites) are diagnosed younger with later-stage disease, have fewer treatment options at diagnosis, and die at younger ages. Inmates with advanced disease are "truly marginalized" (Maddocks, 2003).

Three key studies have enabled the comparison of the incidence of several medical conditions across three distinct US populations: state and federal prisoners (Maruschak, 2008), jail inmates (Maruschak, 2006), and the general population (US Department of Health and Human Services, 2004). The first two studies were conducted by the US Census Bureau on behalf of the Bureau of Justice Statistics; both studies employed a two-stage sampling design that began with the selection of prisons in the first stage followed by the selection of inmates in the second stage. The first stage began with the pre-selection of a limited number of target jails (234), state prisons (21), and federal prisons (3); additionally, a stratified randomized sample was used to increase the total number of eligible jails (465), state prisons (301), and federal prisons (40). Inmates in the target institutions were then chosen by computer using a random start point and predetermined skip interval. Face-to-face self-report interviews with 14,499 jail inmates, 6,982 state prisoners, and 3,686 federal prisoners were conducted without cross-referencing individuals' health records (Wilper et al., 2009). The third study was conducted by the National Center for Health Statistics, part of the Centers for Disease Control (CDC), which has been gathering data since the early 1960s and has conducted the National Health and Nutrition Examination Survey continuously since 1999 (US Department of Health and Human Services, 2004). This study used nationally representative samples that were selected "annually using a complex, multistage sampling design that employs probability, stratified, and cluster sampling to produce U.S. national prevalence estimates" (Ostchega et al., 2011, p. 2). The National Health and Nutrition Examination Survey involves both a face-to-face self-report interview and a physical exam in a standardized environment (US Department of Health and Human Services, 2004).

Both inmate study populations were overwhelmingly male, under 35 years of age, and disproportionately black or Hispanic. While initial rates (i.e., rates without adjustments for age) of diabetes, hypertension, prior myocardial infarction, and persistent asthma appeared comparable to those for the general population in free society, the age-standardized rates were higher in all named categories except prior myocardial infarction among jail inmates (Wilper et al., 2009). Of the more than 20 percent of inmates taking medication for any reason when entering prison or jail, between 26 percent (federal) and 42 percent (jail) stopped taking medication after incarceration. On balance, the data confirm that inmates report more serious health problems at earlier ages compared to age-matched noninstitutionalized peers. Moreover, the most common inmate-reported maladies relate directly to three of the four most common causes of death in prison (heart disease, cancer, respiratory disease, and cerebrovascular disease).

Another study (Binswanger, Krueger, and Steiner, 2009) used a different branch of the National Center for Health Statistics. The same two inmate datasets were compared with the results of the National Health Interview Survey, which employed a continuous cross-sectional probability sampling design to capture a representative sample of households and noninstitutional group quarters (e.g., college dormitories); the target sample size was 35,000, which was generated from 40,000 households with approximately 75,000 to 100,000 individuals who were surveyed each year (US Department of Health and Human Services, 2010). Data from the National Center for Health Statistics for 2002, 2003, and 2004 for adults in free society were compared with the inmate studies. Age- and gender-adjusted results indicate that the prevalence of hypertension, diabetes, myocardial infarction, asthma, arthritis, cervical cancer, and hepatitis is higher for inmates across all age categories as compared to adults in free society; when adjusted for a range of sociodemographic factors and alcohol consumption, these findings hold true for all conditions except myocardial infarction, angina, and diabetes (Binswanger, Krueger, and Steiner, 2009). This list of common maladies directly relate to all four of the most common causes of death in prison.

Inmate Mortality

The top four causes of death in the general population and in the state inmate population are shown in Table 9.2. The top two causes of death, common to both populations, accounted for roughly one-half of all deaths; when combined, these four causes of death accounted for two-thirds of all deaths in state prisons during the index period. Male inmates had a 72 percent higher death rate than female inmates (Mumola, 2007). Older inmates had higher death rates in all categories except suicide in inmates under 35 years of age, which contrasts with international data showing suicide as the leading cause of prison deaths worldwide (Fazel and Baillargeon, 2011). Inmates aged 45 and older accounted for two-thirds of all US inmate deaths. Overall, black and Hispanic state prisoners had identical death rates (206 per 100,000), which were markedly lower than the death rate for white inmates (343 per 100,000). The aggregate inmate population aged 15 to 64 had an overall mortality rate that was 19 percent lower than the mortality rate for the same age group in free society, though these numbers varied sharply by race. Death rates for white and Hispanic prisoners were slightly higher than rates for their free counterparts as compared to blacks in free society; blacks were 57 percent less likely to die while incarcerated (Mumola, 2007).

A population-based retrospective study of 1,807 inmate cancer patients contained in the cancer registry of the University of Texas Medical Branch (Galveston) were compared with two cohorts in free society: the

Table 9.2 The Four Leading Causes of Death, General Population Compared to the Prison Population, 2002–2004 (percentages of all deaths)

	General Population	State Prison Population
1	Heart disease (25)	Heart disease (27)
2	Cancer (23)	Cancer (23)
3	Respiratory disease (6)	Liver disease (10)
4	Cerebrovascular disease (5)	AIDS (7)

Sources: Kochanek et al., 2011; Mumola, 2007.

Surveillance, Epidemiology, and End Results (SEER) registry cohort, comprising a random sample of 179,757 patients; and an age-matched, gender-matched, and race-matched SEER population (called MSEER), comprising 6,124 patients (Mathew et al., 2005). The incidence of cancer was higher for inmates than for both nonincarcerated cohorts, in terms of the overall incidence of all cancers, as well as when matched by gender, race, and specific cancer type. Moreover, survival was significantly poorer for inmates (21 months median) than for each comparison cohort of patients from SEER (55 months) and MSEER (54 months). Lung cancer, non-Hodgkins lymphoma, and hepatic carcinoma were more common in the inmates than in the MSEER cohort ($p < 0.001$ for all comparisons); the same three cancers also caused more deaths among inmates than among the SEER cohort ($p < 0.0001$ for all comparisons).

As compared to the risk of death in free society, male and female inmates of all races have a significantly heightened risk of death after release, particularly immediately following release. One study (Rosen, Schoenbach, and Wohl, 2008) comprises a population based in North Carolina only, limited to black and white males aged 20 to 69 who were incarcerated ($n = 169,795$) or died ($n = 376,029$) between the years 1980 (all) and 2004 (inmates) or 2005 (general population). Both white and black former prisoners had a higher incidence of death from homicide, accidents, substance abuse, HIV/AIDS, liver disease, and liver cancer compared with the general population. Compared with the free population, white former prisoners had deaths from cardiovascular disease, lung cancer, respiratory diseases, and diabetes at least 30 percent higher than expected; in these categories, black former prisoners had lower than expected mortality.

An earlier retrospective cohort study looked at all causes of death in any state for former inmates ($n = 30,237$) released from the Washington State Department of Corrections from July 1999 through December 2003 (Binswanger et al., 2007). All inmates were followed starting with their release from prison and ending with their reincarceration or death, unless they were still living at the conclusion of the study. The mean follow-up period was 1.9 years. This study came to similar conclusions. The study cohort (ages 18 to 84) included both males and females, though again the majority of inmates were male (87 percent) non-Hispanic whites (62 percent), with 91 percent of those who identified as Hispanic also identifying as white. Causes of death included (in descending order of prevalence) drug overdose, cardiovascular disease, homicide, suicide, cancer, and motor vehicle accidents. Homicide, suicide, and overdose were most common in those under 45 years of age; cardiovascular disease and cancer were highest in those aged 45 and older. As compared to the risk of death for people in free society without a history of incarceration, the risk of death for released inmates was 3.5 times higher. The weeks immediately following release posed the greatest risk; for example, the adjusted overdose risk was 129 times greater for released inmates than for the general population. Mortality rates did not return to the general population baseline over the study period. In sum, the causes of death reflect the illnesses noted as most common in the incarcerated: heart disease, cancer, substance abuse and dependence, mental illness, and liver disease.

Defining Hospice Care, Palliative Care, and Disease-Directed Therapy

When comparing and contrasting disease-directed therapy (conventional treatment) with hospice or palliative care, the defining elements are the goals of care, the services provided, the health-care personnel delivering the care, where the care is usually delivered, regulations and practice standards, and financing. Cancer can serve as an illustrative example. Disease-directed treatment for cancer focuses on the goal of eliminating the disease or condition; when cure is not possible, containing the spread of the disease or slowing the progression of the disease takes priority. All appropriate therapies are open to consideration. These might include surgery, conventional radiation, Gamma knife, chemotherapy, chemoembolization (Liver Cancer Network, 2011), radio-frequency ablation ("Radio Frequency Ablation of Liver Tumors," 2011), targeted immunologic, biologic, or hormonal therapies, conventional and advanced stem cell–based therapies including transplantation of rejection-resistant customized body parts (Naik, 2011; Rettner, 2011), and clinical trials. The "burden of treatment" threshold is very high, meaning that even severe treatment symptoms and increased risk of disability or death are acceptable in the name of disease eradication or containment. Extensive imaging studies and genetic testing are not uncommon before, during, and after treatment; testing for the BRCA1 or BRCA2 gene mutations in breast/ovarian cancers ("BRCA1 and BRCA2," 2009) or testing for the FLT3 and other mutations in acute myeloid leukemia (Rockova, 2011) are examples. Treatment is usually provided by a physician specialist. For hospitalization or outpatient clinic intervention for the management of side effects, allied health professionals would be involved on an as-needed basis. There is usually an evidence-based standard of care. Treatment and symptom control measures are usually billed on a fee-for-service basis or under an established managed-care protocol.

In contrast to disease-directed therapy, hospice could not be more different, in all respects, for cancer patients. Hospice was established as a separate category of care by Medicare in the 1980s (Miller and Mike, 1995). Patients must have a prognosis of six months or less to live, and the goal of care is a patient-defined dying experience that neither hastens nor impedes the dying process. Comfort and patient choice take the highest priority. An interdisciplinary team delivers this care; team members include doctors and nurses, social workers, chaplains, home health aides, ancillary health professionals, and volunteers. Care is provided in the patient's home or a homelike setting, including either free-standing hospice houses or assisted-living and skilled-care nursing facilities. The family, as defined by the patient, is considered the unit of care in hospice, not just the patient. All aspects of the individual receive attention, including their medical, psychosocial, relational, instrumental, spiritual, and existential needs. Diagnostic procedures and invasive or "curative" interventions are reserved for circumstances where comfort remains the highest goal—for example, radiation for a spinal cord compression. Hospice-care financing is "carved out" of other medical care, is paid for on a per diem basis for all-inclusive services (home visits, medications, durable medical equipment, and bereavement care), and is covered by all public (Medicare/ Medicaid) and most private health-care funders. The National Hospice and Palliative Care Organization (NHPCO) has promulgated disease-specific criteria for consideration of hospice, predicated on measurable markers. The NHPCO website (www.nhpco.org) contains valuable additional information on hospice and palliative care, and materials drawn from that website (NHPCO, 2009, 2010a) serve as the source for most of the description of hospice elements here.

Palliative care contains elements of both hospice and disease-directed therapy, and can be applied to both sets of goals. The Center to Advance Palliative Care (CAPC, www.capc.org) offers both a definition (CAPC, 2011a) and a chart comparing palliative care to geriatrics, hospice, and case management (CAPC, 2011b). Broadly speaking, the medical definition of "to palliate" is to relieve or ameliorate suffering, whether induced by disease or injury. However, a more narrow definition has emerged and is used to describe the interdisciplinary health-care teams, usually hospital-based, who see patients with very serious illness or injury. These teams listen closely to patients and their loved ones, act as arbiters between specialty health-care teams and patients/families, provide context regarding an injury or illness, and make recommendations to increase comfort and diminish suffering. They also continuously assess the stated treatment goals of the patient/family, and provide counsel on whether the interventions being employed or recommended are in sync with those stated goals, as well as whether the expressed goals are consistent with the patient's condition and prognosis. From this unique vantage point, palliative-care teams can be guardians of the patient's comfort while helping the patient and their family grapple realistically with which goals and treatments best suit a particular patient and in a particular set of circumstances.

Inmate Health-Care Entitlement, Financing, and Standards of Care

Inmates' Legal Entitlement to Health Care

When any government (federal, state, or local) deprives an individual of their freedom against their will for breaking the law, then that government entity assumes a number of responsibilities. One of the most important of these is the provision of medical care, and forty years of jurisprudence related to health care for inmates can be distilled into two simple precepts. First, inmates are entitled to health care. Second, the standard of care for medical services for prisoners shall be comparable to that which free citizens can obtain outside of prison. Admittedly, the devil is in the details, and interpretation and implementation of these precepts can vary widely. When a government entity fails in its responsibility to provide adequate health care, the courts have the authority and the power to impose their will.

Several landmark legal decisions have framed the provision of health care for detainees. In *Estelle v. Gamble* (1976), the Supreme Court held that "deliberate indifference to serious medical needs of prisoners constitutes the unnecessary and wanton infliction of pain, proscribed by the Eighth Amendment." The justices added that "denial of medical care is surely not part of the punishment which civilized nations may impose for crime." In *Ramos v. Lamm* (1980), the Court held that either "repeated examples of negligent acts which disclose a pattern of conduct by the prison medical staff" or "proving there are such systemic and gross deficiencies in staffing, facilities, equipment, or procedures that the inmate population is effectively denied access to adequate medical care" was sufficient to demonstrate "deliberate indifference." Both acts of commission and acts of omission can constitute deliberate indifference. In *Wellman v. Faulkner* (1983), the Federal 7th Circuit Court stated that imprisoning entities must "provide persons in its custody with a medical care system that meets minimal standards of adequacy." Then in *Gates v. Cook* (2004), the Supreme Court sided with death-row inmates in determining that providing insufficient mental health care is also a violation of the Eighth Amendment; with this decision, mental health was included as an essential element of overall health care. That said, there is a prohibition against inmate participation in clinical trials, which is promulgated by the National Commission for the Protection of Human Subjects of Biomedical and Behavioral Research (1974–1978) and published in the Belmont Report (US Department of Health, Education and Welfare, 1979). The guiding principle is that the vulnerability of the inmate population outweighs the potential benefits of experimental or unproven therapies (Lerner, 2007; Wang and Wildeman, 2011).

To date, there are no published analyses of the cost of prison health-care litigation (Hill et al., 2006). It is worth noting that little of the litigation to date has focused on the needs of elderly or dying prisoners. As that population grows, so will use of the legal system to challenge and compel departments of corrections to provide for the myriad health care, housing, safety, and programming needs of an increasingly vulnerable and infirm inmate population. Still unknown is how prison systems and the judiciary will determine which treatments fall under the umbrella of the community standard of care and which need not be made available to inmates. A strong argument can be made that inmates aged 65 and older should receive the same benefits as Medicare recipients, and any efforts to limit inmate access (based on expense) to newer treatments approved for people in free society will undoubtedly be challenged in court. Prisoners' Legal Services (a Massachusetts-based advocacy organization) reported in 2010 that "health care is now the most common issue that [prisoners contacting them] raise" (Thompson, 2010, p. 636).

It is noteworthy that although appropriate health care is mandated and the adequacy of that care is alluded to by the courts, "adequacy" is left undefined; courts have signaled a reluctance to intervene on questions of adequacy of care. "Where a prisoner has received some medical attention and the dispute is over the adequacy of the treatment, federal courts are generally reluctant to second guess medical judgments" (Thompson, 2010, p. 638). Moreover, the existence of a community standard of care is no guarantee it will always be met in free society, much less in prisons (Cohn, 1999).

This ambiguity results in many examples of prisoners' efforts to pursue disease-directed therapy being frustrated through delays in treatment, the unnecessary repetition of tests, or serial referrals to specialists (Thompson, 2010); the risk of experiencing deliberate indifference masquerading as health care may be greater when health care is privatized (Bedard and Frech, 2007; von Zielbauer and Plambeck, 2005). All four top causes of inmate deaths while incarcerated require timely and consistent treatment to prevent disease progression, extend life, and improve quality of life. By contrast, from a correctional administration's perspective, a more aggressive course of treatment will also be significantly more expensive, regardless of its chances of success.

Prison Health-Care Costs and Financing

As inmates age, their security (Kerbs and Jolley, 2007), housing, programming, and health-care needs evolve (Aday, 2003; Aday and Krabill, 2011). A wide range of needs related to advancing age and infirmity have been identified (Curran, 2000), and sound recommendations abound (Aday, 1994b; Anno et al., 2004; California Performance Review, 2004; Gibbons and Katzenbach, 2006; Hill et al., 2006). Undoubtedly, decreased staff-to-inmate ratios and expanded budgets will be required to address older inmates' needs, including infrastructure retrofitting, new construction of segregated housing, special diets, age-specific programming, and work-assignment accommodations for various disabilities (mobility, sight, hearing) that may be coupled with difficulties completing activities of daily living (dressing, eating, toileting, transferring). The premium price extracted from most departments of correction and public safety for medical care and treatment of advanced disease could also see explosive growth.

For example, in 2006 the California Department of Corrections and Rehabilitation reported that inmates aged 55 and older accounted for 5 percent of all inmates, but that they also accounted for over 22 percent of the costs of off-site hospital admissions (Hill et al., 2006, p. 4). In 2009, 1 percent of the inmate population accounted for one-third of outside medical costs (Vesely, 2010, p. 32). Various sources place the yearly cost per older inmate (aged 55 and older) at three times that of a younger inmate (Lundstrom, 1994; Mitka, 2004). This figure has remained fairly constant over the years, thus raising many concerns about the potential financial strains that older inmates pose to correctional budgets in the long run. Additionally, further strain on the budgets of departments of public safety and corrections is inevitable given the aging infrastructure of the current prison system, the need for retrofitting of existing prisons, the need for new public prisons, and the need for secure public and private long-term care facilities for elderly inmates (Mara, 2002). Interestingly, public support for large prison budgets may be waning. Recent opinion polls suggest that the public may be shifting its support toward smaller prison budgets, but it is unclear if this shift represents a temporary detour or a permanent change in public opinion (Greenberg, Quinlan, and Rosner, 2011).

The method of funding inmate health care amplifies the adverse financial impact of an aging and increasingly infirm prison population. Again, the ballooning cost of inmate health care echoes the national dialogue on Medicare's exploding costs as the general population ages. Prisons are mandated to provide care equivalent to the community standard, but the consumers (prisoners) have little or no incentive to contain costs, and prison administrators often lack the power to negotiate costs.

Standards of Care for Community Hospice, Palliative Care, and Disease-Directed Therapy

Hospice care in free society today is largely guided by Medicare, state hospice certification bodies, the National Hospice and Palliative Care Organization, and the Joint Commission on the Accreditation of Health-Care Organizations (JCAHO, www.jointcommission.org). Medicare has established the conditions of participation (US Department of Health and Human Services, 2008) that hospices must follow to be eligible for Medicare reimbursement. Specific standards of care are published by the National Hospice and Palliative Care Organization for the general public (NHPCO, 2010b) and are revised periodically. Standards are included that stress quality assurance and continuous quality improvement. Additionally, individual states often implement mechanisms for licensing hospices that largely conform to Medicare's conditions of participation and may include state-specific requirements; that said, licensure is important because it enables state reimbursement via Medicaid. For hospices affiliated with hospitals or health systems, the cyclical accreditation process by the JCAHO includes hospice-specific standards.

Palliative care is practiced across a variety of settings and it is still evolving, which means that standards are more difficult to define. The American Academy of Hospice and Palliative Medicine (AAHPM, www .aahpm.org) provides guidelines for practice and position papers on a variety of topics (AAHPM, 2006a, 2006b, 2006c, 2007b). Palliative-care teams can be hospital- or community-based, formally structured or more informally organized, and may or may not include members who are board-certified in palliative medicine (AAHPM, 2007a).

Standards of care for disease-directed therapy vary based on the severity of the condition; the patient's age, co-morbidities, and underlying overall health; availability of a given therapy; coverage; and patient preference. For example, a broad range of options for cancer therapy was outlined earlier. Which of those therapies would be the standard of care would depend first on the type, location, and stage of the cancer. These standards are generally derived through the clinical trials process in concert with the National Institutes of Health (NIH, www.nih.gov) and the condition-specific professional medical organizations like the American Society of Clinical Oncology (ASCO, www.asco.org) and the American Cancer Society (ACS, www.cancer.org). It is naive, however, to suggest that a treatment like Provenge (Thara et al., 2011) for hormone-resistant advanced prostate cancer would be available for or desirable to all eligible patients in free society, especially given the $93,000 cost and the sophisticated processes involved in producing a dose. Moreover, such costs and treatments may be difficult (if not impossible) to secure in correctional contexts.

Standards of Care for Correctional Hospice, Palliative Care, and Disease-Directed Therapy

In correctional settings, there are also specific standards of care for hospice. The first iteration of these standards grew out of the GRACE project, funded by the Robert Wood Johnson Foundation's (2009) Promoting Excellence in End-of-Life Care program; Volunteers of America was a collaborator on this project as well (Grace Project, 2000). The original standards were promulgated for free-society populations (and then adapted to prison settings) using the National Hospice and Palliative Care Organization's standards of practice (NHPCO, 2000). A major revision of the quality guidelines for hospice and end-of-life care in correctional settings was completed about a decade later (NHPCO, 2009); these revised guidelines form the foundation for hospice care in prisons and jails in the United States today. The multidisciplinary committee responsible for the revision was comprised largely of geographically diverse members of existing exemplary prison hospices. Members had access to the draft NHPCO standards (NHPCO, 2010b), brought their own expertise, and had the benefit of descriptive published reports from some of the first prison hospices in the country (Barens, 1998; Bauersmith and Gent, 2002; Boyle, 2002; Evans, Herzog, and Tillman, 2002; Linder, Enders, et al., 2002; Linder, Knauf, et al., 2002; Maull, 2005). They also benefited from the published descriptive (Bick, 2002) and empirical (Lin and Mathew, 2005) studies on care and symptom management in prisons.

The paucity of specialty health-care services, particularly palliative-care teams, in correctional settings is particularly unfortunate. There are no published reports of in-house palliative-care teams in any correctional setting in the United States. Hence, inmates will likely encounter a palliative-care team only if and when they are seen in a community inpatient or outpatient setting.

Standards of care for disease-directed therapy for prisoners mirror those in the free community, with a few caveats. The availability and access of treatment is complicated by the need to transport and guard prisoners, the rigors of scheduling for some treatments (for instance, radiation is usually daily for a fixed period of time), and the proximity to and cost of a specific treatment (Gibbons and Katzenbach, 2006; Hill et al., 2006; Thompson, 2010). With those factors in mind, there is abundant evidence that in free society, ethnic/racial minorities, particularly blacks and Hispanics, who compose the majority of prison and jail populations, have a greater preference for disease-directed therapy over hospice compared to whites; moreover, ethnic and racial minorities are less likely to complete an advance medical directive or to voluntarily choose to limit disease-directed therapy or extraordinary life-preserving interventions (Dubler, 1998). Consequently, a disproportionately high number of inmates will want to pursue the standard of care for disease-directed therapy.

These findings are consistent across multiple studies of hospice utilization, including a random-digit-dialed convenience survey of 220 blacks and 253 whites in Cincinnati (Ludke and Smucker, 2007); a secondary analysis of the National Mortality Followback Survey using death certificates and interviews with relatives for 23,000 decedents in 1993 (Greiner, Perera, and Ahluwalia, 2003); and an analysis of CDC death-certificate records and the Centers for Medicare and Medicaid Services hospice claims in 2002 (Connor et al., 2008).

Likewise, findings from studies on advance care planning have consistently documented how racial and ethnic minorities share a preference for disease-directed treatment. For example, a face-to-face survey study with 139 interviews from consecutive patients (51 African Americans, 39 Hispanics, 49 non-Hispanic whites) at the University of Miami School of Medicine's general medicine clinic found that larger proportions of Hispanics (42 percent) and blacks (37 percent) preferred life-sustaining treatments (regardless of risks) as compared with whites (14 percent) (Caralis et al., 1993). In a retrospective cohort study of approximately 400,000 nursing-home residents in California, Massachusetts, New York, and Ohio between November 1998 and October 1999 (Kiely et al., 2001), whites were more likely than blacks, in all of these states, to have a living will, a do-not-resuscitate order, and a surrogate decisionmaker. Similar conclusions were found in a secondary analysis of the 1996 Medical Expenditure Panel Survey, which comprised a nationally representative sample of 3,747 nursing-home residents. According to this analysis: "African Americans are about one-third as likely as Caucasians to have living wills and one-fifth as likely as Caucasians to have [do-not-resuscitate] orders; Hispanics are about one-third as likely as Caucasians to have [do-not-resuscitate] orders and just as likely as Caucasians to have living wills . . . even after controlling for health and other demographic factors" (Degenholtz et al., 2002, p. 378). In sum, the results of these three studies are congruent with general trends in the literature (see, e.g., Baker, 2002; Johnstone and Kanitsaki, 2009).

Differences Between Hospice in Correctional Settings and Free Society

There are important differences between hospice behind bars and in the larger community outside of prison. Departments of corrections are ultimately responsible for paying for inmate health care; prisoners are currently ineligible for public or private health insurance. As a consequence, prison hospices are not bound by the Medicare conditions of participation, so patients need not meet predefined criteria to be admitted to and remain in prison hospice. This carries some benefits. For example, prison hospices do not have to follow the eligibility rule requiring that an inmate have a prognosis of six months or less to live. Inmates too ill to remain in the general population who have a terminal condition can be transferred to hospice even if their demise is not imminent. Moreover, the prohibition of disease-directed therapies for hospice patients in free society does not apply to prison, so the transition from curative to comfort care can be more gradual and can include concurrent disease-directed and hospice interventions, an approach sometimes called simultaneous care (Hui et al., 2010; Meyers et al., 2011; Meyers and Linder, 2003; Meyers et al., 2004). Hence, AIDS patients, for example, can continue to receive highly active antiretroviral therapy (HAART) while under hospice care, and prisoners with end-stage kidney disease can continue dialysis if they choose to do so. Another positive difference is that inmate volunteers are available to sit vigil around the clock, ensuring that no inmate dies alone unless that is their desire. This benefit is sorely missed in community hospices. That said, the goals of hospice (allowing a disease to take its course, neither hastening nor delaying death) still apply.

Negative differences may include having fewer options for management of pain and other acute symptoms, having fewer health professionals who are highly skilled in palliative and end-of-life care, discontinuity of treatment approaches from one shift to the next, rotating medical and correctional staff to include those not trained in or sympathetic to hospice philosophy, and many impediments to care brought about by dilapidated and difficult-to-modify physical facilities (Bick, 2002; Hoffman and Dickinson, 2011; Linder, Knauf, et al., 2002; Linder and Meyers, 2011; Zimmermann, 2009). The absence of some hospice team members from the prison setting, notably home health aides, physical and occupational therapists, and dietitians, is also problematic, as is limited access to adaptive medical equipment and the space to operate it. Another striking difference between elder-care services in prison compared to free society is that the primary models to improve quality and contain health-care costs in free society "depend on some combination of patient self-management and informal support," neither of which is readily adaptable to prisons (Hill et al., 2006, p. 6). Finally, correctional systems are notoriously inflexible, slow to adapt, and usually averse to innovation.

Innovations, Interventions, and Challenges of Prison Hospice

Hospice has long been recognized as the standard of care for terminally ill patients who have a prognosis of six months or less to live and who have exhausted available disease-directed or curative treatment options or who have elected to focus on comfort and pursue primarily palliative interventions. The past two decades (1990–2010) have seen the rise of a fledgling prison hospice movement nationwide. In 2004, a national survey of prison hospices by Anno et al. found twenty-five established correctional hospice programs with between one and fifty additional programs in the planning stages at the federal, state, and local levels across the United States and its territories. More recently, in 2011, Hoffman and Dickinson published the findings from a survey that identified sixty-nine known prison hospice programs. Hence the United States is slow to increase access to prison hospice programs, as evidenced by this limited number of programs. Such findings suggest that the United States has a great need for expanded access to such programs given the aging demography of its prisons.

Initial Prison Hospice Planning

The successful integration of hospice into the prison setting is greatly facilitated when correctional staff and supervisors are included in the planning process and participate in specialized training, and when the program has support from the warden's office (Barens, 1998). Infrastructure and staff attitudes have presented the greatest obstacles to the smooth integration of hospice services into prisons. Additionally, aging physical facilities are not easily modified or renovated to accommodate the special needs and preferred services traditionally provided to individuals in hospice settings. For example, the chaplain (Keith Knauf) at the California Medical Facility in Vacaville explained during an interview that while showers are common in prison, bathtubs are not typically available. Hospices often need bathtubs or modified bathing facilities to accommodate nonambulatory patients. Ideally, Knauf has noted that there should be an area where a prisoner on a gurney could be bathed. If just showers are available, outfitting them with grab bars and seats for use by disabled individuals, with room to accommodate a staff assistant, is an acceptable (though cumbersome) alternative.

Inmate Volunteers

Many prison hospices use inmate volunteers; most programs impose stringent pre-screening criteria and provide extensive initial and ongoing training. Use of inmate volunteers provides several specific benefits, including around-the-clock inmate availability to sit vigil with dying prisoners, ensuring that no inmate dies alone unless desired; experiential understanding of prison life; and links to friends outside the hospice unit.

Given the evidence that successful rehabilitation reduces recidivism (Esperian, 2010; Pew Center on the States, 2011), one area rich with research opportunities involves formally evaluating how the hospice volunteer experience behaviorally affects the inmate volunteer, both during their remaining time in prison and upon release; one positive qualitative phone interview study of fourteen prison hospice program coordinators (Bronstein and Wright, 2006) and numerous anecdotal reports (e.g. Barens, 1998; Beeler, 2006; Cichowlas and Chen, 2010) suggest that these programs do have positive effects on inmate volunteers. That said, determining which inmate work assignments or volunteer activities are transformative for inmates and contribute to successful reintegration into free society deserves high priority and can potentially pay huge financial and societal dividends.

Limiting Care

Those who have experienced inferior health care based on race and socioeconomic status are often deeply suspicious of any recommendation to forego disease-directed intervention, despite the inexorable trajectory of terminal illness and the reality that comfort-focused care is more appropriate and more humane. A report of an archetypical case study of this phenomenon in free society is available elsewhere (Linder, 2004). That said, suspicions regarding health-care workers and their recommendations can run high among minorities, who have have been subjected to ethical violations within the Tuskegee experiment (Freimuth et al., 2001; Jones, 1993; Roy, 1995) and the circumstances surrounding the HeLa cancer-cell line (Skloot, 2010), which represent two powerful examples of the systemic neglect or outright harm visited on the disadvantaged among us by the dominant (white) culture and its health-care providers.

Advance Medical Directives

Advance medical directives enable individuals to appoint a surrogate decisionmaker and express treatment preferences should they be unable to speak for themselves, and are usually used to restrict or limit care. In prison, there are inherent conflicts of interest that effectively eliminate readily available proxies for various reasons:

- Inmates are forbidden from having power over other inmates.
- Individuals' health-care providers are excluded from serving as proxies because prison personnel have an apparent if not an actual conflict of interest if asked to serve as an inmate's proxy.
- The complicated and often conflicted long-distance relationships an inmate has with his or her biological family mean that family members are often unavailable or unwilling to serve in this capacity.

- Many departments of corrections restrict or outright forbid any contact between freed convicted felons and those still in custody, eliminating the prison "family" from serving as surrogates even after they gain their freedom.

As noted earlier, individuals who have lower socioeconomic status, lower literacy, and less education, and those who are members of an ethnic or racial minority, are less likely to complete an advanced medical directive (Johnstone and Kanitsaki, 2009; Kwak and Haley, 2005; Murphy and Palmer, 1996), and are less inclined to opt to restrict the care they receive if they do want care (see also Waters, 2001; Dubler, 1998). That said, user-friendly tools to facilitate end-of-life decisionmaking are available (Enders, 2004; "The 'Go Wish' Game," 2009; Steinhauser et al., 2000); these alternatives seem to overcome many of the literacy and health-literacy obstacles in prison-based settings.

Resuscitation and Do-Not-Resuscitate Orders

Most prison hospice programs do not require enrolled patients to have a do-not-resuscitate order, though such orders are routinely discussed. During high-profile medical emergencies, departments of corrections must consider many stakeholders, including the inmate's biological family, other inmates, prison administration, and the courts. Foregoing resuscitation of an inmate in the prison setting, even when doing so follows an inmate's expressed preference, could be seen by some stakeholders as yet another example of deliberate indifference. Conversely, resuscitation in the prison setting, particularly when performed in view of an inmate audience, is a very public display of prison administration and corrections staff going to great lengths to preserve an inmate's life and can counter suspicions of deliberate indifference. That said, some departments of corrections do not offer the do-not-resuscitate option to gravely ill inmates (Dubler, 1998), meaning in effect that resuscitation must always be attempted. *Commissioner of Corrections v. Myers* (1979) set the troubling precedent that prison policy can supersede an individual's right to refuse care or treatment.

Physician's Order for Life-Sustaining Treatment

Recently a new instrument regarding end-of-life care has been added, the physician's order for life-sustaining treatment (see http://www.ohsu.edu/polst). The order allows first-responders more latitude when summoned to help a terminally ill patient *in extremis*. States adopting this treatment paradigm then produce guidance for health-care professionals; Oregon is a good example (Center for Ethics in Health Care, 2009). The physician's order should be enforceable within, and more importantly beyond, the prison's walls, enhancing the portability that an individual's preferences will be followed and ensuring greater continuity of care across different settings. So far, twelve states and parts of another have adopted this paradigm; moreover, sixteen states and portions of six others are at some stage of evaluating or implementing this treatment paradigm ("State POLST Contact List," 2011). Its penetration into prison systems is an area rich with opportunity for ongoing and future research, but currently no evidence is available that addresses its use in correctional settings.

Hastened Death

It is only a matter of time before the more challenging issues on the frontier of hastened death make their way behind prison walls. The term *hastened death* refers to a range of actions, many of which are already legal in some or all states, that may accelerate the dying process for those with terminal illness. This continuum includes the discontinuation of dialysis for end-stage renal disease or failure; the refusal of food and fluids; palliative sedation, a practice in which the death-hastening impact is hotly debated in the palliative-care literature (Cassell and Rich, 2010; Jansen, 2010a, 2010b; Orentlicher, 1997); and assisted suicide or euthanasia. It is doubtful that assisted dying would be available to inmates in the foreseeable future, even in states where the practice is legal for members of free society. However, in two landmark decisions regarding a constitutional right to assisted suicide (*Vacco v. Quill,* 1997; *Washington v. Glucksberg,* 1997), the Supreme Court suggested a right to aggressive palliative care (Burt, 1997), affirmed the principle of double effect (i.e., when good or legitimate acts may also result in bad effects), and noted a "care-giver obligation to address pain and suffering at the end of life" (Dubler, 1998, p. 154), particularly for vulnerable groups who are unable to ease their own suffering.

In sum, prisons and the judiciary will have to determine if and under what circumstances inmates will be permitted to elect one or another of these options. Additionally, these decisions are laden with questions of biomedical ethics, the answers to which have broad implications not just for inmates at the end of life, but also with respect to treatment of late-stage disease, the overall costs of health care in prison, and the value of a human life.

Dementia

Dementia, including Alzheimer's disease, will present increasing challenges to prisons and jails. The diverging trajectories for physical versus mental decline in inmates with dementia will translate into the need for lower staff-to-inmate ratios and will carry a substantial financial premium above and beyond the average cost per person per year of incarceration. Legal challenges regarding the use of physical or chemical restraints on demented inmate patients are a near certainty. Prisons will be in the unenviable position of providing close supervision and custodial oversight for individuals who can neither remember the reasons for their incarceration nor the rules and prohibitions of appropriate inmate behavior.

On a more philosophical note, Rich (2004) raises the question of identity. Should an advance medical directive continue in force for an individual in the free population as dementia progresses? He ponders whether the patient with advanced dementia is essentially a different person. Assuming for a moment that his suggestion is true or at least legally arguable, it raises the companion issue of whether we are justified in continuing the incarceration of an individual whose memory and thought processes are so altered from those of the inmate originally imprisoned as to raise the same identity conundrum.

Non-Prison-Based Options for Inmate End-of-Life Care

Medical Parole and Compassionate Release

Medical parole may be granted whether an inmate is dying or simply profoundly disabled or ill with no imminent threat of death. If the circumstances of these cases change radically and individuals become more functional, in some instances medical parole can be revoked and the individual could be returned to prison ("Big Hurdles Remain," 2011; Sacramento Bee Staff, 2011).

Compassionate release usually applies to inmates who are in the terminal phase of an illness; release usually includes care by a hospice team; frequently, permanent placement involves relatives or a skilled-care facility. Generally, compassionate release is not revocable should the patient's medical condition dramatically improve, but it is usually granted only when that possibility is minuscule.

The biggest problems with most medical parole or compassionate-release programs in the United States is the requirement that the inmate no longer pose a threat to society in order to begin the process, and thus, frequently, the inmate dies before the process can be completed (Anno et al., 2004; Beck, 1999). The dire fiscal situations currently faced at the local, state, and federal levels may lead to widespread reconsideration of these policies. For example, California recently revised its compassionate-release policy ("Big Hurdles Remain," 2011; McGreevy and Dolan, 2010; California State Senate, 2010), and a handful of inmates have been freed (Sacramento Bee Staff, 2011; Stanton, 2011a, 2011b, 2011c). The savings can be substantial, by some estimates as much as $200 million per year in California (McGreevy and Dolan, 2010). The savings to the California Department of Corrections and Rehabilitation for just one of the first three inmates granted medical parole will be $750,000 per year; the total annual potential savings for some of those inmates who are eligible for medical parole in California is estimated at up to $2 million per year (McGreevy and Dolan, 2010).

Nonetheless, resistance remains strong. The first inmate to be granted a medical parole hearing under a new California law, a quadriplegic, paralyzed from the neck down, was denied medical parole despite estimated medical costs of $650,000 per year, which will escalate dramatically if he requires outside hospitalization (*Sacramento Bee,* 2011). When medical parole is granted, real net savings result, as it is no longer necessary to transport or guard these individuals and thus substantial cost is shifted away from corrections. Finally, there will likely be additional resistance at the federal and state levels to any plans that would shift a significant portion of the costly care for aging inmates from prisons to Medicare, Medicaid, and other public funding streams.

Project for Older Prisoners

In 1989, Jonathon Turley established the Project for Older Prisoners (POPS), which performs three functions related to older prisoners: individual case evaluations, state reports and recommendations for reform, and legislative drafting (see Turley 2007). The program performs a systematic and comprehensive evaluation of older prisoners (prisoners who may or may not be physically infirm or at the end of life) at a given institution and makes recommendations for the release of individual inmates who are identified as representing both a low risk of recidivism and a negligible threat to public safety, as is often the case with prisoners receiving end-of-life care. Currently, the program is active in five states (Louisiana, Maryland, Michigan, North Carolina, and Virginia) and the District of Columbia. Yet there is reluctance or resistance in many states; in California, POPS programs have yet to be initiated despite a recommendation from an independent panel chaired by former governor George Deukmejian (Corrections Independent Review Panel, 2004) and the recent Supreme Court order to reduce the prison population (Stanton, Doyle, and Yamamura, 2011).

In testimony to Congress in 2007, Turley pointed out that older inmates are physiologically older than their chronological age and that their housing costs are higher (often by a factor of three) when compared to the costs associated with the housing of younger inmates; moreover, he indicated that the crisis facing correctional entities today results from the confluence of four factors—acute demographic shifts in prison populations, budget shortfalls, overcrowding, and high recidivism rates—but that POPS could help to alleviate the adverse outcomes related to these factors (see Turley 2007). Court-ordered reductions in inmate populations often result in the least-desirable outcome—the release of younger inmates who are less expensive to house, but who also represent a greater risk to society and are more likely to recidivate. Moreover, the retention of older inmates appears counterproductive, because they are more expensive to house and to care for medically, and represent a significantly smaller risk to the public safety. There is a clear inverse correlation between age and recidivism, meaning that increased age translates directly into dramatically decreased rates of recidivism. Thus, Turley cites federal data reporting a 31.6 percent rate of recidivism for released prisoners under 40 years of age, which is much higher than the 11 percent rate of recidivism for prisoners aged 40 and older. Clearly, age is a necessary but not sufficient predictor of successful reintegration into the community and desistance in further criminal activity.

Federal Bureau of Prisons Programs

The Federal Bureau of Prisons is making a more concerted effort at drug education, residential and nonresidential treatment for the incarcerated (with a substantive curriculum and time off for participation), and transitional housing and support (community transition) for reentry. This bold experiment continues to generate valuable data allowing a better comparison between incarceration with and without treatment for substance abuse (Pelissier et al., 2000; Pelissier et al., n.d.). Moreover, the federal effort has expanded significantly, from 5,887 participants in 1990, to 21,832 in 1995, to 44,571 in 2000, to 98,172 in 2010 (US Department of Justice, 2010). Though not confined to an older population, older inmates are included in the substance abuse treatment efforts of the Federal Bureau of Prisons, and a compound effect on recidivism for older inmates is expected in relation to the interaction between age and treatment.

Criminal Justice Transition Coalition Recommendations

Additional concrete recommendations can be found in the Criminal Justice Transition Coalition's report *Smart on Crime* (Sloan et al., 2008). Given the inverse correlation between age and recidivism, the coalition recommends expansion of programs for the early release of all eligible elderly offenders to home detention. The coalition voices support for the Second Chance Act, specifically the pilot program called Elderly and Family Reunification for Certain Nonviolent Offenders, under which the Bureau of Prisons is authorized "to set up one or more demonstration projects at [bureau facilities] for qualified individuals" (Sloan et al., 2008, p. 67). Eligibility criteria include the following: inmates who are not imprisoned for a life sentence; inmates who have served the greater of ten years or 75 percent of their term of imprisonment; and inmates who do not have convictions for crimes of violence, sex offenses, or other offenses described in the relevant code (18 U.S.C. § 2332b(g)(5)(B) or USC 18 chapter 37).

Conclusion

There is broad agreement that a large population of older and infirm inmates, both in absolute numbers and as a percentage of the total prison population, will continue to grow over the coming decades. That said, large public systems like public safety and corrections departments take a long time to adapt to change, and the coming changes in the demographics and health status of the adult prison population will require significant adaptation in personnel, infrastructure, public policy, and the allocation of ever more scarce resources. How will the United States address the aging prison population relative to end-of-life care? How will society deal with exploding health-care costs that are often associated with the last six months of life? Will the country continue to block or delay the early release of low-risk inmates, including those who are often disabled by terminal illnesses at the end of life? How society responds to these vexing issues will determine the future of the corrections system nationwide. While adaptations to address these issues are making their way into some of the country's prisons and jails, two questions remain to be answered. Are we making substantial enough changes to the system to avoid continued financial and socio-legal problems? My interpretation of the evidence is that we are not. Can we take enough evasive action to significantly alter our course to avoid catastrophic problems? That remains to be seen.

10

Community Reentry and Aging Inmates

Kristie R. Blevins and Anita N. Blowers

From the 1980s to the present day, "get tough on crime" legislation and stricter sentencing policies have dramatically increased the number of individuals sentenced to prison each year in the United States (Auerhahn, 2002; Mauer, 2002). Additionally, the average length of prison sentences has grown. The result of these trends is that more offenders than ever before are being sentenced to prison and being held in institutional facilities for longer terms. The majority of offenders, however, will not die in prison. Most inmates will be released back into the community, though many of them will be in their senior years when their discharge occurs (Auerhahn, 2002).

Each year, more than 700,000 inmates are released from prisons in the United States (Visher, 2007). Some offenders are released because they have served their maximum sentences, while others are discharged via early-release mechanisms such as parole, crowding provisions, or compassionate release due to terminal illnesses. Whatever the reason for release, the reentry of inmates has implications not only for the individuals being released, but also for their families and the community at large. In fact, inmate release can affect community finances, public safety, levels of homelessness, civic participation, and public health (Visher, 2007; Williams and Abraldes, 2007).

Prisoner release in the United States has so far been unsuccessful. For example, in a study of former inmates released through various methods in fifteen states, more than half of former prisoners were rearrested within the first couple of years after release (Solomon, Kachnowski, and Bhati, 2005). These results are consistent with other research examining recidivism rates of former inmates (Hughes, Wilson, and Beck, 2001; Langan and Levin,

2002). The alarming failure rate of prisoners who reenter society has come to the attention of academics, journalists, politicians, and policymakers at the local, state, and federal levels (Pager, 2006; Visher, 2007), and it is clear that the reentry process must be thoroughly evaluated and modified to become more effective. Accordingly, researchers have begun to examine what works to make community reentry more successful (see, e.g., Listwan, Cullen, and Latessa, 2006; Petersilia, 2004). In general, evaluations indicate that substance abuse treatment, vocational training, and programs designed specifically for violent offenders can lead to reduced recidivism and fewer technical violations during reentry (Seiter and Kadela, 2003).

At present, most research on prisoner reentry tends to generalize among all inmates coming out of prison. This information is certainly crucial, but exploring issues relating to the successful reentry of unique inmate populations, such as older prisoners, might provide additional insight into methods of facilitating successful reentry and reintegration. Thus, this chapter focuses attention on the special needs (e.g., housing, employment, familial relationships, and health-care issues) that aging inmates face as they deal with reintegrating back into society. The first part of the chapter provides an overview of the considerations that must be taken into account when designing and implementing reentry programs for older inmates. The second part examines current initiatives directed toward reentry of older prisoners and policy implications that need to be addressed to effectively manage this population. The chapter concludes with a review of the sociopolitical and policy-based obstacles that complicate the reentry of older federal and state prisoners into society.

The Aging Inmate Population

The aging prison population has inevitably resulted in more geriatric inmates being released from prison than ever before, but there has been little research specifically concerning the reentry and reintegration of older former prisoners (Williams and Abraldes, 2007). Reentry into society is stressful for former inmates of any age as they attempt to find jobs, housing, and physical and mental health care, and reestablish connections with friends and family in the community (Binswanger et al., 2007; Petersilia, 2003). However, reentry "becomes even more problematic for older prisoners, as these inmates are both quantitatively and qualitatively different from other prisoners" (Stojkovic, 2007, p. 115). Prisons currently work under the assumption that incoming prisoners will be incarcerated young and released young (Ornduff, 1996). However, elderly prisoners have different needs than the rest of the prison population, and as a result need to be treated differently, as discussed throughout this book and elsewhere (see, e.g., Aday, 2003; Ornduff, 1996).

Although there is no clear-cut consensus, most researchers recommend that correctional agencies adopt age 50 as the chronological starting point for defining older inmates (Aday, 2003; Stojkovic, 2007). Because of the unhealthy lifestyles of many individuals before incarceration and the lack of medical care associated with unhealthy lifestyles, the physiological age of an inmate usually surpasses their chronological age (Aday, 2003; Kerbs, 2000b). The reason for the lower boundary that defines prisoners as "old," "elderly," or "geriatric" stems from the fact that criminal offenders tend to have many health issues related to poverty, substance abuse, unhealthy lifestyles, and other social issues (e.g., more frequent exposure to communicable diseases) (Aday, 2003; Loeb and AbuDagga, 2006; Williams and Abraldes, 2007). The resulting medical problems of offenders are often compounded by the lack of appropriate health care and living conditions. Once in prison, inmates tend to age more quickly as compared to individuals on the outside (Aday, 2003; Williams and Abraldes, 2007). Considering the typically unhealthy and stressful conditions faced by offenders both before and during prison, it has been estimated that many prisoners are seven to ten years older physiologically than they are chronologically (Rikard and Rosenberg, 2007). Inmates tend to have shorter life expectancies than individuals on the outside (Auerhahn, 2002), and the hastened aging of inmates can be measured by examining the higher rates of chronic disease and illness among inmates as compared to nonincarcerated individuals (Aday, 2003; Colsher et al., 1992).

In the late 1970s, there were approximately 6,500 inmates aged 55 and older in US prisons (Bureau of Justice Statistics, 2001). Following that period, the correctional orientation in the country became more punitive in nature, resulting in harsher sentencing practices. During the 1980s and 1990s, the average age of the prison population increased substantially. By 2000, the number of inmates aged 55 and older had grown to over 50,000, an increase of more than 750 percent (Bureau of Justice Statistics, 2001). Since 2000, the number of older inmates has continued to increase; at the end of 2009, there were 79,100 inmates (5.1 percent of the total prison population) aged 55 and older. That number doubles when the age for determining who is an "older" inmate is reduced to 50; hence, there were 160,700 prisoners aged 50 and older at the end of 2009, accounting for 10.4 percent of the total prison population (West, Sabol, and Greenman, 2010). Older inmates account for the largest percentage of growth among prisoners (Harrison and Beck, 2004), and some speculate that older inmates will make up about one-third of the prison population by 2020 (Enders, Paterniti, and Meyers, 2005; Neely, Addison, and Craig-Moreland, 1997).

There are multiple explanations for the aging of the prison population. First, the "get tough on crime" movement and the accompanying harsher sentencing practices have limited the discretion of judges when considering mitigating factors such as age, health issues, and risk to public safety when sentencing offenders (Rikard and Rosenberg, 2007; Smyer and Burbank, 2009; Yates and Gillespie, 2000). The consequence is that a greater number of older people are being sentenced to prison for crimes committed later in life (Kerbs, 2000a). Second, increased use of strict sentencing related to drug crimes, as well as mandatory-minimum sentences, truth-in-sentencing policies that require inmates to complete a certain percentage of their sentences (usually 85 percent) before being considered for release, and second- and third-strike legislation have resulted in longer confinement sentences for many offenders (Snyder et al., 2009; Yorston and Taylor, 2006). Because they are serving longer sentences, numerous inmates do not become eligible for release until well after they have turned 50 years old (Kerbs, 2000b).

Overall, there are four groups of geriatric prisoners. The first group comprises those who have spent most of their lives in prison for crimes committed when they were young. The second group comprises those who have lived a relatively crime-free life but were caught engaging in criminal acts in their older years (Ornduff, 1996; Yates and Gillespie, 2000). The third group consists of older career criminals who tend to commit less serious crimes but spend time in prison sporadically throughout their lives after getting caught for each offense (Aday, 1994a). Finally, the fourth group includes older inmates who have landed in prisons as part of the deinstitutionalization and transinstitutionalization movements, in which individuals with mental illnesses go to prisons rather than state hospitals or other care facilities (Williams and Abraldes, 2007; Yates and Gillespie, 2000).

Although the system's front-end policies (e.g., sentencing policies) have contributed to the nation's aging prison population, more conservative policies at the back-end of the system (i.e., at the point of release from prison) also have played a role. Specifically, it is harder than ever for inmates to qualify for early release from prison via parole or postrelease supervision. In fact, Williams and Abraldes (2007) noted that there is no longer a balance between sentencing and release, because fewer inmates are able to meet release criteria. The same types of "get tough" legislation that incarcerate more individuals for longer periods of time also often place constraints on parole boards and other release mechanisms. The fact that several states have abolished discretionary parole (Petersilia, 1999) intensifies the problem by eliminating one option for early release for inmates who would otherwise be eligible. Among the states that still offer discretionary parole, most of them have implemented strict guidelines for parole-board members and other decisionmaking entities, making it more difficult for inmates to be considered suitable for discretionary release (Higgins and Severson, 2009).

There is no indication that current conservative sentencing and release policies will be modified in the near future. Given that prison populations will likely continue to grow, and the vast majority of individuals entering prison will be released (Petersilia, 1999; Pollock, 2004), prisoner reentry into society will remain an important topic for decades. Additionally, because inmates are spending more time behind bars, there will be an exponential growth in the number of elderly inmates being released from prison. Thus, it is imperative that correctional administrators begin to address the special challenges older inmates encounter as they reintegrate back into society.

The Relationship Between Age and Crime and the Risk of Releasing Older Inmates

Overall, inmate reentry into society poses a risk for public safety (Listwan, Cullen, and Latessa, 2006; Solomon, Kachnowski, and Bhati, 2005). As mentioned previously, there is a high probability that the majority of those released from prison will be rearrested within a few years after discharge (Austin, 1986; Hughes, Wilson, and Beck, 2001; Langan and Levin, 2002; Solomon, Kachnowski, and Bhati, 2005). These findings, however, should not be generalized to older inmates for one main reason: their age. When comparing an older individual's arrest rate before entering prison with his or her arrest rate after release from prison, there are almost always significantly fewer arrests after prison (Austin, 1986; Smyer and Burbank, 2009). The lower rate of arrest after prison is explained, in part, by the maturation effect (Austin, 1986). The literature on correlates of crime has consistently found that people tend to commit fewer crimes as they get older, regardless of the control variables used, such as type of offense, race, and gender (Smyer and Burbank, 2009). In fact, in their study of a male cohort, Kurlychek, Brame, and Bushway (2006) maintain that the risk of committing additional crimes decreases drastically at six to seven years after arrest, even among young offenders. Moreover, they found that offenders' rates of recidivism become very similar to those of nonoffenders at about seven years after arrest.

The relationship between age and crime holds true for individuals who have served both short and long prison terms. Indeed, the number of rearrests among those on parole declines sharply with age (Austin and Hardyman, 2004). Older releasees tend to have very low recidivism rates (Holman,

1998) and, in general, are less likely to have future contact with the criminal justice system as compared to younger former inmates (Goetting, 1983). Overall, older releasees are less likely than any other group of former prisoners to get sent back to prison (Williams and Abraldes, 2007).

While the literature is clear in establishing that older individuals commit less crime (Aday, 2003), older former prisoners should not automatically be considered as low risk to the community. There are always exceptions to any pattern, including the relationship between age and crime (Moffitt, 1993). Although it has been established time and time again that older prisoners pose the lowest risk to public safety upon release, some older releasees will inevitably end up back in prison for committing a new crime or for violating their conditions of parole or postrelease supervision. Aside from age, there are social, financial, and medical issues that should be considered. These are important risk factors for all releases, but they may create particularly salient barriers to the successful reentry and reintegration of older former prisoners. Each issue is important in its own right, but the problems are often interrelated, and the cumulative effects of the barriers might make successful reintegration even more difficult. The following discussion describes the most common barriers and risk factors that could compromise successful community reintegration for older inmates upon release from prison.

Physical and Mental Health Issues

One of the biggest challenges correctional administrators face in caring for older inmates is meeting the health-care needs of this population. It is estimated that as many as 85 percent of older inmates have multiple medical issues (on average three or more chronic conditions), often accompanied by mental health problems (Aday, 1994a; Loeb, Steffensmeier, and Myco, 2007; Williams and Abraldes, 2007). These medical issues stem from unhealthy lifestyles both before and during their time in prison (Loeb, Steffensmeier, and Lawrence, 2008). In addition to reporting more health issues, inmates report having poorer perceptions of their health status, and have lower utilization of primary health-care services than among the general population (Greifinger, 2007).

Common medical issues experienced by older inmates and older released prisoners include arthritis, chronic obstructive pulmonary disease, heart disease, cancer, diabetes, liver and kidney problems from alcohol and drug abuse, paralysis from gunshot wounds, hepatitis, and sensory loss including vision or hearing problems (Aday, 2003; Binswanger et al., 2007; Colsher et al., 1992; Loeb and AbuDagga, 2006; McCarthy, 1983; Williams and Abraldes, 2007). The majority of older inmates also are dealing with a variety of mental health problems. As the older inmate population increases, correctional facilities will be faced with an even greater onslaught of mental health issues. Currently there are more mentally ill individuals in correctional facilities than in mental hospitals and institutions throughout the United States (Williams et al., 2006), and this number is likely to continue to soar as the number of elderly prisoners continues to rise. In 2004–2005, throughout the United States, the number of individuals with serious mental illnesses in jails and prisons was over three times greater than the number in hospitals (Torrey et al., 2010). A review of national surveys and individual state reports by Torrey et al. (2010) indicates that at least 15–20 percent of jail and prison inmates are seriously mentally ill. Disorders such as schizophrenia, personality disorders, depression, bipolar disorder, severe anxiety, and posttraumatic stress have been frequently reported to be higher among inmates than among the nonincarcerated population (Anno et al., 2004; Hammett, Roberts, and Kennedy, 2001b; Maruschak and Beck, 2001; Williams and Abraldes, 2007). Since mental disorders become more prevalent as individuals age, older prisoners are even more likely than the general inmate population to face problems with mental illness (Aday, 2003). For example, older inmates tend to have significantly higher rates of depression, generalized anxiety, and schizophrenia than do younger inmates (Aday, 2003; Williams and Abraldes, 2007; Wilson and Barboza, 2010).

Older inmates also suffer disproportionately with cognitive impairment associated with the aging process (e.g., slower reflexes), while others will experience more severe impairments such as dementia (Williams and Abraldes, 2007; Wilson and Barboza, 2010). Estimates suggest that the prevalence of dementia among inmates is likely to be two to three times higher than the prevalence among individuals outside prison (Wilson and Barboza, 2010). At the very least, many older inmates and former prisoners suffer from minor psychological issues that are associated with the experience of being incarcerated (Crawley and Sparks, 2006). For example, prisoners must adapt to regimented structure and scheduling, and they often must cope with issues such as boredom, crowded conditions, fear for personal safety, and isolation from family and friends. These factors may lead to psychological problems such as heightened anxiety and depression (Haney, 2001).

Mentally ill inmates returning to the community are often confronted with the double label of "ex-con" and "mental patient" (Draine et al., 2005). Older inmates have the additional stigma of being labeled as "old." Thus, older offenders with mental health issues may have to work harder to find social acceptance in the community. Moreover, the availability of inpatient and outpatient programs equipped to address prisoners with mental health issues following release into the community is not sufficient to serve those in need. The public mental health system is faced with an increasing lack of resources, and many of the programs that do exist are unwilling to serve correctional populations or individuals recently released from incarceration (Hodge, 2007). Therefore, most mentally ill persons who are released from jails and prisons receive little, if any, psychiatric aftercare. This lack of treatment may lead to higher recidivism among releasees with psychiatric issues as compared to other released prisoners (Torrey et al., 2010).

As inmates age, they are more likely to require the use of multiple medications for both physical and mental health conditions (Williams and Abraldes, 2007), and this presents challenges to correctional administrators. A study of the Texas Department of Criminal Justice found that approximately 89 percent of older prisoners were prescribed at least one medication and that the average older inmate received medications from over seven different drug classifications (Williams et al., 2010). Although during incarceration inmates typically receive their medications as prescribed, it is not uncommon for older inmates to be released without being given a supply of their medications; and even if they are given such a supply, it is usually only a small supply to last them a short period of time (Williams and Abraldes, 2007).

Another concern is that most inmates do not have health insurance or financial assistance for health care at the point of release. Even if they qualify for Medicare or Medicaid, inmates are usually unable to apply for the benefits until after they secure a permanent postrelease address (Williams, 2007; Williams and Abraldes, 2007). Since it can take a long period of time before the benefits are activated, some former prisoners go without needed medical care and medicines for substantial periods after release. The lack of medications for some conditions, especially mental illnesses, may contribute to a releasee's return to criminal behavior due to a psychotic episode or to obtain other types of medication. Thus, even when individuals have received adequate health and substance abuse treatment services while in prison, they often face limited access and insufficient linkages to community-based health care on release (Hammett, Roberts, and Kennedy, 2001b).

Employment

It is common for former inmates to encounter problems trying to secure employment upon release from prison (Pager, 2003; Petersilia, 2001, 2003), and employment rates for individuals with criminal histories tend to be very low (Western, Kling, and Weiman, 2001). Having a criminal record, especially one that includes incarceration, is often a stumbling block in obtaining a job for individuals of any age because of the inherent exclusions from certain types of jobs. This is particularly true for offenders convicted of violent and sex offenses (i.e., crimes that are commonly associated with older prisoners) (Kerbs, 2000b). Most often, former offenders tend to gravitate toward work as manual laborers, since they often lack the educational background needed for other careers (Aday, 2003). The problem, of course, is that older former prisoners are confronted with physical health problems that often impede their ability to work as manual laborers. Additionally, mental health problems that are typically experienced by older former inmates will also severely limit their employment opportunities. Furthermore, older adults in general often face ageism, as employers may be reluctant to hire older workers. Thus, it is no surprise that finding employment will be particularly challenging for the older former prisoner (Goetting, 1983; Nagin and Waldfogel, 1998).

Because stable employment is very important to reintegration and because those who have steady work tend to have lower rates of recidivism (Harer, 1994; Travis, 2005a), unemployment is considered a risk factor for former prisoners (Seiter and Kadela, 2003). If the individual does not have a consistent income, he or she may turn to crime in order to provide basic necessities and support for family members. Moreover, unemployment is also related to other potential risk factors such as strained familial relationships, increased levels of anxiety that may worsen physical or mental health problems, the discouragement of offenders from seeking needed health care, and the potential reduction in participation in prosocial community activities (see Gillis, 2000; Motiuk, 1996).

Family Relationships

The successful reentry and reintegration of former inmates is associated with access to healthy family relationships. High levels of support from family members during and after incarceration increase the odds of effective reentry (Shapiro and Schwartz, 2001; Visher, 2007; Visher and Travis, 2003). Support from families can be difficult to obtain because the incarceration of a loved one often causes both financial and emotional strain for the family (Austin and Hardyman, 2004). For example, there might be resentment for the crime that was committed or the family might lose the primary wage earner when he or she is imprisoned. Even if family members wish to continue their relationships with the offender, doing so might not be an option because of the location of the correctional facility (Conover, 2000). While most prisoners are from urban areas, major prison facilities are usually located in remote areas, sometimes many hours away from the inmates' communities of origin. Additionally, the families of many prisoners do not have or cannot afford transportation to facilities for regular visits (Austin and Hardyman, 2004). Prison administrative policies and restrictions on visitation also may make visitation less likely (Austin and Hardyman, 2004; Conover, 2000). Consequently, prisoners serving long sentences often have limited interaction with family members and usually struggle to maintain ordinary relationships with them (Aday, 1994a).

Family relationships might be strained, deteriorated, or completely absent by the time an inmate is released (Austin and Hardyman, 2004; Flanagan, 1981; Hairston, 1991). The longer the term of imprisonment, the less likely prisoners are to be able to maintain stable relationships with their family members. Relationships that deteriorated during the incarceration can be difficult, if not impossible, to restore upon release. Additionally, the likelihood of restoring and maintaining familial relationships after release is often related to location and opportunities. It will be unlikely that an independent releasee will be able to live in the same community as his or her family if there are no opportunities for employment and stable housing (Austin and Hardyman, 2004). Older offenders, due to their advanced age and often longer incarceration, will face even greater challenges upon release as they try to reestablish family relationships that have been lost or damaged (Aday, 2003; Goetting, 1983; Rikard and Rosenberg, 2007). As the years pass, often with limited phone or person-to-person contact, family members are more likely to sever contacts with inmates (Austin and Hardyman, 2004; Conover, 2000). Additionally, older prisoners may find that family members are dealing with their own challenges regarding the aging process, and family members may be deceased by the time older prisoners are released (Rikard and Rosenberg, 2007).

Ties to the Community

Most inmates will reenter either the same communities from which they came or communities that are similar to those in which they resided before prison (Pogorzelski et al., 2005), and it has been shown that community characteristics are related to the success or failure of returning inmates (Austin and Hardyman, 2004). For example, communities with high levels of unemployment and poverty and a low level of collective efficacy among residents have higher crime and recidivism rates (Lynch and Sabol, 2001; Sampson, 2001). Unfortunately, these characteristics describe the communities to which the majority of older inmates are returning (Pogorzelski et al., 2005), and their negative attributes (e.g., lack of prosocial opportunities and presence of deviant peers) can contribute to increased failure rates of older releasees.

It should be noted that the recidivism factor is not the only concern when examining community characteristics; it is also important to think about the well-being of the releasee. The issue of personal safety is very important for older former prisoners because it is less likely that they will be able to physically defend themselves if they are targeted as victims (Williams and Abraldes, 2007). If they are physically injured during an offense committed against them, the likelihood of them being able to live independently will decrease.

Another issue related to the community is stable housing. There is a severe lack of transitional housing—halfway houses or other specialized group homes—for inmates coming out of prison. Most inmates exit prison with no savings, no real source of income, and no benefits (Petersilia, 2001), yet they are expected to find a suitable permanent residence (as a condition of release) on their own. The lack of funds makes it difficult enough for releasees to find permanent housing, but this problem is exacerbated by financial agencies and property managers that may be less likely to provide services to older and disadvantaged individuals (Austin and Hardyman, 2004) or deny applicants who have criminal records (Pogorzelski et al., 2005). Further, some affordable housing options (e.g., public or subsidized housing) may not be accessible to former offenders because of restrictions on residents with criminal records or histories of substance abuse or mental illness. For instance, offenders with violent or drug-related crimes are often denied access to public housing. Even nonviolent offenders may be denied access to public housing because of their conditions of supervision, and they may be evicted from public housing if they reside with someone who commits a new criminal offense (Pogorzelski et al., 2005).

Being able to secure appropriate housing is especially difficult for older prisoners. Older inmates with health issues have an even tougher time finding appropriate housing, as they may not be able to live independently, and private nursing homes and assisted-living facilities are often reluctant to accept former offenders. Older prisoners with health issues have even more pronounced difficulties. A study by Visher and Mallik-Kane (2007) found that inmates with physical health problems were less likely to secure housing before their release and more likely to move around after release than were prisoners without health issues. Given the high rate of health problems among older inmates, one can expect that securing housing will be extremely challenging for these prisoners.

Research on prisoner reentry clearly indicates that former prisoners without stable housing are less likely to report to their mandatory appointments with supervision officers, seek medical care, and consistently take their prescribed medications (Hammett, Roberts, and Kennedy, 2001b). It will also be more difficult to obtain a job and public benefits if they are not able to provide agencies with permanent addresses. In short, lack of stable housing can contribute to unsuccessful reentry by affecting a releasee's ability to address his or her treatment needs and reducing their capability to abide by conditions of release.

Institutional Dependency and the Prisonization Effect

Another factor that may contribute to success or failure during reentry concerns the amount of time spent in prison. Older inmates who have spent long terms in prison may become "prisonized" in that they may become accustomed to the regimented structure of prison life, may internalize the values of the prison subculture, and may lose their sense of independence and self-esteem (Austin and Hardyman, 2004; Flanagan, 1981; Snyder et al., 2009; Williams and Abraldes, 2007). Having lost almost all contact with the outside world, many of these individuals build their primary support mechanisms among other inmates within the prison walls. Over time, prisoners adapt to the environments to which they are confined and become dependent on the prison and its culture to provide structure and direction. Upon release, older inmates are less likely to know how to properly survive outside of the routinization of the institution and therefore face additional challenges when adapting to life in free society (Snyder et al., 2009). Likewise, they may not have received the life skills (e.g., balancing a checkbook, utilizing technology, etc.) or employment training needed to properly reintegrate into the community, and many do not have family members, friends, or other community contacts who can offer economic or emotional support and guidance (Aday, 2003; Crawley and Sparks, 2006).

While most inmates look forward to being released, some inmates experience so much anxiety related to their potential release that they actually wish to remain in prison, where things are more predictable (Aday, 2003; Aday and Webster, 1979; Crawley and Sparks, 2006). For those who are released against their wishes, their high levels of anxiety may increase the risk of mental health crises or suicide after they return to the community (Williams and Abraldes, 2007). In fact, suicide is a leading cause of death among former inmates (Binswanger et al., 2007). A few former prisoners even go so far as committing new crimes to intentionally get caught so that they can return to a correctional institution (Williams and Abraldes, 2007).

Policy Implications for the Reentry of Older Inmates

As previously discussed, older inmates pose a relatively low risk to public safety. Individually, however, risk levels vary according to individual characteristics and environmental and social factors such as employment, exposure to criminal peers and relatives, substance use, and mental health issues (Van Voorhis, Braswell, and Lester, 2000). Consequently, each individual should be examined and assessed for their risk of recidivism, with consideration of age and other factors discussed in this chapter. The individual's exposure to particular risk factors, as well as the cumulative effects of any combination of factors, should be considered when determining their risk of recidivism. Even if a releasee is considered to be medium or high risk, this risk can be significantly lowered, and the odds of successful reintegration greatly increased, with appropriate reentry and transition procedures that address their risk factors and their physical and emotional needs (see Petersilia, 2004).

Interviews and surveys conducted with older inmates have revealed that they are concerned about being released to live in free society. They have anxiety about housing, transportation, personal relationships, medical care, employment, substance abuse, and personal safety outside of the institution (Crawley and Sparks, 2006; Loeb, Steffensmeier, and Myco, 2007). Hence, this discussion now turns to the policies and practices that may assist older inmates in improving the fit between their unique bio-psycho-social needs and the tasks related to successful reentry.

One area of primary importance to older inmates' successful reentry is their access to medical care. Studies have shown that former inmates have a higher probability of dying after they are released than while they are incarcerated. Binswanger et al. (2007), in their study of former prisoners in the state of Washington, examined death rates for former inmates as compared to other state residents for approximately two years after release. They found that former inmates were three and a half times more likely to die as compared to other residents in the state. Given that older prisoners experience many health problems (Loeb, Steffensmeier, and Myco, 2007), this rate might be even higher for elderly releasees. Accordingly, it is imperative that older inmates be connected with health-care providers in the community as early as possible. An intermediary, perhaps a correctional counselor or social worker, should serve as a representative to help set up appointments for the releasee and to ensure that new service providers have access to proper records. Ideally, this process would start well before release, with the intermediary working with the inmate beginning three to six months prior to release and continuing the relationship during and after release into the community.

It is critical that community service and public health officials are able to review documents containing the releasee's physical and mental health histories and the services provided to them during their incarceration (Snyder et al., 2009). The intermediary also should help the offender apply for or reestablish Medicare or Medicaid benefits as soon as possible. The procedures and paperwork associated with these types of processes can be complicated, so it is important to provide appropriate assistance to ensure that the application for much needed federal and state benefits is both quick and successful. In addition, prison administrators must realize that the transition to community service providers will take time, so releasees should be given an ample supply of their prescription medications when leaving the facility (Hammett, Roberts, and Kennedy, 2001b; Williams and Abraldes, 2007). Older inmates should receive training and education while still in prison so they can effectively manage their medical needs once released (when and how to take medications, when follow-up medical exams are needed, etc). Upon release, older offenders should be closely monitored, preferably by an intermediary or specialized case worker, to ensure that their medical needs are being met.

It is likely that inmates will have more access to medical and other nonmandated services while they are in prison as compared to when they are released (Hammett, Roberts, and Kennedy, 2001a). This is not to say that the services are better in prison than they are in the community; rather, inmates know where to go within the facility to receive medical and other services. After release, former prisoners often find it difficult to receive the services that were readily available in the institution. Even if they know where to obtain the services outside prison, there might be transportation or financial issues that preclude them from getting the assistance they need. It is important that policymakers and practitioners understand the difficulties that many older former prisoners will face when attempting to obtain health care in the community, and implement policies that will help ease the transition into the community. For example, thorough screening and preventive measures should be taken before an older inmate is released to ensure that he or she is provided with assistive devices as needed (e.g., eyeglasses and hearing aids). While such devices are costly, it may be fiscally advantageous in the long term to provide them, because adequate vision and hearing may promote increased independence and community interaction while preventing social isolation and depression (Williams and Abraldes, 2007).

Another recommendation is that a standard safety assessment should be conducted by a caseworker once an older former prisoner secures a permanent residence. Housing should be inspected and basic modifications should be made to help provide a safe environment so that older releasees can live more independently. Simple improvements such as the installation of hand rails and good lighting will not only increase feelings of independence, but also likely prevent serious injuries, such as from falling, that could lead to more problems. If older former prisoners have ambulatory impairments, they should be provided with tools such as canes, walkers, or wheelchairs that will help them become more mobile (Williams and Abraldes, 2007).

Other assessments should be tailored to older releasees and should be conducted both before and after release to identify levels of independence and risks of suicide or mental health breakdowns (Higgins and Severson, 2009; Williams and Abraldes, 2007). Evaluating a former prisoner's activities of daily living (e.g., eating, dressing, and bathing) can help determine the extent to which he or she will be capable of living independently. For those prisoners who require specialized housing needs such as assisted-living arrangements, it is critical that prison officials work with inmates long before release to secure appropriate housing upon discharge. As discussed previously, securing housing for former inmates can be difficult because of limited funds and the many restrictions they may face when applying for either private or public housing (Pogorzelski et al., 2005). Given the extensive time it might take to find suitable permanent housing, practitioners should focus on providing stable temporary housing for former prisoners immediately after release so that caseworkers will have ample time to help releasees acquire a permanent residence.

When needed, the reentry process also should include life-skills training, job training, and help in reconnecting or rebuilding relationships with family or other prosocial members in the community (Aday, 2003; Crawley and Sparks, 2006). Life-skills training is needed to reorient the inmates so they can develop the competencies needed to acclimate to and successfully live in modern society. Older inmates have two major challenges to successful reentry. First, many older prisoners have been removed from general society for a lengthy time and thus need to reorient themselves to changes in society. Second, they must also reconsider how they will care for themselves if they have physical and mental health limitations related to the aging process. Consequently, the type of training older inmates require to live successful, independent lives may be quite different from the type of training needed by younger inmates.

Additionally, services should be offered to help inmates maintain and improve family relationships (Shapiro and Schwartz, 2001). Prisons should promote policies and procedures that encourage visitation to help inmates maintain relationships with prosocial family members and other community contacts. For those inmates whose personal relationships are dysfunctional, counseling and support should be made available both before and immediately after release (Snyder et al., 2009; Visher, 2007). This type of counseling is particularly critical for those prisoners who have spent many years behind bars, as they are likely to experience greater challenges when reconnecting with family members and friends who can provide support networks upon release.

Releasees should know where they can go to obtain health services and medications, and their care history and needs should be shared with health agencies. During incarceration, inmates should be encouraged to engage with community resources, and community agencies should be encouraged to reach out to inmates early in their incarceration so inmates can arrange for medical assistance, appropriate housing, mentorship, benefits, and other needed services upon release (Williams and Abraldes, 2007). Unfortunately, there are few community agencies designed to work with people coming out of prisons. This opportunity is even more limited for older former prisoners, because some community agencies exclude older offenders from their services due to lack the resources or inability to manage the unique needs of these individuals (Aday and Webster, 1979; Curran, 2000).

Clearly, an important component of the successful reentry of older inmates is an early start to discharge planning (Snyder et al., 2009), preferably three to six months before the release date. Comprehensive reentry strategies include clear communication with and collective efforts among community service providers, such as community corrections personnel, social workers, and medical and mental health-care providers. An initial component of this collective effort should include detailed assessments for each releasee concerning the availability of physical and mental health-care treatment and benefits, employment, transitional and permanent housing, transportation, community supervision, and other treatment needs (e.g., substance abuse or behavioral counseling). This type of assessment should include information from the inmate, his or her records, as well as services available in the community to which the inmate will be released. This type of assessment and service provision takes time, necessitating that the reentry process begin well before release and continue through the postrelease transition until the releasee has been integrated into the community (Visher and Travis, 2003). Strong collaborations will help to prevent gaps between agencies working to provide services for job placement, health care, housing, counseling, and other treatment needs (Hammett, Roberts, and Kennedy, 2001b; Pettus and Severson, 2006; Travis and Petersilia, 2001). Thus, it will be beneficial for older releases if prisons foster close working relationships with community providers and use case managers or other intermediaries to coordinate efforts between agencies. Visher (2007) suggests incorporating such an intermediary in the form of a "reentry coach" or "life coach" to provide former inmates with the assistance and guidance they need. Such a broker can help with everything from medical care to housing and employment (Pager, 2006). In ideal situations, the intermediary would be notified of the release date and time and would meet the releasee at the prison gate, accompany him or her into the community, and introduce the former prisoner to his or her service providers.

Because older inmates constitute an increasingly larger part of the population being released from prison (Visher, 2006, 2007), federal and state efforts must expand to meet the reentry needs of these older former offenders (Curran, 2000). Efforts aimed at effective community treatment and programming for former prisoners are apt to save corrections systems millions of dollars each year (Welsh, 2004). Additionally, correctional staff and service providers located in the community will need training in how to tailor their services to meet older offenders' unique bio-psycho-social needs. These workers will need to learn how to tailor the main components of reentry programming, such as the use of intensive case management following release, to the needs of older offenders as well as to the physical and mental deterioration that can accompany the aging process (Goetting, 1983; Higgins and Severson, 2009; Williams and Abraldes, 2007). Moreover, reentry workers will also need training in "aging networks." As part of the Older Americans Act, enacted in 1965, aging networks across the nation have been established to better coordinate the federal, state, and local agencies that deliver social services and programming targeted to the needs of older adults living in the community. These aging networks provide a great resource, but historically the community providers involved with these networks have not reached out and coordinated their services with correctional facilities (Higgins and Severson, 2009).

Initiatives Directed Toward Reentry of Older Prisoners

It is generally estimated that the current cost of providing housing, programming, and medical care to older offenders is three to four times that for younger offenders (Aday, 2003; Kerbs, 2000a; Williams and Abraldes, 2007). Because elderly inmates account for a disproportionate share of correctional costs, legislators and policymakers have begun to understand that older prisoners who are seen as posing a relatively low risk to public safety should be considered for early release (Chiu, 2010; Kerbs, 2000a; Smyer and Burbank, 2009; Stojkovic, 2007).

An example of one promising reentry approach for older inmates is the Project for Older Prisoners (POPS), which uses a case-management strategy that connects correctional systems with law schools. This program—currently active in five states (Louisiana, Maryland, Michigan, North Carolina, and Virginia) and the District of Columbia, as discussed in Chapter 9—is designed precisely for the early release for older nonviolent offenders who have served a substantial proportion of their sentences for their specific crimes (Aday, 2003; Ornduff, 1996; Rikard and Rosenberg, 2007; Turley, 2007; Yates and Gillespie, 2000). In this program, law-school students volunteer to develop reintegration plans for older prisoners who are deemed candidates for early release. The assessment for early release takes into account information about the offender (e.g., criminal history, chemical dependence and health history, employment background, ties to the family), and includes interviews with the offender, correctional staff, and victims, and a determination of the offender's recidivism risk. If the inmate appears to be a good candidate for the program, the students then assist the offender with developing release strategies that address residential, employment, and financial plans. The assessment findings and release strategies are then presented to the appropriate parole or pardon board (Turley, 2007). To date, the POPS program has helped with the release and reentry of hundreds of older prisoners; moreover, most participants have successfully reintegrated back into society at a low rate of recidivism (Turley, 2007; Williams and Abraldes, 2007), which bodes well for the maintenance of public safety.

Another successful effort aimed at helping older former inmates reintegrate into society is the Senior Ex-Offender Program (SEOP). This program is sponsored by a local senior center in San Francisco and helps older former offenders secure employment and various types of treatment (e.g., substance abuse and vocational training), as well as social, medical, and mental health support. Representatives from the senior center act as intermediaries and mentors for the releasees and help them to become productive members of society (see Williams and Abraldes, 2007).

Geriatric- and medical-release programs have also been used successfully for the early release of older inmates. To be eligible for medical release, inmates must meet a number of requirements, usually related to their age, medical condition, and risk to public safety. A recent review of state policies indicates that fifteen states and the District of Columbia allow for the processes for early release of geriatric inmates. Jurisdictions use various combinations of strategies such as discretionary parole, inmate furloughs, and medical or compassionate release (for a complete review of these policies, see Chiu, 2010). While legislators are increasingly willing to consider early release for those older prisoners who are seen as posing a relatively low risk to public safety, a review of these policies indicates that jurisdictions rarely use these provisions. Chiu (2010) suggests that four factors contribute to states' unwillingness to utilize early releases for older offenders: political considerations and public sentiment, narrow eligibility criteria, procedures that discourage inmates from applying for release, and challenges associated with compliance as well as a lengthy referral and review processes. While geriatric- and medical-release strategies can be useful, more studies need to be conducted to determine the real cost savings to taxpayers. In addition, states need to more carefully pilot and evaluate their programs and more research needs to be conducted to develop effective risk- and needs-assessment instruments to ensure that reentry programs and supervision plans for older offenders can be successfully implemented (Chiu, 2010). While some standardized risk and needs assessments, such as the Level of Service Inventory—Revised have been extensively validated on offenders of all ages (see Latessa and Smith, 2007), assessments might be even more accurate if they are developed based on unique populations such as elderly offenders (Travis, 1989).

Conclusion

Any person being released from prison will likely face obstacles when reentering society and trying to successfully reintegrate into the community. Former inmates will have to overcome barriers concerning employment, public benefits, personal relationships, and abiding by (when applicable) their general and specific conditions of release. These offenders are moving from a place where everything was structured and provided for them, to a place (with which they may not be very familiar) where they will have to obtain their own shelter, food, and transportation. Aside from meeting their own needs related to daily living, they may also have to abide by conditions of release that include frequent meetings with supervising officers and treatment providers. They must find transportation to these meetings, which sometimes interferes with work schedules, thus putting their jobs at risk. Service providers and supervising officials must be careful not to set releasees up for failure because of technical violations issued when individuals cannot meet all of the demands placed on them.

Reentry for older inmates is especially challenging because they often have additional medical and mental health issues that require immediate and continuing treatment and medications. Their health-care issues can be exacerbated by financial burdens resulting from the lack of private medical insurance or public benefits that have not been granted or restored. They also have added difficulties finding employment and appropriate housing. Moreover, older inmates often deal with the challenges of reentry at times in their lives when they are typically ill-equipped to manage their own affairs, and are expected to navigate complicated bureaucracies to meet their needs upon release (Stojkovic, 2007). Accordingly, those working with elderly releasees should attempt to place just as much, if not more, emphasis on helping them to succeed rather than focusing on minor technical violations that would result in failure. While new crimes committed by releasees certainly should not be ignored, it is important to remember that there is more to measuring reintegration than just recidivism. Thus, measures of successful reentry should also include factors related to successful living outside of prison (e.g., employment and educational endeavors) (Lynch, 2006; Visher, 2007).

Current conservative sentencing policies have resulted in more individuals being sentenced to prison, and in longer sentences of incarceration. As a result, the prison system is in crisis, suffering from problems such as severe overcrowding and the elimination of many correctional programs (Cullen and Gilbert, 1982; Pratt, 2009). Because of limited space and funding, some policymakers have been exploring ways to create space and reduce costs through early-release programs. These types of programs that specifically target nonviolent older inmates can be effective at both reducing the number of prisoners and saving money, particularly in relationship to funds spent on the delivery of medical and mental health services for older inmates. Cost-benefit analyses suggest that incorporating successful treatment programs into the reentry process can save taxpayers millions of dollars in incarceration costs (Roman et al., 2007; Welsh, 2004; Zhang, Roberts, and Callanan, 2006). These savings can be even greater for elderly inmates because of the increased costs associated with incarcerating these individuals.

Academics and policymakers have suggested that community corrections options, such as house arrest, electronic monitoring, halfway houses or other group homes, or state nursing homes, might be better suited for older offenders than prisons (Aday, 2003; Snyder et al., 2009). Another helpful solution would be for correctional agencies to consider early release for older inmates who suffer from a variety of physical or mental health problems (Smyer and Burbank, 2009; Williams and Abraldes, 2007). Such selective decarceration of low-risk older inmates could result in social, fiscal, and safety benefits not only for the releasees, but also for correctional systems and communities at large (Kerbs, 2000a; Stojkovic, 2007).

The prevailing correctional philosophy cannot be ignored when considering community reentry. Although rehabilitative efforts do exist, the conservative ideology from the 1980s to the present day has fashioned an overall correctional orientation aimed toward incapacitation, retribution, and deterrence through harsher punishment (Pratt, 2009). For example, it is known that older prisoners convicted of homicide are less likely than any other type of prisoner to commit additional crimes and are therefore the lowest risk to the safety of the community (Austin and Hardyman, 2004). Although these types of offenders are extremely low-risk, community members are typically opposed to early release of murderers, as well as many other types of offenders (e.g., pedophiles). Realistically, though, the vast majority of inmates will not die in prison, and most of them will be released into the community either when they complete their sentences or through some type of early-release mechanism. Hopefully, members of the public will come to understand the importance of reentry programs and will begin to support strategies that improve the success of reintegration efforts.

It is clear that early, intensive, and consistent individual case planning and management is necessary for the successful reentry of older inmates into society. These plans should be initiated while older offenders are still in custody, and case managers should continue to provide support throughout the older offenders' full transition into society (Roberts, Kennedy, and Hammett, 2004; Taxman, 2007; Visher, 2007). It is also important that the professionals who are working to assist older inmates be provided with specialized training in gerontology so that they can better understand the needs of older inmates, and better facilitate their reentry into society. For example, some parole officers located in Denver, Colorado, are given specialized training to support their reentry work with older offenders (Mitchell, 2010).

Finally, it is important that reentry initiatives for older inmates incorporate a multidisciplinary team approach in which community service providers, correctional staff, and public health professionals work together in a collaborative fashion to better understand the unique challenges faced by older inmates and to ensure that these individuals are prepared for successful transition back into the community (Higgins and Severson, 2009). The exponential growth in the size of the older prison population and in the costs associated with housing these inmates requires that we look for better solutions. In order to properly assist the older offenders in navigating a smooth and successful transition from prison to the community, we must focus attention on developing age-specific reintegration strategies. In doing this, we must keep in mind that reentry is not just about the individual who is leaving prison, but also affects and is in turn affected by the community and the older offenders' family relationships and social ties. Just as the releasee can influence their community and the people around them, so too can the community and the people involved in the older offender's life contribute to their successful or unsuccessful transition into society (Visher, 2007).

11

Future Considerations

John J. Kerbs and Jennifer M. Jolley

As noted at the start of this book, the scholarly literature regarding older prisoners in the United States has developed over the past four decades (1970–present) to address a wide array of topics with increasingly sophisticated research designs and methodologies. Almost all of the published research on older inmates to date has primarily focused on the identification and description of their bio-psycho-social problems and criminogenic needs. For example, as discussed throughout this book, we know that older prisoners report having chronic health problems, psychological problems, and social stressors including the threat of victimization at the hands of younger inmates (Aday, 2003; Aday and Krabill, 2011; Kerbs and Jolley, 2007, 2009b). We also know that, criminologically speaking, older offenders are not incarcerated for trivial matters. Older men are incarcerated primarily for violent and sex offenses (Aday, 1994b; Flynn, 1998, 2000; Kerbs, 2000a), while older women are largely imprisoned for violent and drug offenses (Aday and Krabill, 2011; Kerbs, 2000a). That said, the big questions that remain almost entirely unanswered by the scholarly literature are related to the monitoring and evaluation of programs, policies, and procedures that affect the correctional care and custody of older offenders, from the point of judicial processing and incarceration through potential release thereafter. In short, how do we effectively and efficiently treat older offenders' bio-psycho-social problems *and* criminogenic needs? Primary research on the important monitoring and evaluation questions is almost nonexistent, but these questions must be answered if the United States is to advance public safety effectively and efficiently without violating the constitutional rights of the vulnerable population of older offenders.

We seek here in this concluding chapter to correct this void in the literature. The chapter begins by reviewing a framework for the development, implementation, and evaluation of effective correctional interventions. Based on this framework, we then identify gaps in the literature, while proposing a new generation of studies that fill identified voids that aim to advance the ability of the US criminal justice system to work effectively and efficiently with older offenders in courts, prisons, and free society thereafter for those who are released. Our proposed studies do not exhaust all possible areas of inquiry, but they do represent a modest and important first step in efforts to gain a better understanding of what works and what does not work with older offenders. Finally, the chapter addresses funding for such research, which will never materialize without adequate support from private foundations, state governments, and the US Department of Justice, whose Office of Justice Programs houses a myriad of funding opportunities.

The Risk-Need-Responsivity Model

The risk-need-responsivity model (Andrews, 2006; Andrews and Bonta, 2006; Andrews and Dowden, 2007; Andrews et al., 1990) is an evidence-based approach to correctional rehabilitation that embodies a series of principles for effective correctional treatment. When these principles are implemented correctly within treatment programs, they can significantly reduce recidivism rates by 25 percent to 60 percent (Gendreau, 1996), but programs that do not adhere to these principles do not reduce recidivism rates—regardless of accessible treatment components (Andrews and Dowden, 2007). The origins of the model (i.e., the development, dissemination, and evaluation of the risk-need-responsivity principles) can be traced to a relatively small group of scholars in the United States and Canada, including Don Andrews, James Bonta, Francis Cullen, Paul Gendreau, Edward Latessa, and Patricia Van Voorhis (Cullen, 2005). These scholars collectively developed an approach to treatment for offenders of all ages that is "fluid and flexible and capable of supporting a range of culturally appropriate contingent penal strategies" (Hannah-Moffat, 2005, p. 30), which is important given the ethnic diversity of the aging prison population in the United States (see Chapter 1 for more details regarding the racial/ethnic diversity of older prisoners).

The principles of effective treatment apply to the interventions that offenders receive as they move through community- and prison-based correctional treatment programs. First, the risk principle requires that all offenders receive a standardized risk assessment that examines empirically identified predictors for future criminal activity (Andrews and Dowden, 2007). In the context of such assessments, risk is defined as the propensity or likelihood of future recidivism as predicted by *static* and *dynamic* factors (Andrews and Dowden, 2007; Gottfredson and Moriarty, 2006). Static risk factors are those that do not change or those that change in only one direction, such as gender and age; in contrast, dynamic risk factors are changeable and include substance abuse and other such treatable criminogenic issues. The level of identified risk (i.e., the propensity to commit future criminal acts) is used to adjust the intensity of service delivery: the structure, duration, and number of services (Andrews and Dowden, 2007; Jolley and Kerbs, 2010). Thus, high-risk offenders (i.e., offenders with a high propensity to reoffend) should be provided with more intensive and extensive services, as this level of service provision has been found to reduce recidivism rates among high-risk offenders (Andrews, Bonta, and Hoge, 1990; Harris, Gingerich, and Whittaker, 2004; Thanner and Taxman, 2003). In contrast, low-risk offenders should receive less intensive and extensive services, as this level of service provision has been found to reduce recidivism rates among low-risk offenders (Andrews and Bonta, 2006; Thanner and Taxman, 2003).

This approach to treatment-matching by risk levels is critical given that research has demonstrated that recidivism rates increase when low-risk offenders are put in high-intensity programs (a mismatch). This happens because such programs pull low-risk offenders away from prosocial peers and activities and force them to attend time-intensive programs with high-risk criminals who model antisocial attitudes, beliefs, and behaviors. Moreover, such programs expose low-risk offenders to greater supervision, which increases the probability of technical violations (Andrews, Bonta, and Hoge, 1990; DeMatteo, Marlowe, and Festinger, 2006; Lowenkamp, Latessa, and Holsinger, 2006). Additionally, research on high-risk offenders in low-intensity programs indicates that such a mismatch leads to programming that does not adequately address intensive treatment needs due to the limited nature of interventions in low-intensity programs.

The second principle in the risk-need-responsivity model requires that evidence-based treatment programs focus on the treatment of *criminogenic* needs, which are defined by the deficits that drive criminal behavior. Conceptually and operationally, criminogenic needs are defined as a subset of dynamic risk factors that, when treated, decrease both the propensity for criminal activity and thus the rates of recidivism. To date, the research has identified eight criminogenic needs: a history of antisocial behavior, antisocial personality patterns, antisocial cognition, antisocial associates, family and marital problems, problems with poor performance and satisfaction in school and work, low levels of involvement and satisfaction with anticriminal leisure activities, and alcohol and drug abuse (Andrews, 2006; Andrews and Bonta, 2006; Andrews and Dowden, 2007).

The third and final principle in the risk-need-responsivity model requires that interventions be generally and specifically responsive to the treatment of criminogenic needs (Andrews and Dowden, 2007). Effective treatment programs that are *generally responsive* match offenders' criminogenic needs with evidence-based programs and interventions (Ferguson, 2002) that have been empirically shown to decrease recidivism rates (Andrews et al., 2006; Andrews and Dowden, 2007). Such programs include behavioral, social-learning, and cognitive-behavioral strategies. *Specifically responsive* treatment programs refine generally responsive services by tailoring such interventions to fit with offenders' demographics, learning styles, motivations, personalities, and strengths (Andrews and Dowden, 2007).

Using these three principles of risk, need, and responsivity, the following sections of this chapter outline an aggressive research agenda to improve the delivery of effective treatment services for older offenders in state and federal prisons. While this research agenda is far from exhaustive, it does represent a needed first step toward answering some of the most pressing questions facing America's graying prison population. Should these studies be implemented, they would provide answers that would help to enhance public safety while advancing the humane and ethical treatment of aging prisoners.

Risk Assessment

If there is one thing that a full and proper implementation of the risk-need-responsivity model requires, it is a comprehensive risk-assessment instrument to determine a prisoner's propensity to commit future crimes. This is an important first step that helps to identify the static and dynamic risk factors that drive an offender's propensity to reoffend. Unfortunately, the best available risk-assessment tools appear to have been validated in various countries using community- and prison-based samples of offenders that were largely under the age of 50 (see, e.g., Hsu, Caputi, and Byrne, 2011; Grann, Belfrage, and Tengstrom, 2000; Mills, Jones, and Kroner, 2005) or unspecified in relation to the average age of offenders in study samples (see, e.g., Hoffman, Stone-Meierhoefer, and Beck, 1978). For example, Singh, Grann, and Fazel (2011) completed a metaregression analysis of violence risk-assessment tools as examined in sixty-eight studies involving 25,980 participants, and their results documented a positive association between increased age and the rate of predictive validity; hence, as age increased, so did the predictive validity of risk-assessments for violence, but the average age of released prisoners across all studies was about 32, which means that many of the studies examined prisoners in their late 20s and early 30s. Moreover, beyond these age-based sampling limitations, only a few studies examined samples that included women, but these studies did provide an indication that the predictive validity of risk-assessment tools was greater for women as compared to men (the intersection of age and gender was not explored adequately for aging men and women in their 50s, 60s, 70s, 80s, and 90s).

That said, future studies are needed to determine if these same risk-assessment instruments are valid for older male and female offenders who are far beyond their 30s—that is, the young-old (50 to 64 years old), the middle-old (65 to 74 years old), and the oldest-old (75 and older).[1] Furthermore, many of the measured constructs in risk-assessment instruments do not appear to be applicable to older offenders in general, and to older prisoners more specifically. For example, the Level of Service Inventory—Revised (commonly used both in the United States and Canada) contains fifty-four questions that can be divided into various empirically supported subsets of criminogenic factors, but ten of these questions appear to be potentially invalid as predictors of risk for older offenders (Andrews and Bonta, 1995). For example, the Level of Service Inventory—Revised asks if the offender was arrested prior to the age of 16; while this may be a good measure of risk for a young adult, it may have little relevance for a 70-year-old offender who has long since started desisting from criminal behavior given the inverse relationship between age and recidivism as discussed in Chapter 8. Other measures used in the Level of Service Inventory—Revised are suspect given developmental differences between younger and older offenders and given a lack of clarity regarding the timing of certain measures. For example, the inventory includes questions about official records of assault/violence, but it does not clarify whether such records are recent or very old. The offender's employment status is also included without regard for potential disabilities or status as a retiree. Additionally, the inventory determines whether the offender has a history of suspension or expulsion from school, but such questions are not necessarily relevant for older prisoners (aged 50 and older) in general or for the oldest-old of prisoners (aged 75 and older). Other questions examine reliance on social assistance as a risk factor, but this may have little to do with any increased risk of recidivism for disabled or retired offenders; indeed, recent research has found social assistance to reduce recidivism rates for those who are unemployed, as compared to those who are unemployed who lack such assistance (Makarios, Steiner, and Travis, 2010). In sum, while the Level of Service Inventory—Revised appears to have a number of relevant measures for risk, many measures appear to be irrelevant and, more importantly, invalid for an aging population of offenders. Thus, future studies should validate such instruments with samples of older offenders (aged 50 and older) with an eye toward evaluating the validity of such instruments for the young-old, the middle-old, and the oldest-old.

Elder Courts

Americans in free society and in prison are, demographically speaking, aging quickly (Aday, 2003; C. G. Camp and G. M. Camp, 1994–2001; G. M. Camp and C. G. Camp, 1991–1993; Collins, Estes, and Bradsher, 2001; Guerino, Harrison, and Sabol, 2012; Vierck and Hodges, 2005; West and Sabol, 2008; West, Sabol, and Greenman, 2010). In free society, the population of citizens aged 65 and older is expected to more than double by 2050, to over 82 million from 31 million in 1990 (Collins, Estes, and Bradsher, 2001). As discussed throughout this book, similar trends are occurring in prison, with the number and proportion of older prisoners increasing each year. These demographic shifts will place an increasingly heavy burden on the courts that are necessarily involved in the judicial and correctional handling of older offenders (Rothman and Dunlop, 2006; Rothman, Dunlop, and Entzel, 2000). Unfortunately, we know very little about "best practices" for the judicial handling of older offenders; nonetheless, some jurisdictions are now creating specialty courts for older citizens, known as "elder courts" (Rothman and Dunlop, 2006). While the idea of a specialty court for aging Americans may appear sound on paper, we know virtually nothing about the ability of these courts to advance, among other things, public safety, treatment for criminogenic needs, services for complex medical and mental health problems, access to social services, and due process protections for an aging population who may require accommodations for physical and cognitive disabilities.

Given these gaps in the literature and the historical use of elder courts with cases that involve nonviolent offenses and mental health problems (i.e., violent offenses and sex offenses were historically excluded from elder courts) (Rothman and Dunlop, 2006), there is a profound need to examine potential differences in outcomes associated with the judicial processing and sentencing of older citizens (regardless of charges and convictions) in specialized elder courts versus regular criminal courts. In terms of research designs, there are at least two ways of studying the relative differences in distal outcomes (i.e., long-term outcomes like rates of recidivism) between elder courts and criminal courts. First, some might argue that a randomized control trial study might represent a "gold standard" for within-jurisdictional studies (Farrington, 2003a, 2003b; Farrington and Welsh, 2006); such a study would take older offenders who are charged with criminal offenses in the same jurisdiction and randomly assign them to either an elder court or a regular criminal court. Theoretically, random assignment ensures that there is no selection bias in the assignment of offenders to either the elder court or the criminal court. This is why random assignment bolsters internal validity: the extent to which the study's results can be credited to the judicial treatment provided by elder courts as compared to the other potential flaws in the study design like any confounding or "omitted variable bias" (i.e., selection bias) that might lead to differences in the outcomes between the two court systems. To the extent that randomization guarantees that the two courts receive similar offenders, any potential difference in outcomes would be the result of differences between these two judicial interventions, which is why randomized control trials can help untangle the effects of the court system from the effects of other variables that might otherwise unduly influence (without random assignment) the outcomes (e.g., rates of recidivism).

Although randomized control trials are considered the gold standard, they are generally expensive, rarely funded, and relatively uncommon in research that involves criminal justice systems (Farrington, 2003b; Farrington and Welsh, 2006). While we think the federal government should fund randomized control trials that compare the effectiveness of elder courts against the effectiveness of generic criminal courts with older citizens, fiscal constraints and a decreased interest in funding such studies in the United States (see Farrington, 2003b; Garner and Visher, 2003) suggest that an alternative approach is needed to advance our access to policy-relevant information on the relative effectiveness of such specialty courts. Moreover, there are many other reasons why randomized control trials may not successfully bolster a study's internal validity, which is the main reason for pursuing them. First, random assignment to elder courts may not appear random to minority-status elders who may refuse to participate given the mistrust between racial/ethnic minorities and researchers who have a history in the United States of violating the human rights of minorities involved in biomedical and social research (Alvidrez and Arean, 2002; Lau, Chang, and Okazaki, 2010; Thomas and Quinn, 1991). Second, those assigned to the "criminal court" (regardless of their racial and ethnic backgrounds) may demand access to the elder court because of the perceived benefits of processing in specialty courts; moreover, a subject's preference in judicial processing could affect the likelihood of agreeing to participate in a randomized control trial, engaging in the assigned court, and completing the judicial intervention (Corrigan and Salzer, 2003). If judicial preferences are suspected as a threat to internal validity that leads to differences in the offenders agreeing to participate in elder versus criminal courts, then researchers could include judicial preference as an independent variable and statistically control for such effects.

That said, nonexperimental or quasi-experimental research designs can provide budget-conscious court systems with useful information that circumvents many of the problems previously noted. Such research designs can compare (without random assignment) the outcomes associated with the judicial processing of older offenders in elder courts versus criminal courts, both within and between jurisdictions. The biggest methodological problem with such studies is the aforementioned threat to internal validity, but such problems can largely be corrected by using a genre of techniques known as propensity score analyses. These techniques have been used for decades (Guo and Fraser, 2010; Luellen, Shadish, and Clark, 2005) to correct for selection biases that threaten the internal validity of studies that seek to identify causal effects in biomedical and social sciences. By definition, propensity scores are represented by the conditional probability (between 0 and 1) that a person will be in one group rather than another (e.g., elder courts versus criminal courts). Propensity score analyses take covariates that are known to potentially affect the outcomes of concern and statistically balance the treatment and control groups on such covariates so that the groups are similar, statistically speaking, with regard to identified covariates. With randomized control trials, random assignment theoretically ensures that each person in the study has a fifty-fifty chance of being placed in either the treatment group or the control group; studies using propensity score analyses statistically adjust or balance the probabilities to be as equal as possible on covariates that are known to potentially influence the outcomes and threaten internal validity. In the end, such analyses statistically "balance two non-equivalent groups on observed covariates to get more accurate estimates of the effects of a treatment on which the two groups differ" (Luellen, Shadish, and Clark, 2005, p. 530). Although propensity score analyses do not adjust for unmeasured or unknown confounding variables, they do remove many of the concerns that social scientists have regarding selection biases that threaten internal validity, which is why we suggest such analyses for studies that do not use randomized control trials.

In terms of studies that examine the differences between elder and criminal courts, we believe that quasi-experimental studies are best, because they allow for real-world comparisons within and between jurisdictions, including studies involving offenders from multiple counties and states. Such multijurisdiction and multistate studies would help to strengthen the external validity of such research: the ability to generalize the results to other populations in other places (Sampson, 2010). Because randomized control trials tend to be implemented in highly controlled settings (e.g., one or two courts in a given jurisdiction) with a limited number of subjects, the results are not generalizable outside of the original settings, but cross-jurisdictional research with propensity score analyses can provide findings that are more generalizable (beyond the scope of a small controlled setting). As Sampson (2010) noted, random assignment may advance internal validity by circumventing selection biases via random assignment of subjects to treatment and control groups, but randomized control trials typically introduce another potential form of bias via selective sampling, because random assignment does not correct for a nonrandom sample selection. In the final analysis, randomized control trials can hurt external validity and the ability to generalize results, which is why propensity score analyses may be preferable when comparing elder courts with regular criminal courts across jurisdictions.

Sentencing Reforms

Given the inverse association between age and crime/recidivism (as discussed in Chapters 2 and 8), there is a serious need for studies that examine alternative sentencing strategies for older offenders and offenders who might otherwise age in place behind bars. While studying the overall effectiveness of specialized elder courts versus mainstream criminal courts in relation to recidivism rates, we could also examine the relative effectiveness for older offenders in community-based supervision (e.g., felony probation) versus prison sentences that are followed by community supervision. Recent research suggests that (as compared to noncustodial sanctions like felony probation) imprisonment may be positively associated with recidivism. As noted by Nagin, Cullen, and Jonson, "compared with noncustodial sanctions, incarceration appears to have a null or mildly criminogenic effect on future criminal behavior" (2009, p. 115). This finding is congruent with some of the earlier research as published by the Bureau of Justice Statistics, which found that the percentage of inmates who successfully completed parole after a first release was highest among prisoners who served less than twelve months as compared to those who served five or more years (Hughes, Wilson, and Beck, 2001). Much of this research that documents the potentially adverse effects of prison on recidivism has been conducted on younger and middle-aged inmates, but there is a need for the replication of such research on older and aging offenders facing felony sentences. The application of randomized control trials seems ethically compromised in this situation, because it would be hard to convince a judge (or the public for that matter) to randomly assign older offenders with felony convictions to either probation or prison. That said, comparisons of recidivism rates for older offenders sentenced to felony probation versus prison and subsequent parole could be accomplished by using propensity score analyses to statistically balance what would largely be nonequivalent groups, so that the study's internal validity is not unduly compromised by selection biases and covariates known to result in differential rates of recidivism.

Finally, multisite studies should examine judicial interventions based on assessed needs, including both supervision needs and criminogenic needs as identified within pre-sentencing investigation reports and as defined within a risk-need-responsivity framework (Andrews and Bonta, 2006; Andrews, Bonta, and Wormith, 2006; Andrews and Dowden, 2007). Although older offenders sentenced to federal and state prisons are growing quickly in both number and proportion, we know little to nothing about the sentencing requirements of these offenders and the role of court-ordered treatment for identified criminogenic needs prior to, during, or after their release. This gap in our knowledge is unfortunate because it undermines our efforts to advance public safety via the treatment of criminogenic needs among a population of aging offenders who are typically serving time for serious violent, sex, and drug-related felonies (Aday, 1994b; Aday and Krabill, 2011; Flynn, 1998, 2000; Kerbs, 2000a). We should also be mindful of the fact (as noted in Chapter 8) that aging offenders start to desist from criminal behavior at around age 31 for violent and sex offenses and age 37 for alcohol and drug offenses (Sampson and Laub, 2003). Given that older prisoners are (by definition) aged 50 and older, most have a high probability of being in the process of desisting from criminal behavior, which bodes well for their potential sentencing to shortened lengths of stay in prison, community-based alternatives to prison, and court-mandated treatment inside or outside of prison for their criminogenic needs (Kerbs and Jolley, 2009b). Of course, all three options should be empirically examined so that felony sentencing schemes can be adjusted to minimize the rates of recidivism via targeted interventions for criminogenic needs.

Prison-Based Research

As noted in Chapter 8, older prisoners (despite the serious nature of their conviction offenses) are very well behaved and thus are good candidates for treatment. As prisoners age into their 30s, 40s, and beyond, they are less likely to engage in prison misconduct (DeLisi, 2003; Cunningham and Sorensen, 2007) and they are less likely to receive disciplinary reports for violence

(Sorensen and Cunningham, 2010). Indeed, less than 10 percent of all older inmates present serious disciplinary problems (McShane and Williams, 1990), which bodes well for their orderly participation in treatment.

Although their advanced age and correspondingly high likelihood of desistance from antisocial behavior suggests that they may be the best candidates for treatment of criminogenic needs, we know very little about programs that attempt to treat such needs. Much of the literature on older inmates' needs is focused on the assessment of their bio-psycho-social needs (as discussed in Chapters 3 and 4), but we must begin to design, implement, monitor, and evaluate programs that treat these needs while simultaneously treating criminogenic needs via generally and specifically responsive treatment programs (Andrews and Bonta, 2006; Andrews and Dowden, 2007). One such program is True Grit, which operates in the Nevada Department of Corrections (Harrison, 2006; Harrison and Benedetti, 2009). This one-size-fits-all program for geriatric inmates (aged 60 and older) provides substance abuse treatment, mental health treatment, end-of-life care, cognitive therapy, sex-offender treatment, wellness and life-skills training, physical-fitness and movement therapy, and discharge planning (Harrison, 2011).

To date, the program has processed 266 inmates, with another 135 geriatric prisoners participating in the program as of 2011. Of the 266 inmates who have passed through the program, 38 died in prison, 91 were paroled or completed their sentence, 37 left the program prior to completion, 78 were dismissed due to programmatic or disciplinary violations, and 22 were transferred to other facilities, including permanent medical facilities (Harrison, 2011). Thus, the majority of inmates ($n = 137$) who have entered True Grit (about 52 percent) have never completed the program due to early departures, premature terminations related to behavioral issues, and transfers to other facilities. Such attrition provides a great opportunity for a quasi-experimental study that compares the recidivism rates of three groups: those who complete True Grit, geriatric prisoners who leave True Grit prematurely, geriatric prisoners who never access True Grit programming. Again, as with our suggested research designs for the comparison of elder courts with regular criminal courts, propensity score analyses (Guo and Fraser, 2010; Luellen, Shadish, and Clark, 2005) could be employed to balance covariates that are known to affect recidivism rates for the three groups under examination in this proposed study. Because True Grit operates with a waiting list for programmatic entry (Harrison, 2011), one could also design a randomized control trial evaluation, with applicants being randomly assigned to True Grit or a control group who receive "regular" services (i.e., the services that are typically accessible to all inmates, regardless of age). Although such an experiment would be expensive and potentially complicated (from an ethical perspective) given that some inmates would be randomly deselected from receiving True Grit services, a randomized control trial evaluation would benefit from fewer threats to internal validity (Farrington, 2003a, 2003b; Farrington and Welsh, 2006; Sampson, 2010).

The utility of age segregation also needs to be rigorously evaluated. Many academics and policymakers have called for the advancement of policies that provide older inmates with access to age-segregated cells, units, and prisons on a voluntary or mandated level (see Chapter 7; also see Kerbs and Jolley, 2007, 2009b). Because most older prisoners reside in the general prison population (Kerbs, 2000a) and few have access to the limited number of age-segregated options in federal and state prisons, the time has come to see if age segregation (1) increases their access to and engagement in bio-psycho-social services; (2) advances positive outcomes relative to their acute and chronic physical and mental health problems; (3) advances their physical safety; (4) increases their access to and engagement in treatment for criminogenic needs; and (5) advances, when applicable, their functional status in relation to basic activities of daily living (i.e., bathing, dressing, eating, toileting, and walking), instrumental activities of daily living (e.g., complete housework, take medications, manage money, shop, communicate, use technology, use transportation), and prison activities of daily living (e.g., dropping to the floor for alarms, standing for headcount, getting to meals, hearing orders, climbing onto a top bunk) (Williams et al., 2006).

At the facility level, randomized control trials appear to be viable and desirable in terms of research design because they can promote the internal validity of the results and determine whether or not age segregation (as compared to mainstreaming older inmates in the general prison population) advances the well-being of aging prisoners on the aforementioned five levels. Quasi-experimental designs that utilize propensity score analyses to balance nonequivalent groups in relation to known covariates that might affect these five outcomes are also viable and desirable because they can strengthen the external validity of such studies, thus allowing for the generalization of results to other units and prisons (Sampson, 2010). Quasi-experimental studies also have the added benefit of permitting comparisons within and across facilities without moving inmates within or between facilities; in short, older prisoners can be maintained where they reside without relocation during the course of any study that compares those living in age-segregated facilities with those in age-integrated facilities.

Finally, we need more research that examines subpopulations of older inmates. For example, we have little understanding of how age, gender, and race conjoin to affect the correctional experiences, bio-psycho-social needs, and physical and mental health outcomes of older men and women from different racial and ethnic groups. Generally speaking (as discussed in Chapter 5), empirical studies need to start documenting between-group differences because not all older prisoners are the same and most research is dominated by nonprobability sampling designs with few (if any) older women from a limited number of facilities and states; although such past studies are of limited utility in relation to the generalizability of results, future studies should make a concerted effort to use probability sampling designs with oversampling for typically underrepresented groups (e.g., older white, African American, and Hispanic women), which would allow for between-group examinations with generalizable results.

More research is also needed regarding the quality of physical and mental health care as experienced by and provided to both older prisoners in general (regardless of gender) and older women in particular. To the extent that female prisoners of all ages are more likely than male prisoners to be placed in rural facilities (Young and Reviere, 2006) that are far removed from urban centers, which are more likely to provide specialized care and treatment, older women with chronic-care conditions (e.g., arthritis, asthma, heart problems, hypertension, diabetes, etc.) in rural facilities may be at increased risk for adverse outcomes if they have difficulties accessing such specialized care and treatment. To date, we have yet to see a study that is theoretically informed with a framework for care (e.g., Campbell, Roland, and Buetow, 2000, as discussed in Chapter 5) that critically examines how older women in prison access health-care structures (buildings, equipment, and staff) and processes (technical care and interpersonal relationships) that conjoin to result in certain outcomes (e.g., changes in health status relative to need, levels of functioning, and symptom relief). We simply need more primary research that examines such issues relative to the types of care they receive (e.g., preventive, acute, and chronic care), the functions of such care (assessment, diagnosis, treatment, and follow-up services), and the short- and long-term outcomes of such care. Finally, whenever possible, such research should be longitudinal in design so that the developmental trajectories of health-care services can be linked, in a causal sense, to physical and mental health outcomes that surface both during a prison sentence and after any potential release.

Reentry Research

As noted in Chapter 10, more than 700,000 inmates are released from prisons each year in the United States (Visher, 2007). The best available data from the Bureau of Justice Statistics indicates that a total of 708,677 federal and state prisoners were released in 2010, which equates to about 1,942 releases per day (Guerino, Harrison, and Sabol, 2012). Although many studies could be proposed to better understand the reentry process for aging inmates, we suggest the monitoring and evaluation of existing (model) reentry programs that specialize in the release of older prisoners. Two key programs readily come to mind—the Project for Older Prisoners (POPS) and the Senior Ex-Offender Program (SEOP) (as discussed in Chapter 10).

The Project for Older Prisoners was originally designed and implemented by Jonathan Turley for older offenders who have served a significant amount of time in prison for largely nonviolent crimes (Aday, 2003; Ornduff, 1996; Rikard and Rosenberg, 2007; Turley, 2007; Yates and Gillespie, 2000). This reintegration program involves law-school students who volunteer to provide case-management and release-planning services to older inmates who are expensive to maintain in prison due to health-related problems and who are at low risk of recidivism because of their advanced age (Kerbs, 2000b). POPS volunteers develop and present parole boards with employment, financial, and residential plans that are to be implemented should the parole board decide to release an aging inmate (Turley, 2007). POPS has been implemented widely in multiple states through multiple law schools and is hailed for having very low rates of recidivism (Turley, 2007; Williams and Abraldes, 2007); nonetheless, evaluations to date have not clarified if the low rates are due to selection biases, wherein law-school volunteers cherry-pick older inmates who are perceived as having the lowest risk of recidivism and thus the lowest threat to public safety—e.g., nonviolent prisoners who are at low risk of recidivism due to advanced age or health problems. Because POPS volunteers can pick any inmate that they so choose, it is impossible to run a randomized control trial evaluation of this program, but a quasi-experimental study that utilizes propensity score analyses to balance covariates and compare prisoners released via POPS with older inmates released via regular parole or after sentence completion without supervision would be helpful in understanding the potential effects of participation in POPS on recidivism rates. The question is simple: Regarding the low rates of recidivism for inmates released via POPS, are these statistical artifacts of selection biases that occur when volunteers cherry-pick releasees? Stated differently, is POPS more effective at reducing recidivism than regular parole or release without supervision for aging inmates?

The same question could be asked of prisoners who participate in the Senior Ex-Offender Program. This program is based in San Francisco and run by a local senior center that helps older released prisoners obtain employment and treatment (e.g., substance abuse and vocational training), as well as medical, mental health, and social services. SEOP provides mentorship and intensive case-management services for releasees (see Williams and Abraldes, 2007), but it is unclear if this reduces recidivism rates when compared to older releasees who do not access such services at senior centers. Such programs raise large questions about the role of community supports and social networks in the potential reduction of recidivism for older releasees. Moreover, such questions are never going to be addressed without funding the monitoring and evaluation of such community-based innovations via comparisons of SEOP's releasees with releasees who are either placed on parole without access to SEOP or released without supervision or postrelease services of any kind after the completion of their sentence.

SEOP's focus on employment and treatment raises other important issues and questions. With regard to the former, research generally finds that the employment of released prisoners helps to advance public safety because it is inversely associated with recidivism (Batiuk et al., 2005; Makarios, Steiner, and Travis, 2010), positively associated with the number of days of crime-free living prior to recidivism (Tripodi, Kim, and Bender, 2010), and an important part of successful reentry (Maruna, 2001; Solomon et al., 2008; Travis, 2005a, 2005b). Moreover, as compared with parolees who have no employment in the first year of release, those with stable or even unstable employment during the first year of parole have a significantly lower likelihood of recidivism (Makarios, Steiner, and Travis, 2010); interestingly, other sources of income, including retirement, disability, or social security, also decrease the likelihood of recidivism, which bodes well for older unemployed inmates who are retired, disabled, or otherwise dependent on social support for one reason or another. Finally, as noted in Chapter 8, employment appears to be an important (primary) predictor of desistance from criminal activities in general across the life-course (Laub and Sampson, 2003; Sampson and Laub, 1993). These studies conjoin to suggest that employment support services through SEOP-type programs could be very helpful in decreasing the likelihood of recidivism among older releasees, but we will never know how effective such programs are as compared to parole without such services if we do not conduct studies that compare SEOP participants with regular parolees. Given that SEOP also provides case-management services for treatment issues, it would also be interesting to see if treatment services via SEOP provide additional reductions in recidivism beyond those potentially related to employment services. Again, a comparison group will be needed to clarify differences in recidivism rates among SEOP participants versus regular parolees.

As a final comment regarding reentry studies, there are plenty of state and federal prisons that could be examining the effectiveness of generic early-release and medical- or compassionate-release programs (as discussed in Chapter 9) that extend far beyond POPS and SEOP. While we have actual examples of such programs and suggested examples of legislation to promote such programs (American Civil Liberties Union, 2012; Kerbs, 2000b; Lundstrom, 1994), we do not have much in the way of long-term evaluations for such programs. At a minimum, it is important to determine if the bio-psycho-social needs of the seriously ill or the actively dying are better met in prison versus the free society for such aging offenders. Though many states (as discussed in Chapter 9) are running correctional nursing homes for infirm inmates, palliative-care programs for seriously ill inmates, and hospice care for the dying, both the cost and the quality of care for such correctional interventions are rarely compared with the cost and quality of parallel programs in free society. Additionally, we know almost nothing about these programs in relation to public safety and the rates of recidivism for the infirm, seriously ill, and dying offenders who spend their final days in free society. Hence, more research is needed in these areas.

Funding Future Research

The various proposed studies reviewed here represent an aggressive approach to answering key questions that must be addressed for the advancement of public safety and the care and custody of aging inmates. Although funding for research related to aging Americans in free society is generally accessible for a variety of topics related to health and aging outside of prison, we realize that funding for the research agenda identified herein is not easily acquired. State and federal support for monitoring and evaluation research on older prisoners has been less than adequate. For example, in fiscal year 2011, there were a total of eighty-seven solicitations for research (i.e., requests for proposals) as vetted by the US Office of Justice Programs through the Bureau of Justice Assistance (thirty-five solicitations), the Bureau of Justice Statistics (seventeen solicitations), the National Institute of Justice (thirty-two solicitations), and the Office of Sex-Offender Sentencing, Monitoring, Apprehending, Registering, and Tracking (three solicitations). Of all eighty-seven solicitations, not one was specific to monitoring and evaluation for older prisoners or (for that matter) older offenders in the community as evidenced by the titles of the solicitations and a cursory review of the content thereof.[2]

As with the failures of the federal government and state governments to directly support such research, private foundations and nonprofit organizations are also slow to fund and implement such research, but it is needed and this need will not dissipate with time (indeed, it will only intensify as the number of aging inmates continues to grow beyond 246,600 in 2010) (Guerino, Harrison, and Sabol, 2012). This is not to say that foundations have been completely removed from funding research related to older prisoners. For example, both the John A. Hartford Foundation and the Jacob & Valeria Langeloth Foundation have funded research on older prisoners over the past decade. Other foundations should be encouraged to follow their example of support for research involving underserved populations.[3]

In an effort to advance our understanding of monitoring and evaluation issues related to older prisoners, we suggest a partnering of resources between prison systems and academics, research think tanks, and funding sources, including private foundations and governmental entities at the local, state, and federal levels. There is clearly a need for such joint efforts, but answers to the next phase of research will require financial and methodological support that can only be achieved through collaborative partnerships. Such support could also extend far beyond the research agenda noted herein to include evaluations of correctional staff training programs for the provision of geriatric services, programs that provide gender-specific services for older women in prison, and other issues as discussed throughout this book. In sum, evaluations of these and other topics will be increasingly important over time as US prisons try to improve the conditions of confinement to meet the special needs of aging inmates. Indeed, if evidence-based corrections is to advance the quality and quantity of correctional programming and services to older inmates, we will need to aggressively fund and resource such research, both now and in the decades to come.

In closing and as a cautionary note, the failure to properly fund, evaluate, and improve services to older prisoners could result in potential legal liabilities for the ever-increasing number and proportion of inmates aged 50 and older in federal and state prisons. As discussed in Chapter 6, a review of legal issues suggests that older prisoners do have certain rights as defined by statutory law, case law, and the US Constitution. Hence, to the extent that adequate funding is allocated to improve care and custody services for older inmates, legal liabilities could be reduced while advancing the humane treatment of this vulnerable and growing population of prisoners with special needs.

Notes

1. These categories were adapted from widely recognized age brackets that have been used in free society to characterize the young-old (65 to 74 years old),

the middle-old (75 to 84 years old), and the oldest-old (85 and older). Given the presence of accelerated aging in prison as discussed throughout this book, older prisoners (on average) present a physiological age that is ten to fifteen years past their chronological age (Mitka, 2004). Thus, a 50-year-old inmate presents (physiologically speaking) more like a 60- to 65-year-old person outside prison. Hence we have adjusted the age brackets associated with these three groups to reflect the difference between the chronological and physiological age of people in prison as compared to people outside prison.

2. See http://www.ojp.usdoj.gov/funding/archived_solicitations_11.htm.

3. See, for example, http://gainscenter.samhsa.gov/cms-assets/documents/66624 -251634.aging-in-correctional-custodyfinal.pdf.

References

Abner, C. (2006). Graying prisons: States face challenges of an aging inmate population. *State News,* 49(10) (November–December): 8–12.

Abrams, A. J. (1984). Forward. In E. S. Newman, D. J. Newman, and M. L. Gewirtz (eds.), *Elderly criminals* (pp. xi–xviii). Boston: Oelgeschlager, Gunn, and Hain.

Abramsky, S. (2004). Lifers. *Legal Affairs* (March–April). http://www.legalaffairs .org/issues/March-April-2004/feature_abramsky_marpar04.msp.

ADA Amendments Act of 2008. Pub. Law 110-325.

Adams, K., and Ferrandino, J. (2008). Managing mentally ill inmates in prisons. *Criminal Justice and Behavior,* 35(8): 913–927.

Adams, W. E., Jr. (1995). The incarceration of older criminals: Balancing safety, cost, and humanitarian concerns. *Nova Law Review,* 19(2): 465–486.

Aday, R. H. (1994a). Aging in prison: A case study of new elderly offenders. *International Journal of Offender Therapy and Comparative Criminology,* 38 (1): 80–91.

———. (1994b). Golden years behind bars: Special programs and facilities for elderly inmates. *Federal Probation,* 58(2): 47–54.

———. (1999). Responding to the graying of American prisons: A 10-year follow-up. Unpublished report. Murfreesboro: Middle Tennessee State University.

———. (2003). *Aging prisoners: Crisis in American corrections.* Westport: Praeger.

———. (2005–2006). Aging prisoners' concerns toward dying in prison. *Omega,* 52: 199–216.

———. (2006). Managing aging prisoners in the United States. In A. Wahidin and M. Cain (eds.), *Ageing, crime, and society* (pp. 210–229). London: Willan.

Aday, R. H., and Krabill, J. J. (2011). *Women aging in prison: A neglected population in the prison system.* Boulder: Lynne Rienner.

Aday, R. H., and Nation, P. (2001). *A case study of older female offenders.* Nashville: Tennessee Department of Corrections.

Aday, R. H., and Shahan, D. (1995). Elderly reactions to a death education program in a nursing home setting. *Gerontology & Geriatrics Education,* 15(1): 3–18.

Aday, R. H., and Webster E. L. (1979). The development of a preliminary model. *Offender Rehabilitation,* 3(3): 271–282.

Age Discrimination in Employment Act of 1967. 29 U.S.C. §§ 621–634 (2011).

Age Discrimination in Employment Act of 1975. 42 U.S.C. §§ 6101–6107 (2011).

Ahalt, C., Binswanger, I. A., Steinman, M., Tulsky, J., and Williams, B. (2012). Confined to ignorance: The absence of prisoners information from nationally representative health data sets. *Journal of General Internal Medicine,* 27(2): 160–166.

Ahn-Redding, H. (2007). *The million-dollar inmate: The financial and social burden of nonviolent offenders.* Lanham: Lexington Books.

Albertson's Inc. v. Kirkingburg. 527 U.S. 555 (1999).

Allen, F. A. (1981). *The decline of the rehabilitative ideal: Penal policy and social purpose.* New Haven: Yale University Press.

Allen, R. S., Phillips, L. L., Roff, L. L., Cavanaugh, R., and Day, L. (2008). Religiousness/spirituality and mental health among older male inmates. *The Gerontologist,* 48(5): 692–697.

Allman, R. M., Sawyer, P., and Roseman, J. M. (2006). The UAB study of aging: Background and prospects of insights into life-space mobility among African Americans and whites in rural and urban settings. *Aging and Health,* 2: 417–428.

Alston, L. T. (1986). *Crime and older Americans.* Springfield, IL: Charles C. Thomas.

Alvidrez, J., and Arean, P. A. (2002). Psychosocial treatment research with ethnic minority populations: Ethical considerations in conducting clinical trials. *Ethics & Behavior,* 12: 103–116.

American Academy of Hospice and Palliative Medicine (AAHPM) (2006a). Clinical practice guidelines. http://www.aahpm.org/Practice/default/quality.html.

——— (2006b). Statement on artificial nutrition and hydration near the end of life. December 8. http://www.aahpm.org/positions/nutrition.html.

——— (2006c). Statement on palliative sedation. September 15. http://www.aahpm.org/positions/sedation.html.

——— (2007a). Certification in hospice and palliative medicine. http://www.aahpm.org.

——— (2007b). Physician-assisted death. February 14. http://www.aahpm.org/positions/suicide.html.

American Civil Liberties Union (2012). *At America's expense: The mass incarceration of the elderly.* Washington, DC.

American Correctional Association (2003). *Directory of adult and juvenile correctional departments, institutions, agencies, and probation and parole authorities.* Lanham: American Correctional Association.

American Law Institute (1962). *Model penal code.* Philadelphia: American Law Institute.

Americans with Disabilities Act of 1990. 42 U.S.C. § 12101 *et seq.* (2011).

Ammar, N. H., and Weaver, R. R. (2005). Restrained voices: Female inmates' views of health services in two Ohio prisons. *Women & Criminal Justice,* 16(3): 67–89.

Anderson, E., and Hilliard, T. (2005). Managing offenders with special health needs: Highest and best use strategies. *Corrections Today,* 67(1): 58–61.

Anderson, J., and McGehee, R. D. (1991). South Carolina strives to treat elderly and disabled offenders. *Corrections Today,* 53(5): 124–127.

———. (1994). Incarceration alternatives: A special unit for elderly offenders and offenders with disabilities. *Forum on Corrections Research,* 6(2): 35–36.

Andrews, D. A. (2006). Enhancing adherence to risk-need-responsivity: Making quality a matter of policy. *Criminology and Public Policy,* 5: 595–602.

Andrews, D. A., and Bonta, J. L. (1995). *The Level of Service Inventory–Revised.* Toronto: Multi-Health Systems.

———. (2006). *The psychology of criminal conduct.* 4th ed. Newark: Lexis-Nexis and Matthew Bender.

Andrews, D. A., Bonta, J. L., and Hoge, R. D. (1990). Classification for effective rehabilitation: Rediscovering psychology. *Criminal Justice and Behavior,* 17: 19–52.

Andrews, D. A., Bonta, J. L., and Wormith, S. J. (2006). The recent past and near future of risk and/or need assessment. *Crime & Delinquency,* 52: 7–27.

Andrews, D. A., and Dowden, C. (2007). The risk-need-responsivity model of assessment and human service in prevention and corrections: Crime-prevention jurisprudence. *Canadian Journal of Criminology and Criminal Justice,* 49: 439–464.

Andrews, D. A., Zinger, I., Hoge, R. D., Bonta, J., Gendreau, P., and Cullen, F. T. (1990). Does correctional treatment work? A clinically relevant and psychologically informed meta-analysis. *Criminology,* 28: 369–404.

Anno, B. (2001). *Correctional health care: Guidelines for the management of an adequate delivery system.* Washington, DC: US Department of Justice, National Institute of Corrections.

——— (2004a). *Addressing the needs of elderly, chronically ill, and terminally ill inmates.* Washington, DC: US Department of Justice, National Institute of Corrections.

——— (2004b). Prison health services: An overview. *Journal of Correctional Health Care,* 10: 287–301.

Anno, B. J., Graham, C., Lawrence, J. E., and Shansky, R. (2004). *Correctional health care: Addressing the needs of the elderly, chronically ill, and terminally ill inmates.* Washington, DC: US Department of Justice, National Institute of Corrections, Criminal Justice Institute.

Armstrong v. Wilson. 124 F.3d 1019 (9th Cir. 1997).

Arndt, S., Turvey, C. M., and Flaum, M. (2002). Older offenders, substance abuse, and treatment. *American Journal of Geriatric Psychiatry,* 10(6): 733–739.

Auerhahn, K. (1999). Selective incapacitation and the problem of prediction. *Criminology,* 37(4): 703–734.

——— (2002). Selective incapacitation, three strikes, and the problem of aging prison populations: Using simulation modeling to see the future. *Criminology and Public Policy,* 1: 353–388.

——— (2003). *Selective incapacitation and public policy: Evaluating California's imprisonment crisis.* Albany: State University of New York Press.

——— (2006). Conceptual and methodological issues in the prediction of dangerous behavior. *Criminology & Public Policy,* 5(4): 801–808.

Auerhahn, K., and McGuire, C. J. (2010). *Revisiting the social contract: Community justice and public safety.* New York: NovaScience.

Austin, J. (1986). Using early release to relieve prison crowding: A dilemma in public policy. *Crime and Delinquency,* 32: 404–502.

Austin, J., Clark, J., Hardyman, P., and Henry, D. A. (1999). The impact of "three strikes and you're out." *Punishment & Society,* 1(2): 131–162.

Austin, J., and Hardyman, P. (2004). The risks and needs of the returning prisoner population. *Review of Policy Research,* 21: 13–29.

Avi-Itzhak, B., and Shinnar, R. (1973). Quantitative models in crime control. *Journal of Criminal Justice,* 1: 185–217.

Bailey, A., and Hayes, J. M. (2006). Who's in prison? The changing demographics of incarceration. *California Counts: Population Trends & Profiles,* 8(1): 1–26.

Baillargeon, J., Binswanger, I. A., Penn, J. V., Williams, B. A., and Murray, O. J. (2009). Psychiatric disorders and repeat incarcerations: The revolving prison door. *American Journal of Psychiatry,* 166(1): 103–109.

Baillargeon, J., Black, S. A., Pulvino, J., and Dunn, K. (2000). The disease profile of Texas prison inmates. *Annals of Epidemiology,* 10: 74–80.

Baker, M. (2002). Economic, political, and ethnic influences on end-of-life decision-making: A decade in review. *Journal of Health & Social Policy,* 14(3): 27–39.

Bales, W. D., and Mears, D. P. (2008). Inmate social ties and the transition to society: Does visitation reduce recidivism? *Journal of Research in Crime and Delinquency,* 45(3): 287–321.

Barens, E. (writer) (1998). *Angola prison hospice: Opening the door.* Video. Produced by the Center on Crime, Communities, and Culture, and the Project on Death in America. http://www.soros.org/initiatives/usprograms/multimedia /angola_20080912.

Barr, D. (2008). *Health disparities in the United States: Social class, race, ethnicity, and health.* Baltimore: Johns Hopkins University Press.

Baskin, D. R., and Sommers, I. B. (1998). *Casualties of community disorder: Women's careers in violent crime.* Boulder: Westview.

Batiuk, M. E., Lahm, K. F., McKeever, M., Wilcox, N., and Wilcox, P. (2005). Disentangling the effects of correctional education: Are current policies misguided? An event history analysis. *Criminal Justice,* 5(1): 55–74.

Bauersmith, J., and Gent, R. (2002). The Broward County jails hospice program: Hospice in the jail. *Journal of Palliative Medicine,* 5(5): 667–670.

Baum, D. (1996). *Smoke and mirrors: The war on drugs and the politics of failure.* Boston: Little, Brown.

Beck, A., and Gilliard, D. (1995). *Prisoners in 1994.* Washington, DC: US Department of Justice, Bureau of Justice Statistics.

Beck, A., and Harrison, P. (2001). *Prisoners in 2000.* Washington, DC: US Department of Justice, Bureau of Justice Statistics.

Beck, J. (1999). Compassionate release from New York State prisons: Why are so few getting out? *Journal of Law, Medicine, & Ethics,* 27(3): 216–239.

Bedard, K., and Frech, T. E. (2007). *Prison health care: Is contracting out healthy?* Departmental Working Papers, Department of Economics, University of California, Santa Barbara. http://www.escholarship.org/uc/item /6vh3429f.

Beeler, A. (2006). Palliative care volunteers: A program of compassion. *Corrections Today,* 68(4): 38–40.

Beiser, V. (1999). Pensioners or prisoners? *The Nation,* 268(18): 28–30.

Benekos, P. J., and Merlo, A. V. (1995). Three strikes and you're out: The political sentencing game. *Federal Probation,* 59(1): 3–9.

Benson v. Terhune. 304 F.3d 874 (9th Cir. 2002).

Bergman, S., and Amir, M. (1973). Crime and delinquency among the aged in Israel. *Geriatrics,* 28(1): 149–157.

Bick, J. (2002). Managing pain and end-of-life care for inmate patients: The California Medical Facility experience. *Journal of Correctional Health Care,* 9: 131–147.

Big hurdles remain to fix medical parole (2011). Editorial. *Sacramento Bee,* May 27, p. A16. http://www.sacbee.com/2011/05/27/3657815/big-hurdles-remain-to-fix-medical.html.

Binswanger, I., Krueger, P., and Steiner, J. (2009). Prevalence of chronic medical conditions among jail and prison inmates in the USA compared with the general population. *Journal of Epidemiology and Community Health,* 63(11): 912–919.

Binswanger, I. A., Stern, M. F., Deyo, R. A., Heagerty, P. J., Cheadle, A., Elmore, J. G., and Koepsell, T. D. (2007). Release from prison: A high risk of death for former inmates. *New England Journal of Medicine,* 356(2): 157–165.

Bintz, M. T. (1974). Recreation for the older population in correctional institutions. *Therapeutic Recreational Journal,* 8: 87–89.

Bishop, A. J., and Merten, M. J. (2011). Risk of co-morbid health impairment among older male inmates. *Journal of Correctional Health Care,* 17(1): 34–45.

Bloom, B. B., Owen, B., and Covington, S. (2003). *Gender-responsive strategies: Research, procedures, and guiding principles for women offenders.* Washington, DC: US Department of Justice, National Institute of Corrections.

Blumenthal, D. (1996). Quality of care: What is it? *New England Journal of Medicine,* 335: 891–894.

Blumstein, A. (1983). Prisons: Population, capacity, and alternatives. In J. Q. Wilson (ed.), *Crime and public policy* (pp. 229–250). San Francisco: Institute for Contemporary Studies Press.

Blumstein, A., and Beck, A. J. (1999). Population growth in U.S. prisons, 1980–1996. In M. Tonry and J. Petersilia (eds.), *Crime & justice: An annual review of research,* vol. 26 (pp. 17–61). Chicago: University of Chicago Press.

Board of Trustees of the University of Alabama v. Garrett. 531 U.S. 356 (2001).

Bolling v. Sharpe. 347 U.S. 497 (1954).

Bond, G. D., Thompson, L. A., and Malloy, D. M. (2005). Lifespan differences in the social networks of prison life. *International Journal of Aging and Human Development,* 61(3): 161–178.

Bonner v. Lewis. 857 F.2d 559 (9th Cir. 1988).

Bourdieu, P. (1986). Forms of capital. In J. G. Richardson (ed.), *Handbook of theory and research for the sociology of education* (pp. 242–258). New York: Greenwood.

Bowker, L. H. (1982). Victimizers and victims in American correctional institutions. In R. Johnson and H. Toch (eds.), *The pains of imprisonment* (pp. 63–76). Beverly Hills: Sage.

Boyle, B. A. (2002). The Maryland Division of Correction hospice program. *Journal of Palliative Medicine,* 5(5): 671–675.

Brahce, C. I., and Bachand, D. J. (1989). In S. Chaneles and C. Burnett (eds.), *Older offenders: Current trends* (pp. 45–60). New York: Haworth.

Brame, R., Bushway, S. D., and Paternoster, R. (2003). Examining the prevalence of criminal desistance. *Criminology,* 41(2): 423–448.

Branco, K. J. (2007). Religious activities, strength from faith, and social functioning among African American and white nursing home residents. *Religion, Spirituality, and Aging,* 19(4): 3–20.

BRCA1 and BRCA2: Cancer risk and genetic testing (2009). May 29. http://www.cancer.gov/cancertopics/factsheet/Risk/BRCA.

Bronstein, L. R., and Wright, K. (2006). The Impact of prison hospice: Collaboration among social workers and other professionals in a criminal justice setting that promotes care for the dying. *Journal of Social Work in End-of-Life & Palliative Care,* 2(4): 85–102.

Brown v. Englander. Civil Action no. 10-cv-257-SM, 2010 U.S. Dist. LEXIS 126245 (D. N.H. Nov. 24, 2010).

Brown v. Plata. 131 S. Ct. 1910 (2011).

Buckaloo, B. J., Krug, K. S., and Nelson, K. B. (2009). Exercise and the low-security inmate: Changes in depression, stress, and anxiety. *The Prison Journal,* 89(3): 328–343.

Buckler, K. G., and Travis, L. F. (2003). Reanalyzing the prevalence and social context of collateral consequence statutes. *Journal of Criminal Justice,* 31: 435–453.

Bureau of Justice Statistics (2001). *Prisoners in 2000.* Washington, DC: US Department of Justice.

——— (2010). *Key facts at a glance: Correctional populations, 1980–2008.* http://bjs.ojp.usdoj.gov/content/glance/tables/corr2tab.cfm.

——— (2011). *Prisoner recidivism analysis tool.* http://bjs.ojp.usdoj.gov/index.cfm?ty=datool&surl=/recidivism/index.cfm#.

Burt, R. A. (1997). The Supreme Court speaks: Not assisted suicide but a constitutional right to palliative care. *New England Journal of Medicine,* 337(17): 1234–1236.

Bushway, S. D., Piquero, A. R., Broidy, L. M., Cauffman, E., and Mazderolle, P. (2001). An empirical framework for studying desistance as a process. *Criminology,* 39(2): 491–515.

Byock, I. R. (2002). Dying well in corrections: Why should we care? *Journal of Correctional Health Care,* 9(2): 102–117.

Caes, G. (1990). *Long-term confinement and the aging inmate population.* Washington, DC: US Department of Justice.

Cain, B., and Fontenot, K. (2001). Managing Angola's long-term inmates. *Corrections Today,* 63(5): 35–38.

Caldwell, C., Jarvis, M., and Rosefield, H. (2001). Issues impacting today's geriatric female offenders. *Corrections Today,* 65(5): 110–113.

California Department of Corrections and Rehabilitation (2008). *Why CDCR developed a parole violation decision making instrument.* http://www.cdcr.ca.gov/PVDMI.

——— (2010). Office of Research, Offender information reports. http://www.cdcr.ca.gov/Reports_Research/Offender_Information_Services_Branch/Offender_Information_Reports.html.

California Legislative Analyst's Office (1999). *The "three strikes and you're out" law's impact on state prisons: An update.* http://www.lao.ca.gov/1999/cal_update/oct_99/oct_99_calupdate.html.

——— (2005). *A primer: Three strikes—The impact after more than a decade.* http://www.lao.ca.gov/2005/3_strikes/3_strikes_102005.htm.

California Performance Review (2004). *Reforming California's youth and adult correctional systems: Inmate/parolee population management.* http://www .cpr.ca.gov/Review_Panel/Inmate_Population_Management.html.

California State Senate (2010, September 28). Parole: Medical Parole—Permanently medically incapacitated inmates. SB1399 Stat. Sacramento, CA: Author.

Camp, C. G. (ed.) (2003). *The corrections yearbook: Adult corrections 2002.* Middletown, CT: Criminal Justice Institute.

Camp, C. G., and Camp, G. M. (1994). *The corrections yearbook 1994: Adult corrections.* South Salem, NY: Criminal Justice Institute.

———. (1995). *The corrections yearbook 1995: Adult corrections.* South Salem, NY: Criminal Justice Institute.

———. (1996). *The corrections yearbook: 1996.* South Salem, NY: Criminal Justice Institute.

———. (1997). *The corrections yearbook: 1997.* South Salem, NY: Criminal Justice Institute.

———. (1998). *The corrections yearbook: 1998.* South Salem, NY: Criminal Justice Institute.

———. (1999). *The corrections yearbook 1999: Adult corrections.* Middletown, CT: Criminal Justice Institute.

———. (2000). *The 2000 corrections yearbook: Adult corrections.* Middletown, CT: Criminal Justice Institute.

———. (2001). *The 2001 corrections yearbook: Adult systems, populations, budgets, staff, facilities, probation, parole, trends.* Middletown, CT: Criminal Justice Institute.

Camp, G. M, and Camp, C. G. (1991). *The corrections yearbook 1991: Adult corrections.* South Salem, NY: Criminal Justice Institute.

———. (1992). *The corrections yearbook 1992: Adult corrections.* South Salem, NY: Criminal Justice Institute.

———. (1993). *The corrections yearbook 1993: Adult corrections.* South Salem, NY: Criminal Justice Institute.

Campbell, S. M., and Roland, M. O. (1996). Why do people consult the doctor? Factors influencing demand for primary medical care. *Family Practice,* 13: 75–83.

Campbell, S. M., Roland, M. O., and Buetow, S. A. (2000). Defining quality of care. *Social Science & Medicine,* 51: 1611–1625.

Campbell, S. M., Roland, M. O., Quayle, J. A., and Buetow, S. A. (1998). Quality indicators for general practice: Which ones can general practitioners and health authority managers agree are important and how useful are they? *Journal of Public Health Medicine,* 20(4): 414–421.

Caralis, P., Davis, B., Wright, K., and Marciel, E. (1993). The influence of ethnicity and race on attitudes toward advance directives, life-prolonging treatments and euthanasia. *Journal of Clinical Ethics,* 4(2): 155–166.

Carmel, S., and Glick, S. M. (1996). Compassionate-emphatic physicians: Personality traits and social-organizational factors that enhance or inhibit this behavior pattern. *Social Science & Medicine,* 43: 1253–1261.

Casper, J. D., Brereton, D., and Neal, D. (1983). The California determinate sentence law. *Criminal Law Bulletin,* 19: 405–433.

Cassell, E., and Rich, B. (2010). Intractable end-of-life suffering and the ethics of palliative sedation. *Pain Medicine,* 11(3): 435–438.

Castle v. Eurofresh Inc. (*Eurofresh* I). Civil Action no. CV 09-8114-PCT-MHM (DKD), 2010 U.S. Dist. LEXIS 21481 (D. Ariz. Mar. 8, 2010).

Castle v. Eurofresh Inc. (*Eurofresh* II). 734 F. Supp. 2d 938 (D. Ariz. Aug. 10, 2010).

Caulkins, J. P., Rydell, C. P., Schwabe, W. L., and Chiesa, J. (1997). *Mandatory minimum drug sentences: Throwing away the key or the taxpayer's money?* Santa Monica: RAND.

Caverley, S. J. (2006). Older mentally ill inmates: A descriptive study. *Journal of Correctional Health Care,* 12(4): 262–268.

Center for Ethics in Health Care (2009). *POLST (Physician Order for Life-Sustaining Treatment): Guidance for Oregon's Health Care Professionals.* Portland. http://www.ohsu.edu/polst/programs/documents/Guidebook2009.pdf.

Center to Advance Palliative Care (CAPC) (2011a). Defining palliative care. http://www.capc.org/building-a-hospital-based-palliative-care-program /case/definingpc.

——— (2011b). Palliative care vs. other services. http://www.capc.org/building-a -hospital-based-palliative-care-program/case/definingpc/designing/presenting -plan/pc_vs_other.

Chaiken, M. R., and Chaiken, J. (1984). Offender types and public policy. *Crime & Delinquency,* 30: 195–226.

Chaiklin, H. (1998). The elderly disturbed prisoner. *Clinical Gerontologist,* 20(1): 47–62.

Chambers, C. D., Lindquist, J. H., White, O. Z., and Harter, M. T. (eds.) (1987). *Elderly victims and deviants.* Athens: Ohio University Press.

Champion, D. J. (1987). Elderly felons and sentencing severity: Interregional variations in leniency and sentencing trends. *Criminal Justice Review,* 12(2): 7–14.

Chaneles, S. (1987). Growing old behind bars. *Psychology Today,* 21(10): 46–51.

Chaneles, S., and Burnett, C. (eds.) (1989). *Older offenders: Current trends.* New York: Haworth.

Chiu, T. (2010). *It's about time: Aging prisoners, increasing costs, and geriatric release.* New York: Vera Institute of Justice.

Choi, N. G., Ransom, S., and Wyllie, R. (2008). Depression in older nursing home residents: The influence of nursing home environmental stressors, coping, and acceptance of group and individual therapy. *Journal of Aging & Mental Health,* 12: 536–547.

Chressanthis, G. A. (1988). Criminal homicide and the elderly offender: A theoretical and empirical analysis. *Journal of Quantitative Criminology,* 4(2): 187–199.

Christian, J., Mellow, J., and Thomas, S. (2006). Social and economic implications of family connections to prisoners. *Journal of Criminal Justice,* 34: 443–452.

Churchill, W. (1910). *Parliamentary debate.* House of Commons, UK, July 10.

Cichowlas, J. A., and Chen, Y. J. (2010). Volunteer prisoners provide hospice to dying inmates. *Annals of Health Law,* 19(1): 127–132.

City of Cleburne v. Cleburne Living Center, Inc. 473 U.S. 432 (1985).

Clark, S. D., Long, D. D., and Schiffman, L. G. (1999). The mind-body connection: The relationship among physical activity level, life satisfaction, and cognitive age among mature females. *Journal of Social Behavior and Personality,* 14: 221–240.

Clear, T., Rose, D., and Ryder, J. (2001). Incarceration and the community: The problem of removing and returning offenders. *Crime and Delinquency,* 47(3): 335–351.

Clear, T. R., Hardyman, P. L., Stout, B., Lucken, K., and Dammer, H. R. (2000). The value of religion in prison: An inmate perspective. *Journal of Contemporary Criminal Justice,* 16(1): 53–74.

Coalition for Federal Sentencing Reform (1998). Nursing homes behind bars: The elderly in prison. http://www.sentencing.org/v2il.html.

Cohen, J. (1983). Incapacitation as a strategy for crime control: Possibilities and pitfalls. In M. Tonry and N. Morris (eds.), *Crime & justice: An annual review of research,* vol. 5 (pp. 1–84). Chicago: University of Chicago Press.

Cohen, S., Gottlieb, B. H., and Underwood, L. G. (2001). Social relationships and health: Challenges for measurement and intervention. *Advanced Mind, Body, Medicine,* 17: 129–141.

Cohn, F. (1999). The ethics of end-of-life care for prison inmates. *Journal of Law, Medicine, & Ethics,* 27(3): 252–259.

Coleman, J. S. (1988). Social capital in the creation of human capital. *American Journal of Sociology,* 94: S95–S120.

Collins, C. A., Estes, C. L., and Bradsher, J. E. (2001). Inequality and aging: The creation of dependency. In C. L. Estes (ed.), *Social policy and aging: A critical perspective* (pp. 137–164). Thousand Oaks, CA: Sage.

Colsher, P. L., Wallace, R. B., Loeffelholz, P. L., and Sales, M. (1992). Health status of older male prisoners: A comprehensive survey. *American Journal of Public Health,* 82(6): 881–884.

Columbia Human Rights Law Review (2011). *A jailhouse lawyer's manual.* 9th ed. New York.

Commission on Safety and Abuse in America's Prisons (2006). *Confronting confinement.* http://www.prisoncommission.org/pdfs/Confronting_Confinement .pdf.

Commissioner of Corrections v. Myers. 379 Mass. 255, 399 N.W.2d 452 (1979).

Conklin, T. J., Lincoln, T., and Tuthill, R. W. (2000). Self-reported health and prior health behaviors of newly admitted correctional inmates. *American Journal of Public Health,* 90(12): 1939–1941.

Connor, S. R., Elwert, F., Spence, C., and Christakis, N. A. (2008). Racial disparity in hospice use in the United States in 2002. *Palliative Medicine,* 22(3): 205–213.

Conover, T. (2000). *New jack: Guarding Sing Sing.* New York: Random.

Cooper, R., and Kaufman, J. (1998). Race and hypertension: Science and nescience. *Hypertension,* 32(5): 813–816.

Cooper, R., and Werner, P. (1990). Predicting violence in newly admitted inmates. *Criminal Justice and Behavior,* 17: 431–477.

Corrections Independent Review Panel (2004). *Reforming corrections.* Sacramento: California Performance Review. http://www.cpr.ca.gov/Review_Panel/pdf/intro to6.pdf.

Corrigan, P. W., and Salzer, M. S. (2003). The conflict between random assignment and treatment preference: Implications for internal validity. *Evaluation and Program Planning,* 26: 109–121.

Cowdrey, L. (2006). Commission: U.S. prisons, jails in need of reform. *Nation's Health,* 36(6): 21.

Cowles, E. L. (1990). Program needs for long-term inmates. In J. M. Quinlan (ed.), *Long-term confinement and the aging inmate population* (pp. 17–25). Washington, DC: US Department of Justice.

Cox, J. F., and Lawrence, J. E. (2010). Planning services for elderly inmates with mental illness. *Corrections Today,* 72(3): 52–57.

Craddock, A. (1996). A comparative study of male and female prison misconduct careers. *The Prison Journal,* 76: 60–80.

Craig v. Boren. 429 U.S. 190 (1976).

Crawley, E. (2005). Institutional thoughtlessness in prisons and its impacts on the day-to-day prison lives of elderly men. *Journal of Contemporary Criminal Justice,* 21(4): 350–363.

Crawley, E., and Sparks, R. (2005a). Hidden injuries? Researching the experiences of older men in English prisons. *Howard Journal,* 44(4): 345–356.

——— (2005b). Older men in prison: Survival, coping, and identity. In A. Liebling and S. Maruna (eds.), *The effects of imprisonment* (pp. 343–365). London: Willan.

——— (2006). Is there life after imprisonment? How elderly men talk about imprisonment and release. *Criminology and Criminal Justice,* 6(1): 63–82.

Crowe, M., Andel, R., Okonkwo, O., Wadley, V., Sawyer, P., and Allman, R. M. (2008). Life-space and cognitive decline in a community-based sample of African American and Caucasian older adults. *Journal of Gerontology: Medical Sciences,* 63: 1241–1245.

Crowther, M. R., Parker, M. W., Atchenbaum, W. A., Larimore, W. L., and Koenig, H. G. (2002). Rowe and Kahn's model of successful aging revisited: Positive spirituality—The forgotten factor. *The Gerontologist,* 42: 613–620.

Cruzan v. Director, Missouri Department of Health. 497 U.S. 261 (1990).

Cullen, F. T. (2005). The twelve people who saved rehabilitation: How the science of criminology made a difference. *Criminology,* 43: 1–42.

Cullen, F. T., and Gilbert, E. (1982). *Reaffirming rehabilitation.* Cincinnati: Anderson.

Cullen, F. T., Wozniak, J. F., and Frank, J. (1985). Rise of the elderly offender: Will a new criminal be invented? *Crime and Social Justice,* 23: 151–165.

Cummings, C. (1999). *Older inmates: The impact of an aging inmate population on the correctional system.* Sacramento: California Department of Corrections.

Cunningham, M. D., and Sorensen, J. R. (2007). Predictive factors for violent misconduct in close custody. *The Prison Journal,* 87: 241–253.

Cunninghis, R. N (1989). The purpose and meaning of activities. In E. S. Deichman and R. Kociecki (eds.), *Working with the elderly* (pp. 150–171). New York: Prometheus.

Curran, N. (2000). Blue hairs in the bighouse: The rise in the elderly inmate population, its effect on the overcrowding dilemma, and solutions to correct it. *New England Journal on Criminal and Civil Confinement,* 26: 225–264.

Curtin, T. (2007). The continuing problem of America's aging prison population and the search for a cost-effective and socially acceptable means of addressing it. *Elder Law Journal,* 15: 473–501.

Dawes, J. (2009). Ageing prisoners: Issues for social work. *Australian Social Work,* 62(2): 258–271.

Death in Custody Reporting Act of 2000. Pub. Law 106-297 C.F.R. (1999).

Deaton, D., Aday, R. H., and Wahidin, A. (2009–2010). The effect of health and penal harm on aging female prisoners' views of dying in prison. *Omega: Journal of Death and Dying,* 60(1): 51–70.

Degenholtz, H. B., Arnold, R. A., Meisel, A., and Lave, J. R. (2002). Persistence of racial disparities in advance care plan documents among nursing home residents. *Journal of the American Geriatrics Society,* 50(2): 378–381.

Delgado, M., and Humm-Delgado, D. (2009). *Health and healthcare in the nation's prisons: Issues, challenges, and policies.* Lanham: Rowman and Littlefield.

DeLisi, M. (2003). Criminal careers behind bars. *Behavioral Sciences and the Law,* 21: 653–669.

DeLuca, H. R. (1998). Managing older inmates: It's more than just time. In D. E. Redburn and R. P. McNamara (eds.), *Social gerontology* (pp. 209–219). Westport: Auburn.

DeMatteo, D. S., Marlowe, D. B., and Festinger, D. S. (2006). Secondary prevention services for clients who are low risk in drug court: A conceptual model. *Crime & Delinquency,* 52: 114–134.

Dershowitz, A. M. (1973). Preventive confinement: A suggested framework for constitutional analysis. *Texas Law Review,* 51: 1277–1324.

——— (1976). Background paper. In Report of the Twentieth Century Fund, Task Force on Criminal Sentencing, *Fair and certain punishment* (pp. 67–130). New York: McGraw-Hill.

Ditton, P. M., and Wilson, D. J. (1999). *Truth in sentencing in state prisons.* Washington, DC: US Department of Justice, Bureau of Justice Statistics.

Do, D., Finch, B., Basurto-Davila, R., Bird, C., Escarce, J., and Lurie, N. (2008). Does place explain racial health disparities? Quantifying the contribution of residential context to the black/white health gap in the United States. *Social Science & Medicine,* 67(8): 1258–1268.

Donabedian, A. (1980). *Explorations in quality assessment and monitoring.* Vol. 1, *The definition of quality and approaches to its assessment.* Ann Arbor: Health Administration.

——— (1988). The quality of care: How can it be assessed? *Journal of the American Medical Association,* 260(12): 1743–1748.

——— (2005). Evaluating the quality of medical care. *Milbank Quarterly,* 83(4): 691–729.

Draine, J., Woff, N., Jacoby, J. E., Hartwell, S., and Duclos, C. (2005). Understanding community re-entry of former prisoners with mental illness: A conceptual model to guide new research. *Behavioral Sciences and the Law,* 23(5): 689–707.

Drake, R. E., Goldman, H. H., Leff, H. S., Lehman, A. F., Dixon, L., Mueser, K. T., and Torrey, W. C. (2001). Implementing evidence-based practices in routine mental health service settings. *Psychiatric Services,* 52(2): 179–182.

Dubler, N. N. (1998). The collision of confinement and care: End-of-life care in prisons and jails. *Journal of Law, Medicine, & Ethics,* 26(2): 149–156.

Dugger, R. L. (1988). Graying of America's prisons: Special care considerations. *Corrections Today,* 50(3): 26–30, 34.

Dunlop, B. D., Rothman, M. B., and Hirt, G. M. (2001). Elders and criminal justice: International issues for the 21st century. *International Journal of Law & Psychiatry,* 24: 285–303.

Dunlop, D. D., Manheim, L. M., Song, J., and Chang, R. W. (2002). Gender and ethnic/racial disparities in health care utilization among older adults. *Journal of Gerontology,* 57B(4), S221–S233.

Edison v. Douberly. 604 F.3d 1307 (11th Cir. 2010).

End-of-life care in corrections: The facts (2008–2009). http://www.nhpco.org/files /public/access/corrections/Corrections_The_Facts.pdf.

Enders, S. (2004). *Simple answers to difficult healthcare questions: Choice.* Carmichael, CA: Autumn Indigo.

Enders, S. R., Paterniti, D. A., and Meyers, F. J. (2005). An approach to develop effective health care decision making for women in prison. *Journal of Palliative Medicine,* 8: 432–439.

Esperian, J. H. (2010). The effect of prison education programs on recidivism. *Journal of Correctional Education,* 61(4): 316–334.

Estelle v. Gamble. 429 U.S. 97, 102 (1976).

Evans, C., Herzog, R., and Tillman, T. (2002). The Louisiana State Penitentiary: Angola prison hospice. *Journal of Palliative Medicine,* 5(4): 553–558.

Ex parte Young. 209 U.S. 123 (1908).

Fair Labor Standards Act of 1938. 29 U.S.C. § 201 *et seq.* (2011).

Falter, R. G. (1999). Selected predictors of health services needs of inmates over age 50. *Journal of Correctional Health Care,* 6(2): 149–175.

Farmer v. Brennan. 511 U.S. 825 (1994).

Farrington, D. P. (1986). Age and crime. In N. Morris and M. Tonry (eds.), *Crime & justice: An annual review of research,* vol. 7 (pp. 189–250). Chicago: University of Chicago Press.

——— (2003a). Methodological quality standards for evaluation research. *Annals of the American Academy of Political and Social Science,* 587: 49–68.

——— (2003b). A short history of randomized experiments in criminology. *Evaluation Review,* 27(3): 218–227.

Farrington, D. P., and Welsh, B. C. (2006). A half century of randomized experiments on crime and justice. *Crime and Justice,* 34(1): 55–132.

Fattah, E. A., and Sacco, V. F. (1989). *Crime and victimization of the elderly.* New York: Springer-Verlag.

Fazel, S., and Baillargeon, J. (2011). The health of prisoners. *Lancet,* 377(9769): 956–965.

Fazel, S., Hope, T., O'Donnell, I., and Jacoby, R. (2004). Unmet treatment needs of older prisoners: A primary care survey. *Age and Ageing,* 33(4): 396–398.

Fazel, S., Hope, T., O'Donnell, I., Piper, M., and Jacoby, R. (2001). Health of elderly male prisoners: Worse than the general population, worse than younger prisoners. *Age and Ageing,* 30(5): 403–407.

Federal Bureau of Investigation (2003). *Age-specific arrest rates and race-specific arrest rates for selected offenses, 1993–2001.* Washington, DC.

Feinberg, G. (1983). Shoplifting by the elderly: One community's innovative response. *Aging,* 341: 20–24.

Feldmeyer, B., and Steffensmeier, D. (2007). Elder crime: Patterns and current trends, 1980–2004. *Research on Aging,* 29: 297–322.

——— (2012). Patterns and trends in elder homicide across race and ethnicity, 1985–2009. *Homicide Studies,* 17(2): 204–223.

Fellner, J. (2007). *Prevalence and policy: New data on the prevalence of mental illness in US prisons.* Washington, DC: Human Rights Watch.

——— (2008). Afterwords: A few reflections. *Criminal Justice and Behavior,* 35(8): 1079–1087.

Ferguson, J. L. (2002). Putting the "what works" research into practice: An organizational perspective. *Criminal Justice and Behavior,* 29: 472–492.

Fiori, K. L., Hays, J. C., and Meador, K. G. (2004). Spiritual turning points and perceived control over the life course. *International Journal of Aging and Human Development,* 59: 391–420.

Fisher, A. A., and Hatton, D. C. (2010). A study of women prisoners' use of co-payments for health care: Issues of access. *Women's Health Issues,* 20: 185–192.

Flanagan, T. J. (1981). Dealing with long-term confinement: Adaptive strategies and perspectives among long-term prisoners. *Criminal Justice and Behavior,* 8: 201–222.

Fletcher, S. K. (2004). Religion and life meaning: Differentiating between religious beliefs and religious community in constructing life meaning. *Journal of Aging Studies,* 18: 171–185.

Florida Corrections Commission (2001). *Annual report of the CMA incarcerating elderly and aging inmates: Medical and mental health implication.* Tallahassee.

Florida Department of Corrections (1993). *Status report on elderly inmates.* Tallahassee.

Florida House of Representatives (1999). *An examination of elder inmates services: An aging crisis.* Tallahassee.

Flynn, E. E. (1992). The graying of America's prison population. *The Prison Journal,* 72(1–2): 77–98.

——— (1998). *Managing elderly offenders: A national assessment.* Washington, DC: National Institute of Justice.

——— (2000). Elders as perpetrators. In M. B. Rothman, B. D. Dunlop, and P. Entzel (eds.), *Elders, crime, and the criminal justice system: Myth, perceptions, and reality in the 21st century* (pp. 43–85). New York: Springer.

Flynn v. Doyle. 672 F. Supp. 2d 858 (E.D. Wis. 2009).

Fogel, C. I. (1993). Hard time: The stressful nature of incarceration. *Issues in Mental Health Nursing,* 14: 367–377.

Foote, C. (1993). *The prison population explosion: California's rogue elephant.* San Francisco: Center on Juvenile and Criminal Justice.

Forsyth, C. J., and Shover, N. (1986). No rest for the weary. *Sociological Focus,* 19(4): 375–386.

Frankel, M. E. (1973). *Criminal sentences: Law without order.* New York: Hill and Wang.

Frankfort-Nachmias, C., and Nachmias, D. (2000). *Research methods in the social sciences.* 6th ed. New York: Worth.

Freimuth, V., Quinn, S., Thomas, S., Cole, G., Zook, E., and Duncan, T. (2001). African Americans' views on research and the Tuskegee syphilis study. *Social Science & Medicine,* 52(5): 797–808.

Freudenberg, N. (2001). Jails, prisons, and the health of urban populations: A review of the impact of the correctional system on community health. *Journal of Urban Health: Bulletin of the New York Academy of Medicine,* 78(2): 214–235.

Fry, L. J. (1987). Older prison inmate: A profile. *Justice Professional,* 2(1): 1–12.

Fry, P. S. (2000). Religious involvement, spirituality, and personal meaning for life: Existential predictors of psychological wellbeing in community-residing and institutional care elders. *Aging and Mental Health,* 4: 375–387.

Furman v. Georgia. 408 U.S. 238 (1972).

Gal, M. (2002). Physical and mental health of older offenders. *Forum on Corrections Research,* 14(2): 15–19.

Gallagher, E. M. (1990). Emotional, social, and physical health characteristics of older men in prison. *International Journal of Aging and Human Development,* 31(4): 251–265.

Garner, J. H., and Visher, C. A. (2003). The production of criminological experiments. *Evaluation Review,* 27(3): 316–335.

Gates v. Cook. 376 F.3d 323, 376 F.3d 323 (5th Cir. 2004).

Gavazzi, S. M., Yarcheck, C. M., Rhine, E. E., and Partridge, C. R. (2003). Building bridges between the parole officer and the families of serious juvenile offenders: A preliminary report on a family-based parole program. *International Journal of Offender Therapy and Comparative Criminology,* 47(3): 291–308.

Gaydon, B. L., and Miller, M. K. (2007). Elders in the justice system: How the system treats elders in trials, during imprisonment, and on death row. *Behavioral Sciences and the Law,* 25: 667–699.

Gayton v. McCoy. 593 F.3d 610 (7th Cir. 2010).

Gendreau, P. (1996). Offender rehabilitation: What we know and what needs to be done. *Criminal Justice and Behavior,* 23: 144–161.

Gibbons, J., and Katzenbach, N. (2006). *Confronting confinement.* New York: Vera Institute of Justice, Commission on Safety and Abuse in America's Prisons.

Gibbs, J. J. (1991). Environmental congruence and symptoms of psychopathology: A further exploration of the effects of exposure to the jail environment. *Criminal Justice and Behavior,* 18: 351–374.

Gillespie, M. W., and Galliher, J. F. (1972). Age, anomie, and the inmate's definition of aging in prison: An exploratory study. In D. P. Kent, R. Kastenbaum, and S. Sherwood (eds.), *Research planning and action for the elderly* (pp. 465–483). New York: Behavioral Publications.

Gilliard, D., and Beck, A. (1998). *Prisoners in 1997.* Washington, DC: US Department of Justice, Bureau of Justice Statistics.

Gillis, C. (2000). Reconceptualizing offender employment. *Forum on Corrections Research,* 12: 32–35.

Glamser, F., and Cabana, D. (2003). Dying in a total institution: The case of death in prison. In C. Bryant (ed.), *Handbook on death and dying* (pp. 495–501). Thousand Oaks, CA: Sage.

Glaze, L. E., and Bonczar, T. P. (2009). *Probation and parole in the United States, 2008.* Washington, DC: US Department of Justice, Bureau of Justice Statistics.

The "Go Wish" game: Values sort cards (2009). http://www.codaalliance.org/gowish cards.html.

Goetting, A. (1983). The elderly in prisons: Issues and perspectives. *Journal of Research in Crime and Delinquency,* 20(2): 291–309.

——— (1984). Elderly in prison: A profile. *Criminal Justice Review,* 9(2): 14–24.

——— (1985). Racism, sexism, and ageism in the prison community. *Federal Probation,* 49(3): 10–22.

Goetting, A., and Howsen, R. (1986). Correlates of prison misconduct. *Journal of Quantitative Criminology,* 2: 49–67.

Goffman, E. (1961). *Asylums: Essays on the social situation of mental patients and other inmates.* Garden City, NY: Anchor.

Golder, S., Ivanoff, A., Cloud, R. N., Besel, K. L., McKiernan, P., Bratt, E., and Bledsoe, L. K. (2005). Evidence-based practice with adults in jails and prisons:

Strategies, practices, and future directions. *Best Practices in Mental Health,* 1(2): 100–132.

Goodman v. Georgia (United States v. Georgia). 546 U.S. 151 (2006).

Gordon, D. R. (1994). *The return of the dangerous classes: Drug prohibition and policy politics.* New York: Norton.

Gorman, B. K., and Read, J. G. (2006). Gender disparities in adult health: An examination of three measures of morbidity. *Journal of Health and Social Behavior,* 47(2): 95–110.

Gottfredson, M. R. (2005). Offender classifications and treatment effects in developmental criminology: A propensity/event consideration. *ANNALS of the American Academy of Political and Social Science,* 602 (November): 46–56.

Gottfredson, S. D., and Moriarty, L. J. (2006). Statistical risk assessment: Old problems and new applications. *Crime & Delinquency,* 52: 178–200.

Grace Project. (2000). End-of-life care standards of practice for inmates in correctional settings. July 17. http://www2.edc.org/lastacts/archives/archivesMay00 /standards.asp.

Grann, M., Belfrage, H., and Tengstrom, A. (2000). Actuarial assessment of risk for violence: Predictive validity of the VRAG and the historical part of the HCR-20. *Criminal Justice and Behavior,* 27(1): 97–114.

Gravlee, C. (2009). How race becomes biology: Embodiment of social inequality. *American Journal of Physical Anthropology,* 139(1): 47–57.

Greenberg, D. (1975). The incapacitative effect of imprisonment: Some estimates. *Law & Society Review,* 9: 541–580.

Greenberg, D. F., and West, V. (2001). State prison populations and their growth, 1971–1991. *Criminology,* 39: 615–654.

Greenberg, S., Quinlan, A., and Rosner, J. (2011). *Poll on the California economy and budget.* University of Southern California and Los Angeles Times. http://www.gqrr.com/index.php?ID=2649.

Greenwood, P. W., and Abrahamse, A. (1982). *Selective incapacitation.* Santa Monica: RAND.

Greifinger, R. (2007). *Public health behind bars: From prisons to communities.* New York: Springer.

Greiner, K. A., Perera, S., and Ahluwalia, J. S. (2003). Hospice usage by minorities in the last year of life: Results from the National Mortality Followback Survey. *Journal of the American Geriatrics Society,* 51(7): 970–978.

Gubler, T., and Petersilia, J. (2006). *Elderly prisoners are dying for reform.* California Sentencing and Corrections Policy Series. Stanford: Stanford University Criminal Justice Center.

Guerino, P., Harrison, P. M., and Sabol, W. J. (2012). *Prisoners in 2010.* Washington, DC: US Department of Justice, Bureau of Justice Statistics.

Guo, S., and Fraser, M. W. (2010). *Propensity score analysis.* Thousand Oaks, CA: Sage.

Guzman v. Cockrell. Civil Action no. 9:10cv111, 2011 U.S. Dist. LEXIS 41646 (E.D. Tex. Apr. 15, 2011).

Haber, D. (2006). Life review: Implementation, theory, research, and therapy. *International Journal of Aging and Human Development,* 63(2): 153–171.

Hairston, C. F. (1988). Family ties during imprisonment: Do they influence future criminal activity? *Federal Probation,* 52: 48–52.

———— (1991). Family ties during imprisonment: Important to whom and for what? *Journal of Sociology and Social Welfare,* 18: 87–104.

Hale v. Arizona. 993 F.2d 1387 (9th Cir. 1993).

Ham, J. N. (1976). *The Forgotten minority . . . An exploration of long-term institutionalized aged and aging male prison inmates.* Washington, DC: US Department of Justice, National Institute of Law.

———— (1980). Aged and infirm male prison inmates. *Aging,* 309–310 (July–August): 24–31.

Hammett, T. M., Roberts, C., and Kennedy, S. (2001a). Health-related issues in prisoner reentry. *Crime and Delinquency,* 47: 390–409.

———— (2001b). Linkages between in-prison and community-based health services. *Journal of Correctional Health Care,* 10: 333–368.

Haney, C. (2001). *The psychological impact of incarceration: Implications for post-prison adjustment.* Washington, DC: Urban Institute.

Hannah-Moffat, K. (2005). Criminogenic needs and the transformative risk subject: Hybridizations of risk/need in penalty. *Punishment & Society,* 7: 29–51.

Harcourt, B. (2001). *Illusion of order: The false promise of broken windows policing.* Cambridge: Harvard University Press.

Harer, M. D. (1994). *Recidivism among federal prisoners released in 1987: A preliminary report.* Washington, DC: Federal Bureau of Prisons.

Harner, H. M., Hentz, P. M., and Evangelista, M. L. (2010). Grief interrupted: The experience of loss among incarcerated women. *Qualitative Health Research,* 21: 454–464.

Harris, F., Hek, G., and Condon, L. (2006). Health needs of prisoners in England and Wales: The implications for prison healthcare of gender, age, and ethnicity. *Health and Social Care in the Community,* 15(1): 56–66.

Harris, P. M., Gingerich, R., and Whittaker, T. A. (2004). The "effectiveness" of differential supervision. *Crime & Delinquency,* 50: 235–271.

Harrison, M. T. (2006). True Grit: An innovative program for elderly inmates. *Corrections Today,* 68(7): 46–49.

———— (2011). True Grit: An innovative structured living program for geriatric prisoners in the Nevada Department of Corrections. Paper presented at the Aging Prisoners Forum, October 8. New York: Fordham University.

Harrison, M. T., and Benedetti, J. (2009). Comprehensive geriatric programs in a time of shrinking resources: "True Grit" revisited. *Corrections Today,* 71(5): 44–47.

Harrison, P. M., and Beck, A. J. (2004). *Prisoners in 2003.* Washington, DC: US Department of Justice, Bureau of Justice Statistics.

Harzke, A. J., Baillargeon, J. G., Pruitt, S. L., Pulvino, J. S., Paar, D. P., and Kelley, M. F. (2010). Prevalence of chronic medical conditions among inmates in the Texas prison system. *Journal of Urban Health: Bulletin of the New York Academy of Medicine,* 87(3): 486–503.

Hassine, V. (2009). *Life without parole: Living in prison today.* 4th ed. New York: Oxford University Press.

Haugebrook, S., Zgoba, K. M., Maschi, T., Morgen, K., and Brown, D. (2010). Trauma, stress, health, and mental health issues among ethnically diverse older adult prisoners. *Journal of Correctional Health Care,* 16(3): 220–229.

Hayes v. Snyder. 546 F.3d 516 (7th Cir. 2008).

Her Majesty's Inspectorate of Prisons (2004). *"No problems—old and quiet": Older prisoners in England and Wales: A thematic review.* London.

Hewitt, J. D., and Clear, T. R. (1983). *The impact of sentencing reform: From indeterminate to determinate sentencing.* Lanham: University Press of America.

Higgins, D., and Severson, M. G. (2009). Community reentry and older adult offenders: Redefining social work roles. *Journal of Gerontological Social Work,* 52: 784–802.

Hill, T., Williams, B., Cobe, G., and Lindquist, K. (2006). *Aging inmates: Challenges for healthcare and custody.* San Francisco: Lumetra.

Hill v. Dekalb Regional Youth Detention Center. 40 F.3d 1176 (11th Cir.1994).

Hodge, S. K. (2007). Providing transition and outpatient services to the mentally ill released from correctional institutions. In R. Greifinger (ed.), *Public health behind bars: From prisons to community* (pp. 461–477). New York: Springer.

Hoffman, H. C., and Dickinson, G. E. (2011). Characteristics of prison hospice programs in the United States. *American Journal of Hospice and Palliative Medicine,* 28: 245–252.

Hoffman, P. B., Stone-Meierhoefer, B., and Beck, J. L. (1978). Salient Factor Score and release behavior: Three validation samples. *Law and Human Behavior,* 2(1): 47–62.

Holman, B. (1998). Nursing homes behind bars: The elderly in prison. *Coalition for Federal Sentencing Reform,* 2(1): 1–2.

Hooyman, N. R., and Kiyak, H. (2011). *Social gerontology: A multidisciplinary perspective.* Boston: Addison-Wesley.

House, J. S., Umberson, D., and Landis, K. R. (1988). Social relationships and health. *Science,* 241: 540–545.

Hsu, C. I., Caputi, P., and Byrne, M. K. (2011). The Level of Service Inventory–Revised (Lsi-R) and Australian offenders: Factor, structure, and specificity. *Criminal Justice and Behavior,* 38(6): 600–618.

Hughes, T., Wilson, D., and Beck, A. (2001). *Trends in state parole.* Washington, DC: US Department of Justice, Bureau of Justice Statistics.

Hui, D., Elsayem, A., Li, Z., De La Cruz, M., Palmer, J. L., and Bruera, E. (2010). Antineoplastic therapy use in patients with advanced cancer admitted to an acute palliative care unit at a comprehensive cancer center: A simultaneous care model. *Cancer,* 116(8): 2036–2043.

Hunt, G., Riegel, S., Morales, T., and Waldorf, D. (1993). Changes in prison culture: Prison gangs and the case of the "Pepsi Generation." *Social Problems,* 40(3): 398–409.

Hutto v. Finney. 437 U.S. 678 (1978).

Hyde, R., Brumfield, B., and Nagel, J. (2000). Female inmate health care requests. *Journal of Correctional Health Care,* 7(1): 91–103.

In re Conroy. 486 A.2d 1209 (N.J. 1985).

Ireland, J. L. (2000). "Bullying" among male prisoners: A review of the research. *Aggression and Violent Behavior,* 5: 201–215.

Jacobs, E., and Spadaro, N. (2003). *Leading groups in corrections: Skills and techniques.* Lanham: American Correctional Association.

James, D. J., and Glaze, L. E. (2006). *Mental health problems of prison and jail inmates.* Washington, DC: US Department of Justice, Bureau of Justice Statistics.

James, M. F. (1992). The sentencing of elderly criminals. *American Criminal Law Review,* 29(3): 1025–1044.

Jansen, L. A. (2010a). Disambiguating clinical intentions: The ethics of palliative sedation. *Journal of Medicine and Philosophy,* 35(1): 19–31.

——— (2010b). Intractable end-of-life suffering and the ethics of palliative sedation: A commentary on Cassell and Rich. *Pain Medicine,* 11(3): 440–441.

Jiang, S., and Winfree, L. T. (2006). Social support, gender, and inmate adjustment to prison life. *The Prison Journal,* 86(1): 32–55.

Johnson v. Avery. 393 U.S. 483 (1969).

Johnson, B. R., Larson, D. B., and Pitts, T. C. (1997). Religious programming, institutional adjustment, and recidivism among former inmates in prison fellowship program. *Justice Quarterly,* 14: 145–166.

Johnson, E. H. (1988). Care for elderly inmates: Conflicting concerns and purposes in prisons. In B. R. McCarthy and R. H. Langworthy (eds.), *Older offenders: Perspectives in criminology and criminal justice* (pp. 157–163). New York: Praeger.

Johnson, G. (2008). Assisted living facilities for geriatric inmates. Appropriations Act, chap. 879, item 387-B. Virginia Department of Corrections and Virginia Parole Board. http://sfc.virginia.gov/pdf/Public%20Safety/September%2024%20mtg/Final% 20Geriatric%20Report%20for%20Item%20387-B%20incl.%20Ex.pdf.

Johnstone, M. J., and Kanitsaki, O. (2009). Ethics and advance care planning in a culturally diverse society. *Journal of Transcultural Nursing,* 20(4): 405–416.

Jolley, J. M., and Kerbs, J. J. (2010). Risk, need, and responsivity: Unrealized potential for the international delivery of substance abuse treatment in prison. *International Criminal Justice Review,* 20(3): 280–301.

Jones, J. H. (1993). Bad blood: The Tuskegee syphilis experiment. New York: Free Press and Maxwell McMillan International.

Jones v. North Carolina Prisoners' Labor Union, Inc. 433 U.S. 119 (1977).

Jordan, B. K., Schlenger, W. E., Fairbanks, J. A., Caddell, J. M. (1996). Prevalence of psychiatric disorders among incarcerated women. *Archives of General Psychiatry,* 53: 513–519.

Junior, V. Y. (2003). Helping female inmates cope with grief and loss. *Corrections Today,* 65(3): 76–79.

Kadish, S. H. (1978). Determinate sentencing: Reform or regression? Proceedings of the Special Conference on Determinate Sentencing, Boalt Hall School of Law, University of California, Berkeley. Washington, DC: US Department of Justice, Law Enforcement Assistance Administration.

Kahana, E. (1982). A congruence model of person-environment interaction. In M. P. Lawton, G. Windley, and T. O. Byerts (eds.), *Aging and the environment: Theoretical approaches* (pp. 98–122). New York: Springer.

Kaufman, J. S. (2008). Epidemiologic analysis of racial/ethnic disparities: Some fundamental issues and a cautionary example. *Social Science & Medicine,* 66(8): 1659–1669.

Kennedy v. Louisiana. 554 U.S. 407 (2008).

Kerbs, J. J. (2000a). Arguments and strategies for the selective decarceration of older prisoners. In M. B. Rothman, B. D. Dunlop, and P. Entzel (eds.), *Elders, crime, and the criminal justice system: Myth, perceptions, and the reality in the 21st century* (pp. 229–250). New York: Springer.

——— (2000b). The older prisoner: Social, psychological, and medical considerations. In M. B. Rothman, B. D. Dunlop, and P. Entzel (eds.), *Elders, crime, and the criminal justice system: Myth, perceptions, and the reality in the 21st century* (pp. 207–228). New York: Springer.

Kerbs, J. J., and Jolley, J. M. (2007). Inmate-on-inmate victimization among older male prisoners. *Crime & Delinquency,* 53(2): 187–218.

——— (2009a). Challenges posed by older prisoners: What we know about America's aging prison population. In R. Tewksbury and D. Dabney (eds.), *Prisons and jails: A reader* (pp. 389–411). New York: McGraw-Hill.

——— (2009b). A commentary on age segregation for older prisoners: Philosophical and pragmatic considerations for correctional systems. *Criminal Justice Review,* 34(1): 119–139.

Kerley, K. R., Allison, M. C., and Graham, R. D. (2006). Investigating the impact of religiosity on emotional and behavioral coping in prison. *Journal of Crime and Justice,* 29(2): 69–93.

Kiely, D. K., Mitchell, S. L., Marlow, A., Murphy, K. M., and Morris, J. N. (2001). Racial and state differences in the designation of advance directives in nursing home residents. *Journal of the American Geriatrics Society,* 49(10): 1346–1352.

King v. CDCR. Civil Action no. S-06-0065 LKK GGH P, 2007 U.S. Dist. LEXIS 51179 (E.D. Cal. July 16, 2007).

King, R. D., Massoglia, M., and Macmillan, R. (2007). The context of marriage and crime: Gender, the propensity to marry, and offending in early adulthood. *Criminology,* 45(1): 33–65.

King, R. S., and Mauer, M. (2001). *Aging behind bars: Three strikes seven years later.* Washington, DC: Sentencing Project.

Kittrie, N. N. (1971). *The right to be different: Deviance and enforced therapy.* Baltimore: Johns Hopkins University Press.

Kochanek, K., Xu, J., Murphy, B., Minino, A., and Kung, H.-C. (2011). *Deaths: Preliminary data for 2009.* Washington, DC: US Department of Health and Human Services, Centers for Disease Control and Prevention, National Center for Health Statistics, National Vital Statistics System. http://www.cdc.gov/nchs/data/nvsr/nvsr59/nvsr59-04.pdf.

Koenig, H. G. (1995). Religion and older men in prison. *International Journal of Geriatric Psychiatry,* 10(3): 219–230.

Koenig, H. G., George, L. K., and Siegler, I. C. (1988). Use of religion and other emotion-regulating coping strategies in older adults. *The Gerontologist,* 25: 303–310.

Koenig, H. G., Johnson, S., Bellard, J., Denker, M., and Fenlon, R. (1995). Depression and anxiety disorder among older male inmates at a federal correctional facility. *Psychiatric Services,* 46(4): 399–401.

Koenig, H. G., McCullough, M. E., and Larson, D. B. (2001). *Handbook of religion and health.* New York: Oxford University Press.

Kohler, B., Ward, E., McCarthy, B., Schymura, M., Ries, L., Eheman, C., and Edwards, B. (2011). Annual report to the nation on the status of cancer, 1975–2007, featuring tumors of the brain and other nervous system. *Journal of the National Cancer Institute,* 103: 1–23.

Korematsu v. United States. 323 U.S. 214 (1944).

Krabill, J., and Aday, R. H. (2005). Exploring the social world of aging female prisoners. *Women & Criminal Justice,* 17(1): 27–55.

Krajick, K. (1979). Growing old in prison. *Corrections Magazine,* 5(1): 32–46.

Kratcoski, P. C. (2000). *Older inmates: Correctional counseling and treatment.* 5th ed. Long Grove, IL: Waveland.

Kratcoski, P. C., and Babb, S. (1990). Adjustment of older inmates: An analysis of institutional structure and gender. *Journal of Contemporary Criminal Justice,* 6(4): 264–281.

Kratcoski, P. C., and Pownall, G. A. (1989). Federal Bureau of Prisons programming for older inmates. *Federal Probation,* 53(2): 28–35.

Kruttschnitt, C., and Gartner, R. (2003). Women's imprisonment. *Crime & Justice,* 30: 1–81.

Kubler-Ross, E. (1969). *On death and dying.* New York: Macmillan.

Kurlychek, M. C., Brame, R., and Bushway, S. D. (2006). Scarlet letters and recidivism: Does an old criminal record predict future offending? *Criminology and Public Policy,* 5(3): 483–504.

Kutrip v. City of St. Louis. 329 Fed. Appx. 683 (8th Cir. 2009).

Kuziemko, I. (2007). *Going off parole: How the elimination of discretionary prison release affects the social cost of crime.* Working Paper no. 13380. Cambridge, MA: National Bureau of Economic Research.

Kwak, J., and Haley, W. E. (2005). Current research findings on end-of-life decision making among racially or ethnically diverse groups. *The Gerontologist,* 45(5): 634–641.

Lamb-Mechanick, D., and Nelson, J. (2000). *Prison health care survey: An analysis of factors influencing per capita costs.* Washington, DC: American Correctional Association.

Langan, P. A., and Levin, D. J. (2002). *Recidivism of prisoners released in 1994.* Washington, DC: US Department of Justice, Bureau of Justice Statistics.

Langan, P. A., Schmitt, E. L., and Durose, M. R. (2003). *Recidivism of sex offenders released from prison in 1994.* Washington, DC: US Department of Justice, Bureau of Justice Statistics.

Latessa, E. J., and Smith, P. (2007). *Corrections in the community.* Cincinnati: Anderson.

Lau, A. S., Chang, D. F., and Okazaki, S. (2010). Methodological challenges in treatment outcome research with ethnic minorities. *Cultural Diversity and Ethnic Minority Psychology,* 16(4): 573–580.

Laub, J. H., Nagin, D. S., and Sampson, R. J. (1998). Trajectories of change in criminal offending: Good marriages and the desistance process. *American Sociological Review,* 63(2): 225–238.

Laub, J. H., and Sampson, R. J. (2003). *Shared beginnings, divergent lives: Delinquent boys to age 70.* Cambridge: Harvard University Press.

Laub, J. H., Sampson, R. J., and Sweeten, G. A. (2008). Assessing Sampson and Laub's life-course theory of crime. In F. T. Cullen, J. P. Wright, and K. R. Blevins (eds.), *Taking stock: The status of criminological theory—Advances in criminological theory,* vol. 15 (pp. 313–333). New Brunswick, NJ: Transaction.

Lawton, M. P. (1983). Environment and other determinants of well-being in older people. *The Gerontologist,* 23(4): 349–357.

Leigey, M. E. (2007). *Life while serving life: Examining the correctional experiences of older inmates serving a life without parole sentence.* Unpublished PhD dissertation, University of Delaware, Newark.

Leigey, M. E., and Hodge, J. P. (2012). Gray matters: Gender differences in the physical and mental health of older inmates. *Women & Criminal Justice,* 22: 289–308.

Leigey, M. E., and Reed, K. L. (2010). A woman's life before serving life: Examining the negative pre-incarceration life events of female life-sentenced inmates. *Women & Criminal Justice,* 20(4): 302–322.

Lemieux, C. M., Dyeson, T. B., and Castiglione, B. (2002). Revisiting the literature on prisoners who are older: Are we wiser? *The Prison Journal,* 82(4): 440–458.

Lemon, B. W., Bengtson, V. L., and Peterson, J. A. (1972). An exploration of the activity theory of aging: Activity types and life satisfaction among in-movers to a retirement community. *Journal of Gerontology,* 27: 511–523.

Lerner, B. H. (2007). Subjects or objects? Prisoners and human experimentation. *New England Journal of Medicine,* 356(18): 1806–1807.

Levitt, L., and Loper, A. B. (2009). The influence of religious participation on the adjustment of female inmates. *American Journal of Orthopsychiatry,* 79(1): 1–7.

Lewis, C. (2006). Treating incarcerated women: Gender matters. *Psychiatric Clinics of North America,* 29: 773–789.

Liang, J., Krause, N., and Bennett, J. (2001). Is giving better than receiving? *Psychology & Aging,* 16: 511–523.

Light, S. C. (1991). Assault on prison officers: Interactional themes. *Justice Quarterly,* 8: 243–262.

Lin, J. T., and Mathew, P. (2005). Cancer pain management in prisons: A survey of primary care practitioners and inmates. *Journal of Pain & Symptom Management,* 29(5): 466–473.

Lin, N. (2000). Inequality and social capital. *Contemporary Sociology,* 29(6): 785–795.

Linder, J. (2004). Oncology. In J. Berzoff and P. Silverman (eds.), *Living with dying: A handbook for end-of-life health practitioners* (pp. 696–724). New York: Columbia University Press.

Linder, J., Enders, S. R., Craig, E., Richardson, J., and Meyers, F. J. (2002). Hospice care for the incarcerated in the United States: An introduction. *Journal of Palliative Medicine,* 5(4): 549–552.

Linder, J., Knauf, K., Enders, S. R., and Meyers, F. J. (2002). Prison hospice and pastoral care services in California. *Journal of Palliative Medicine,* 5(6): 903–908.

Linder, J., and Meyers, F. (2007). Palliative care for prison inmates: "Don't let me die in prison." *Journal of the American Medical Association,* 298(8): 894–901.

—— (2009). End-of-life care in correctional settings. *Journal of Social Work in End-of-Life & Palliative Care,* 5(1–2): 27–33.

—— (2011). Palliative care for prison inmates: "Don't let me die in prison." In S. McPhee, M. Winker, M. Rabow, P. S. Z., and A. Markowitz (eds.), *Care at the close of life: Evidence and experience* (pp. 457–469). New York: McGraw-Hill.

Lindsey v. McGinnis. No. 93-2290, 1994 U.S. App. LEXIS 9926 (6th Cir. 1994).

Lipton, D., Martinson, R., and Wilks, J. (1975). *The effectiveness of correctional treatment: A survey of treatment evaluation studies.* New York: Praeger.

Listwan, S. J., Cullen, F. T., and Latessa, E. J. (2006). How to prevent prisoner reentry programs from failing: Insights from evidence-based corrections. *Federal Probation,* 70: 19–25.

Litvan, L. M. (1998). Can "three strikes" reduce crime? *Investors Business Daily,* November 30, 1998, pp. A1, A26.

Litwin, H., and Shiovitz-Ezra, S. (2006). The association between activity and wellbeing in later life: What really matters? *Ageing & Society,* 26: 225–242.

Liver Cancer Network (2011). Chemoembolization. http://www.livercancer.com /treatments/chemoembolization.html.

Lo Gerfo, M. L. (1980–1981). Three ways of reminiscing in theory and practice. *International Journal of Aging and Human Development,* 12(1): 39–48.

Loeb, S. J., and AbuDagga, A. (2006). Health-related research on older inmates: An integrative review. *Research in Nursing & Health,* 29(6): 556–565.

Loeb, S. J., and Steffensmeier, D. (2006). Older male prisoners: Health status, self-efficacy beliefs, and health-promoting behaviors. *Journal of Correctional Health,* 12(4): 269–278.

Loeb, S. J., Steffensmeier, D., and Lawrence, F. (2008). Comparing incarcerated and community-dwelling older men's health. *Western Journal of Nursing Research,* 30: 234–249.

Loeb, S. J., Steffensmeier, D., and Myco, P. M. (2007). In their own words: Older male prisoners' health beliefs and concerns for the future. *Geriatric Nursing,* 28: 319–329.

Long, A. B. (2008). Introducing the new and improved Americans with Disabilities Act: Assessing the ADA Amendment Acts of 2008. *Northwestern University Law Review Colloquy,* 103: 217–229.

Long, L. M. (1992). Study of arrests of older offenders: Trends and patterns. *Journal of Crime and Justice,* 15(2): 157–175.

Longino, C. F., Jr., and Kart, C. S. (1982). Explicating activity theory: A formal replication. *Journal of Gerontology,* 37: 713–722.

Love v. Westville Correction Center. 103 F.3d 558 (7th Cir. 1996).

Lowenkamp, C. T., Latessa, E. J., and Holsinger, A. M. (2006). The risk principle in action: What have we learned from 13,676 offenders and 97 correctional programs? *Crime & Delinquency,* 52: 77–93.

Ludke, R. L., and Smucker, D. R. (2007). Racial differences in the willingness to use hospice services. *Journal of Palliative Medicine,* 10(6): 1329–1337.

Luellen, J. K., Shadish, W. R., and Clark, M. H. (2005). Propensity scores: An introduction and experimental test. *Evaluation Review,* 29: 530–558.

Lundstrom, S. (1994). Dying to get out: A study on the necessity, importance, and effectiveness of prison early release programs for elderly inmates suffering from HIV disease and other terminal-centered illnesses. *BYU Journal of Public Law,* 8(1): 155–188.

Lynch, J. P. (2006). Prisoner reentry: Beyond program evaluation. *Criminology and Public Policy,* 5(2): 401–412.

Lynch, J. P., and Sabol, W. J. (2001). *Prisoner re-entry in perspective.* Washington, DC: Urban Institute.

Mabli, J., Holley, C. S. D., Patrick, J., and Walls, J. (1979). Age and prison violence: Increasing age heterogeneity as a violence-reducing strategy in prisons. *Criminal Justice & Behavior,* 6(2): 175–186.

MacKenzie, D. L. (1987). Age and adjustment to prison: Interactions with attitudes and anxiety. *Criminal Justice and Behavior,* 14(4): 427–447.

——— (2000). Evidence-based corrections: Identifying what works. *Crime and Delinquency,* 46(4): 457–471.

Maddocks, I. (2003). Commentary: Prisoners with advanced disease—A truly marginalized population. *Journal of Pain & Palliative Care Pharmacotherapy,* 17(3–4): 139–140.

Magee, C. G., Hult, J. R., Turalba, R., and McMillan, S. (2005). Preventive care for women in prison: A qualitative community health assessment of the

Papanicolaou Test and follow-up treatment at a California state women's prison. *American Journal of Public Health,* 95(10): 1712–1717.

Makarios, M., Steiner, B., and Travis, L. F. (2010). Examining the predictors of recidivism among men and women released from prison in Ohio. *Criminal Justice and Behavior,* 37(12): 1377–1391.

Malinchak, A. A. (1980). *Crime and gerontology.* Englewood Cliffs, NJ: Prentice Hall.

Mara, C. M. (2002). Expansion of long-term care in the prison system: An aging inmate population poses policy and programmatic questions. *Journal of Aging and Social Policy,* 14(2): 43–61.

Mara, C. M., and McKenna, C. (2000). "Aging in place" in prison: Health and long-term care needs of older inmates. *The Public Policy and Aging Report,* 10(4): 1, 3–8.

Marquart, J. W., and Merianos, D. E. (1997). Health condition and prisoners: A review of research and emerging areas of inquiry. *The Prison Journal,* 77(2): 184–208.

Marquart, J. W., Merianos, D. E., and Doucet, G. (2000). The health-related concerns of older prisoners: Implications for policy. *Aging and Society,* 20(1): 79–96.

Martinez, P., Benson E., Harrison, K., Lansing, C., and Munson, M. (1999). *Elderly offenders in Texas prisons.* Austin: Criminal Justice Policy Council.

Martinson, R. (1974). What works? Questions and answers about prison reform. *The Public Interest,* 35: 22–54.

Maruna, S. (2001). *Making good: How ex-convicts reform and rebuild their lives.* Washington, DC: American Psychological Association.

Maruschak, L. M. (2006). *Medical problems of jail inmates.* Washington, DC: US Department of Justice, Bureau of Justice Statistics.

——— (2008). *Medical problems of prisoners.* Washington, DC: US Department of Justice, Bureau of Justice Statistics.

Maruschak, L. M., and Beck, A. J. (2001). *Medical problems of inmates, 1997.* Washington, DC: US Department of Justice, Bureau of Justice Statistics.

Massachusetts Board of Retirement v. Murgia. 427 U.S. 307 (1976).

Masters, R. (1994). *Counseling criminal justice offenders.* Thousand Oaks, CA: Sage.

Mathew, P., Elting, L., Cooksley, C., Owen, S., and Lin, J. (2005). Cancer in an incarcerated population. *Cancer,* 104(10): 2197–2204.

Mauer, M. (2002). Analyzing and responding to the driving forces of prison population growth. *Criminology and Public Policy,* 1: 389–392.

——— (2007). The hidden problem of time served in prison. *Social Research,* 74(2): 701–706.

Mauer, M., King, R. S., and Young, M. C. (2004). *The meaning of "life": Long prison sentences in context.* Washington, DC: Sentencing Project.

Maull, F. (2005). The prison hospice movement. *Explore* (New York) 1(6): 477–479.

McCarthy, M. (1983). The health status of elderly inmates. *Corrections Today,* 45(1): 64–65, 74.

McCorkle, R. C. (1992). Personal precautions to violence in prison. *Criminal Justice and Behavior,* 19(2): 160–173.

——— (1993). Fear of victimization and symptoms of psychopathology among prison inmates. *Journal of Offender Rehabilitation,* 19(1–2): 27–41.

McDonald, D. (1999). Medical care in prisons. In M. Tonry and J. Petersilia (eds.), *Crime & justice: An annual review of research,* vol. 26 (pp. 427–478). Chicago: University of Chicago Press.

McGlynn, E. A., Asch, S. M., Adams, J., Keesey, J., Hicks, J., DeCristofaro, A., and Kerr, E. A. (2003). The quality of health care delivered to adults in the United States. *New England Journal of Medicine,* 348: 2635–2645.

McGreevy, P., and Dolan, J. (2010). Governor signs bill to allow medical parole for incapacitated inmates. *California Healthline: The Daily Digest of News, Policy and Opinion,* September 29. http://www.californiahealthline.org/articles /2010/9/29/governor-signs-bill-to-allow-medical-parole-for-incapacitated -inmates.

McGuckin v. Smith. 974 F.2d 1050 (9th Cir. 1992).

McShane, M. D., and Williams, F. P., III (1990). Old and ornery: The disciplinary experiences of elderly prisoners. *International Journal of Offender Therapy and Comparative Criminology,* 34(3): 197–212.

Metzler, C. (1981). *Senior citizens in Massachusetts state correctional facilities from 1972–1979.* Boston: Massachusetts Department of Corrections.

Meyers, A. R. (1984). Drinking, problem drinking, and alcohol-related crime among older people. In E. S. Newman, D. J. Newman, and M. L. Gewirtz (eds.), *Elderly criminals* (pp. 51–66). Boston: Oelgeschlager, Gunn, and Hain.

Meyers, F. J., Carducci, M., Loscalzo, M. J., Linder, J., Greasby, T., and Beckett, L. A. (2011). Effects of a problem-solving intervention (COPE) on quality of life for patients with advanced cancer on clinical trials and their caregivers: Simultaneous care educational intervention (SCEI)—Linking palliation and clinical trials. *Journal of Palliative Medicine,* 14(4): 465–473.

Meyers, F. J., and Linder, J. (2003). Simultaneous care: Disease treatment and palliative care throughout illness. *Journal of Clinical Oncology,* 21(7): 1412–1415.

Meyers, F. J., Linder, J., Beckett, L., Christensen, S., Blais, J., and Gandara, D. R. (2004). Simultaneous care: A model approach to the perceived conflict between investigational therapy and palliative care. *Journal of Pain & Symptom Management,* 28(6): 548–556.

Miller, P. J., and Mike, P. B. (1995). The Medicare hospice benefit: Ten years of federal policy for the terminally ill. *Death Studies,* 19(6): 531–542.

Miller, S. J., Dinitz, S., and Conrad, J. P. (1982). *Careers of the violent: The dangerous offender and criminal justice.* Lexington, MA: Lexington Books.

Miller v. Hinton. 288 Fed. Appx. 901 (4th Cir. 2008).

Mills, J. F., Jones, M. N., and Kroner, D. G. (2005). An examination of the generalizability of the LSI-R and Vrag probability bins. *Criminal Justice and Behavior,* 32(5): 565–585.

Mitchell, K. (2010). Elderly parolees get help in reintegrating. *Denver Post,* August 03. http://www.denverpost.com/ci_15663717.

Mitford, J. (1973). *Kind and usual punishment: The prison business.* New York: Random.

Mitka, M. (2004). Aging prisoners stressing health care system. *Journal of the American Medical Association,* 292(4): 423–424.

Moffitt, T. E. (1993). Adolescence-limited and life-course-persistent antisocial behavior: A developmental taxonomy. *Psychological Review,* 100: 674–701.

Moore, E., and Unwin, T. (2002). Ohio's older inmates. *Ohio Corrections Research Compendium,* 1: 36–44.

Moore, E. O. (1989). Prison environments and their impact on older citizens. *Journal of Offender Counseling, Services, & Rehabilitation,* 13(2): 175–191.

Morris, N. (1974). *The future of imprisonment.* Chicago: University of Chicago Press.

Morton, J. B. (1992). *An administrative overview of the older inmate.* Washington, DC: US Department of Justice, National Institute of Corrections.

———— (1993). Training staff to work with elderly and disabled inmates. *Corrections Today,* 55(1): 42, 44–47.

———— (1994). Training staff to work with special needs offenders. *Forum on Corrections Research,* 6(2): 32–34.

Morton, J. B., and Anderson, J. C. (1982). Elderly offenders: The forgotten minority. *Corrections Today,* 44(6): 14–16, 20.

Motiuk, L. (1996). Targeting employment patterns to reduce offender risk and needs. *Forum on Corrections Research,* 12: 32–35.

Mumola, C. J. (2005). *Suicide and homicide in state prisons and local jails.* Washington, DC: US Department of Justice, Bureau of Justice Statistics.

———— (2007). *Medical causes of death in state prisons, 2001–2004.* Washington, DC: US Department of Justice, Bureau of Justice Statistics.

Murphy, S. T., and Palmer, J. M. (1996). Ethnicity and advance care directives. *Journal of Law, Medicine, & Ethics,* 24(2): 108–117.

Nagin, D. S. (1978). General deterrence: A review of the empirical evidence. In A. Blumstein, J. Cohen, and D. Nagin (eds.), *Deterrence and incapacitation: Estimating the effects of criminal sanctions on crime rates* (pp. 95–139). Washington, DC: National Academy of Sciences.

———— (1998). Deterrence and incapacitation. In M. Tonry (ed.), *The handbook of crime and punishment* (pp. 345–368). New York: Oxford University Press.

Nagin, D. S., Cullen, F. T., and Jonson, C. L. (2009). Imprisonment and reoffending. *Crime and Justice,* 38(1): 115–200.

Nagin, D. S., and Waldfogel, J. (1998). The effects of conviction on income through the life cycle. *International Review of Law and Economics,* 18: 25–40.

Naik, G. (2011). Lab-made trachea saves man: Tumor-blocked windpipe replaced using synthetic materials, patient's own cells. *Wall Street Journal,* July 8.

National Cancer Institute (NCI) (2010). *Median age of cancer patients at death, 2003–2007, by primary cancer site, race, and sex: SEER cancer statistics review, 1975–2007.* Washington, DC.

National Hospice and Palliative Care Organization (NHPCO) (2000). Standards of practice for hospice programs. http://nhpco.org/i4a/pages/index.cfm?pageid =5308.

———— (2009). Facts and figures: Hospice care in America. http://www.nhpco .org/files/public/Statistics_Research/NHPCO_facts_and_figures.pdf.

———— (2010a). Facts and figures: Hospice care in America. http://www.nhpco .org/files/public/Statistics_Research/Hospice_Facts_Figures_Oct-2010.pdf.

———— (2010b). *Standards of practice for hospice programs* [standards of practice manual]. http://www.nhpco.org/files/public/quality/Standards/NHPCO _STANDARDS_2010CD.pdf.

National Institute of Corrections (2002). *Services for families and their children.* Bureau of Justice Statistics Special Report. Longmont, CO.

Neely, C. L., Addison, L., and Craig-Moreland, D. (1997). Addressing the needs of elderly offenders. *Corrections Today,* 59(5): 102–123.

Nellis, A., and King, R. S. (2009). *No exit: The expanding use of life sentences in America*. Washington, DC: Sentencing Project.

Newman, D. J. (1984). Elderly offenders and American crime patterns. In E. S. Newman, D. J. Newman, and M. L. Gewirtz (eds.), *Elderly criminals* (pp. 3–16). Boston: Oelgeschlager, Gunn, and Hain.

Newman, E. S., and Newman, D. J. (1984). Public policy implications of elderly crime. In E. S. Newman, D. J. Newman, and M. L. Gewirtz (eds.), *Elderly criminals* (pp. 225–242). Boston: Oelgeschlager, Gunn, and Hain.

Noonan, M. E., and Carson, E. A. (2011). *Prison and jail deaths in custody, 2000–2009: Statistical tables*. Washington, DC: US Department of Justice, Bureau of Justice Statistics.

O'Connor, T. P. (2004). What works: Religion as a correctional intervention. Pt. 1. *Journal of Community Corrections*, 14(1): 11–22, 27.

O'Connor, T. P., and Duncan, J. B. (2008). Religion and prison programming: The role, impact, and future direction of faith in correctional systems. *Social and Behavioral Rehabilitation in Prisons, Jails, and the Community*, 11(6): 81–96.

O'Lone v. Estate of Shabazz. 482 U.S. 342 (1987).

Olmstead v. L.C. 527 U.S. 581 (1999).

Orentlicher, D. (1997). The Supreme Court and physician-assisted suicide: Rejecting assisted suicide but embracing euthanasia. *New England Journal of Medicine*, 337(17): 1236–1239.

Ornduff, J. (1996). Releasing the elderly inmate: A solution to prison overcrowding. *Elder Law Journal*, 4: 173–200.

Osborn, C. Y., et al. (2010). Racial disparities in the treatment of depression in low-income persons with diabetes. *Diabetes Care*, 33(5): 1050–1054.

Osborn, S. G., and West, D. (1979). Marriage and delinquency: A post-script. *British Journal of Criminology*, 18: 254–256.

Ostchega, Y., Porter, K., Hughes, J., Dillon, C., and Nwankwo, T. (2011). *Resting pulse rate reference data for children, adolescents, and adults: United States, 1999–2008*. Washington, DC: Centers for Disease Control and Prevention.

Ouimet, M., and LeBlanc, M. (1996). The role of life experiences in the continuation of the adult criminal career. *Criminal Behavior and Mental Health*, 6: 73–97.

Packer, H. L. (1968). *The limits of the criminal sanction*. Stanford: Stanford University Press.

Pager, D. (2003). The mark of a criminal record. *American Journal of Sociology*, 108: 937–935.

——— (2006). Evidence-based policy for successful prisoner reentry. *Criminology and Public Policy*, 5(3): 505–514.

Pargament, K. (1990). God help me: Toward a theoretical framework of coping for the psychology of religion. *Research in the Social Scientific Study of Religion*, 26: 195–224.

Pastore, A. L., and Maguire, K. (2010). *Sourcebook of criminal justice statistics*. http://www.albany.edu/sourcebook.

Paz, S. R. (2007). Accommodating disabilities in jails and prisons. In R. Greifinger (ed.), *Public health behind bars: From prisons to communities* (pp. 42–55). New York: Springer.

Pelissier, B., Rhodes, W., Saylor, W., Gaes, G., Camp, S., Vanyur, S., and Wallace, S. (2000). *TRIAD Drug Treatment Evaluation Project: Final report of three-year outcomes*. Pt. 1. Washington, DC: Federal Bureau of Prisons, US Board of Prisons, Office of Research and Evaluation.

Pelissier, B., Wallace, S., O'Neil, J., Gaes, G., Camp, S., Rhodes, W., and Saylor, W. (n.d.). *Federal prison residential drug treatment reduces substance use and arrests after release*. Washington, DC: Federal Bureau of Prisons.

Pennsylvania Department of Corrections v. Yeskey. 524 U.S. 206 (1998).

Pennsylvania Prison Society. (2012). *Virtual visitation*. http://www.prisonsociety .org/progs/ifs_fvv.shtml.

Petersilia, J. (1999). Parole and prisoner reentry in the United States. *Crime and Justice*, 26: 479–529.

——— (2001). Prisoner reentry: Safety and reintegration challenges. *The Prison Journal*, 18(3): 360–375.

——— (2003). *When prisoners come home: Parole and prisoner reentry*. New York: Oxford University Press.

——— (2004). What works in prisoner reentry? Reviewing and questioning the evidence. *Federal Probation*, 68: 4–8.

Pettit, B., and Western, B. (2004). Mass imprisonment and the life course: Race and class inequality in U.S. incarceration. *American Sociological Review*, 69(2): 151–169.

Pettus, C. A., and Severson, M. (2006). Paving the way for effective reentry practice: The critical role and function of the boundary spanner. *The Prison Journal*, 86: 206–229.

Pew Center on the States (2010). *Prison count 2010*. http://www.pewcenteronthe states.org/uploadedFiles/Prison_Count_2010.pdf.

——— (2011). *State of recidivism: The revolving door of America's prisons*. Public Safety Performance Project. Washington, DC.

Philips, B. U., Jr., Gong, G., Hargrave, K. A., Belasco, E., and Lyford, C. P. (2011). Correlation of the ratio of metastatic to non-metastatic cancer cases with the degree of socioeconomic deprivation among Texas counties. *International Journal of Health Geographics*, 10: 1–6.

Phipps v. Sheriff of Cook County. 681 F. Supp. 2d 899 (N.D. Ill. 2009).

Piquero, A. R., Farrington, D. P., and Blumstein, A. (2003). The criminal career paradigm. *Crime and Justice*, 30: 359–506.

——— (2007). *Key issues in criminal career research: New analyses of the Cambridge study in delinquent development*. Cambridge: Cambridge University Press.

Pitkala, K. H., Blomquist, L., Routasalo, P., Saarenheimo, M., Karvinen, E., Oikarinen, U., and Mantyranta, T. (2004). Leading groups of older people: A description and evaluation of the education of professionals. *Educational Gerontology*, 30: 821–833.

Pitre v. Cain. 131 S. Ct. 8 (2010).

Pogorzelski, W., Wolff, N., Pan, K. Y., and Blitz, C. L. (2005). Behavioral health problems, ex-offender reentry policies, and the "Second Chance Act." *American Journal of Public Health*, 95: 1718–1724.

Pollock, J. M. (2002). Parenting programs in women's prisons. *Women & Criminal Justice*, 14(1): 131–154.

——— (2004). *Prisons and prison life: Costs and consequences*. New York: Oxford.

Porcella, K. (2007). The past coming back to haunt them: The prosecution and sentencing of once deadly but now elderly criminals. *St. John's Law Review*, 81: 369–397.

Porter, N. D. (2011). *The state of sentencing 2010: Developments in policy and practice*. Washington, DC: Sentencing Project.

Potter, E., Cashin, A., Chenoweth, L., and Jeon, Y. (2007). The healthcare of older inmates in the correctional setting. *International Journal of Prisoner Health,* 3: 204–213.

Powell, J. L. (2006). *Social theory and aging.* Lanham: Rowman and Littlefield.

Pratt, T. C. (2009). *Addicted to incarceration: Corrections policy and the politics of misinformation in the United States.* Thousand Oaks, CA: Sage.

Price, C. A. (2006). *Aging inmate population study.* Raleigh: North Carolina Department of Correction.

The price of punishment: Growing old in jail—Follow-up conversation with sixty-four year old inmate (2000). WBUR radio broadcast, Boston.

Prison Reform Trust. (2007). *Bromley briefings: Prison fact file.* London.

Procunier v. Martinez. 416 U.S. 396 (1974).

Purcell v. Pennsylvania Department of Corrections. Civil Action no. 00-181J, 2006 U.S. Dist. LEXIS 42476 (W.D. Pa. Mar. 31, 2006).

Quetelet, A. (1831, 1984). *Research on the propensity for crime at different ages.* Translated by F. Sylvester Sawyer. Cincinnati: Anderson.

Quinn, C. (2009). The right to refuse medical treatment or to direct the course of medical treatment: Where should inmate autonomy begin and end? *New England Journal on Criminal and Civil Confinement,* 35: 453–487.

Radio frequency ablation of liver tumors (2011). July 13. Retrieved July 29, 2011, from http://www.radiologyinfo.org/en/info.cfm?pg=rfaLiver.

Ramos v. Lamm. 639 F.2d 559; 485 F. Supp. 122 (10th Cir. 1980).

Reed, M. B., and Glamser, F. D. (1979). Aging in a total institution: The case of older prisoners. *The Gerontologist,* 19(4): 354–360.

Regan, J. J., Alderson, A., and Regan, W. M. (2002). Psychiatric disorders in aging prisoners. *Clinical Gerontologist,* 26(1–2): 117–124.

Rehabilitation Act of 1973. Pub. Law 93-112, 87 Stat. 355 (1994) (codified as amended at 29 U.S.C. §§ 701–796).

———. Section 504, 29 U.S.C. § 794 (2011).

Reimer, G. (2008). The graying of the U.S. prison population. *Journal of Correctional Health Care,* 14(3): 202–208.

Religious Land Use and Institutionalized Persons Act of 2000. 42 U.S.C. §§ 2000cc–2000cc-5 (2011).

Rettner, R. (2011). Man gets world's first synthetic trachea. *My Health News Daily,* July 8. http://www.msnbc.msn.com/id/43689818/ns/health-health_care /t/man-gets-worlds-first-synthetic-trachea.

Rhine E. E., Neff, A. R., and Natalucci-Persichetti, G. (1998). Restorative justice, public safety, and the supervision of juvenile offenders. *Corrections Management Quarterly,* 2: 40–48.

Rhodes v. Chapman. 452 U.S. 337 (1981).

Rich, B. (2004). Current legal status of advance directives in the United States. *Wien Klin Wochenschr,* 116(13): 421–426.

Rideau, W., and Sinclair, B. (1982). Growing old in prison. *Angolite,* 7(4): 33–40.

Ries, L., Young, J., Keel, G., Eisner, M., Lin, Y., and Horner, M.-J. (2007). *Cancer survival among adults: U.S. SEER program, 1988–2001: Patient and tumor characteristics.* SEER Survival Monograph. Bethesda, MD: National Institutes of Health.

Riggins v. Nevada. 504 U.S. 127 (1992).

Rikard, R. V., and Rosenburg, E. (2007). Aging inmates: A convergence of trends in the American criminal justice system. *Journal of Correctional Health Care,* 13: 150–162.

Robert Wood Johnson Foundation (2009). Promoting excellence in end-of-life care. October 15. http://www.rwjf.org/files/research/AHC.final.pdf.

Roberts, C., and Kennedy, S., and Hammet, T. M. (2004). Health-related issues in prisoner reentry. *Crime and Delinquency,* 47(3): 390–409.

Robbins, I. P. (1996). George Bush's America meets Dante's Inferno: The Americans with Disabilities Act in prison. *Yale Law & Policy Review,* 15: 49–112.

——— (1999). Managed health care in prisons as cruel and unusual punishment. *Journal of Criminal Law and Criminology,* 90(1): 195–238.

Rockova, V. (2011). Risk stratification of intermediate-risk acute myeloid leukemia: Integrative analysis of a multitude of gene mutation and gene expression markers. *Blood,* 118(4): 1069–1076.

Rodstein, M. (1975). Crime and the aged. *Journal of the American Medical Association,* 234(6): 639.

Rogers, A., Hassell, K., and Nicholaas, G. (1999). Demanding patients? *Analyzing the use of primary care.* Oxford: Oxford University Press.

Roman, J., Brooks, L., Lagerson, E., Chalfin, A., and Tereshchenko, B. (2007). *Impact and cost-benefit analysis of the Maryland Reentry Partnership Initiative.* Washington, DC: Urban Institute.

Rosefield, H. A. (1993). The older inmate: "Where do we go from here?" *Journal of Prison and Jail Health,* 12(1): 51–58.

Rosen, D. L., Schoenbach, V. J., and Wohl, D. A. (2008). All-cause and cause-specific mortality among men released from state prison, 1980–2005. *American Journal of Public Health,* 98(12): 2278–2284.

Rosner, M. W., Wiederlight, M., Harmon, R. B., and Cahn, D. J. (1991). Geriatric offenders examined at a forensic psychiatric clinic. *Journal of Forensic Sciences,* 36(6): 1722–1731.

Rosner, R., Wiederlight, M., and Schneider, M. (1985). Geriatric felons examined at a forensic psychiatry clinic. *Journal of Forensic Sciences,* 30(3): 730–740.

Rothman, M. B., and Dunlop, B. D. (2006). Elders and the courts: Judicial policy for an aging America. *Journal of Aging and Social Policy,* 18(2): 31–45.

Rothman, M. B., Dunlop, B. D., and Entzel, P. (eds.) (2000). *Elders, crime, and the criminal justice system: Myth, perceptions, and reality in the 21st century.* New York: Springer.

Rowe, J. W., and Kahn, R. L. (1997). Successful aging. *The Gerontologist,* 37: 433–440.

Roy, B. (1995). The Tuskegee syphilis experiment: Medical ethics, constitutionalism, and property in the body. *Harvard Journal of Minority Public Health,* 1(1): 11–15.

Rubenstein, D. (1982). The older person in prison. *Archives of Gerontology and Geriatrics,* 1(3): 287–296.

——— (1984). The elderly in prison: A review of the literature. In E. S. Newman, D. J. Newman, and M. L. Gewirtz (eds.), *Elderly criminals* (pp. 153–168). Boston: Oelgeschlager, Gunn, and Hain.

Ruddell, R., and Winfree, L. T., Jr. (2006). Setting aside criminal convictions in Canada: A successful approach to offender reintegration. *The Prison Journal,* 86(4): 452–469.

Sabath, M. J., and Cowles, E. L. (1988). Factors affecting the adjustment of elderly inmates to prison. In B. McCarthy and R. Langworthy (eds.), *Older offenders: Perspectives in criminology and criminal justice* (pp. 178–195). New York: Praeger.

Sabol, W. J., Couture, H., and Harrison, P. M. (2007). *Prisoners in 2006.* Washington, DC: US Department of Justice, Bureau of Justice Statistics.

Sabol, W. J., West, H. C., and Cooper, M. (2009). *Prisoners in 2008.* Washington, DC: US Department of Justice, Bureau of Justice Statistics.

Sacramento Bee (2011). Under criticism, corrections pushes parole for sick inmates. March 2. http://blogs.sacbee.com/capitolalertlatest/2011/03/under-criticism-corrections-pu.html#mi_rss=Capitol%20Alert#storylink=misearch.

Sampson, R. (2001). How do communities undergird or undermine human development? Relevant contexts and social mechanisms. In A. Booth and A. Crouter (eds.), *Does it take a village? Community effects on children, adolescents, and families* (pp. 3–30). Mahwah, NJ: Lawrence Erlbaum.

—— (2010). Gold standard myths: Observations on the experimental turn in quantitative criminology. *Journal of Quantitative Criminology,* 26: 489–500.

Sampson, R. J., and Laub, J. H. (1990). Crime and deviance over the lifecourse: The salience of adult social bonds. *American Sociological Review,* 55: 608–627.

—— (1993). *Crime in the making: Pathways and turning points throughout life.* Cambridge: Harvard University Press.

—— (2003). Life-course desisters? Trajectories of crime among delinquent boys followed to age 70. *Criminology,* 41: 555–592.

—— (2005). When prediction fails: From crime-prone boys to heterogeneity in adulthood. *Annals of the American Academy of Political and Social Science,* 602: 73–79.

Sampson, R. J., Laub, J. H., and Wimer, C. (2006). Does marriage reduce crime? A counterfactual approach to within-individual causal effects. *Criminology,* 44: 465–508.

Santos, M. G. (2003). *Profiles from prison.* Westport: Praeger.

Sapers, H. (2011). Interview with Howard Sapers, Correctional Investigator of Canada: Review of data on older prisoners in Canada's federal penitentiaries in 2011. Ottawa: Government of Canada, Office of the Correctional Investigator, July 22.

Sapp, A. D. (1989). Arrests for major crimes: Trends and patterns for elderly offenders. In S. Chaneles and C. Burnett (eds.), *Older offenders: Current trends* (pp. 19–44). New York: Haworth.

Savage, J., and Kanazawa, S. (2002). Social capital, crime, and human nature. *Journal of Contemporary Criminal Justice,* 18(2): 188–211.

Schrag, P. (1998). *Paradise lost: California's experience, America's future.* Berkeley: University of California Press.

Schmidt v. Odell. 64 F. Supp. 2d 1014 (D. Kan. 1999).

Seiter, R. P., and Kadela, K. R. (2003). Prisoner reentry: What works, what does not, and what is promising. *Crime and Delinquency,* 49: 360–388.

Sell v. United States. 539 U.S. 166 (2003).

Shannon, L. W. (1991). *Changing patterns of delinquency and crime: A longitudinal study in Racine.* Boulder: Westview.

Shapiro, C., and Schwartz, M. (2001). Coming home: Building on family connections. *Corrections Management,* 5: 52–61.

Shavit, Y., and Rattner, A. (1988). Age, crime, and the early life course. *American Journal of Sociology,* 93: 1457–1470.

Sheu, M., et al. (2002). Continuity of medical care and risk of incarceration in HIV-positive and high-risk HIV-negative women. *Journal of Women's Health,* 11(8): 743–751.

Shichor, D. (1984). Patterns of elderly lawbreaking in urban, suburban, and rural areas: What do arrest statistics tell us? In W. Wilbanks and P. K. H. Kim (eds.), *Elderly criminals* (pp. 53–68). New York: University Press of America.

Shimkus, J. (2004). The graying of America's prisons: Corrections copes with care for the aged. *Correct Care,* 18(3): 1, 16. http://www.ncchc.org/pubs/CC /archive/18-3.pdf.

Shinnar, S., and Shinnar, R. (1975). The effects of the criminal justice system on the control of crime: A quantitative approach. *Law & Society Review,* 9: 581–611.

Shover, N. (1985). *Aging criminals.* Beverly Hills: Sage.

——— (1996). *Great pretenders: Pursuits and careers of persistent thieves.* Boulder: Westview.

Siever, R. (2005). HMOs behind bars: Constitutional implications of managed health care in the prison system. *Vanderbilt Law Review,* 58(4): 1365–1404.

Silfen, P., David, S. B., Kliger, D., Eshel, R., Heichel, H., and Lehman, D. (1977). The adaptation of the older prisoner in Israel. *International Journal of Offender Therapy and Comparative Criminology,* 21(1): 57–65.

Singh, J. P., Grann, M., and Fazel, S. (2011). A comparative study of violence risk assessment tools: A systematic review and metaregression analysis of 68 studies involving 25,980 participants. *Clinical Psychology Review,* 31: 499–513.

Skloot, R. (2010). *The immortal life of Henrietta Lacks.* New York: Crown.

Sloan, V., et al. (2008). *Smart on crime: Recommendations for the next administration and Congress, 2009.* Washington, DC: Criminal Justice Transition Coalition.

Smyer, T., and Burbank, P. M. (2009). The U.S. correctional system and the older prisoner. *Journal of Gerontological Nursing,* 35(12): 32–37.

Smyer, T., Gragert, M. D., and LaMere, S. (1997). Stay safe! Stay healthy! Surviving old age in prison. *Journal of Psychosocial Nursing,* 35(9): 10–17.

Snell, T. L., and Morton, D. C. (1994). *Women in prison.* Washington, DC: US Department of Justice, Bureau of Justice Statistics.

Snyder, C., van Wormer, K. V., Chadha, J., and Jaggers, J. W. (2009). Older adult inmates: The challenge for social work. *Social Work,* 54(2): 117–124.

Solomon, A. L., Kachnowski, V., and Bhati, A. (2005). *Does parole work? Analyzing the impact of postprison supervision on rearrest outcomes.* Washington, DC: Urban Institute.

Solomon, A. L., et al. (2008). *Putting public safety first: 13 parole supervision strategies to enhance reentry outcomes.* Washington, DC: Urban Institute.

Sorensen, J., and Cunningham, M. D. (2010). Conviction offense and prison violence: A comparative study of murderers and other offenders. *Crime & Delinquency,* 56(1): 103–125.

Stand Up for What's Right and Just (SURJ) (2009). SURJ seeks volunteer attorneys to assist with POPS program. April 21. http://www.surj.org/news/?p=47.

Stanton, S. (2011a). Quadriplegic prisoner is first in California to get medical parole hearing. *Sacramento Bee,* May 19. http://www.sacbee.com/2011/05/19 /3637751/quadriplegic-prisoner-is-first.html.

——— (2011b). Third state prison inmate released under new medical parole law. *Sacramento Bee,* June 16. http://blogs.sacbee.com/crime/archives/2011/06 /third-state-pri.html.

——— (2011c). "Three-strikes" inmate wins state's first medical parole. *Sacramento Bee,* June 16. http://www.sacbee.com/2011/06/16/3704535/three-strikes-inmate-wins-states.html.

Stanton, S., Doyle, M., and Yamamura, K. (2011). U.S. Supreme Court says California must reduce prison population. *Sacramento Bee,* May 24. http://www.sacbee.com/2011/05/24/3649095/us-supreme-court-says-california.html #ixzz1UMgcSoxx.

State POLST contact list (2011). http://www.ohsu.edu/polst/programs/state+programs.htm.

Stedman, R. S. (2002). Toward a social psychology of place: Predicting behavior from place-based cognitions, attitude, and identity. *Environment and Behavior,* 34: 561–581.

Steffensmeier, D. J. (1987). Invention of the "new" senior citizen criminal: An analysis of crime trends of elderly males and elderly females, 1964–1984. *Research on Aging,* 9(2): 281–311.

Steffensmeier, D. J., and Harer, M. D. (1987). Is the crime rate really falling? An "aging" U.S. population and its impact on the nation's crime rate, 1980–1984. *Journal of Research in Crime and Delinquency,* 24(1): 23–48.

Steinhauser, K. E., Christakis, N. A., Clipp, E. C., McNeilly, M., McIntyre, L., and Tulsky, J. A. (2000). Factors considered important at the end of life by patients, family, physicians, and other care providers. *Journal of the American Medical Association,* 284(19): 2476–2482.

Stephan, J. J., and Karberg, J. C. (2003). *Census of state and federal correctional facilities, 2000.* Washington, DC: US Department of Justice.

Stephenson, B. L., Wohl, D. A., Kaplan, A. H., Golin, C. E., Hsiao-Chuan, T., and Stewart, P. (2005). Effect of release from prison and re-incarceration on the viral loads of HIV-infected individuals. *Public Health Reports,* 120(1): 84–88.

Sterns, A. A., Law, G., Sed, C., Keohane, P., and Sterns, R. S. (2008). Growing wave of older prisoners: A national survey of older prisoners' health, mental health, and programming. *Corrections Today,* 70(4): 70–72, 74, 76.

Stevens, N., and Van Tilburg, T. (2000). Stimulating friendship in later life: A strategy for reducing loneliness among older women. *Educational Gerontology,* 26: 15–35.

Stevenson, R. G., and McCutchen, R. (2006). When meaning has lost its way: Life and loss behind bars. *Illness, Crisis, and Loss,* 14(2): 103–119.

Stojkovic, S. (2007). Elderly prisoners: A growing and forgotten group within correctional systems vulnerable to elder abuse. *Journal of Elder Abuse and Neglect,* 19: 97–117.

Stojkovic, S., and Lovell, R (1997). *Corrections: An introduction.* Cincinnati: Anderson.

Strupp, H., and Willmott, D. (2005). *Dignity denied: The price of imprisoning older women in California.* San Francisco: Legal Services for Prisoners with Children.

Sundaram, V. (2009). *Yearning for freedom: California's golden girls.* http://prisonmovement.wordpress.com/2009/02/09/yearning-for-freedom-californias-golden-girls.

Superintendent of Belchertown State School v. Saikewicz. 370 N.E.2d 417 (Mass. 1977).

Taft, B., and Wilkinson, R. (1999). *A comprehensive approach to addressing the needs of aging prisoners.* Columbus: Ohio Department of Rehabilitation and Correction.

Taxman, F. S., (2007). Reentry and supervision: One is impossible without the other. *Corrections Today,* 69(2): 98–105.

Taylor v. Ortiz. 410 Fed. Appx. 76, 79–80 (10th Cir. 2010).

Teller, F. E., and Howell, R. J. (1981). The older prisoner: Criminal and psychological characteristics. *Criminology,* 18(4): 549–555.

Tennessee v. Lane. 541 U.S. 509 (2004).

Thanner, M. H., and Taxman, F. S. (2003). Responsivity: The value of providing intensive services to high-risk offenders. *Journal of Substance Abuse Treatment,* 24: 137–147.

Thara, E., Dorff, T. B., Pinski, J. K., and Quinn, D. I. (2011). Vaccine therapy with sipuleucel-T (Provenge) for prostate cancer. *Maturitas,* 69(4): 296–303.

Theobald, D., and Farrington, D. P. (2011). Why do the crime-reducing effects of marriage vary with age? *British Journal of Criminology,* 51: 136–158.

Thigpen, M., and Hunter, S. (1998). *Hospice and palliative care in prisons special issues in corrections.* Longmont, CO: US Department of Justice, National Institute of Corrections Information Center.

Thivierge-Rikard, R., and Thompson, M. (2007). The association between aging inmate housing management models and non-geriatric health services in state correctional institutions. *Journal of Aging & Social Policy,* 19(4): 39–56.

Thomas, J., and Zaitzow, B. H. (2006). Conning or conversion? The role of religion in prison coping. *The Prison Journal,* 86: 242–259.

Thomas, S. B., and Quinn, S. C. (1991). The Tuskegee syphilis study, 1932 to 1972: Implications for HIV education and AIDS risk education programs in the black community. *American Journal of Public Health,* 81: 1498–1504.

Thompson, J. H. (2010). Today's deliberate indifference: Providing attention without providing treatment to prisoners with serious medical needs. *Harvard Civil Rights–Civil Liberties Law Review,* 45(2): 635–654.

Thor v. Superior Court. 855 P.2d 375 (Cal. 1993).

Thornburgh v. Abbott. 490 U.S. 401 (1989).

Tobin, P., and Metzler, C. (1983). *Typology of older prisoners in Massachusetts state correctional facilities, 1972–1982.* Boston: Massachusetts Department of Corrections.

Toch, H. (2006). *Living in prison: The ecology of survival.* Washington, DC: American Psychological Association.

Torrey, E. F., Aaron, D., Kennard, A. D., Eslinger, S. D., Lamb, R., and Pavle, J. (2010). *More mentally ill persons are in jails and prisons than hospitals: A survey of the states.* Alexandria, VA: National Sheriff's Association. http://www.sheriffs.org/userfiles/file/FinalJailsvHospitalsStudy.pdf.

Toseland, R. (1995). Group work with the elderly and family caregivers. New York: Springer.

Toyota Motor Manufacturing, Kentucky, Inc. v. Williams. 534 U.S. 184 (2002).

Travis, L. (1989). *Risk classification in probation and parole.* Cincinnati: University of Cincinnati, Risk Classification Project,.

Travis, J. (2005a). *But they all come back: Facing challenges of prisoner reentry.* Washington, DC: Urban Institute.

——— (2005b). Prisoner reentry: The iron law of imprisonment. In R. Muraskin (ed.), *Key correctional issues* (pp. 64–71). Upper Saddle River, NJ: Prentice Hall.

Travis, J., and Petersilia, J. (2001). Reentry reconsidered: A new look at an old question. *Crime and Delinquency,* 47(3): 291–313.

Tripodi, S. J., Kim, J. S., and Bender, K. (2010). Is employment associated with reduced recidivism? *International Journal of Offender Therapy and Comparative Criminology,* 54(5): 706–720.

Turesky, D. G., and Schultz, J. M. (2010). Spirituality among older adults: An exploration of the developmental context, impact on mental and physical health, and integration into counseling. *Journal of Religion, Spirituality, and Aging,* 22: 162–179.

Turley, J. (2007). *Promoting inmate rehabilitation and successful release planning.* Statement before the House Committee on the Judiciary, Subcommittee on Crime, Terrorism, and Homeland Security, 110th Congress, Washington, DC.

Turner, M. G., Sundt, J. L., Applegate, B. K., and Cullen, F. T. (1995). "Three strikes and you're out" legislation: A national assessment. *Federal Probation,* 59(3): 16–35.

Turner, S., and Trotter, C. (2010). Growing old in prison? A review of national and international research on ageing offenders. South Melbourne: Department of Justice.

Turner v. Safley. 482 U.S. 78 (1987).

Uggen, C. (2000). Work as a turning point in the life course of criminals: A duration model of age, employment, and recidivism. *American Sociological Review,* 67: 529–546.

Uggen, C., Manza, J., and Thompson, M. (2006). Citizenship, democracy, and the civic reintegration of criminal offenders. *Annals of the American Academy of Political and Social Science,* 605: 281–310.

United States v. Georgia (Goodman v. Georgia). 546 U.S. 151 (2006).

US Census Bureau (2011). *Statistical abstract of the United States.* http://www.census.gov/compendia/statab/2011/tables/11s0006.pdf.

US Department of Health, Education, and Welfare (DHEW), National Commission for the Protection of Human Subjects of Biomedical and Behavioral Research (1979). *The Belmont report: Ethical guidelines for the protection of human subjects of research.* http://www.mri.edu.eg/mri/The%20Belmont%20Report.pdf.

US Department of Health and Human Services (DHHS) (2004). *National Health and Nutrition Examination Survey (NHANES).* http://www.cdc.gov/nchs/data/nhanes/nhanes_03_04/overviewbrochure_0304.pdf.

———— (2008). *Medicare and Medicaid programs: Hospice conditions of participation.* from http://edocket.access.gpo.gov/2008/pdf/08-1305.pdf.

———— (2010). *National Health Interview Survey: The principal source of information on the health of the U.S. population.* http://www.cdc.gov/nchs/data/nhis/brochure2010January.pdf.

US Department of Justice (2010), Federal Bureau of Prisons. *The Federal Bureau of Prisons annual report on substance abuse treatment programs fiscal year 2010: Report to the Judiciary Committee, United States Congress.* http://www.bop.gov/inmate_programs/docs/annual_report_fy_2010.pdf.

Vacco v. Quill. No. 95-1858 (US Supreme Court 1997).

Van den Haag, E. (1975). *Punishing criminals: Concerning a very old and painful question.* New York. Basic.

Van Voorhis, P., Braswell, M., and Lester, D. (2000). *Correctional counseling and rehabilitation.* Cincinnati: Anderson.

Vega, M., and Silverman, M. (1988). Stress and the elderly convict. *International Journal of Offender Therapy and Comparative Criminology,* 32(2): 153–162.

Vesely, R. (2010). Another aging population: More states considering early-release programs for older, infirm inmates. *Modern Healthcare,* 40(13): 32.

Vierck, E., and Hodges, K. (2005). *Aging: Lifestyles, work, and money.* Westport: Greenwood.

Visher, C. A. (2006). Effective reentry programs. *Criminology and Public Policy,* 5(2): 299–302.

——— (2007). Returning home: Emerging findings and policy lessons about prisoner reentry. *Vera Institute of Justice,* 20(1): 93–102.

Visher, C. A., and Mallik-Kane, K. (2007). Reentry experiences of men with health problems. In R. Greifinger (ed.), *Public health behind bars: From prisons to community* (pp. 434–460). New York: Springer.

Visher, C. A., and Travis, J. (2003). Transitions from prison to community: Understanding individual pathways. *Annual Review of Sociology,* 29: 89–113.

Vitiello, M., and Kelso, C. (2004). A proposal for a wholesale reform of California's sentencing practice and policy. *Loyola of Los Angeles Law Review,* 38: 903.

Vito, G. F., and Wilson, D. G. (1985). Forgotten people: Elderly inmates. *Federal Probation,* 49(1): 18–23.

Vogeli, C., Shields, A. E., Lee, T. A., Gibson, T. B., Marder, W. D., Weiss, K. B., and Blumenthal, D. (2007). Multiple chronic conditions: Prevalence, health consequences, and implications for quality, care management, and costs. *Journal of General Internal Medicine,* 22(3): 391–395.

von Hirsch, A. (1976). *Doing justice: The choice of punishments.* New York: Hill and Wang.

——— (1984). The ethics of selective incapacitation: Observations on the contemporary debate. *Crime & Delinquency,* 30: 175–194.

von Hirsch, A., and Hanrahan, K. (1981). Determinate penalty systems in America: An overview. *Crime & Delinquency,* 27(3): 289–316.

von Zielbauer, P., and Plambeck, J. (2005). As health care in jails goes private, 10 days can be a death sentence. *New York Times,* February 27. http://www.ny times.com/2005/02/27/nyregion/27jail.html?.

Wahidin, A. (2004). *Older women in the criminal justice system: Running out of time.* London: Jessica Kingsley.

Wahl, H., and Oswald, F. (2010). Environmental perspectives on aging. In D. Dannefer and C. Phillipson (eds.), *The Sage handbook of social gerontology* (pp. 111–124). Thousand Oaks, CA: Sage.

Walmsley, R. (2006). *World female imprisonment list: Women and girls in penal institutions, including pre-trial detainees/remand prisoners.* London: King's College London, School of Law, International Centre for Prison Studies.

Wang, E. A., and Wildeman, C. (2011). Studying health disparities by including incarcerated and formerly incarcerated individuals. *Journal of the American Medical Association,* 305(16): 1708–1709.

Washington v. Glucksberg. No. 96-110 (US Supreme Court 1997).

Washington v. Harper. 494 U.S. 210 (1990).

Waters, C. M. (2001). Understanding and supporting African Americans' perspectives of end-of-life care planning and decision making. *Qualitative Health Research,* 11(3): 385–398.

Webster, J. D., Bohlmeijer, E. T., and Westerhof, G. J. (2010). Mapping the future of reminiscence: A conceptual framework for research and practice. *Research on Aging,* 32: 527–564.

Webster, J. D., and Gould, O. (2007). Reminiscence and vivid personal memories across adulthood. *International Journal of Aging and Human Development,* 64: 149–170.

Wellman v. Faulkner. 715 F.2d 269, nos. 81-3060, 81-3061 (7th Cir. 1983).

Welsh, B. C. (2004). Monetary costs and benefits of correctional treatment programs: Implications for offender reentry. *Federal Probation,* 68: 9–13.

West, H., and Sabol, W. (2008). *Prisoners in 2007.* Rockville, MD: US Department of Justice, Bureau of Justice Statistics.

——— (2009). *Prison inmates at midyear 2008: Statistical tables.* Rockville, MD: US Department of Justice.

West, H. C., Sabol, W. J., and Greenman, S. J. (2010). *Prisoners in 2009.* Washington, DC: US Department of Justice, Bureau of Justice Statistics.

Western, B., Kling, J. R., and Weiman, D. D. (2001). The labor market consequences of incarceration. *Crime and Delinquency,* 47: 410–427.

White v. Napoleon. 897 F.2d 103 (3d Cir. 1990).

Wiegand, N. D., and Burger, J. C. (1979). The elderly offender and parole. *The Prison Journal,* 59(2): 48–57.

Wilbanks, W. (1984a). The elderly offender: Placing the problem in perspective. In W. Wilbanks and P. K. H. Kim (eds.), *Elderly criminals* (pp. 1–16). New York: University Press of America.

——— (1984b). The elderly offender: Sex and race variations in frequency and pattern. In W. Wilbanks and P. K. H. Kim (eds.), *Elderly criminals* (pp. 41–52). New York: University Press of America.

Wilbanks, W., and Kim, P. K. H. (eds.) (1984). *Elderly criminals.* New York: University Press of America.

Wilbanks, W., and Murphy, D. D. (1984). The elderly homicide offender. In E. S. Newman, D. J. Newman, and M. L. Gewirtz (eds.), *Elderly criminals* (pp. 79–92). Boston: Oelgeschlager, Gunn, and Hain.

Williams, B., and Abraldes, R. (2007). Growing older: Challenges of prison and reentry for the aging population. In R. Greifinger (ed.), *Public health behind bars: From prisons to community* (pp. 56–72). New York: Springer.

Williams, B., Baillargeon, J., Lindquist, K., Walter, L., Covinsky, K., Whitson, H., and Steinman, M. (2010). Medication prescribing practices for older prisoners in the Texas prison system. *American Journal of Public Health,* 100(4): 756–761.

Williams, B. A., Lindquist, K., Hill, T., Baillargeon, J., Mellow, J., Greifinger, R., and Walter, L. C. (2009). Caregiving behind bars: Correctional officer reports of disability in geriatric prisoners. *Journal of the American Geriatric Society,* 57: 1286–1292.

Williams, B. A., Lindquist, K., Sudore, R. L., Strupp, H. M., Willmott, D. J., and Walter, L. C. (2006). Being old and doing time: Functional impairment and adverse experiences of geriatric female prisoners. *Journal of the American Geriatrics Society,* 54: 702–707.

Williams, J. (2006). *The aging inmate population: Southern states' outlook.* Atlanta: Southern Legislative Conference of the Council of State Governments.

Williams, N. H. (2007). Prison health and the health of the public: Ties that bind. *Journal of Correctional Health Care,* 12(2): 80–92.

Williams v. Meese. 926 F.2d 994 (10th Cir. 1991).

Wilper, A. P., Woolhandler, S., Boyd, J. W., Lasser, K. E., McCormick, D., Bor, D. H., and Himmelstein, D. U. (2009). The health and health care of U.S. prisoners: Results of a nationwide survey. *American Journal of Public Health,* 99(4): 666–672.

Wilson, D. G., and Vito, G. F. (1986). Imprisoned elders: The experience of one institution. *Criminal Justice Policy Review,* 1(4): 399–421.

Wilson, J., and Barboza, S. (2010). The looming challenge of dementia in corrections. *Correct Care,* 24(2): 12–14.

Wilson, J. Q. (1975). *Thinking about crime.* New York: Random.

Wilson, K. S., and Spink, K. S. (2006). Exploring older adults' social influences for physical activity. *Activities, Adaptation, and Aging,* 30(3): 47–60.

Wines, E. C. (ed.) (1871). *Transactions of the national congress on penitentiary and reformatory discipline held at Cincinnati, Ohio, October 12–18, 1870.* Albany, NY: Weed, Parsons.

Wolff, N., Blitz, C. L., Shi, J., Siegel, J., and Bachman, R. (2007). Physical violence inside prisons: Rates of victimization. *Criminal Justice and Behavior,* 34(5): 588–599.

Wolff v. McDonnell. 418 U.S. 539, 555–556 (1974).

Wolfgang, M. E., Figlio, R. M., and Sellin, T. (1972). *Delinquency in a birth cohort.* Chicago: University of Chicago Press.

Woods v. Goord. 01 Civ. 3255 (SAS) (DFE), 2002 U.S. Dist. LEXIS 7157 (S.D. N.Y. Apr. 23, 2002).

Wooldredge, J. D. (1991). Correlates of deviant behavior among inmates of U.S. correctional facilities. *Journal of Crime and Justice,* 14: 1–25.

———— (1994). Inmate crime and victimization in a southwestern correctional facility. *Journal of Criminal Justice,* 22(4): 367–381.

———— (1998). Inmate experiences and psychological well-being. *Criminal Justice and Behavior,* 26: 235–250.

Wooldredge, J. D., Griffin, T., and Pratt, T. (2001). Considering hierarchical models for research on inmate behavior: Predicting misconduct with multilevel data. *Justice Quarterly,* 18: 202–232.

Worden, J. W. (2008). *Grief counseling and grief therapy: A handbook for the mental health practitioner.* New York: Springer.

Workforce Investment Act of 1998. Section 188, 29 U.S.C. § 2938 (2011).

World prison brief: Entire world—Prison population totals (2010). http://www .prisonstudies.org/info/worldbrief/wpb_stats_print.php?area=all&category =wb_poptotal.

World prison brief: Female prisoners worldwide (2010). http://www.prisonstudies .org/info/worldbrief/wpb_stats.php?area=all&category=wb_female.

Wright, J. D., and Rossi, P. H. (1986). *Armed and considered dangerous: A survey of felons and their firearms.* New York: Aldine de Gruyter.

Wright, K. N. (1993). Prison environment and behavior outcomes. *Journal of Offender Rehabilitation,* 20(1): 93–113.

Wright, K. N., and Bronstein, L. (2007). Creating decent prisons: A serendipitous finding about prison hospices. *Journal of Offender Rehabilitation,* 44(4): 1–16.

Yates, J., and Gillespie, W. (2000). The elderly and prison policy. *Journal of Aging and Social Policy,* 11: 167–175.

Yeskey v. Pennsylvania Department of Corrections. 118 F.3d 168 (3d Cir. 1997).

Yorston, G. (2006). Aging prisoners: Crisis in American corrections. *Criminal Behaviour and Mental Health,* 16(2): 131–132.

Yorston, G., and Taylor, P. J. (2006). Commentary: Older offenders–No place to go? *Journal of the American Academy of Psychiatry and Law,* 34: 333–337.

Young, D. S. (1998). Health status and service use among incarcerated women. *Family and Community Health,* 21(3): 16–31.

——— (1999). Ethnicity and health service use in a women's prison. *Journal of Multicultural Social Work,* 7(3–4): 69–93.

——— (2000). Women's perception of health care in prison. *Health Care for Women International,* 21: 219–234.

Young, V. D., and Reviere, R. (2006). *Women behind bars: Gender and race in U.S. prisons.* Boulder: Lynne Rienner.

Zalman, M. (1977–1978). The rise and fall of the determinate sentence. *Wayne Law Review,* 24: 45–94, 857–937.

Zamble, E. (1992). Behavior and adaptation in long-term prison inmates. *Criminal Justice and Behavior,* 19: 409–425.

Zatz, N. D. (2008). Working at the boundaries of markets: Prison labor and the economic dimension of employment relationships. *Vanderbilt Law Review,* 61: 857–958.

Zhang, S. X., Roberts, R. E. L., and Callanan, V. J. (2006). The cost benefits of providing community-based correctional services: An evaluation of a statewide parole program in California. *Journal of Criminal Justice,* 34: 341–350.

Zimbardo, P. G. (1994). *Transforming California's prisons into expensive old age homes for felons: Enormous hidden costs and consequences for California's taxpayers.* San Francisco: Center on Juvenile and Criminal Justice.

Zimmermann, N. (2009). Starting a prison hospice program. *Illness, Crisis, & Loss,* 17(4): 349–361.

Zimring, F. E. (1983). Sentencing reform in the states: Lessons from the 1970s. In M. Tonry and F. E. Zimring (eds.), *Reform and punishment: Essays on criminal sentencing* (pp. 101–121). Chicago: University of Chicago Press.

Zimring, F. E., and Hawkins, G. (1995). *Incapacitation: Penal confinement and the restraint of crime.* New York: Oxford University Press.

The Contributors

Ronald H. Aday is a professor in the Department of Sociology and Anthropology at Middle Tennessee State University. His research interests include older prisoners, older women in prison, women serving life, death and dying, and aging and social policy.

Kathleen Auerhahn is an associate professor and graduate chair in the Department of Criminal Justice at Temple University. Her research interests center around the intersection of inequality and social control and include the ethics and efficacy of criminal justice policy, adjudication and sanctioning processes and outcomes, and the relationship between social-structural inequality and legal discourse.

Kristie R. Blevins is an associate professor in the School of Justice Studies at Eastern Kentucky University. Her research interests include corrections, wildlife crime, and the occupational reactions of criminal justice employees.

Anita N. Blowers is an associate professor in the Department of Criminal Justice and Criminology and a core faculty member in the Gerontology Program at the University of North Carolina, Charlotte. Her research focuses on older offenders and the criminal justice system, elder abuse and neglect, sentencing, and criminal justice policy.

Jennifer M. Jolley is a National Institute of Mental Health (NIMH) postdoctoral fellow and Ruth L. Kirschstein National Research Service Award

279

recipient at the Cecil G. Sheps Center for Health Services Research, University of North Carolina, Chapel Hill. Her research, which is federally funded through the NIMH, focuses on the prevention of repeat maltreatment in child-welfare systems; the design and implementation of community, correctional, and forensic programs that address interpersonal violence; older prisoners; and the reentry of federal and state prisoners into society.

Naoki Kanaboshi is an assistant professor in the Department of Criminal Justice at Grand Valley State University. His research focuses on the rights of prisoners and their family members.

John J. Kerbs is an associate professor in the Department of Criminal Justice at East Carolina University. His research focuses on the safety and victimization of older prisoners; the bio-psycho-social needs of older prisoners; service delivery systems for older offenders, both during their incarceration and after release to community-based supervision; school safety; and the prevention of repeat maltreatment in child-welfare systems.

Jennifer J. Krabill is a research associate at the Tennessee Center for Gerontology and Geriatric Research. She is currently a graduate student in higher education at Middle Tennessee State University. Her research interests include senior-center programming, older incarcerated women, prison programs and policies, religion behind bars, and mental health and prison adjustment.

Margaret E. Leigey is an associate professor in the Department of Criminology at the College of New Jersey. Her research focuses on the correctional experiences of special inmate populations, including older inmates, life-sentenced inmates, female inmates, and juveniles incarcerated in adult prisons.

John F. Linder is a retired licensed clinical social worker from the University of California, Davis, Medical Center. His research focuses on end-of-life and palliative care, prison hospice, the aging prison population, health-care disparities, hastened death including assisted suicide, and spirituality and end-of-life care.

Index

About the Book

Within two decades—if not sooner—at least one in three prisoners in the United States will be a "senior citizen." Our prisons, however, were designed for a much younger population. *Senior Citizens Behind Bars* critically explores the unique set of challenges that older prisoners pose for the criminal justice system.

Examining the lack of fit between the needs of older inmates and the correctional policies and practices that govern efforts to meet those needs, the authors confront such tough issues as health care, inmate victimization, and end-of-life care. Their rigorous, evidence-based analysis of both problems and solutions is a seminal contribution carefully designed for scholars and practitioners alike.

John J. Kerbs is an associate professor of criminal justice at East Carolina University. **Jennifer M. Jolley** is a National Institute of Mental Health postdoctoral fellow in the Cecil G. Sheps Center for Health Services Research at the University of North Carolina, Chapel Hill.